BIBLE APPLICATION LESSONS AND PRAYERS

365 Days Divine Inspirations For Daily Living

By

James Taiwo

Copyright © 2016 by James Taiwo

All rights reserved. No part of this publication may be reproduced, distributed, or transmitted in any form or by any means, including photocopying, recording, or other electronic or mechanical methods, without the prior written permission of the publisher, except in the case of brief quotations embodied in critical reviews and certain other noncommercial uses permitted by copyright law.

Unless otherwise noted, Scripture quotations are taken from the New King James Version®, (NKJV). Copyright © 1982 by Thomas Nelson. Used by permission. All rights reserved.

Scripture quotations marked (NIV) are taken from the Holy Bible, New International Version®, NIV®. Copyright © 1973, 1978, 1984, 2011 by Biblica, Inc.™ Used by permission of Zondervan. All rights reserved. **www.zondernvan.com**

Scripture quotations marked (KJV) are taken from the Holy Bible, King James Version (Public Domain)

« Dedication »

To God, who makes all things possible for those that trust Him.

« Contents »

« PREFACE » 1

« DAY 1 » 2

« DAY 30 » 33

« DAY 60 » 64

« DAY 90 » 98

« DAY 120 » 129

« DAY 150 » 159

« DAY 180 » 190

« DAY 210 » 221

« DAY 240 » 251

« DAY 270 » 281

« DAY 300 » 313

« DAY 330 » 345

« DAY 360 » 379

« DAY 365 » 384

« Note To The Reader » 385

« Connect With James Taiwo » 386

« About The Author » 387

« PREFACE »

God requires everyone to establish and maintain a consistent relationship with him, but the task is gradually becoming an impossible mission for people of our time due to our never-ending busy schedules. A daily reminder of God's word to keep His love afresh in our hearts can only result to our blessing. This book provides some opportunities that many people have long desired. It enhances personal growth and helps to build Godly principles.

While I would have loved to delve into other topic areas in book writing, I felt God's strong desire to make this particular book a priority project. I chose to follow God's leading with a clear understanding that His ways are not always the same as ours. *Who am I to challenge God's decision if He chooses to act as he wishes?* I responded to the Creator's call and sought His face to understand the message meant for this book, and I wrote as He inspired.

This book would have remained an uncompleted and abandoned project, but since it has a root traceable to God, the enemy's windstorm could not stop it. Now available in your hands is a "mission accomplished" project that is set to help everyone who reads it.

God's divine inspirations expressed through this book make it suitable to benefit anyone who lay hands on it. It is suitable to leading a person to enjoy God to a maximum extent. The book will benefit global community as it positively impacts both the Christians and non Christians. Here is a book that provides an opportunity everyone needs to live a Godly lifestyle; raise a happy family, and also have hope of qualifying for a delightful eternal life that God has prepared for His people.

« DAY 1 »

Jesus Christ Regained The Authority That Humanity Lost

Focus Passage: Genesis 1, 2, 3

God created all things by his divine power to showcase his glory as the scripture stated,

> *"In the beginning God created the heavens and the earth. The earth was without form, and void; and darkness was on the face of the deep. And the Spirit of God was hovering over the face of the waters. Then God said, "Let there be light"; and there was light"* **(Genesis 1:1-3).**

Lesson:
God created all things by his power for his pleasure, and he specially created human beings to take dominion over other creatures. Adam and Eve who were the first humans created lost their authority due to their disobedience to God; however, God sent his Son Jesus Christ to reclaim the lost dominion for us. That is, believers now have victory through death and resurrection of Jesus Christ. Situations will submit to people that confess their beliefs in Jesus Christ. The scripture stated,

"Therefore God also has highly exalted Him and given Him the name which is above every name, that at the name of Jesus every knee should bow, of those in heaven, and of those on earth, and of those under the earth, and that every tongue should confess that Jesus Christ is Lord, to the glory of God the Father" **(Philippians 2:9-11).**

Prayer:
Praise God for Jesus Christ has regained the dominion that Adam and Eve lost in the Garden of Eden! Praise God for Jesus Christ has handed me the authority that I needed to succeed on earth. Since I am no more an ordinary person, I proclaim my victory over every situation of life. I triumph in the name of Jesus Christ over sickness, financial problem, marital problem, career problem, and other problems. Through the authority acquired in the name of Jesus Christ, I dominate all situations to establish my victory and I shall remain victorious forever!

Amen.

« DAY 2 »

God Can Handle Complex Problems For The Benefit Of His Children

Focus Passage: Matthew 1

Mary and Joseph had a healthy courtship and thought of getting married to start a family, but something else happened that almost ruined their plan. Mary was found pregnant with no man to be held accountable! She was pregnant of the Holy Spirit. Joseph was confused about the inexplicable situation, and Mary also was embarrassed. However, God himself intervened as bible reported,

> *"Now the birth of Jesus Christ was as follows: After His mother Mary was betrothed to Joseph, before they came together, she was found with child of the Holy Spirit. Then Joseph her husband, being a just man, and not wanting to make her a public example, was minded to put her away secretly. But while he thought about these things, behold, an angel of the Lord appeared to him in a dream, saying, "Joseph, son of David, do not be afraid to take to you Mary your wife, for that which is conceived in her is of the Holy Spirit. And she will bring forth a Son, and you shall call His name Jesus, for He will save his people from their sins"* **(Matthew 1:18-21).**

Lesson:
God knows how to solve any difficult problem for his people and earn them testimony. The Creator also knows how to rally necessary supports for his divine plan – whether people understand it or not. Hence, believers must reserve their trust in God, and believe that he will do whatever he has promised. A difficult situation will not be a barrier for God to act since he is the Creator. He will earn his saints testimony by making their challenges become a stepping-stone unto promotion and breakthrough. Therefore, believers are encouraged to keep trusting God for he will show up in due time to manifest his glory in their lives. Our steadfast faith will allow God to perfect his miracle in our lives.

Prayer:
Dear God, I know you are with me always, and you will perfect all that concerns me! You will attend to my needs and fight my battles to have victory. All I am asking now is the grace to completely trust you! Help me to reserve my trust in you. Let me keep professing, "My God shall perfect all that concerns me to earn me testimony!" For in the name of Jesus Christ I make my requests.

Amen.

« DAY 3 »

Believers Must Properly Handle Their Failure And Convert It To Success

Focus Passage: Genesis 4, 5, 6

The two brothers (Cain and Abel) offered their sacrifices to God, but God accepted Abel's offering and rejected Cain's offering. Cain was raged and developed bitterness against his brother whose sacrifice was accepted, and he killed him. The scripture reported,

> *"In the course of time Cain brought some of the fruits of the soil as an offering to the Lord. And Abel also brought an offering—fat portions from some of the firstborn of his flock. The Lord looked with favor on Abel and his offering, but on Cain and his offering he did not look with favor. So Cain was very angry, and his face was downcast. Then the Lord said to Cain, "Why are you angry? Why is your face downcast? If you do what is right, will you not be accepted? But if you do not do what is right, sin is crouching at your door; it desires to have you, but you must rule over it." Now Cain said to his brother Abel, "Let's go out to the field." While they were in the field, Cain attacked his brother Abel and killed him"* **(Genesis 4:3-8 NIV).**

Lesson:
Children of God must know how to properly handle their failure to prevent it from degenerating into actions that can lead them into making costly mistakes. Believers must understand that a failure does not symbolize an end of life, and they must know how to properly handle it. If a failure is properly handled, it can become a motivating factor that leads someone into having success. Failure exposes a person to see things differently and act differently – which eventually will make him/her produce better result than an earlier time.

Besides, believers must know how to admit their mistakes and make necessary restitution to God, and to whoever is concerned. They should also have habit of forgiving themselves, and know how to pick up their pieces and transform them into success. The Bible consists of numerous examples of people who gathered their pieces and become successful. David, Paul, Peter, and many others have once failed in their lifetime, yet they were still able to make meaningful impacts that many people still reference today.

Prayer:
Dear God, please teach and empower me to transform my failures into success. Let your Holy Spirit empower me into making proper decisions; let him give me momentum needed to transform any negative situation into a positive one. Again, do not let the enemy successfully keep me down over any failure, but let me stay lifted to operate in victory throughout the days of my life. For in the name of Jesus Christ I make my requests.

Amen.

« DAY 4 »

Envy Is Evil, And It Can Lead Anyone Into Making Irreparable Mistakes

Focus Passage: Matthew 2

King Herod attempted to trick the Wise Men into exposing the birthplace of Jesus Christ so that he could kill him. However, the people outsmart him and made his plan fail. Meanwhile, to the shame of the cruel king, he still went ahead to kill all Jesus' age mates. The scripture reported,

> *"...Then Herod, when he saw that he was deceived by the wise men, was exceedingly angry; and he sent forth and put to death all the male children who were in Bethlehem and in all its districts, from two years old and under, according to the time which he had determined from the wise men"* **(Matthew 2:16).**

Lesson:
Children of God are to be careful not to envy others, since it is a practice that violates God's law, and it incurs terrible consequences. When envy (jealousy) is not controlled, it blindfolds a person to make terrible mistakes that can cause irreparable damage. Christians must ensure to guide their thoughts not to allow the plague of jealousy to have root in their lives. Instead of yielding to the desires of the devil, we should rather give our hearts to the Holy Spirit and let him control us. To achieve this, we must consistently study the word of God and pray. As we expose ourselves to godliness, the Holy Spirit will take over lives to make it positively productive and be relevant for God's kingdom. Jehovah will indeed honor people that allow his Holy Spirit to take control of their lives!

Prayer:
Dear God, I understand that jealousy is a plague, and it is sinful. I don't want to entertain the plague in my life; therefore, I pray that you please empower me through your Holy Spirit to act godly as bible requires. Give me strength to only entertain thoughts that are edifying and are pleasant to you. Please let my thoughts and actions benefit people around me, and also glorify you name. For in the name of Jesus Christ I make my requests.

Amen.

« DAY 5 »

God's Judgment On This Earth Is Imminent; Humanity Only Have A Choice To Repent Before It Is Too Late

Focus Passage: Genesis 7, 8, 9

The first generation that lived on earth aggravated God with their sins, and the Creator was determined to wipe them off. However, he found Noah and his family faithful, and he saved them. Others were destroyed with flood. The scripture reported,

> *"The Lord then said to Noah, "Go into the ark, you and your whole family, because I have found you righteous in this generation. Take with you seven pairs of every kind of clean animal, a male and its mate, and one pair of every kind of unclean animal, a male and its mate, and also seven pairs of every kind of bird, male and female, to keep their various kinds alive throughout the earth. Seven days from now I will send rain on the earth for forty days and forty nights, and I will wipe from the face of the earth every living creature I have made." And Noah did all that the Lord commanded him. Noah was six hundred years old when the floodwaters came on the earth"* **(Genesis 7:1-6 NIV).**

Lesson:
God is God of justice that repays people for their activities. Although he doesn't pass instant judgment like Old Testament era, but his principle remains unchanged. He will punish the wicked people and bless those that are righteous. Jehovah is an impartial God, and he will not spare our present world from its wickedness. He will judge this present world as he did for the first generation. (God judged the previous generation with flood; he also judged Cities of Sodom and Gomorrah with fire - Genesis 7, 19). People of our generation only have an option to repent from our sins and return to God with faithful services. Humanity must exercise repentance before it is too late. In due time, God will destroy this sinful planet with fire and replace it with a new one that is void of sin (Revelation 21:1-4). Only people who have repented of their sins will qualify for the new planet to be created. They shall rejoice in the presence of God forever.

Prayer:
Dear God, I understand that you will soon destroy this present sinful planet. You will cast it to hell fire together with the evil dwellers. I also understand that you will create a new planet that is void of evil for those who have faithfully serve you. Therefore, I submit myself at your feet to ask for the forgiveness of my sins. I am sorry for all my past mistakes, and I repent from them. I also confess my faith in your Son Jesus Christ, and I accept him as my personal Lord and Savior. Please write my name in your book of life to qualify for the eternal joy that is preserved for your saints. For in the name of Jesus Christ I make my requests.

Amen.

« DAY 6 »

Jesus' Power Is Still Very Much Active To Perform Miracles For People That Believe In It

Focus Passage: Matthew 3

John baptized Jesus Christ in Jordan River, and God immediately validated his ministry with visible signs. The scripture reported the incident as stated,

> "When He had been baptized, Jesus came up immediately from the water; and behold, the heavens were opened to Him, and He saw the Spirit of God descending like a dove and alighting upon Him. And suddenly a voice came from heaven, saying, "This is my beloved Son, in whom I am well pleased" **(Matthew 3:16-17)**.

Lesson:
Heaven confirmed the ministry of Jesus Christ with visible signs immediately John baptized him. God's audible voice was heard concerning him stating, *"This is my beloved Son, in whom I am well pleased."* Not only did heaven confirmed Jesus' ministry, but earth also confirmed it. Earth dwellers witnessed Jesus' ministry in full flesh with visible signs and wonders. The blind saw, lame walked, and dead rose! Meanwhile, the ministry of Jesus Christ has not ended but still active till today. Jesus' power still performs miracles today in people's lives when they exercise their faith in him. That is, impossibilities will continue to become possibilities for people who have confessed their faith in Jesus Christ. However, the greatest demonstrative power of Jesus is his ability to save souls. Faith in Jesus Christ will save anyone from the pit of hell to God's palace of heaven!

Prayer:
Praise God Jesus' ministry is still very much active with more signs and wonders to be witnessed. Since I am a follower of Jesus Christ I have all the rights to perform miracles as well. Starting from my life and extending to others, I shall witness Christ's salvation, healing, deliverance, and other testimony. I am an ordained child of God commissioned to showcase God's power, and songs of victory shall be my portion always! Praise Jesus Christ for his saving grace and power of miracles.

Amen!

« DAY 7 »

Humanity Have A Choice To Either Obey God's Laws And Be Blessed, Or Reject Them And Be Punished

Focus Passage: Genesis 10,11,12

The people of first generation ganged up to rebel against God and his plan for them to live peacefully and dominate the earth. They attempted to violate God's creation law that required humanity to procreate and multiply to flourish the earth. The first-generation-people wanted to remain in one location and build a tower that would reach heaven. Therefore, God was dissatisfied, and he confused their languages which ultimately made their mission fail. The scripture reported,

> *"And the whole earth was of one language, and of one speech. And it came to pass, as they journeyed from the east, that they found a plain in the land of Shinar; and they dwelt there. And they said one to another, Go to, let us make brick, and burn them thoroughly. And they had brick for stone, and slime had they for morter. And they said, Go to, let us build us a city and a tower, whose top may reach unto heaven; and let us make us a name, lest we be scattered abroad upon the face of the whole earth. And the Lord came down to see the city and the tower, which the children of men builded. And the Lord said, Behold, the people is one, and they have all one language; and this they begin to do: and now nothing will be restrained from them, which they have imagined to do. Go to, let us go down, and there confound their language, that they may not understand one another's speech"* **(Genesis 11:1-7 KJV).**

Lesson:

All people must understand the fundamental principle of creation: God made humans; humans did not make God! We only have a choice to either accept God's plans or reject them. Obedience to God's plans will lead us into receiving his blessings, and our disobedience to his laws will make us receive his punishments. Meanwhile, God offers grace of forgiveness and restoration for anyone who has derailed from his laws. He reserves his forgiveness for anyone who repents and returns to him. Such repentant soul will have a renewed opportunity to enjoy God's divine purposes for his/her life.

Prayer:

Dear God, please give me grace to walk within your plans so that I can prosper! Do not let me act contrarily to your laws so that I will not incur your wrath and be punished. Let your Holy Spirit guide me in all I do to satisfy you so that it can prosper throughout the days of my life. For in the name of Jesus Christ I make my requests.

Amen.

« DAY 8 »

Temptations Are Bound To Come; Believers Must Remain Steadfast And Resist Devil To Flee

Focus Passage: Matthew 4

Satan tempted Jesus Christ with food when he was hungry; he challenged him to turn stones into breads to satisfy his hunger. However, Jesus refused to fall for the enemy's trap, and he commanded him to get lost. Satan had no choice than to flee immediately. It is reported,

> *"Then Jesus was led up by the Spirit into the wilderness to be tempted by the devil. And when He had fasted forty days and forty nights, afterward He was hungry. Now when the tempter came to Him, he said, "If you are the Son of God, command that these stones become bread." But He answered and said, "It is written, 'Man shall not live by bread alone, but by every word that proceeds from the mouth of God'"..."Again, the devil took Him up on an exceedingly high mountain, and showed Him all the kingdoms of the world and their glory. And he said to Him, "All these things I will give you if you will fall down and worship me." Then Jesus said to him, "Away with you, Satan! For it is written, 'You shall worship the Lord your God, and Him only you shall serve.'" Then the devil left Him, and behold, angels came and ministered to Him"* **(Matthew 4:1-4; 4:8-11).**

Lesson:
Satan is an enemy of God's people, and he is skilled at tempting them during their weak moments. The enemy sets traps to bring distractions with the hope that believers would stumble into them. However, we (Christians) have God that cares for us! He won't allow the enemy to have upper hands over us since it is stated in the bible, *"No temptation has overtaken you except what is common to mankind. And God is faithful; he will not let you be tempted beyond what you can bear. But when you are tempted, he will also provide a way out so that you can endure it"* **(1 Corinthians 10:13 NIV).**

To overcome Satan's temptations, Christians must evaluate surrounding circumstances and be sensitive to the leadership of the Holy Spirit. We can not afford to make irrational decisions during trials. We must test all spirits and not be quick to attempting anything that comes to mind, since the enemy is prone to bringing many irrelevant suggestions during trial moments. Also, believers must evaluate every suggestion, prophecy, and/or inspiration with the standard of the bible. More so, it is important that Christians remain prayerful and ensure they keep their testimony during their trial moments.

Prayer:
Dear God, please help me to always live a life that is consistent with bible standard. Do not let me yield to Satan's temptation, but empower me through the Holy Spirit to test spirits, thoughts, suggestions, and inspirations so that I can prevail at all times. Help me to always live victoriously over temptations, and let my practices result to the glorifications of your Holy Name. For in the name of Jesus Christ I make my requests.

Amen.

« DAY 9 »

Godliness With Contentment Is A Great Gain

Focus Passage: Genesis 13, 14, 15

Abundance of blessing created frictions between Abram and his nephew Lot. Lot (and his servants) became greedy with wealth and they wanted to dominate Abram's rightful possessions. However, Abram played maturity and allowed peace to reign. The scripture reported,

> *"And Abram said unto Lot, Let there be no strife, I pray thee, between me and thee, and between my herdmen and thy herdmen; for we be brethren. Is not the whole land before thee? Separate thyself, I pray thee, from me: if thou wilt take the left hand, then I will go to the right; or if thou depart to the right hand, then I will go to the left. And Lot lifted up his eyes, and beheld all the plain of Jordan, that it was well watered every where, before the Lord destroyed Sodom and Gomorrah, even as the garden of the Lord, like the land of Egypt, as thou comest unto Zoar. Then Lot chose him all the plain of Jordan; and Lot journeyed east: and they separated themselves the one from the other. Abram dwelled in the land of Canaan, and Lot dwelled in the cities of the plain, and pitched his tent toward Sodom"* **(Genesis 13:8-12 KJV).**

Lot accepted Abram's offer to take whatever property he desired. He chose the best part of the land as his portion. His portion later became the Cities of Sodom and Gomorrah, which God destroyed due to their sins. Meanwhile, God visited and blessed Abram after the departure of Lot. Abram' blessing outlasted him – and his blessing could still be felt among God's believers today.

Lesson:
Every child of God must learn how to live a satisfied life. We must be contented with whatever we have. We mustn't be obsessed with other people's possessions. Even when we are at the point of needs, we are expected to trust God for his provisions and not attempt to steal other people's belongings. In addition, as God's children, we must pray for God's guidance before we accept any offer that is presented to us. Not all that glitter is gold. Believers must allow God to guide our thoughts into making decisions that will lead to our long-term blessings. We will never regret any day of our lives if we operate under the divine guidance of God.

Prayer:
Dear God, please teach me how to be contented with whatever I have. Please do not let me be obsessed with other people's wealth! Help me to stay within my limits and remain happy. Please prosper me in all my ways, and let the testimony of your goodness ever flourish my life. For in the name of Jesus Christ I make my requests.

Amen.

« DAY 10 »

Christianity Requires Consistent Act Of Godliness

Focus Passage: Matthew 5:1-26

Jesus Christ called few people "blessed" because they have exceptional characters that God requires. Jesus said:

1. Blessed *are* the poor in spirit, For theirs is the kingdom of heaven **(Matthew 5:3)**
2. Blessed *are* those who mourn, For they shall be comforted **(Matthew 5:4)**
3. Blessed *are* the meek, For they shall inherit the earth **(Matthew 5:5)**
4. Blessed *are* those who hunger and thirst for righteousness, For they shall be filled **(Matthew 5:6)**
5. Blessed *are* the merciful, For they shall obtain mercy **(Matthew 5:7)**
6. Blessed *are* the pure in heart, For they shall see God **(Matthew 5:8)**
7. Blessed *are* the peacemakers, For they shall be called sons of God **(Matthew 5:9)**
8. Blessed *are* those who are persecuted for righteousness' sake, For theirs is the kingdom of heaven **(Matthew 5:10)**
9. Blessed are you when they revile and persecute you, and say all kinds of evil against you falsely for My sake **(Matthew 5:11)**

Lesson:
Born-again Christians must possess character traits that reflect Jesus' teachings (*Matthew 5:1-26*). We must demonstrate exceptional characters that glorify Christ and are heavenly worthy. Sons and daughters of God must be meek, merciful, enduring, and be lovers of righteousness. We must live a plausible lifestyle that glorifies God and put devil to shame.

Prayer:
Dear God, please help me not to be a nominal Christian but a practicing Christian that takes godliness seriously. Enable me with grace to live a serious Christian lifestyle that is worthy of your kingdom. Let your Holy Spirit empower me to live a life that is in compliance with your laws so that I can prosper throughout the days of my life. For in the name of Jesus Christ I make my requests.

Amen.

« DAY 11 »

Human Counsels May Be Faulty, But Anyone That Listens To God Will Never Regret

Focus Passage: Genesis 16, 17

Sarai advised Abram (her husband) to have a child outside their wedlock to substitute for her barrenness. Abram considered the suggestion appropriate and he impregnated Hagar (Sarai's servant), but the decision became a complicated family problem. Sarai later had her own son, and rivalry developed between the two women. Therefore, Abram was forced to cast out Hagar and the child she bore for him, and his failures degenerated into a generational problem that persisted till today. The generations of Sarai's son (Isaac) and Hagar's son (Ishmael) remains at loggerhead till now! The scripture reported Abram's action that led to a generational problem,

> *"Now Sarai Abram's wife bare him no children: and she had an handmaid, an Egyptian, whose name was Hagar. And Sarai said unto Abram, Behold now, the Lord hath restrained me from bearing: I pray thee, go in unto my maid; it may be that I may obtain children by her. And Abram hearkened to the voice of Sarai. And Sarai Abram's wife took Hagar her maid the Egyptian, after Abram had dwelt ten years in the land of Canaan, and gave her to her husband Abram to be his wife. And he went in unto Hagar, and she conceived: and when she saw that she had conceived, her mistress was despised in her eyes. And Sarai said unto Abram, My wrong be upon thee: I have given my maid into thy bosom; and when she saw that she had conceived, I was despised in her eyes: the Lord judge between me and thee. But Abram said unto Sarai, Behold, thy maid is in thine hand; do to her as it pleaseth thee. And when Sarai dealt hardly with her, she fled from her face"* **(Genesis 16:1-6 KJV).**

Lesson:

Abram (later became Abraham) was a friend of God whom he loved very much, but he stumbled in faith at a point in his life, and his failure became a generational problem; believers must learn from this and be careful not to abuse their God's-given grace because it may lead to an unimaginable complicated problem. It is wise to always listen to God and obey his instructions. We must trust God for his promises, and pursue his counsel above any other advice people may give us. People can only counsel us based on what they know, (and sometimes base on their selfish ambition). Believers must make it a priority to listen to God's voice than to follow human's suggestions that have many uncertainties! Whenever we are in difficult situation and it appears some odds are against us, we must seek God's face in prayer and fasting, and we must study our bible (word of God). Meanwhile, believers should not avoid seeking godly counsels from people whose lives have challenged us. As we engage in spiritual activities to know God's mind over any matter, he will guide us to make accurate decisions that will benefit us and lead to the praise of his name.

Prayer:
Dear God, please teach me how to wait on your promises until they are fulfilled. Give me a patient heart that allows you to rule in my situations. Do not let me be over anxious to make irrational decisions that may lead to making mistakes. Help me to be sensitive in the Holy Spirit to seek your face in prayers, fasting, and studying of your word. Also, direct me to seeking godly counsels that will benefit my life and also glorify your name. For in the name of Jesus Christ I make my requests.

Amen.

« DAY 12 »

Christian Couples Must Live In Love, Joy, And Harmony; They Must Also Practice Forgiveness To Honor God

Focus Passage: Matthew 5:27-48

Jesus Christ taught his followers how to keep dignity of their marriages. They must exercise forgiveness in their marriages to make it work. Jesus said,

> *"Furthermore it has been said, 'Whoever divorces his wife, let him give her a certificate of divorce.' But I say to you that whoever divorces his wife for any reason except sexual immorality causes her to commit adultery; and whoever marries a woman who is divorced commits adultery"... "You have heard that it was said, 'You shall love your neighbor and hate your enemy.' But I say to you, love your enemies, bless those who curse you, do good to those who hate you, and pray for those who spitefully use you and persecute you* **(Matthew 5:31-32; Matthew 5:43-44).**

Lesson:

Christians must honor their marriages and ensure they do their best to make it work. Christian couples must understand that they are not only accountable to each other, but they are also accountable to God; therefore, they must ensure to prioritize godliness and sanctity of their marriage. That is, Christian couples must serve God and be trustworthy. Each party must maintain honesty and not act contrarily to the prosperity of their home. More importantly, couples must exercise forgiveness to promote their marriage unity. They must forgive each other as Christ forgave their sins. It is important that Christian couples understand Jesus' stand on subject of divorce: Jesus discourages divorce, and he requires married couples to exercise forgiveness and live in harmony!

Prayer:

Dear God, please bless my marriage and bless my home. Also bless all Christian couples as well. Let your true love reign in our marriages; empower us through your Holy Spirit to shut doors against bitterness, rage, unforgiveness, and dishonesty. Let our couples live in love and purity that will send a positive message to unbelievers to challenge them to serve you also. Please glorify yourself in our marriages, and let us always peacefully celebrate the joy of our salvation. For in the name of Jesus Christ I make my requests.

Amen.

« DAY 13 »

God Blesses Diligent Hands; He Pays Less Attention To Slothful People

Focus Passage: Genesis 18, 19

God planned to destroy Sodom and Gomorrah (due to their sins), and he chose to give a courtesy notice to his friend Abraham about his decision. Abraham seized the opportunity to intercede for the two cities, but he eventually ran out of luck. The scripture reported,

> *"And the Lord said, "Shall I hide from Abraham what I am doing, since Abraham shall surely become a great and mighty nation, and all the nations of the earth shall be blessed in him?"* **(Genesis 18:17-18).**
>
> Abraham interceded:
> *"And Abraham came near and said, "Would you also destroy the righteous with the wicked? Suppose there were fifty righteous within the city; would you also destroy the place and not spare it for the fifty righteous that were in it? Far be it from you to do such a thing as this, to slay the righteous with the wicked, so that the righteous should be as the wicked; far be it from you! Shall not the Judge of all the earth do right?" So the Lord said, "If I find in Sodom fifty righteous within the city, then I will spare all the place for their sakes"* **(Genesis 18:23-26).**

Lesson:
Believers are expected to utilize every opportunity they have to tap into God's reservoir of blessings. We must be ready to make the full use of our opportunity so that we can prosper in this world. That is, believers cannot be slothful and expects God's prosperity to abide. Despite our exercises of faith and prayers, we are still required to work hard to receive God's blessings! It is not unbiblical for a Christian to be a millionaire or billionaire! God's is ever willing to showcase his glory through our blessings, and therefore we must give him chance to bless us through our works. God cannot bless emptiness, there has to be something we put on the table for him to bless! Once we are diligent, the Creator will demonstrate his strength and bless us, and he will make the testimony of our prosperity send a loud message to the unbelievers. They will emulate us, and make attempt to serve our God so that they can be blessed also.

Prayer:
Dear God, I understand it is true that you only bless diligent hands; therefore, I want to be diligent in my works. Help me to pursue my career in a way that will incur your blessings. Please bless my works, and let whatever I lay my hands on prosper! Please showcase your glory in my life, so that unbelievers can hear my testimony and be challenged to serve you also. For in the name of Jesus Christ I make my requests.

Amen.

« DAY 14 »

God Respects True Worshipers; He Dishonors People's Pleaser

Focus Passage: Matthew 6:1-18

Christians are to be selfless and ensure their activities are focus on glorifying God only. We must not labor to receive human praises as Jesus Christ said,

> *"So when you give to the needy, do not announce it with trumpets, as the hypocrites do in the synagogues and on the streets, to be honored by others. Truly I tell you, they have received their reward in full. But when you give to the needy, do not let your left hand know what your right hand is doing, so that your giving may be in secret. Then your Father, who sees what is done in secret, will reward you"* **(Matthew 6:2-4 NIV).**

Lesson:

God respects true worshipers, but he dishonors people's pleaser. The Creator expects us to give him honest services without seeking for people's acceptance and gratuity. Meanwhile, we must not operate with pretense to create holiness impression. Our services to God and people must come from a pure heart for them to be acceptable. Jehovah knows how to reward faithful services, and he will reward us. Other people will hear our testimony of God's goodness, and they will praise him on our behalves.

Prayer:

Dear God, please help me to offer selfless services to you so that your name can be praised. Help me not to pursue selfish desires, but let my services come from a pure heart so that they can be acceptable to you. Please flood my life with your bounty of goodness from now and evermore! For in the name of Jesus Christ I make my requests.

Amen.

« DAY 15 »

God's Defense For His People Are Mostly Based On Honoring His Name

Focus Passage: Genesis 20, 21, 22

Abraham asked Sarah his wife to call him brother in front of King Abimelech because he feared for his life. The man thought Abimelech's men might snatch his wife and kill him. Abraham's decision was unwise, but God took control of the situation for the sake of the covenant he had with him. The scripture reported how Abraham's irrational decision could have made him lose his wife to a gentile king,

> *"And Abraham said of Sarah his wife, She is my sister: and Abimelech king of Gerar sent, and took Sarah. But God came to Abimelech in a dream by night, and said to him, Behold; thou art but a dead man, for the woman which thou hast taken; for she is a man's wife. But Abimelech had not come near her: and he said, Lord, wilt thou slay also a righteous nation? Said he not unto me, She is my sister? And she, even she herself said, He is my brother: in the integrity of my heart and innocence of my hands have I done this. And God said unto him in a dream, Yea, I know that thou didst this in the integrity of thy heart; for I also withheld thee from sinning against me: therefore suffered I thee not to touch her. Now therefore restore the man his wife; for he is a prophet, and he shall pray for thee, and thou shalt live: and if thou restore her not, know thou that thou shalt surely die, thou, and all that are thine"* **(Genesis 20:2-7 KJV).**

Lesson:

God will protect his own people to glorify his name. He does not always relate with us base on the level of our steadfastness, but he goes out of his ways to help for the sake of glorifying his name. Hence, believers must be restful in God, and trust that he will perfect all that concerns us. While some situations need instant attention, others need patience, and we must allow the Creator to take control of those situations. Our God neither sleeps nor slumbers; he will surely take control of any difficult situation that confronts us, and his solutions will earn us lasting victory and testimony that will put Satan to shame, and glorify his name. In addition, believers must be reminded of God's promises in the bible that states, *"These things I have spoken to you, that in me you may have peace. In the world you will have tribulation; but be of good cheer, I have overcome the world"* **(John 16:33).**

Prayer:

Dear God, please teach me how to trust you during adversity. Help me to demonstrate unshakable faith that will honor you! Give me courage to profess statement of faith during adversity: *"I know my God whom I serve, and he will deliver me from every challenge of life!"* When tables are turned against my enemies, let me return to testify to your goodness in the assembly of your people. For in the name of Jesus Christ I make my requests.

Amen.

« DAY 16 »

Christians Should Not Be Anxious, We Have God Of Universe Working On Our Behalves

Focus Passage: Matthew 6:19-34

Jesus Christ asked his followers to be full of faith and always remain joyous. Jesus said,

> *"Therefore I say unto you, Take no thought for your life, what ye shall eat, or what ye shall drink; nor yet for your body, what ye shall put on. Is not the life more than meat, and the body than raiment? Behold the fowls of the air: for they sow not, neither do they reap, nor gather into barns; yet your heavenly Father feedeth them. Are ye not much better than they? Which of you by taking thought can add one cubit unto his stature? And why take ye thought for raiment? Consider the lilies of the field, how they grow; they toil not, neither do they spin: And yet I say unto you, That even Solomon in all his glory was not arrayed like one of these. Wherefore, if God so clothe the grass of the field, which today is, and tomorrow is cast into the oven, shall he not much more clothe you, O ye of little faith? Therefore take no thought, saying, What shall we eat? or, What shall we drink? Or, Wherewithal shall we be clothed? (For after all these things do the Gentiles seek :) for your heavenly Father knoweth that ye have need of all these things. But seek ye first the kingdom of God, and his righteousness; and all these things shall be added unto you. Take therefore no thought for the morrow: for the morrow shall take thought for the things of itself. Sufficient unto the day is the evil thereof"* **(Matthew 6:25-34 KJV).**

Lesson:

Christians are expected to be joyous (and not be anxious) during difficult situations. Satan loves to outsource scary situations to challenge believers' faith, and we must not allow him to have field day! The enemy's goal is to scare us into doubts and make us compromise our precious faith in God. We must maintain our steadfastness and keep professing positively during difficult situation until we see things turn around positively. As we demonstrate solid and unshakable faith in God, he will arise to fight our battles and earn us victory. Our faith action will return blessings for us, and it will earn us reasons to glorify God.

Prayer:

Dear God, please help me to demonstrate unwavering faith in you, and let me stop worrying about life challenges. Open my eyes and alert my senses to understand that I have God of the universe working on my behalf; he won't stop his works until he has awarded me complete victory! When all problems are over, let me return to testify to your goodness in the assembly of your people. For in the name of Jesus Christ I make my requests.

Amen.

« DAY 17 »

Godly Riches Lead To More Blessing

Focus Passage: Job 1, 2

Job was a billionaire of his time (by the economic standard); he was humble and served God with his wealth to the extent that his services became a subject of discussion between God and Satan. The scripture reported about Job,

> *"There was a man in the land of Uz, whose name was Job; and that man was blameless and upright, and one who feared God and shunned evil. And seven sons and three daughters were born to him. Also, his possessions were seven thousand sheep, three thousand camels, five hundred yoke of oxen, five hundred female donkeys, and a very large household, so that this man was the greatest of all the people of the East. And his sons would go and feast in their houses, each on his appointed day, and would send and invite their three sisters to eat and drink with them. So it was, when the days of feasting had run their course, that Job would send and sanctify them, and he would rise early in the morning and offer burnt offerings according to the number of them all. For Job said, "It may be that my sons have sinned and cursed God in their hearts." Thus Job did regularly" ... So Satan answered the Lord and said, "Does Job fear God for nothing? Have you not made a hedge around him, around his household, and around all that he has on every side? You have blessed the work of his hands, and his possessions have increased in the land. But now, stretch out your hand and touch all that he has, and he will surely curse you to your face!" And the Lord said to Satan, "Behold, all that he has is in your power; only do not lay a hand on his person"* **(Job 1:1-5; 9-12).**

Lesson:

It is possible for people to be rich and still faithfully serve God at the same time. For example, Job in the bible was rich and faithfully served God (Job 1:1-5). God who gives riches does not expect us to abuse its use, but he expects us to utilize them for his honor. However, it takes true humility for rich people to serve God. Any rich person who expects his/her services to be acceptable to God must be willing to separate him/herself from whatever wealth has been acquired. That is, the person must be ready to serve God with simplicity of mind without seeking publicity or obtaining special attention. Also, a rich person who is willing to appease God must be willing to serve under other people's leadership without flexing muscles. Also, a godly and rich person must not segregate, but equally attend to both the poor and rich people alike. God will honor and multiply the riches of anyone who chooses to walk in the path of righteousness for the sake of glorifying his name. Such individual will also be rewarded in heaven.

In addition, believers must understand that God can make everyone rich but he does measure our blessings base on what we can handle. Jehovah will not bless us beyond what we can handle; he won't give us benefits that can distant us from him. Therefore, any Christian who desires riches should first ask him/herself a honest question, *"If God blesses me with much riches will I still remain faithful to him?"*

Prayer:
Dear God, please make me a trustworthy Christian who is not obsessed with riches. Let me be someone whose heart is sold out for you for better for poor! Let me be selfless in my services and serve you with all my resources without seeking for any form of kickback. I surely know you will reward my faithfulness with much benefits; please bless me once you have tested and found me trusted! For in the name of Jesus Christ I make my requests.

Amen.

« DAY 18 »

Christians Must Represent Christ Well On Earth By Always Acting Honorably

Focus Passage: Matthew 7

God expects his children to be straightforward people, and not be hypocritical. Hypocrites point out other people's mistakes and cover theirs. No believer should be found with activities that focus on destroying other people's reputations. We ought not to get involved in any business of digging dirt to blackmail others. Rather, believers should focus on self-improvement that will glorify God. Jesus Christ said,

> *"Judge not, that you be not judged. For with what judgment you judge, you will be judged; and with the measure you use, it will be measured back to you. And why do you look at the speck in your brother's eye, but do not consider the plank in your own eye? Or how can you say to your brother, 'Let me remove the speck from your eye'; and look, a plank is in your own eye? Hypocrite! First remove the plank from your own eye, and then you will see clearly to remove the speck from your brother's eye"* **(Matthew 7:1-5).**

Lesson:
Christians are people of integrity, and we must act honorably at all times. We must venture to correct people in love and help them to recognize whatever is needed to make improvement. Our mission must not be to destroy others. We must not engage in activities that can damage other peoples' reputation, or negatively affect them in any other way. Christ delights noble services, and he will honor us if we act as his true ambassadors on earth.

Prayer:
Dear God, please give me the strength needed to focus on my personal improvement so that I can prosper. Also let my engagements be to benefit others, and not to mar them. Help me not to act contrarily to the bible by judging people and passing damaging comments on them. Please let my activities honor you always so that you can be pleased to bless me. For in the name of Jesus Christ I make my requests.

Amen.

« DAY 19 »

Difficult Situations Will Make Children Of God Stronger!

Focus Passage: Job 3, 4

Job sought for inner peace during his trial moments; he lamented and sought for real comfort, but he found none. He experienced persistent trouble that he had tried all his life to avoid. At a point during his distress, Job preferred death to life; he cursed the period of his childbirth and he wished he was never born. Job lamented,

> *"Why did I not die at birth? Why did I not perish when I came from the womb? Why did the knees receive me? Or why the breasts, that I should nurse? For now I would have lain still and been quiet, I would have been asleep; Then I would have been at rest with kings and counselors of the earth, who built ruins for themselves, or with princes who had gold, who filled their houses with silver; or why was I not hidden like a stillborn child, like infants who never saw light?"* **(Job 3:11-16).**

Lesson:

Children of God are currently living in an imperfect world, and challenges of life are inevitable! It has become almost impossible to live problem-free in our present world. Yet, we serve God that is ever faithful to help us overcome every adversity. Horrific situations will not be able to stop God's light of faithfulness from shining on us. Believers will sail to victory in every situation! However, most challenges have some elements of blessing embedded in them. They force believers to grow in faith and trust God more! When the period of darkness is over, Believers always come out stronger and better to live more victoriously! That is, God uses tough situations to perfect his purposes in our lives.

Prayer:

Dear God, please give me strong faith to handle challenges of life. No matter how tough the situation is, help me to maintain my steadfast faith in you. Let my trials become my testimony so that other people can hear about it and praise your name. Again, let all things work together for your good purposes in my life! For in the name of Jesus Christ I make my requests.

Amen.

« DAY 20 »

Believers Share The Same Authority That Jesus Used To Perform Miracles

Focus Passage: Matthew 8:1-17

Jesus Christ was fond of performing miracles to ease people's tension and solving their problems. Some instances of Jesus' miracles are referenced as quoted:

1. "When He had come down from the mountain, great multitudes followed Him. And behold, a leper came and worshiped Him, saying, "Lord, if you are willing, you can make me clean." Then Jesus put out *His* hand and touched him, saying, "I am willing; be cleansed." Immediately his leprosy was cleansed. **(Matthew 8: 1-3)**.
2. "Now when Jesus had entered Capernaum, a centurion came to Him, pleading with Him, saying, "Lord, my servant is lying at home paralyzed, dreadfully tormented." And Jesus said to him, "I will come and heal him." **(Matthew 8: 5-7)**
3. "Now when Jesus had come into Peter's house, He saw his wife's mother lying sick with a fever. So He touched her hand, and the fever left her. And she arose and served them" **(Matthew 8: 14-15)**.
4. When evening had come, they brought to Him many who were demon-possessed. And He cast out the spirits with a word, and healed all who were sick" **(Matthew 8: 16)**.

Lesson:
When Jesus Christ lived on earth, he took away people's pain and healed their sickness to make them trust God and serve him. Jesus' life played out as prophesied by Prophet Isaiah, *"Surely He has borne our griefs And carried our sorrows; Yet we esteemed Him stricken, Smitten by God, and afflicted. But He was wounded for our transgressions, He was bruised for our iniquities; The chastisement for our peace was upon Him, And by His stripes we are healed"* **(Isaiah 53:4-5)**. Meanwhile, Jesus has left the earth since 2,000 years ago but his ministry is still very much relevant and active in our present days! God's authority invested into Jesus' name will work in our days to earn us solution to our problems.

Prayer:
Dear Jesus Christ, I understand that your power is still very much active to solve people's problems; therefore, I proclaim my victory in you today: I declare my victory over all my challenges – family, health, finance, career, and others. Today, I stand on my feet to declare that my victory is total and it shall be permanent! For in the name of Jesus Christ I make my requests.

Amen.

« DAY 21 »

God's Corrections Make Christians Become Better And Stronger

Focus Passage: Job 5, 6, 7

Eliphaz perceived Job's problem was unusual, and he assumed he must have sinned against God. Eliphaz was wrong in his assumption, but his speech made sense as compared to God's standard of righteousness. Eliphaz said,

> *"Behold, happy is the man whom God corrects; Therefore do not despise the chastening of the Almighty. For He bruises, but He binds up; He wounds, but His hands make whole. He shall deliver you in six troubles, yes, in seven no evil shall touch you. In famine He shall redeem you from death, And in war from the power of the sword. You shall be hidden from the scourge of the tongue, and you shall not be afraid of destruction when it comes. You shall laugh at destruction and famine, and you shall not be afraid of the beasts of the earth"* **(Job 5:17-22).**

Lesson:

God cares for his people and he will deliver them from their troubles. The Creator chastises; reproof, corrects, and instructs people to bring them into compliance of his laws. War, famine, diseases, sicknesses, and others are not strong enough to perpetually affect God's children. They will pave way for God's children to have victory! Touch situation is not necessarily evil for God's children; it helps toughen their muscles to become more resilient and determine to succeed. Once adversity is over, God's children will rise to become stronger than ever before. Adversity also benefits God, since it eventually brings more glory to his name once his children have their expected victory. Satan is the only party that loses battle during adversity. He drops his head and walk away in defeat when God's children celebrate their victory. Children of God will always shout for victory and praise his name!

Prayer:

Dear God, what a wonderful privilege I have to be called your child! I am the most fortunate person created to bring you praise songs. Your Son Jesus Christ has earned me victory through his death on the cross; therefore, Satan cannot rejoice over me anymore! I am more than conqueror through Christ that lives in me! Therefore, I receive your grace to keep professing your faithfulness in every situation. I will shout the shout of victory and praise your name in the assembly of your people – Forever! Thanks to Jesus Christ for giving me such a great privilege of becoming the partaker of his benefits. Hallelujah!

Amen!

« DAY 22 »

The Authority Of Jesus Christ Consist Of Complete Package Anyone Needs For Total Deliverance

Focus Passage: Matthew 8:18-34

Tempest wind blew against the boat that transported Jesus Christ and his disciples, and Jesus arose to rebuke it. And the wind immediately stopped to everyone's amazements. The scripture reported,

> *"Now when He got into a boat, His disciples followed Him. And suddenly a great tempest arose on the sea, so that the boat was covered with the waves. But He was asleep. Then His disciples came to Him and awoke Him, saying, "Lord, save us! We are perishing!" But He said to them, "Why are you fearful, O you of little faith?" Then He arose and rebuked the winds and the sea, and there was a great calm. So the men marveled, saying, "Who can this be, that even the winds and the sea obey Him?" (Matthew 8:23-27).*

Lesson:
Jesus Christ possesses all power needed to speak into every human situation. He has authority over both visible and invisible forces, and whatever he says or does is final! Both the living and nonliving things submit to the authority of Jesus Christ. Jesus' authority also goes into the future to perform miracles for anyone that chooses to trust him. Jesus calms storms, cast out devils, heal the sick, and raise the dead! The list of what Jesus' power can do is endless. Followers of Jesus Christ ought to consider themselves fortunate since much benefit are available for them to enjoy. A person who confesses his/her faith in Jesus Christ will experience his remarkable power of deliverance and victory in every aspect of his/her life. To have absolute right-of-use in Jesus' power, it is necessary that a person first confess him (Jesus Christ) as his/her personal Lord and Savior (Romans 10:9-10).

Prayer:
Dear Jesus, I am glad that you have power to perform miracles to help people that follow you. Since I am your follower, I claim my right to use the authority of your name to have my victory; therefore, I rebuke whatever wind blowing against my life in the name of Jesus! I challenge devil, and I command all his manipulations and attacks against my life to be destroyed! I stand firm as a child of God to proclaim my dominance over every aspect life. I shall prosper at home, and I shall prosper in the field. I shall be above and not beneath, and I my testimony shall abide to the glory of God. For in the name of Jesus Christ I make my declarations.

Amen!

« DAY 23 »

Christians Are Not To Condemn Anyone; We Are Lift Up Lives

Focus Passage: Job 8, 9, 10

Bildad challenged Job and accused him of sin of self-righteousness for not accepting that he had done something wrong to incur terrible wrath of God. Bildad was wrong to presume Job as a sinner. Indeed Job was an imperfect human being, but his problem did not relate to his past sins. His problem was God-approved scenario created to glorify God. (The secret behind Job's trials was mentioned in Job 2:1-6). Bildad accused Job as stated,

> *"Then Bildad the Shuhite answered and said: "How long will you speak these things, and the words of your mouth be like a strong wind? Does God subvert judgment? Or does the Almighty pervert justice? If your sons have sinned against Him, He has cast them away for their transgression"* **(Job 8:1-4).**

Lesson:

Christians must desist from judging other people – for especially when they are going through trials. It is easy for anyone to demoralize people and pass judgment base on what he/she observes, but believers must have different behavior. We are God's children who read bible, and are possessive of the Holy Spirit. Therefore, we cannot be irrational and judge people base on our limited knowledge. We are to represent Christ in people's lives by praying and encouraging them into righteousness. Our jobs as Christians are to offer people moral supports, and give them sense of hope. Meanwhile, the fact that we must care for needy people does not mean that we should support their bad practices; however, we must ensure not to complicate their problems. God will surely honor us if we represent him well to make unbelievers turn to serve him.

Prayer:

Dear God, please make me a Christian who is relevant in the lives of other people. Help me not to focus on people's weaknesses, but let me be an agent of positive change in their lives. Help me to represent you well by making positive contributions that will challenge unbelievers to come closer and serve you. Please let your light so shine around me so that all people can see it and glorify your name. For in the name of Jesus Christ I make my requests.

Amen.

« DAY 24 »

Christians Are To Demonstrate Exemplary Lifestyle That Will Challenge Unbelievers To Consider Serving Christ

Focus Passage: Matthew 9:1-17

The Pharisees were Jesus' persistent enemies; they criticized him on everything he did. The Pharisees had some negative words for Jesus for performing miracles and serving common people. For example, they argued that Jesus supposedly a holy man should not be relating with sinners. The scripture described some Pharisees' actions as quoted,

> "While Jesus was having dinner at Matthew's house, many tax collectors and sinners came and ate with him and his disciples. 11 When the Pharisees saw this, they asked his disciples, "Why does your teacher eat with tax collectors and sinners?" On hearing this, Jesus said, "It is not the healthy who need a doctor, but the sick. But go and learn what this means: 'I desire mercy, not sacrifice.' For I have not come to call the righteous, but sinners" *(Matthew 9:10-13 NIV).*

Lesson:
Christians are expected to be less critical of others; we are supposed to be source of positive motivation for people instead. We are expected to care and be supportive of people to help them materialize their potentials. For us to achieve this purpose, we must be dead to self! That is, we must not be jealous of other people's success. Their success should not be considered as threat! We must be unbiased and be willing to point people's attention towards positive direction that will benefit their lives. Also, we must be ready to celebrate people's achievement. As Jesus' ambassador, we must ensure to engage in practices that will aid his light shining brighter, so that unbelievers can be challenged to receive his salvation

Prayer:
Dear Jesus Christ, please help me to be disciplined and be less critical of others. Help me to represent you well on earth so that I can be blessed. Please give me strength to support good courses that will benefit people and also promote your gospel. Let your light so shine in me so that unbelievers can be motivated to serve you and qualify for your kingdom. For in the name of Jesus Christ I make my requests.

Amen.

« DAY 25 »

God Can't Be Compared With Humans; Humanity Should Tremble Before Him

Focus Passage: Job 11, 12, 13

Zophar accused Job of pretense, and insisted he was a stern sinner who deserved his suffering. Zophar was wrong. He never witnessed Job committing a sin, yet he accused him of wrongdoing. Zophar said,

> *"...Know therefore that God exacts from you less than your iniquity deserves"* **(Job 11:6).**

Lesson

Humans are humans, and God is God. We humans are limited in knowledge, but God is omnipotent. He knows all things, and could adequately respond to them. Therefore, we humans must be careful not to mismatch our opinions with reality of God's standard. God's standard is by far different from ours. Humans have limited and subjective opinions, but God has a firm and unbiased standard. He has limitless knowledge, but he has chosen to share limited knowledge with us, so that we won't claim rivalry with him. The Creator hates having us as his rival; he prefers we depend on him in all situations. Hence, our actions (as believers) must not present us as God's rivals. We must remain humble and dependable on him to receive his benefits.

Prayer:

Dear God, please help me to be disciplined, and not compare myself with you. Do not let me equate myself with you. You are God, and I am human. You are far better than me in all ramifications! Therefore, I choose to submit myself before you for knowledge and strength. I will not question your authority, neither will I usurp it. I will maintain my position as a man/woman who pursue justice and make positive contributions to others people's lives. I will be instrumental to other people's progress, and I will serve you with all my strength. Please keep me steady and firm to remain your true child forever. For in the name of Jesus Christ I make my requests.

Amen.

« DAY 26 »

Signs And Wonders Will Never Be Wanted In The Lives Of People That Demonstrate Unwavering Faith In God

Focus Passage: Matthew 9:18-38

The woman whom Jesus Christ healed of her blood flow problem deserved much credit for holding firmly in faith until she experienced her deliverance. The woman initiated her own healing by saying to herself,

> *"If only I may touch His (Jesus) garment, I shall be made well"* **(Matthew 9:21)**. Of course, Jesus healed her.

Lesson:
Healing and deliverance belong to any child of God who demonstrates unwavering faith. God will not ignore any persistent Christian who cries to him for help; he will come to his/her aids to help, so that unbelievers can hear it and be challenged to serve him also. Therefore, sons and daughters of God must make God proud by demonstrating unwavering faith in their situations. We (believers) must confess faith and claim our healing and deliverance ahead of time to challenge God into action. Our faith will honor God and put devil to shame. Indeed, God's signs and wonders will never be wanted for people who demonstrate their unwavering faith in him.

Prayer:
Dear God, please give me strength to demonstrate unwavering faith in you. Let my faith in you be resolute so that I can have all-round victory and so that I can share the testimony of your goodness to the ends of the ends of the earth. Let my faith in you lead to my salvation, deliverance, healing, and promotion - To glorify your name. For in the name of Jesus Christ I make my requests.

Amen.

« DAY 27 »

Faith Reserved In God Will Never Fail; Jehovah Will Prove Himself Faithful

Focus Passage: Job 14, 15, 16

Job professed his faith in God despite the horrific trials that he went through. The man managed to proclaim,

> *"For there is hope for a tree, if it is cut down, that it will sprout again, and that its tender shoots will not cease. Though its root may grow old in the earth, and its stump may die in the ground, yet at the scent of water it will bud and bring forth branches like a plant"* **(Job 14:7-9).**

Lesson:

The faithfulness of God ever remains the same; no situation can change his nature. He will remain a good God – no matter how good or bad a situation may appear. Therefore, believers ought to remain hopeful in God over whatever circumstance they may face. God who has proven himself faithful in the past will prove Himself faithful again. He will not disappoint, but he will help his children prevail in all situations. The same God who turned situations around for faithful men and women in the bible is still the same one that we (Christians) serve today. He will help us like he'd helped Job, Daniel, Joseph, Deborah, Hannah, and others. God is ever faithful, and he will turn any terrible situation to a good one for his faithful children. Jehovah will ultimately make his children have a big laughter, and praise his holy name.

Prayer:

Dear God, you are beautiful beyond descriptions, and your power is indescribable! You are the supreme God who reigns over men's affairs. I surely know that you are in charge of my situations, and you will turn them around for my blessings. Let God of Job be my God; let God of Daniel be my God; let God of Shadrach, Meshach, and Abednego be my God! Let God who turns impossibilities into possibilities be my God! I bring all my life situations before him that he may turn them around for my benefits and for his glory. Let the whole world hear of God's goodness in my life and praise his holy name. Let my life remain an embodiment of testimony to the name of God from now on, and forever! For in the name of Jesus Christ I make my requests.

Amen.

« DAY 28 »

The Greatest Demonstration Of Jesus' Power Is Not Miracles Of Healing, But Salvation

Focus Passage: Matthew 10:1-2

Jesus Christ called out his disciples, and impacted them with power to preach his gospel. Christ also anointed them with power and authority to cast out devils and heal all kind of diseases. It is reported,

> *"And when He had called His twelve disciples to Him, He gave them power over unclean spirits, to cast them out, and to heal all kinds of sickness and all kinds of disease" (Matthew 10:1).*

Lesson:
Jesus Christ has all power needed to overcome Satan anytime any day! Christ is not only the Savior of the world, but he is also the most powerful being in existence. God has endowed his authority on him to perform all kinds of miracles, and also to root out the works of Satan. (Philippians 2:9-11). However, The Savior has not chosen to hoard his power and authority, he has shared them with his followers. He still shares them today to as many that will believe in his name. Therefore, sons and daughters of God will triumph over Satan in this world! Meanwhile, the greatest demonstration of Jesus' power is not miracles of healing and deliverances; his greatest work is reflected through his salvation capability! Jesus has power to save people from the pathway of hell fire, and earn them the gift of eternal life. Those who believe Jesus Christ will not only triumph over Satan in this world, but they will also inherit the gift of eternal life in heaven.

In addition, Jesus Christ who commanded his disciples to evangelize gospel is still calling all his followers today to do the same thing. Every Christian is called to preach gospel of Jesus Christ so that unbelievers can have their privilege of salvation, and go to heaven. Believers who heed the call of Christ to evangelize gospel will receive the imperishable crowns of glory in heaven. They will shine like the bright stars radiating beauty from the center of God's heart.

Prayer:
Dear Jesus Christ, I am ready to preach your gospel; here I am, send me! Give me grace to preach your unbiased truth of the gospel in every locality. Enable me with strength to proclaim your good news of salvation to people near and beyond, so that they can come to your knowledge and be saved. Please anoint my head with oil of gladness, and let my life radiate your beauty from now on, and forever more! For in your holy name - Jesus Christ - I make my requests.

Amen.

« DAY 29 »

Believers Must Be Sensitive To Only Offer Counsel Based On Holy Spirit Guidance

Focus Passage: Job 17, 18, 19

Job called his friends *"Miserable comforters"* for their insensitive counsels **(Job 16:2)**. Job also painfully responded to his friends' criticisms and said,

> *"Why do you persecute me as God does, and are not satisfied with my flesh?"* **(Job 19:22)**. Meanwhile, Job's friends initially got involved during his adversity to offer moral supports, but they eventually turned to become his critics. They ended up condemning him with their insensitive speeches with claims that he had probably done something wrong to deserve his horrific situation.

Lesson:

Christians must be sensitive to counsel people in some fashions that will glorify God. We must be careful not to miscommunicate our intentions whenever we attempt to help. We must portray Christ's examples by lifting up downcast souls with our words of encouragement. We must not be insensitive and be rash in our approach. Our ultimate goal must be to encourage any fallen believer and help him/her stand. If our efforts lead to the backslidden of others fellows, to what advantage is that? Therefore we have to be careful not to chase people away from God's kingdom with our attitudes. We must be mindful of how we approach people and express our love to them. Our prime focus must be to let people around us feel the warmness of Christ's love and adequately respond. Believer must always remember that "love" is very important to God, and we must demonstrate it to all people - always!

Prayer:

Dear God, please help me to be sensitive to the needs of people around me. Let my life radiate your beauty to others. Give me grace to help others recognize their self-worth and sense of value. Let my efforts motivate others to act positively and keep depending on you. Please anoint me with your Holy Spirit to be your true ambassador in the lives of everyone around me, so that your name can be praised everywhere throughout the world. For in the name of Jesus Christ I make my requests.

Amen.

« DAY 30 »

Satan Harassed Jesus; He Will Also Harass Christians – Believers Must Not Compromise

Focus Passage: Matthew 10:21-42

Jesus Christ warned his disciples to prepare for enemies' persecutions, which are imminent. Believers must set their mind to overcome the persecutions and remain steadfast in their faith. Jesus said,

> *"And you will be hated by all for my name's sake. But he who endures to the end will be saved* **(Matthew 10:22).**" Jesus also said, *"Therefore whoever confesses me before men, him I will also confess before my Father who is in heaven"* **(Matthew 10:32)**.

Lesson:
Christians will face persecutions in this world for the sake of their faith in Christ, but they are assured of great rewards in heaven if they remain unshifted. Satan, the enemy of righteousness has always been Jesus' enemy from inception. He hates Christ, and would do anything to hurt him. Satan pursued Jesus to the point of death on the Cross of Calvary. However, Jesus won his battle against the enemy when he resurrected from the grave on the third day. Christ completely silenced Satan with the power of his resurrection and his divine blood! Meanwhile, Satan has not stopped being upset against Jesus; he attacks Christians (Jesus' followers) throughout the world with great fury. Meanwhile, believers must be encouraged to refute the enemy and stomp their feet in defiance to his harassments. No child of God should give in for the devil - He is a bastard enemy deserving the deepest part of hell fire! Followers of Jesus Christ who remain steadfast in faith and faithfully serve God to the end will be greatly rewarded in heaven. In the meantime, believers can claim their victory over Satan's onslaught by confessing the authority of Jesus' name, blood, and resurrection. Any believer under persecution must proclaim "I rebuke devil and I overcome him by the blood of Jesus Christ for it is written "And they overcame him by the blood of the Lamb and by the word of their testimony, and they did not love their lives to the death"" (Revelation 12:11).

Prayer:
Dear God, please help me to keep the testimony of your Son Jesus Christ unto the end. Help me to triumph over Satan and all his harassments. Anoint me with your oil of gladness to keep shining in the face of adversity and proclaim Christ's gospel to the ends of the end. Since Jesus overcame Satan, I will overcome him also. Therefore, I command Satan to get lost from my life. I rebuke him and I defeat all his assaults against my destiny. I break the power of Satan by the blood of Jesus Christ for it is written: "... They overcame him by the blood of the Lamb and by the word of their testimony, and they did not love their lives to the death" (Revelation 12:11). I proclaim my deliverance today, and I claim God's strength to keep living an overcomer's life from now on, and forever. For in the name of Jesus Christ I make my declarations.

Amen!

« DAY 31 »

A Person Who Arrogates God's Divine Glory To Him Or Herself Will Fail

Focus Passage: Job 20, 21

Zophar one of Job's friends tried to persuade him to accept their accusation that sin had brought crises to his life. However, Job maintained his innocence. Zophar persuasively questioned Job,

> *"Do you not know this of old, since man was placed on earth, that the triumphing of the wicked is short, and the joy of the hypocrite is but for a moment? Though his haughtiness mounts up to the heavens, and his head reaches to the clouds, yet he will perish forever like his own refuse; those who have seen him will say, 'Where is he?'"* **(Job 20:4-7)**. Job responded, *"Listen carefully to my speech, and let this be your consolation. Bear with me that I may speak, and after I have spoken, keep mocking. "As for me, is my complaint against man? And if it were, why should I not be impatient? Look at me and be astonished; Put your hand over your mouth. Even when I remember I am terrified, and trembling takes hold of my flesh. Why do the wicked live and become old, yes, become mighty in power?"* **(Job 21:2-7)**.

Lesson:

God's ways are different from man's way, and no one should behave as if he/she is as knowledgeable as God. Yes, we humans have knowledge, but we are no match with God! He is far more intelligent than us. The Creator can simply make foolishness out of our wisdom, therefore we should tremble before him, and desist from any action that may present us as if we rob shoulder with him. In like fashion, every Christian must be careful not to attempt to equate him or herself with God in speech or deed. We are truly endowed with grace and power through Jesus Christ, but we must still carry out all our exercises in humility before God. Meanwhile, an arrogant person who steps on people and challenge God's authority will not go unpunished. Also, a person who arrogantly speaks or does things as if he/she is God will have much to account for in the presence of his/her Creator! The best anyone can do is to serve God with respect, and treat others with fairness and honor.

Prayer:

Dear God, I am no match with you; therefore, I will not compare myself with you! You are God, and I am a man/woman. You are greater than all, and I respect you for that. Please, I do not want to offend you in any way; neither do I want to equate myself with you. Please give me grace to serve you with due honor, and let me respect everyone you have planted into my world. Give me the spirit of humility to treat others with respect, so that your name can be glorified always. Again, please make me your true child who radiates your beauty at all times! For in the name of Jesus Christ I make my requests.

Amen.

« DAY 32 »

Satan Can Use Adversity To Tempt Anyone, But Believers Have The Choice To Resist His Temptation

Focus Passage: Matthew 11

John the Baptist was disappointed in Jesus for not bailing him out of Herod's prison. (Herod jailed John for proclaiming God's kingdom). The preacher sent a message to Jesus challenging him of his messiah title. He asked if he was the true messiah. However, Jesus responded in an amazing manner as the scripture reported,

> *"Now when John had heard in the prison the works of Christ, he sent two of his disciples, And said unto him, Art thou he that should come, or do we look for another? Jesus answered and said unto them, Go and shew John again those things which ye do hear and see: The blind receive their sight, and the lame walk, the lepers are cleansed, and the deaf hear, the dead are raised up, and the poor have the gospel preached to them. And blessed is he, whosoever shall not be offended in me"* **(Matthew 11:2-6 KJV).**

Lesson:

Satan can use adversity to tempt anyone to deny God, but believers have the choice to resist the temptation. Every Christian must understand that Satan is the brain behind adversity, and his motive is to cause anyone to derail from his/her prestigious Christian journey. The enemy's ultimate goal is to make a believer lose his /her salvation and miss opportunity of making heaven. However, Satan who tempts does not have power of victory - Believers do! Christians must exercise their right in the bible by rebuking the devil, and ask him to get lost as the scripture stated, *"submit to God. Resist the devil and he will flee from you"* **(James 4:7)**. Christians will overcome Satan's temptations by praying and confessing the word of God always. Also, believers must not entertain compromise thoughts. Every child of God must be full of the Holy Spirit to satisfy God in thoughts and deeds, and also to overcome Satan.

Prayer:

Dear God, please help me live an overcomer's live in this world. Give me power to resist Satan and his temptations. Let me be sensitive through the Holy Spirit to understand and do your will at all times. Empower me to keep serving you in the sight of adversity so that devil can be ashamed, and so that the world might praise you on my behalf. Let your songs of victory ever be in my mouth, and let me ever serve you throughout the days of my life. Please do these things, and many more. For in the name of Jesus Christ I make my requests.

Amen.

« DAY 33 »

Believers Must Not Allow Challenges Of Life Severe Their Relationship With God

Focus Passage: Job 22, 23, 24

Job remained steadfast in God and confessed his faith despite various trials that he went through. Job had lost all his ten children in one day, he lost all his businesses, and he was also suffering from a stricken sickness. Amidst all his challenges, the man Job professed,

> *"But He (God) knows the way that I take; when He has tested me, I shall come forth as gold"* **(Job 23:10).**

Lesson:

Afflictions should not separate Christians from their God. Indeed situations of life may be tough and peaceful moments may be far from our radar, yet we (believers) must still trust God. Our relationship with God must not know any boundary. That is, we should not allow any challenge of life dictate how much we will trust God. God of the good times is also God of the bad times. He knows how to make bad situations turn good for his children. Whatever situation that may appear as insurmountable problem today will soon become a testimony for his children, and they will praise his name.

Truly, it may be difficult to put on good attitude during trials, but believers must still do the right thing. We can still trust God during adversity to prove devil wrong and make him ashamed! Any Christian who suffers any hardship should look up to God and keep confessing his/her faith in him. The fellow should keep praising God and wait for his salvation. Surely, our good God will show up in time of need to glorify his name.

Prayer:

Dear God, I ask you to please give me strength to trust you during trials and temptations so that your name can be glorified, and so that devil be put to shame. Please give me unbeatable faith that subdues mountains. Help me to keep positive attitude even when Satan expects me to be sad. Let my faith prove devil wrong! Give me victory over all life challenges; when all trials are over, let me stand in the midst of your congregation to testify to your goodness. Let the songs of your praises ever fill my mouth even from now on and forever more! For in the name of Jesus Christ I make my requests.

Amen.

« DAY 34 »

Jehovah Will Not Entertain Anyone That Attempt To Either Stop Or Negatively Influence His Works

Focus Passage: Matthew 12:1-23

The Pharisees failed in their attempts to use Law of Moses to discredit Jesus' ministerial activities. They failed to realize that Jesus' ministry was masterminded by God himself, and nothing can change it. A confrontation instance between the Pharisees and Jesus Christ was reported,

> *"At that time Jesus went on the Sabbath day through the corn; and his disciples were hungry, and began to pluck the ears of corn and to eat. But when the Pharisees saw it, they said unto him, Behold, thy disciples do that which is not lawful to do upon the Sabbath day. But he said unto them, Have ye not read what David did, when he was an hungry, and they that were with him; How he entered into the house of God, and did eat the shewbread, which was not lawful for him to eat, neither for them which were with him, but only for the priests? Or have ye not read in the law, how that on the Sabbath days the priests in the temple profane the Sabbath, and are blameless? But I say unto you, That in this place is one greater than the temple. But if ye had known what this meaneth, I will have mercy, and not sacrifice, ye would not have condemned the guiltless. For the Son of man is Lord even of the Sabbath day"* **(Matthew 12:1-8 KJV)**.

Lesson:
God's work is very special to him, and he will not entertain anyone who attempts to either stop or negatively influence it. Jehovah cares about his work very much, and he will do whatever necessary to preserve it. Since, gospel activities are God's work, all people ought to be cautious and ensure their pride and selfish interest does not affect it. Anyone who chooses to support God's work will prosper, but whoever negatively affects it will pay a heavy price.

Prayer:
Dear God, please give me a heart that support your work; let me contribute my best efforts to support your work so that I can prosper! Do not let me get involve in any actions that can negatively impact your kingdom; let my actions contribute to the promotion of your kingdom, so that your name can be glorified among the people - Always! For in the name of Jesus Christ I make my requests.

Amen.

« DAY 35 »

Christians Are Expected To Wisely Utilize Their God-Given Grace To Benefit Other People

Focus Passage: Job 25, 26, 27

Bildad inappropriately counseled his friend Job during his distress. His words were right but they did not apply to Job's situation. Bildad was busy teaching Job theology when he ought to have given him moral supports. Job had lost everything he had: He lost his family, business, and health. Yet, all Bildad could do was to talk about God's dominion, peace, and strength. Job didn't need those teaching at that point in his life! Bildad words are quoted,

> *"Dominion and fear belong to Him; He makes peace in His high places. Is there any number to His armies? Upon whom does His light not rise? How then can man be righteous before God? Or how can he be pure who is born of a woman? If even the moon does not shine, and the stars are not pure in His sight, how much less man, who is a maggot, and a son of man, who is a worm?"* **(Job 25:2-6).**

Lesson:

Christians are expected to wisely utilize their God-given grace to benefit other people. We (believers) must be sensitive to people around us and make positive contributions to their lives. Our practices ought not to tear anyone down under whatever circumstance. We must know how to appropriate our spiritual activities to benefit people around us. To what advantage is any spiritual activity that leads others to depression and loss of self-esteem? Believers must learn from Jesus Christ who gave sense of value to people around him so that he could save them. Christ made everyone around him feel special so that he could win their souls! In like manner, Christians' activities must not tear people down; they must motivate people to draw closer to God so that they can be saved. Indeed, believers can truly be Christ's ambassadors in people's lives by asking for more of fullness of the Holy Spirit in their lives!

Prayer:

Dear God, please give me grace to be sensitive to the needs of others; let me be sensitive to other people's needs and appropriately attend to their needs. Let my efforts lead to an upliftment of people's lives, and not to tear them down. Please let me be your true ambassador on earth so that everyone around me can be motivated to serve you according to your expectations. For in the name of Jesus Chris I make my requests.

Amen.

« DAY 36 »

Believers Ought To Keep Distance From People That Trivialize Gospel And Make Slurs Against God

Focus Passage: Matthew 12:24-50

The Pharisees falsely accused Jesus Christ of using evil spirit to cast out devils. However, Jesus questioned their logic to make them realize how much they have missed the point. Jesus also warned his critics to be careful of committing an unpardonable sin with their actions. The scripture reported,

> *"Now when the Pharisees heard it they said, "This fellow does not cast out demons except by Beelzebub, the ruler of the demons." But Jesus knew their thoughts, and said to them: "Every kingdom divided against itself is brought to desolation, and every city or house divided against itself will not stand. If Satan casts out Satan, he is divided against himself. How then will his kingdom stand? And if I cast out demons by Beelzebub, by whom do your sons cast them out? Therefore they shall be your judges. But if I cast out demons by the Spirit of God, surely the kingdom of God has come upon you. Or how can one enter a strong man's house and plunder his goods, unless he first binds the strong man? And then he will plunder his house. He who is not with Me is against Me, and he who does not gather with Me scatters abroad"* **(Matthew 12:24-30).** Jesus warned his critics against unpardonable sin and said, *"Therefore I say to you, every sin and blasphemy will be forgiven men, but the blasphemy against the Spirit will not be forgiven men. Anyone who speaks a word against the Son of Man, it will be forgiven him; but whoever speaks against the Holy Spirit, it will not be forgiven him, either in this age or in the age to come"* **(Matthew 12:31-32).**

Lesson:
Believers must be careful not to allow their critics persuade them to sin against God. We sometimes run into a few individuals who care less about God, and who are consumed with worldly characters. Those people may joke and make slurs against God; they would be quick to question bible beliefs and trivialize God's principles. Believers must keep a distance with those folks! Our associations must cherish and honor things of God. We must not be part of any associations that disrespect God in any fashion or form. Jehovah will honor believers who make him proud in all ramifications, but he will keep a distance from any arrogant person who lightly esteems his principles.

Prayer:
Dear God, please teach me how to respect you. Do not let me associate myself with insensitive people who are careless with their words and actions. Enable me with grace to maintain godly principles that will always glorify your name, so that you can be happy with me at all times. For in the name of Jesus Christ I make my requests.

Amen.

« DAY 37 »

Believers Must Remain Hopeful In God Until Things Turn Around For Their Advantages

Focus Passage: Job 28, 29

Job was let down by his friends during distress; they sought for a way to condemn him rather than lifting up his spirit. However, the man was determined to remain hopeful: He shuns all criticisms and recounted his past deeds to motivate himself. Job referenced his past good deeds as stated,

> *"When the ear heard, then it blessed me, and when the eye saw, then it approved me; because I delivered the poor who cried out, the fatherless and the one who had no helper. The blessing of a perishing man came upon me, and I caused the widow's heart to sing for joy. I put on righteousness, and it clothed me; my justice was like a robe and a turban. I was eyes to the blind, and I was feet to the lame. I was a father to the poor, and I searched out the case that I did not know. I broke the fangs of the wicked, and plucked the victim from his teeth"* **(Job 29:11-17).**

Lesson:

Children of God must remain hopeful in God always. We (believers) must not wait until things turn to our favor before we can profess our faith in God. In fact, the proof of our trust in God is to positively confess his power when things are yet to favor us. We ought not to wait till things favor us before we can shout "God is good!" However, the proof of our faith will make devil ashamed and yield God more glory. Jehovah will forever stand by people of faith to show Himself strong on their behalves. He will beat down their enemies and earn them victory. The Creator won't stop until he has made those who trust him the beacon of his praise.

Prayer:

Dear God, please help me to exercise strong faith in you during my trial period, so that devil can be ashamed and your name be glorified. Help me to stay positive and remain hopeful in you in all situations. Do not let me waver in faith, but let me remain steadfast so that devil can be ashamed, and glory be given to your name. Do not let me be carried away with whatever people say or do rather let my focus remain to trust you. Help me to patiently wait for your help until my change comes. When all trials are over, let me have all causes to testify to your goodness and sing your songs of praise. Please do these things and many more. For in the name of Jesus Christ I make my requests.

Amen.

« DAY 38 »

Every Christian Must Grow And Develop Into Maturity

Focus Passage: Matthew 13:1-30

Jesus Christ used farming process to narrate the story of God's kingdom. Some seeds sown by a farmer would germinate while others will fall short of his expectations. Those seeds that grow and bear fruits are compared to faithful Christians, others are considered as backsliders. Jesus narrated,

> *"... And as he sowed, some seed fell by the wayside; and the birds came and devoured them. Some fell on stony places, where they did not have much earth; and they immediately sprang up because they had no depth of earth. But when the sun was up they were scorched, and because they had no root they withered away. And some fell among thorns, and the thorns sprang up and choked them. But others fell on good ground and yielded a crop: some a hundredfold, some sixty, some thirty"... "Therefore hear the parable of the sower: When anyone hears the word of the kingdom, and does not understand it, then the wicked one comes and snatches away what was sown in his heart. This is he who received seed by the wayside. But he who received the seed on stony places, this is he who hears the word and immediately receives it with joy; yet he has no root in himself, but endures only for a while. For when tribulation or persecution arises because of the word, immediately he stumbles. Now he who received seed among the thorns is he who hears the word, and the cares of this world and the deceitfulness of riches choke the word, and he becomes unfruitful. But he who received seed on the good ground is he who hears the word and understands it, who indeed bears fruit and produces: some a hundredfold, some sixty, some thirty"* **(Matthew 13:4-8; 13:18-23).**

Lesson:

Christianity have stages that include germination stage, growth stage, and fruit bearing stage. Every Christian is expected to undergo the three important stages. No one should fall short of the complete three stages! A person reaches germination stage at a moment he/she accepts Jesus and confesses him as Lord. The second stage is crucial since it requires commitments. A person who has become born-again must be committed to Jesus Christ. He/she must daily exercise his/her faith in God by studying bible, praying, and fellowshipping with other brethren. Every Christian ought to grow as Christ demands. Therefore, the second stage - which is the development mode - must involve a Christian applying God's principles received through bible study and other teachings to his/her daily life. The third stage involves fruit bearing. Every Christian must bear good and positive fruits for God. Anyone at the third stage is considered to be matured. He must preach to others; he must lead others to Christ, and he must demonstrate Christ to his/her equals, and people in other stages of Christianity. However, the third stage is the ultimate goal of Christ. He saves people to transform them to his gospel sharer (Evangelists). Hence, anyone who hides or hoard gospel is acting against the will of Christ. Everyone must proclaim gospel so that other people can be saved as well.

Prayer:
Dear God, please make me someone who grows in faith and reaches maturity. Since I have begun my work with you as a Christian, help me to grow! Let me study your word for my improvement and development. Let my growth lead to maturity, and let me be productive for you. Please make me an effective Christian who shares your gospel to people around me. Indeed someone lead me to Christ; let me lead others to Christ as well! Please empower me to share your gospel and be your true representative on earth. Let your name be praised over my life, and let me be worthy to receive your crown of honor in heaven. For in the name of Jesus Christ I make my requests.

Amen.

« DAY 39 »

Children Of God Must Not Be Irrational In Their Approach, But Be Sensitive In The Holy Spirit

Focus Passage: Job 30, 31

Job scolded his friends for their insensitive and ungodly counsels. (His friend kept condemning him when they ought to have lifted up his spirit to keep trusting God). Job's patience was exhausted, and he vented his frustration,

> *"Now they mock at me, men younger than I, whose father I disdained to put with the dogs of my flock"* **(Job 30:1)**.

Lesson:
Children of God must act godly at all times. We must allow Holy Spirit to teach and lead us how to be involved in every situation - For especially those that we have limited knowledge about. We must not be irrational in our approach and behaviors. Our efforts must be void of unnecessary confrontations. We must be careful to pass positive messages to others - For especially when they are under difficult situations. However, we must not rationalize a situation and refuse to tell the truth of God's word, but we must be sensitive to pass our messages in humane form. We must not share gospel to condemn anyone. Also, we must not demean people in the name of counseling! Our motivations must be to make people draw closer to God and serve him well. Also, our effort must be to help alleviate people's pains, and make them set their hope in God. Jehovah will indeed bless any Christian who represents him well in the lives of others; the fellow will have much benefit to enjoy from the Creator in this life, and the one to come.

Prayer:
Dear God, please help me to be your true ambassador in the lives of other people. Anoint me through your Holy Spirit to make positive contributions into the lives of other people. Let my efforts draw people closer to you. Let my approach teach people how to set their hope in you in whatever circumstance of their lives. Again, please give me grace to represent you well on earth so that the fame of your name can extend to all regions of the earth. For in the name of Jesus Christ I make my request.

Amen.

« DAY 40 »

Heaven Is Specially Prepared For God's Saints; Hell Is Specially Prepared For Satan And His Followers

Focus Passage: Matthew 13:31-58

Everything about the End Time season is summarized in Matthew Chapter 13, which testified that Jesus Christ will soon return to rapture his saints to heaven,

1. Jesus sowed seed of salvation into the world.
2. Satan also sowed seed of wickedness into the world.
3. Those who have responded to Jesus Christ, and have received his salvation offer will go to heaven.
4. God's angels will gather and cast wicked people to hell fire.
5. Meanwhile, God's angels will gather righteous people and send them to heaven.
6. The righteous people will rejoice in God's kingdom, but
7. The wicked people will regretfully live in hell fire.

Lesson:
Heaven is a special place designed and prepared for God's saints, but hell fire is created for Satan and his followers. God's saints are the people who have confessed Jesus Christ as their personal Lord and Savior, and served him well on earth. Unbelievers are those who have rejected Jesus' testimony; they have refused to confess him as Lord, and they are regarded as Satan's followers. However, the door of salvation of Jesus Christ is yet to close, and anyone can cross-platform from hell's pathway to heaven's pathway. Whoever humbly comes to Jesus Christ will be saved. Meanwhile, the door of salvation will eventually close against those who remain defiant to Jesus' offer of salvation. The grace of salvation will immediately cease after rapture. Therefore, it is essential that everyone seriously considers the salvation offer of Jesus Christ today and respond appropriately, since the window of opportunity will not open indefinitely.

Prayer:
Dear God, what profits does a man has by gaining the whole world and losing his soul to Satan in hell fire. I do not want to get burnt in hell fire; neither do I want to make hell my permanent home! Therefore, I respond to the salvation offer of your Son Jesus Christ today: I (*mention your name*) confess Jesus Christ as my personal Lord and Savior. I confess my sins and repent from them. I yield my complete life to Jesus Christ, and I promise to serve him throughout the days of my life. Please keep me heavenly worthy, and let my name be permanently registered in the book of life. At the end of my earthly journey, let me meet you in heaven to rejoice in your everlasting peace and success. For in the name of Jesus Christ I make my requests.

Amen.

« DAY 41 »

No Person Should Bank On Self-Righteousness As A Means Of Appeasing God

Focus Passage: Job 32,33

Elihu scolded Job for his claim of self-righteousness. He rebuked Job as quoted,

> *"Surely you have spoken in my hearing, and I have heard the sound of your words, saying, 'I am pure, without transgression; I am innocent, and there is no iniquity in me. Yet He finds occasions against me, He counts me as His enemy; He puts my feet in the stocks, He watches all my paths."* ***(Job 33:8-11)***.

Lesson:
No Christian should bank on self-righteousness as a means of appeasing God. Indeed, no human righteousness would be good enough to satisfy God's requirements of holiness as the scripture emphasized, "But we are all like an unclean thing, and all our righteousness are like filthy rags; We all fade as a leaf, And our iniquities, like the wind, Have taken us away" ***(Isaiah 64:6)***. Instead of claim of self-righteousness, we (Christians) ought to humble ourselves before God and strive daily to serve him better. In other words, no believer should assume he/she has arrived! No one should claim he/she is more spiritual and has attained an upper level of faith. Believers must each day seek God's face, and serve him with humility. We must carefully obey God and make sizable efforts to meet all his expectations, so that we can prosper on earth and be qualified for heaven.

Prayer:
Dear God, what profit do I earn with a claim of self-righteousness? Absolutely nothing! You are pleased with humble people, but detest arrogant people. Therefore, I ask for your grace to live a humble life before you always. Give me grace to daily strive to meet all your expectations so that I can qualify for your kingdom! Please, let every effort I make before you result to the glory of your name, and be void of selfishness and self-righteousness. Please keep my feet firm in your kingdom from now on and forevermore. For in the name of Jesus Christ I make my requests.

Amen.

« DAY 42 »

Christians Must Be Spiritually Inclined To Satisfy God's Desires

Focus Passage Matthew 14:1-21

King Herod was overly excited during his birthday party to the extent that he subjected his authority to a small girl's demand. The girl forced the king's hands to kill John the Baptist against his own wish. The scripture reported,

> *"...When Herod's birthday was celebrated, the daughter of Herodias danced before them and pleased Herod. Therefore he promised with an oath to give her whatever she might ask. So she, having been prompted by her mother, said, "Give me John the Baptist's head here on a platter. And the king was sorry; nevertheless, because of the oaths and because of those who sat with him, he commanded it to be given to her. So he sent and had John beheaded in prison. And his head was brought on a platter and given to the girl, and she brought it to her mother"* **(Matthew 14:6-11).**

Lesson:
Christians must ensure to be ruled by the Holy Spirit, and not by their emotion. No child of God should mistake emotional leading for the leadership of the Holy Spirit. There is much possibility that anyone can mistake his/her human feelings as a leadership of the Holy Spirit; therefore, believers must be careful! We must weigh every decision based on bible standard, and we must examine every thought to ensure flesh is not in control. For a believer to be truly led by the Holy Spirit, he/she must be prayerful (He must prayerfully consider any proposition). Also, a believer who wants to be spiritually inclined must be filled with the word of God, and give his/her life to prayer and fasting. Those spiritual activities will severe the flesh to have little or no chance to manifest. Meanwhile, whatever anyone considers as inspirational must not violate the scripture. A quick means of evaluating whether an inspiration is godly or not is to ask: "Is this thought or inspiration godly; is it praiseworthy; does it benefit God, and does it benefit other people?" Any inspiration that fails the questions must outrightly be rejected. God expects his children to grow in his grace, live peaceably with him, and benefit others. People who duly obey him and stand by his leadership will ever prevail in every aspect of their lives.

Prayer:
Dear God, please baptize me with your Holy Spirit, and let me satisfy you in everything I do so that your name can be glorified in my life. Do not let me give in for Satan's devises and yield to the craving of flesh. Don't let me be ruled by emotion, but let me be ruled by your Holy Spirit! Anoint me with grace to live a sanctified life; obey your word; benefit your kingdom, and benefit other people around me. Let my life bring glory to your name from now on, and forever more. For in the name of Jesus Christ I make my requests.

Amen.

« DAY 43 »

A Good Christian Is Expected To Be Wise And Make Good Decisions

Focus Passage: Job 34,35

Elihu faulted Job with some unfounded sins, and accused him of wickedness. Elihu argued that nothing else could have brought Job much jeopardy than sin. [However, Elihu was wrong. Job's crisis had nothing to do with his sin. He underwent a God-approved temptation from Satan **(Job 1:6-12)**]. Elihu mistakenly claimed,

> *"What man is like Job, who drinks scorn like water, who goes in company with the workers of iniquity, and walks with wicked men? For he has said, 'It profits a man nothing that he should delight in God"* **(Job 34:7-9)**.

Lesson:
Christians must be careful to adequately process their mind and make wise decisions. A good Christian will not pass any judgment based on inaccurate or incomplete information. Also, a good Christian will not segregate or stereotype people based on their race, gender, culture, background, or others. More importantly, a good Christian who expects God to be happy with him/her will be sensitive to people's needs; he/she will not be found in a position to heap coal of fire on other people's injury. God reserves a befitting place for godly and sensitive Christians in his kingdom. They will wine and dine with him eternally!

Prayer:
Dear God, please make me a sensitive Christian who seeks welfare of others. Enable me with grace to make positive contributions into the lives of others. Let my efforts add to people's joy, peace, and promotion. Please let me remain your good child who will be qualified to participate in your heavenly banquette. For in the name of Jesus Christ I make my requests.

Amen.

« DAY 44 »

Believers Must Take Caution Not To Be Drifted With Distractions

Focus Passage: Matthew 14:22-26

Peter walked on water with Jesus Christ when none of his team members could demonstrate the courage; however, the same Peter began to sink into the water when his faith wavered. The scripture reported,

> *"...And Peter answered Him and said, "Lord, if it is You, command me to come to You on the water." So He said, "Come." And when Peter had come down out of the boat, he walked on the water to go to Jesus"* **(Matthew 14:28-29)**. Peter was distracted as reported, *"But when he saw that the wind was boisterous, he was afraid; and beginning to sink he cried out, saying, "Lord, save me!" And immediately Jesus stretched out His hand and caught him, and said to him, "O you of little faith, why did you doubt?" And when they got into the boat, the wind ceased"* (Matthew 14:30-32).

Lesson:
Believers must always affix their faith on Jesus Christ to successfully live overcomer's lives on earth. We must focus on Jesus to receive courage and have our needs met. Indeed, believers have tendency to be distracted by many surrounding factors, but we must be determined not to be distracted. Distractions will cause us to lose grip and doubt God's power. However, to hold firm our grips, we must keep confessing God's words - even when our mind refuses to cooperate with our confessions. The more we declare God's promises, the more his peace will reign supremely in our heart - which will eventually contribute to our victory and progress.

Prayer:
Dear God, please teach me how to trust you in all ramifications of life. Let my faith in you be absolute. Enable me with grace to keep confessing your words into my life until my positive change is conspicuous. Please empower me through your Holy Spirit to live an overcomer's life by daily confessing your word into my life! Let my declarations lead to my spiritual growth, and lead to my victory. For in the name of Jesus Christ I make my requests.

Amen.

« DAY 45 »

God's Creative Power Is Awesome And Unimaginable

Focus Passage: Job 36,37

God's majesty was proclaimed throughout Job Chapter 36 and 37. Elihu rightly described God as the only supernatural one who reigns supremely over the earth. Indeed God is the greatest of all beings, and all people ought to proclaim his goodness! God created everything that we see today as Elihu analyzed,

> "*As for* the Almighty, we cannot find Him; *He is* excellent in power, *in* judgment and abundant justice; He does not oppress" **(Job 37:23)**.

Lesson:

God's greatness can be easily analyzed by considering our surrounding environment. His creative power can be seen by mere looking at cloud formation: They set in layers and appear as mountains. God decorated the sky with amazing color formations - The beauty of sunrise from west is amazingly different from that of sunset at the east. The twilight radiates its own special beauty also. God - in his infinitesimal wisdom also created living beings and made them specially different from each other. He also created plantations, and made water run through its courses! Perhaps the most amazing creative power of God at display is the creation of human beings. Humans specially made in the resemblance of God are blessed to demonstrate remarkable exercises! In fact, the list of God's goodness and his creative power is endless, and his wisdom is unsearchable! Hence, since God is such a dominant and an incomparable deity, all living beings ought to submit and honor him. Humans specially made in God's image should bring quality praises before him at all times.

Prayer:

Dear God, what an awesome God you are! You are such a wonderful and powerful God that made all things, and you deserve my praises at all times. Who else could have done all these great wonders that I see and feel today? No one besides you! You are such an awesome God! Please endow me with grace to keep bringing quality praises to you always. Empower me to use my imaginations to describe your beauty and sing your praises. Please do not let your songs of praises ever elude my mouth. Shower your grace on me to keep singing your songs of praises from now on, and forever more. For in the name of Jesus Christ I make my requests.

Amen.

« DAY 46 »

God's Laws Should Not Be Mistaken For Any Human Rule Of Law Since They Are Not The Same

Focus Passage: Matthew 15:1-20

Jesus Christ rebuked the Pharisees for stretching God's laws to make them irrelevant. The Pharisees scared and drove people away from God's laws by adding unnecessary clauses to them to either provide loopholes or make them become irrelevant. Jesus Christ rebuked the Pharisees and said,

> *"But he answered and said unto them, why do ye also transgress the commandment of God by your tradition? For God commanded, saying, Honor thy father and mother: and, He that curseth father or mother, let him die the death. But ye say, Whosoever shall say to his father or his mother, It is a gift, by whatsoever thou mightest be profited by me; And honor not his father or his mother, he shall be free. Thus have ye made the commandment of God of none effect by your tradition"* **(Matthew 15:3-6 KJV).**

Lesson:

God's laws are sacred and impactful, and they must be duly obeyed. God's laws should not be mistaken for any human rule of law since they are not the same. Human laws may be vague and imperfect, but God's laws have no shortcoming. Therefore, no one should consider him/herself to be above God's laws. No one should claim he/she knows more than God and attempt to help fix his mistakes. God's laws are inerrant and perfect - They are void of imperfections! All people are to obey God and duly serve him to receive his salvation and benefits. Meanwhile, the warning to respect and abide by God's laws is not limited to unbelievers only, believers also should be careful not to mishandle God's laws. We must be careful to do away with any doctrines and influences that may water down the scriptures (God's Book of Law). Also, believers must be careful not to allow their human traditions and religion activities cast shadow on God's laws to make them become irrelevant. Any doctrine, human tradition, custom, or beliefs that lessen bible impacts must be out rightly rejected. God will honor anyone who stands with his righteousness, but he will reject the dissident of his words.

Prayer:

Dear God, please help me to be careful not to tamper with your commandment so that I can prosper. Empower me through your Holy Spirit to stand with your righteousness and do your will at all times. Do not let me be trapped with human traditions and misappropriate your words. Let me consider your words to be final rule of law, and let me abide by them. Please let me duly fear you and obey your instructions so that I can prosper on earth, and also make it to your eternal kingdom. For in the name of Jesus Christ I make my requests.

Amen.

« DAY 47 »

God And Humans Are Incomparable In Power

Focus Passage: Job 38, 39, 40

God questioned Job to force him into subjection. The questions caught both Job and his friends off guard, and they became silent. God said to Job,

> *"Who is this who darkens counsel by words without knowledge? Now prepare yourself like a man; I will question you, and you shall answer Me. "Where were you when I laid the foundations of the earth? Tell me, if you have understanding. Who determined its measurements? Surely you know! Or who stretched the line upon it? To what were its foundations fastened? Or who laid its cornerstone..."* ***(Job 38:2-6)***.

Lesson:

God is greater than all beings, and he cannot be compared with anyone. A person who compares him/herself with God is basically foolish. God has more knowledge, more wisdom, and more demonstrative power than anyone! He is the greatest of all beings in existence. God created all things, and no one created him. He has power to do and undo anything as he wishes. Meanwhile, despite his dominant power and authority, the Creator has chosen to do good for everyone. He is a good God, and he does no evil to anyone. God hates evil, and he hates evil workers also. He offers options of repentance and grace of salvation for all people; however, he punishes insolent and obstinate ones. God remains the judge of the universe; his greatness and dominion will last eternally. Those who love God and serve him well will receive his immeasurable benefits in heaven, but those who reject the salvation offer of his Son Jesus Christ will have their place in hell fire prepared for Satan and his followers. (Matthew 25:41).

Prayer:

Dear God, please make me your choice child who will bring quality praises to you at all times. Please help me to serve you well so that I can qualify for your kingdom. Please give me grace to recognize your supremacy, and serve you well. Do not let me yield to temptation of arrogating your glory to myself. Don't let me compare you with anyone else. Also, help me to daily live my life in humility before you, so that your name can be glorified over my life. For in the name of Jesus Christ I make my requests.

Amen.

« DAY 48 »

Faith And Traditions Are Not The Same; Christians Must Act In Faith

Focus Passage: Matthew 15:21-39

A mother with a demon-possessed child resisted tradition that could have made her miss her breakthrough. Jesus threw tradition against her to check her faith level, and she passed the test. The woman walked up to Jesus and said,

> "...Have mercy on me, O Lord, thou son of David; my daughter is grievously vexed with a devil. But he answered her not a word. And his disciples came and besought him, saying, Send her away; for she crieth after us. But he answered and said, I am not sent but unto the lost sheep of the house of Israel. Then came she and worshipped him, saying, Lord, help me. But he answered and said, It is not meet to take the children's bread, and to cast it to dogs. And she said, Truth, Lord: yet the dogs eat of the crumbs which fall from their masters' table. Then Jesus answered and said unto her, O woman, great is thy faith: be it unto thee even as thou wilt. And her daughter was made whole from that very hour" **(Matthew 15:22-28 KJV).**

Lesson:
Children of God must remain persistent in their prayers to have their expectations met. God expects us to make our petitions before him without wavering faith. We must keep making our requests until we have received his overflowing blessings. Meanwhile, believers still have temptation of faithlessness to resist. We must resist any circumstance that may manipulate us into doubting God's power. Jehovah can do all things, and he will do us good if will keep asking and have unwavering faith in him.

Prayer:
Dear God, please give me strength to keep looking up to you in faith till I have all my expectations met. Give me strength to keep asking until my joy is full. Do not let me give in for any pressure that can make me doubt your capacity. Let me keep praying and trusting you until my testimony is full to the glory of your name. For in the name of Jesus Christ I make my requests.

Amen.

« DAY 49 »

God Is Big Enough To Turn Any Bad Situation Around For Anyone That Submit To Him

Focus Passage: Job 41, 42

Job realized his mistakes after he was scolded by God, and he repented. He humbled himself before the Creator and asked for his forgiveness. Job said,

> *"I know that you can do everything, And that no purpose of yours can be withheld from you. You asked, 'Who is this who hides counsel without knowledge?' Therefore I have uttered what I did not understand, Things too wonderful for me, which I did not know. Listen, please, and let me speak; you said, 'I will question you, and you shall answer Me.' "I have heard of you by the hearing of the ear, But now my eye sees you. Therefore I abhor myself, and repent in dust and ashes." **(Job 42:2-6).***

Lesson:

People who humble themselves before God will receive his forgiveness and blessings. In contrast, the prideful and unrepentant sinners will have no place before God. Indeed, Jehovah is big enough to turn any bad situation around for those who submit before him. It doesn't cost him anything to transform a situation at the snap of his fingers. However before any miracle can happen, we must submit before him and make him feel like the real king of our lives. A live example of this can be seen in the life of Job. He lost everything to distress, but God restore everything back - with more additions - when he submitted himself before God **(Job 42:12-17).** God turned Job's situations around for good. A once sick, poor, and depressed Job became a wealthy, healthy, happy, and father of ten children. He even lived long to see his 4th generation descendants. Isn't God great? Yes he is! Hence, we (believers) must learn how to fix our eyes on Jesus Christ and remain committed to him. Whatever trial or temptation that may confront us today will soon transform itself into multiple blessings in our lives.

Prayer:

Dear God, please keep me humble before you so that I can be qualified for your blessings. Again teach me how to trust you and submit to your instructions so that I can prosper! Let your Holy Spirit guide my life to yield to your corrections. As I trust and obey you, let all my life challenges transform into blessings. Let me keep climbing higher and higher until your goodness become fully materialized in my life - So that I can share the testimony throughout the world, and so that unbelievers can see and know that my God can do anything for anyone who serve him. Please do these things and many more for me. For in the name of Jesus Christ I make my requests.

Amen.

« DAY 50 »

Christians Can Only Successfully Run Christ's Mission Through The Help Of The Holy Spirit

Focus Passage: Matthew 16

Jesus Christ rebuked Peter for giving room for Satan to manipulate him against his ministry. Peter attempted to persuade Jesus to avoid his sacrificial salvation mission and change course for an alternative means, but Jesus discovered Satan hiding behind the disciple and rebuked him. The scripture reported Peter's action and Jesus reaction

> *"...From that time Jesus began to show to His disciples that He must go to Jerusalem, and suffer many things from the elders and chief priests and scribes, and be killed, and be raised the third day. Then Peter took Him aside and began to rebuke Him, saying, "Far be it from You, Lord; this shall not happen to you!" But He turned and said to Peter, "Get behind Me, Satan! You are an offense to me, for you are not mindful of the things of God, but the things of men"* **(Matthew 16:21-23)**

Lesson:

Christians operate as God's vessels to help carry out Christ's prime mission of saving souls. We are not the commander-in-chief of the mission, but we are the servants. We cannot run Christ's mission in flesh and expect it to prosper. We can only successfully run mission through the help of the Holy Spirit. Again, to comply with God's standard in life and ministry, we must allow his divine Holy Spirit to lead us. No other means of having spiritual success than that! It is important that we do not attempt to run Christ's ministry to satisfy the craving of flesh - which are not limited to pride, selfishness, gluttony, immorality, injustice, and all other ungodliness. Flesh is in enmity with God, and no one can satisfy God in flesh. Therefore, whatever a Christian does must primarily intend to glorify God - and nothing else. However, the Creator knows how to honor people who serve him well. He reserves his heavenly bank of treasures for Christians who are not obsessed with material and selfish gains. The rewards of faithful Christians will not be limited to earthly treasures only, but they will also have multiple benefits to possess in heaven as well.

Prayer:

Dear God, please make me a sensitive Christian who aims at only satisfying your desires always. Give me the gift of discernment to differentiate between godly spirit and evil spirit. Do not let me yield to the craving of flesh so that I will not sin against you. Please empower me through your divine Holy Spirit to live holy and acceptable life before you always, so that I can qualify for your blessings on earth and in heaven. For in the name of Jesus Christ I make my requests.

Amen.

« DAY 51 »

God Will Help His Children That Prioritize His Interest Above Theirs

Focus Passage: Genesis 23, 24

Abraham wanted his son Isaac to inherit his covenant of blessing that God made with him; therefore, he asked his servant to get him a wife that celebrated her religion view. God perceive his faithful and made his wish manifest. He made his servant found Rebekah who later become the mother of Jacob (and Esau). The scripture described Isaac's wife selection,

> *"...And he said O Lord God of my master Abraham, I pray thee, send me good speed this day, and shew kindness unto my master Abraham. Behold, I stand here by the well of water; and the daughters of the men of the city come out to draw water: And let it come to pass, that the damsel to whom I shall say, Let down thy pitcher, I pray thee, that I may drink; and she shall say, Drink, and I will give thy camels drink also: let the same be she that thou hast appointed for thy servant Isaac; and thereby shall I know that thou hast shewed kindness unto my master. And it came to pass, before he had done speaking, that, behold, Rebekah came out, who was born to Bethuel, son of Milcah, the wife of Nahor, Abraham's brother, with her pitcher upon her shoulder. And the damsel was very fair to look upon, a virgin, neither had any man known her: and she went down to the well, and filled her pitcher, and came up. And the servant ran to meet her, and said, Let me, I pray thee, drink a little water of thy pitcher. And she said, Drink, my lord: and she hasted, and let down her pitcher upon her hand, and gave him drink. And when she had done giving him drink, she said, I will draw water for thy camels also, until they have done drinking. And she hasted, and emptied her pitcher into the trough, and ran again unto the well to draw water, and drew for all his camels"* **(Genesis 24:12-20 KJV).**

Lesson:

God will help his children who prioritize his interest above theirs! He sees the intention of everyone's mind, and he knows whether a person is set out to genuinely satisfy his desire or not. Jehovah will send aid to the path of his righteous observers; he will provide for their needs so that they can have enough resources and momentum needed to adequately serve him. Hence, Christians are encouraged to serve God with integrity of their hearts. Their faithful services will not only prosper God's kingdom, but it will reciprocate blessings into their lives also.

Prayer:

Dear God, please help me to serve you with honesty and integrity so that I can enjoy your benefits and also prosper your kingdom. Let my activities come from honest mind; let there be no iota of deception in me, and let my services be acceptable before you always. For in the name of Jesus Christ I make my requests.

Amen.

« DAY 52 »

Much Indescribable Benefits Are Reserved In Heaven For People That Faithfully Serve Jesus To The End

Focus Passage: Matthew 17

Peter witnessed the transfiguration experience of Jesus Christ and he could not get over it. Even though they were literally in the jungle when it happened, he still begged Jesus Christ to allow him to build a tent there (so that he could permanently live with the experience there). The transfiguration experience that blew Peter's mind is as described,

> "Now after six days Jesus took Peter, James, and John his brother, led them up on a high mountain by themselves; and He was transfigured before them. His face shone like the sun, and His clothes became as white as the light. And behold, Moses and Elijah appeared to them, talking with Him. Then Peter answered and said to Jesus, "Lord, it is good for us to be here; if you wish, let us make here three tabernacles: one for you, one for Moses, and one for Elijah" **(Matthew 17:1-4).**

Lesson:

Christians will have everlasting hilarious experience with Jesus Christ in heaven. Believers will first be transformed from terrestrial beings to celestial being, and we will be decorated with honor that will last eternally! We – Christians – will rejoice in the presence of God; we will forget any pain and affliction that we might have suffered on earth. We would be referred as God's first born who has passed through hurdles of live without compromise. God will decorate us with crown of beauty that will never fade. He will give us new names, and establish his kingdom with us forever! Congratulations to those who have confessed Jesus Christ as their personal Lord and Savior – for theirs is the kingdom of God!

Prayer:

Dear God, I understand that heaven is not meant for mediocre, but it is meant for serious Christians who faithfully walk before you on earth. I want to qualify for heaven; therefore, I confess Jesus Christ as my personal Lord and Savior, and I will faithfully serve him unto the end. Please give me all it takes to remain faithful to you until your Son Jesus Christ returns to rapture the saints to heave. For in the name of Jesus Christ I make my requests.

Amen.

« DAY 53 »

Parents Should Be Clever To Make Their Children Maximize Their Potentials

Focus Passage: Genesis 25, 26

Esau and Jacob were two sons of Isaac and Rebekah; the two siblings were both gifted and made their contributions to the family. Esau hunted animals for family dinner and Jacob rear family livestock (He also helped in the kitchen). However their parents failed to maximize their potentials; therefore, they divided the children with their bias affections. Isaac preferred Esau because he hunted games, and Rebekah loved Jacob because he helped with domestication. Eventually, rivalry erupted between the children and it degenerated into bitter rage to the extent that one sought an opportunity to kill the other. The scripture stated,

> *"...Now Jacob cooked a stew; and Esau came in from the field, and he was weary. And Esau said to Jacob, "Please feed me with that same red stew, for I am weary." Therefore his name was called Edom. But Jacob said, "Sell me your birthright as of this day." And Esau said, "Look, I am about to die; so what is this birthright to me?" Then Jacob said, "Swear to me as of this day." So he swore to him, and sold his birthright to Jacob. And Jacob gave Esau bread and stew of lentils; then he ate and drank, arose, and went his way. Thus Esau despised his birthright"* **(Genesis 25:29:33)** ... *"But he (Isaac) said, "Your brother came with deceit and has taken away your blessing"* **(Genesis 27:35)**... *"So Esau hated Jacob because of the blessing with which his father blessed him, and Esau said in his heart, "The days of mourning for my father are at hand; then I will kill my brother Jacob"* **(Genesis 27:41-46)**.

Lesson:

Parents should be clever in dealing with their children to make them maximize their potentials. A wise and godly parent will not prefer one child to another since they are all gifts of God with special unique qualities. Every parent should be sensitive to recognize and master his/her child's potentials and help them demonstrate their best. God is interested in making every child great, and it is the work of the parents to help their children meet the expectation. However, unimaginable consequences amount when a parent fails his/her duty. Satan will tend to take the advantage to act against the child's future. Hence, parents should safeguard their children's future by being sensitive, prayerful and impactful.

Prayer:

Dear God, please give me wisdom to appropriately train my child/children in a way to will make them maximize their potential. Please help me to assist them in fulfilling what you have destined their lives for! Guide me through your Holy Spirit to assist them in making decisions that will enhance their growth and be productive for the society and your kingdom. For in the name of Jesus Christ I make my requests.

Amen.

« DAY 54 »

God's Measurement Of Human's Wealth Will Be Based On Lifestyle That Impact Others

Focus Passage: Matthew 18:1-20

Jesus Christ preached God's kingdom to his audience and used children's illustration to buttress his points. He stated that no one would be fit to enter God's kingdom except he/she has a soft and tender heart like little children. Jesus' disciples asked,

> *"Who then is greatest in the kingdom of heaven?" Then Jesus called a little child to Him, set him in the midst of them, and said, "Assuredly, I say to you, unless you are converted and become as little children, you will by no means enter the kingdom of heaven. Therefore whoever humbles himself as this little child is the greatest in the kingdom of heaven. Whoever receives one little child like this in My name receives Me"* **(Matthew 18:1-20).**

Lesson:
The world's definition of greatness is different from heaven's definition of greatness. People in the world describe greatness with preferences to material wealth and positions; however, God's measurement of human's wealth is based on quality of life they lived, and how they impact others. A person who has gained the whole world to his/her advantage may not meet God's standard of greatness if he/she has denied the Lordship of Jesus Christ! The bible stated, *"For what will it profit a man if he gains the whole world, and loses his own soul?"* **(Mark 8:36).** In addition God's wealth recognition involves openness and contrite spirit. That is, anyone who expects to enter heaven must not resent others. He/she must love God, love people, and have forgiving spirit. The person must walk plainly and humbly before God, and live in honesty. Also, a person who aims at seeing God on the last day must have teachable spirit and be ready to yield to godly corrections. Hence, anyone who aims at reaching heaven must step to the plate and seriously work to comply with God standard.

Prayer:
Dear God, there is no benefit in gaining the whole world and missing heaven; therefore, I am ready to yield my complete life to you! I will give you my complete life and serve you with all I have. I will stop pretense but comply with your laws with all honesty. Please give me a tender heart to be receptive of your words. Give me grace to receive and forgive others, and give me a teachable spirit to follow godly teachings. Anoint me with your oil of gladness to pursue things that benefit your kingdom and prosper others, so that I can be fit for your kingdom. For in the name of Jesus Christ I make my requests.

Amen.

« DAY 55 »

Nothing Can Stop God From Fulfilling His Promises On His Children

Focus Passage: Genesis 27, 28

Jacob became the recipient of God's promises to Abraham his grandfather. Isaac (Jacob's father) proclaimed blessings on him based on God's divine promises to Abraham. Jacob would not only be a great person, but he would also have plentiful descendants to inherit his blessings. Isaac proclaimed,

> *"May God Almighty bless you, and make you fruitful and multiply you, that you may be an assembly of peoples; And give you the blessing of Abraham, to you and your descendants with you, that you may inherit the land in which you are a stranger, which God gave to Abraham"* **(Genesis 28:3-4)**.

Lesson:
God's promises over his children will surely come to pass. Jehovah who has all things at disposal will ensure his promises do not fall to the ground as the psalmist stated, "For You have magnified Your word above all Your name" **(Psalm 138:2)**. Hence, we (believers) must be rest assured that our heavenly Father will definitely take care of their businesses. Nothing can stop him from fulfilling his promises over us. Whatever challenge that anyone currently faces will not be big enough to stop God from fulfilling his promises, since his words are yea and amen **(2 Corinthians 1:20)**! Even if darkness of sorrow covers the earth, our God will still shine his beautiful light on us. He will forgive our sins and heal our land. Jehovah will surely show us his loving-kindness, and ensure that we (his children) sail unto victory in every circumstance of life.

Prayer:
Dear God, I believe your word that stated, "For all the promises of God in Him *are* Yes, and in Him Amen, to the glory of God through us" **(2 Corinthians 1:20)**; therefore, I ask that you please shine your light on every situation of my life and earn me victory. Transform my current challenge into blessing so that my face can shine to the glory of your name. Since I am your son/daughter - a spiritual Jew and a descendant of Abraham let your goodness overtake my life in all ramifications of life. Bless me so much and make my cup run over so that unbelievers can be motivated to serve you also. Please let my blessings become source of blessings for other people as well! For in the name of Jesus Christ I make my requests.

Amen.

« DAY 56 »

Forgiveness Is The Key To Heaven. Christ Forgave Us; We Must Forgive Others Also

Focus Passage: Matthew 18:21-35

Jesus Christ plainly explained the meaning of forgiveness to Peter with a challenge not to keep record of offenses. Jesus illustrated his point with a use of an ambiguous number of error counts as the only basis for keeping unforgiveness. Jesus basically asked his followers not to keep record of offenses, but rather forgive others. The scripture reported,

> "...Then Peter came to Him and said, "Lord, how often shall my brother sin against me, and I forgive him? Up to seven times?" Jesus said to him, "I do not say to you, up to seven times, but up to seventy times seven" **(Matthew 18:21-22)**.

Lesson:
Forgiveness of sin and salvation of souls are the central focus of Jesus' ministry, and his followers must learn how to forgive others also. Christ first demonstrated forgiveness by sacrificing his own life for us - the sinners - as the scripture stated, *"While we were still sinners, Christ died for us"* **(Romans 5:8)**. Therefore if we are saved by grace, we ought to extend the same grace to others by forgiving their offenses. We must represent Christ by all standard and forgive those who have wronged us. Besides, God requires all people to demonstrate forgiveness before they can be accepted to heaven. (Matthew 6:14).

Prayer:
Dear God, please give me grace and strength to forgive people who have wronged me. Help me to live up to your standard of grace and forgiveness that you established on the cross. Give me a tender heart like little children to forgive, so that I can be acceptable to your kingdom. For in the name of Jesus Christ I make my requests.

Amen.

« DAY 57 »

No Man Or Woman Is Big Enough To Fit God's Position

Focus Passage: Genesis 29, 30

Leah and Rachel idolized their husband (Jacob) as God. Leah sought to earn Jacob's affection by bearing more children; Rachel also blamed Jacob for her state of barrenness with the hope he had all the solutions needed. The scripture reported,

> *"Now when Rachel saw that she bore Jacob no children, Rachel envied her sister, and said to Jacob, "Give me children, or else I die!" **(Genesis 30:1).*** However, Jacob was short of meeting his wife expectations - which only God can handle.

Lesson:
Human beings are not God, and no one should presume him/herself or any other person as God. Only God has infallible traits, but others have one shortcoming or the other. Humans are limited in what they can do, but God has limitless capacity. He can do and undo any situation. He can make rain to fall in the morning and make sun to shine in the evening. God made days and nights; he created all things, and no one created him. Therefore, it is unwise for anyone to arrogate God's glory to him/herself, or arrogate the same glory to another human being. All people must come humbly before God and tender their requests to him. He knows how to answer prayers, and he will make all things beautiful in their time for those who trust him. The omnipotent God who has all things at his disposal will definitely answer the prayers of his people.

Prayer:
Dear God, please teach me how to pray! Help me to focus my attentions and prayers to you only. Do not let me arrogate your glory to myself or to someone else's. Let my prayers reach your throne of grace to yield me plentiful results, so that my mouth can be full with the testimony of your goodness. By the way, I am sorry for all my faithless actions. I am also sorry for seeking help from fallible human beings when I should have run to you. From now on, give me grace to keep looking unto you for every needed help until my joy is full. Please do these and many more! For in the name of Jesus Christ I make my requests.

Amen.

« DAY 58 »

Marriage Is The Oldest Institution Created By God For Humanity To Enjoy

Focus Passage: Matthew 19

The Pharisees questioned Jesus on subject of divorce, and they referenced Law of Moses to justify its validity. Meanwhile Jesus responded,

> *"Moses, because of the hardness of your hearts, permitted you to divorce your wives, but from the beginning it was not so. And I say to you, whoever divorces his wife, except for sexual immorality, and marries another, commits adultery; and whoever marries her who is divorced commits adultery"* **(Matthew 19:8-9).**

Lesson:

God started marriage institution in the Garden of Eden, and he still loves marriage till today. Jehovah prefers marriage to divorce; he is interested in seeing people making their best efforts to sustain their marriages. Meanwhile, marriage is expected to take place between a mature man and a mature woman. Marriage is not meant for immature people. Also, marriage instituted in the Garden of Eden is meant to take place between a man and a woman only. However, since marriage institution is very important to God, all people ought to consider it sacred and honor it. Spouses should genuinely love each other, and be committed to their marriages. Couples must maintain openness, and be supportive of each other. If any party make a mistake, he/she should confess it to the other party so as to maintain trust and genuine commitment. It is important that spouses learn how to forgive each other so as to have peace, mutual love, respect, and exercise fear of God.

Prayer:

Dear God, please give me grace to be committed to my marriage. Help me to give all it takes to make my marriage work so that your name can be glorified. Please teach me and my spouse how to submit to each other. Help us to trust and love each other. Also help us to love and serve you, so that we can be blessed and make it to heaven. Enrich my marriage with every needed blessing; bless our children to radiate the beauty of your goodness. Please provide every support my marriage need, so that we can become a beacon of praise to your holy name. For in the name of Jesus Christ I make my requests.

Amen.

« DAY 59 »

Fake God Is Under Someone Else's Control, But The Real God Is In Control Of Everyone

Focus Passage: Genesis 31:30

Laban lamented that someone has stolen his gods. His missing foreign gods were so much precious to him to the extent that he disrupted Jacob's entourage on their journey to search their belongings. Laban patted every pocket and searched all tents to ensure no one got away with his gods. However, it was an unfortunate situation for Laban to find it difficult to align himself with the real God of heaven who cannot be stolen. Laban had lived with Jacob who served the real God for at least 14 years, and had watched him become prosperous as a result of his services to his God. However, Laban's obsessions to foreign (fake) gods blinded him so much that he could not change course to serve the real God that Jacob was serving. Laban still lamented to Jacob,

> "...and now you have surely gone because you greatly long for your father's house, but why did you steal my gods?" **(Genesis 31:30)**.

Lesson:

There is a big difference between the real God and the fake god. The real God cannot be stolen, but the fake god can end up in someone's pocket. No one can oppress the real God, but every fake god is under the control of someone else. Therefore, it is pure foolishness for a person to serve a foreign god under whatever name or title. Meanwhile, foreign items and articles that fall under description of foreign gods are countless. They range from material wealth to human thoughts and imaginations. For example, a carved image, a cloth, a job, or a motor vehicle can be an idol, jewelry, children, partner, and money as well. In other words, anything that attempt to occupy God's position in anybody's mind has become his/her idol. Meanwhile, the real God called Jehovah is jealous of his name, and he will not allow his glory to be shared with anything or anyone else; therefore, he will not bless idol worshippers. Worse still, God will not accept an idol worshipper into his kingdom on the last day. It is therefore important that people search their heart to ensure that God of heaven (the real god) is taking his rightful place there.

Prayer:

Dear God, please uphold me with your right hand of righteousness to devote my complete life to you. Do not let me substitute your position for any other god - be it a person, material, or other deity. Give me a contrite spirit to serve you well and give you due honor always. Do not let me provoke you with sin of idolatry and incur your wrath. Help me to clearly reverence your greatness and serve you well so that I can be blessed in this life, and also be acceptable to your heavenly kingdom. For in the name of Jesus Christ I make my requests.

Amen.

« DAY 60 »

God Will Reward His Faithful Servants In This World, And The New One To Come

Focus Passage: Matthew 20:1-16

God will reward people who serve him without partiality. Jesus taught his disciples that everyone who serves God will be rewarded without any special preferences; however, God's rewards to his people will be satisfying and refreshing. Christ narrated a story to buttress his point as quoted,

> *"So when even was come, the lord of the vineyard saith unto his steward, Call the laborers, and give them their hire, beginning from the last unto the first. And when they came that were hired about the eleventh hour, they received every man a penny. But when the first came, they supposed that they should have received more; and they likewise received every man a penny. And when they had received it, they murmured against the goodman of the house, Saying, These last have wrought but one hour, and thou hast made them equal unto us, which have borne the burden and heat of the day. But he answered one of them, and said, Friend, I do thee no wrong: didst not thou agree with me for a penny? Take that thine is, and go thy way: I will give unto this last, even as unto thee. Is it not lawful for me to do what I will with mine own? Is thine eye evil, because I am good? So the last shall be first, and the first last: for many be called, but few chosen"* **(Matthew 20:8-16 KJV).**

Lesson:

God is the best "businessperson" that anyone can ever imagine. He is very skilled at investing his resources where it will yield him much result. Something peculiar about God's business tactics is that he is very honest and reaps off no one. He rewards those who serve him in adequate proportions, and he pays everyone to the last penny. Jehovah's rewards to his faithful servants are ever refreshing and they last eternally. People who have served God well will not only earn much personal rewards on earth and heaven only, but their descendants will also eat the fruits of their labor. They will find favor before God and men. Since there is much benefit kept in stock for people who faithfully serve God, everyone ought to strive with their time, energy, and other resources to get involved in his kingdom business. Meanwhile, people should not only focus on serving God to receive earthly blessings only, they should also strive to enter his kingdom since Jesus Christ has stated, "The first shall be last, and the last shall be first" **(Matthew 20:16).**

Prayer:

Dear God, please train me to invest my time, energy, and other resources into aiding your kingdom so that I can prosper. Help me to use all I have to propagate gospel and promote your kingdom. Please let my household and I have much benefit to receive from you in this life and the next one to come. Again, please qualify me for your eternal kingdom so that my earthly services will not be in vain! For in the name of Jesus Christ I make my requests.

Amen.

« DAY 61 »

Disobedience Has Bitter Consequences, But Obedience Yield Blessings

Focus Passage: Genesis 33, 34, 35

Dinah the daughter of Jacob brought much trouble to her family with her act of disobedience. She crossed her family borderline and trespassed until a gentile forced her into an unholy relationship and violated her. Dinah's brothers therefore took laws into their hands and sought for revenge - but all to leading their family into more troubles. Their actions eventually forced the entire family of Jacob to flee the comfort of their settlement for fear of reprisal. Jacob lamented to his disobedient children,

> "*...You have troubled me by making me obnoxious among the inhabitants of the land, among the Canaanites and the Perizzites; and since I am few in number, they will gather themselves together against me and kill me. I shall be destroyed, my household and I*" **(Genesis 34:30).**

Lesson:
God loves obedient children, and he will do whatever necessary to protect and provide for them. People who trust God will enjoy his divine blessings: whatever they have will be secured, and new doors of opportunity will be opened for them also. Meanwhile, those who live in disobedience have the risk of losing whatever they have. They may also miss any new opportunity on their path! Satan also seizes the moment of disobedience to carry out his onslaught. The enemy loves to make disobedient people bear consequences and live in regret. Disobedient people also have high risk of not making heaven, since God considers act of disobedience a sin. However, since there are many benefits to gain in obedience and many benefits to lose in disobedience, believers ought to do their best to cooperate with God at all times.

Prayer:
Dear God, please help me to love you dearly and obey you so that I can prosper. Let serving you be an easy task for me; give me grace to resist temptation of disobedience so that Satan - the enemy - will have nothing to claim from my life. Please let your holy spirit empower me to do your will always! For in the name of Jesus Christ I make my requests.

Amen.

« DAY 62 »

Jesus Christ Endured All Hardship To Secure Salvation For Mankind

Focus Passage: Matthew 20:17-34

Jesus Christ knew what dangers lied ahead of his earthly ministry; he told his disciples that the ending part would not be so easy. The Son of God explained to his disciples that he would be betrayed by a friend and be persecuted by his enemies till the point of death. However, despite the full awareness of the dangers ahead of him, Jesus still continued to relentlessly pursue his ministry; he was determined to finish his special mission of creating salvation pathway for humanity. Jesus said to his disciples,

> *"Behold, we are going up to Jerusalem, and the son of man will be betrayed to the chief priests and to the scribes; and they will condemn him to death, and deliver him to the gentiles to mock and to scourge and to crucify. And the third day he will rise again"* **(Matthew 20:18-19).**

Lesson:
No one should forget the great work of salvation that Jesus Christ accomplished on the cross to save humanity. The Son of God endured persecutions of the enemies and ensured that he preached, suffered, died, and resurrected to save humanity. Yes, Christ endured enemies' harassments to die for the sake of saving humanity! Hence, everyone who claims to appreciate Christ's significant efforts of salvation ought to confess him as Lord and accept him as his/her personal Savior.

Prayer:
Dear Lord Jesus Christ, I thank you for sacrificing your life for the sake of saving a poor sinner like me. I couldn't thank you enough, and the best way to appreciate you is to confess and believe that you are the Savior of the world. Also, I must accept you as my personal Lord and Savior to be saved. Therefore, I make my declaration of faith in you today: I confess that you (Jesus Christ) are my personal Lord and Savior. I also confess my sins and repent from them. Please forgive my sins and accept me as your son/daughter so that I can qualify for your kingdom. From now on, I declare that I am yours, and I will serve you forever! Praise God I am now saved. Thank you Jesus Christ for your saving grace.

Amen

« DAY 63 »

Jealousy Can Make Anyone Lose His Lifetime Benefit

Focus Passage: Genesis 36, 37, 38

Joseph had a dream from God that he would one day become a prominent leader that everyone in his family will honor. His brothers became jealous and hated him once he shared the dream with them, and they hope something horrific would happen to him. Joseph's brothers first conspired to kill him, but they eventually sold him to slavery. The scripture reported Joseph's brothers' actions,

> *"Now when they saw him afar off, even before he came near them, they conspired against him to kill him. Then they said to one another, "look, this dreamer is coming! come therefore, let us now kill him and cast him into some pit; and we shall say, 'some wild beast has devoured him.' We shall see what will become of his dreams!" ... "And they sat down to eat a meal. then they lifted their eyes and looked, and there was a company of Ishmaelite, coming from Gilead with their camels, bearing spices, balm, and myrrh, on their way to carry them down to Egypt. So Judah said to his brothers, "What profit is there if we kill our brother and conceal his blood? Come and let us sell him to the Ishmaelite, and let not our hand be upon him, for he is our brother and our flesh." And his brothers listened. Then midianite traders passed by; so the brothers pulled Joseph up and lifted him out of the pit, and sold him to the Ishmaelite for twenty shekels of silver. And they took Joseph to Egypt"* **(Genesis 37:18-20; Genesis 37:25-28).**

Lesson:

A good Christian is expected to be selfless and not be jealous of others. Children of God ought to be satisfied with whatever they have - without getting obsessed with other people's belonging or achievements. The main fact here is that every child of God has a unique quality that can make him/her great in life; everyone should concentrate on his/her unique qualities to be the best he/she can be. However, jealousy will make a person shift focus from what may benefit him/her to pursue other people's dream, wealth, and ambition. Worse still, jealousy is a direct sin that violates god's commandment **(exodus 20:17)**. Hence, everyone who is named after Christ must desist from jealousy, and have a contrite spirit to demonstrate selfless attitude towards others. A true Christian will help other people to pursue their goals to have success. Meanwhile, God will reward those who help others; Jehovah will reciprocate their act of kindness with multiple blessings.

Prayer:

Dear God, please keep me humble to appreciate your grace and goodness in my life. Help me to be satisfied with whatever I have, and not be jealous of others. Do not let me entertain selfish thought or engage in any action that may obstruct other people's progress. Let me be an agent of positive change in the lives of others so you can be happy and bless me! For in the name of Jesus Christ I make my requests.

Amen.

« DAY 64 »

Believers Must Avoid Mistaking Human Traditions As God's Standard

Focus Passage: Matthew 21:1-22

Jesus Christ violated unpopular Jewish traditions that contradicted God's laws. He disrupted temple merchants and also allowed people to shout hosanna to his praise. Those actions triggered outrage from his opposing traditionalist and Jewish sects who were determined to kill him. Meanwhile, they had no choice than to wait and allow the Son of God to fully manifest his ministry according to God's commission. Some actions of Jesus that triggered bitter jealousy and rage from his opponents are as quoted,

> "...And the disciples went, and did as Jesus commanded them, And brought the ass, and the colt, and put on them their clothes, and they set him thereon. And a very great multitude spread their garments in the way; others cut down branches from the trees, and strawed them in the way. And the multitudes that went before, and that followed, cried, saying, Hosanna to the son of David: Blessed is he that cometh in the name of the Lord; Hosanna in the highest. And when he was come into Jerusalem, all the city was moved, saying, Who is this? And the multitude said, This is Jesus the prophet of Nazareth of Galilee. And Jesus went into the temple of God, and cast out all them that sold and bought in the temple, and overthrew the tables of the moneychangers, and the seats of them that sold doves, And said unto them, It is written, My house shall be called the house of prayer; but ye have made it a den of thieves. And the blind and the lame came to him in the temple; and he healed them. And when the chief priests and scribes saw the wonderful things that he did, and the children crying in the temple, and saying, Hosanna to the son of David; they were sore displeased, And said unto him, Hearest thou what these say? And Jesus saith unto them, Yea; have ye never read, Out of the mouth of babes and sucklings thou hast perfected praise?" **(Matthew 21:6-16 KJV).**

Lesson:

Children of God must know how to draw a line between human traditions and God's laws, because they are incomparable. Human's rules are subject to God's rules, since he has the final authority. Therefore, believers must be careful not to assume any popular opinion as God's acceptable standard. Jehovah will honor us for observing his commandments, and he will preserve his best treasures for us in his kingdom. In addition, believers also must understand that we have unbeatable power of God residing in us. God will honor our statements and also validate our actions with signs and wonders. Demons will submit to our authority, and whatever we command to bind on earth will be declared "bound" in heaven **(Matthew 18:18)**. Therefore, we must exercise our authority over every buying and selling spirit that may be attempting to operate in our heart - which is God's temple.

Prayer:

Praise God for his son Jesus Christ has come to set the captives free. All buying and selling spirit and all human traditions are now forced to be in subjection to Jesus' authority! Since I am a believer in Jesus Christ, I therefore proclaim my victory over all buying and selling spirit that may be attempting to operate in my life. I also receive the unbeatable power of God to stand against heresy and god-forbidden opinions that contradict bible. I claim the strength of the Holy Spirit to say no to sinful activities and say yes to Godly activities. By faith in Jesus Christ, I receive God's power to live triumphantly every day of my life, and the testimony of Jesus Christ will forever fill my mouth. For in the name of Jesus Christ I make my faith declarations.

Amen.

« DAY 65 »

A Good Christian Must Act Honorably To Glorify God

Focus Passage: Genesis 39, 40

Joseph rejected request of Potiphar's wife to fornicate with her for the sake of not wanting to sin against God. When given the sinful offer, Joseph responded,

> *"...look, my master does not know what is with me in the house, and he has committed all that he has to my hand. There is no one greater in this house than I, nor has he kept back anything from me but you, because you are his wife. How then can I do this great wickedness, and sin against God?"* **(Genesis 39:8).**

Lesson:
A true child of God must be able to say "I am not doing this or that because I don't want to sin against God!" the creator is really interested in people who will stand up for his righteousness and serve him well at this end time period. Therefore, believers who have confessed Jesus Christ as their Lord and Savior must make God proud. Every Christian must know what he/she stands for. That is, everything cannot be acceptable to a Good Christian. He/she must be able to say "yes" or "no" to comply with God's standard of holiness. However, believers' acts of holiness must not be based on outward actions and appearances only. True act of holiness must start from within - including human thoughts and indoor activities. Those who duly obey God will see him on the last day, but anyone who plays double standard with God will have no place in heaven. Jehovah who requires holiness will only accept those who practice it into his heavenly kingdom.

Prayer:
Dear God, please give me strength to say "no" to sin and "say" yes to righteousness. Baptize and empower me with your Holy Spirit to live a sanctified life before you. Give me grace to run from sin and live in holiness so that I can be acceptable to your kingdom. Please edify me by the truth of your word (bible) so that I will not be disappointed on the last day. For in the name of Jesus Christ I make my requests.

Amen.

« DAY 66 »

God's Spirit Will Help Believers Have Remarkable Success Where Others Have Failed

Focus Passage: Matthew 21:23-46

The Pharisees questioned Jesus Christ with an intension of trapping him; however, Christ silenced them with an unprecedented response. Once the hypocrite realized the messiah was already a step higher in the game, they became quiet. The scripture reported the scenario,

> *"And when he was come into the temple, the chief priests and the elders of the people came unto him as he was teaching, and said, By what authority doest thou these things? and who gave thee this authority? And Jesus answered and said unto them, I also will ask you one thing, which if ye tell me, I in like wise will tell you by what authority I do these things. The baptism of John, whence was it? from heaven, or of men? And they reasoned with themselves, saying, If we shall say, From heaven; he will say unto us, Why did ye not then believe him? But if we shall say, Of men; we fear the people; for all hold John as a prophet"* **(Matthew 21:23-26 KJV).**

However, the Pharisees who attempted to manipulate Jesus were skilled religion scholars. Yet, they could not subdue Jesus who had not received any formal education. Jesus was also much younger in age than many of his critics. The Son of God was able to outwit his opponents because God's spirit dwelled in him. Likewise, followers of Jesus Christ will rule over their challenges since they possess the spirit of Christ dwelling in them.

Lesson:
A person who has the spirit of God operating in him/her will prevail over trials and temptations of life. God's spirit comes with strength, knowledge, and understanding. He (Holy Spirit) also comes with power that no human wisdom can suppress. Meanwhile, for anyone to have the invincible Spirit of God, his/her ways must be right with God. The fellow must have yielded his/her life to God by confessing his son Jesus Christ as Lord. Also, he/she must follow God's instructions. Once the necessary conditions are met, God will release his spirit on the fellow to live victoriously on earth.

Prayer:
Dear God, please baptize me with your Holy Spirit to live a victorious life on earth. Give me strength and wisdom that prevail in all situations. Let your spirit transform my life to lose and bind in every situation as necessary. Empower me to prevail in all situations, and let my adversaries stumble before me so that I can have your name praised in the assembly of your people. Please do these things and many more. For in the name of Jesus Christ I make my requests.

Amen.

« DAY 67 »

God's Plans Will Fulfill On His Children In Spite Any Odd They Might Face

Focus Passage: Genesis 41, 42

Joseph had a rough life despite his beautiful dreams of becoming a prominent leader someday. Everyone closed to him disappointed him – except God. His brothers deserted him and sold him to slavery; Potiphar jailed him for an offense he did not commit, and pharaoh's chief butler – who promised him heaven on earth, abandoned him once he left prison. Meanwhile, God remained faithful to Joseph – despite all his predicaments. Through God's divine arrangement, Joseph was elevated to a position of honor: a powerful king pharaoh who had no pre-knowledge of Joseph's existence became God's tool of helping Joseph to actualize his dreams. The king had a dream that baffled him, and no one could interpret it; therefore, his cabinets were forced to seek for Joseph who was the only one qualified for the task. He interpreted the dream, and the king promoted him. King Pharaoh said to Joseph,

> *"...in as much as God has shown you all this,* there is *no one as discerning and wise as you. You shall be over my house, and all my people shall be ruled according to your word; only in regard to the throne will I be greater than you."* And pharaoh said to Joseph, *"see, I have set you over all the land of Egypt"* **(Genesis 41:39-41).**

Lesson:

God will fulfill his plans on his children in spite any odds that may come their ways. Children of God have right access to the treasure of God, and they will enjoy them to the fullness. Although circumstances of life may sometimes come as storm, and it may appear as if the whole world is collapsing on us. Various forms of disappointment may come our way: people may slander us, desert us, and abuse us. We may face injustice, and people force us to pay what we did not owe. Yet, God is faithful to carry us through journey of life and help us prevail. Once we remain on his side, he will fulfill his ultimate plans on us. Even when we fall short of his expectations, Jehovah will still prove Himself faithful, and ensure that our hope is not dashed. He will ensure that none of negative circumstances can stop his promises of goodness from getting fulfilled on us. In fact, the creator will turn every challenge we face to our stepping-stones of fulfilling his promises in our lives.

Prayer:

Dear God, I believe that you are God of gods and Lord of lords. You are strong and able to fulfill all your promises of goodness in my life. Therefore, I am praying that you put me in the book of your remembrance by turning all my predicaments into a stepping-stone of my greatness. Let all my life events and happening cooperate with your promises. Please lift me up beyond any human suppression and oppression. Let my dreams and aspirations come into materialization. Empower me to walk according to your plans until my face fully shine to the glorification of your name. For in the name of Jesus Christ I make my requests.

Amen.

« DAY 68 »

Treasures Of God's Kingdom Will Be Awarded To Serious Christians

Focus Passage: Matthew 22:1-22

Jesus Christ warned people who are preoccupied with cares of the world and think less of God to change their practices, unless they risk losing an opportunity of going to heaven. Christ shed light on this teaching with a story of a rich man who invited his close friends for his daughter's wedding. The friends disappointed him; therefore, he revoked their invitations and punished them. The rich man also substituted his friends' invitations for another that focused on inviting common people to his prestigious ceremony. Jesus' narrated the story as stated,

> *"The kingdom of heaven is like a king who prepared a wedding banquet for his son. He sent his servants to those who had been invited to the banquet to tell them to come, but they refused to come. "Then he sent some more servants and said, 'Tell those who have been invited that I have prepared my dinner: My oxen and fattened cattle have been butchered, and everything is ready. Come to the wedding banquet.' "But they paid no attention and went off—one to his field, another to his business. The rest seized his servants, mistreated them and killed them. The king was enraged. He sent his army and destroyed those murderers and burned their city. "Then he said to his servants, 'The wedding banquet is ready, but those I invited did not deserve to come. So go to the street corners and invite to the banquet anyone you find"* **(Matthew 22:1-9 NIV).**

Lesson:
God preserves his heavenly kingdom for people who take his commandments seriously. Treasures of God's kingdom will not be awarded to people with nonchalant attitude who care less about God and his instructions. Both the unbelievers and those who blindly pursue worldly cares as if they are the life ultimate price will be turned away from entering heaven. Only people who have expressed their faith in Jesus Christ and have consistently walked with him will be accepted to God's kingdom. Hence, anyone who aims at seeing God and enjoy his eternal kingdom should take the important step of confessing Jesus Christ as his/her Lord, and consistently walk with him.

Prayer:
Dear God, I understand that heaven is meant for serious Christians who daily walk with you. Therefore, I ask for your grace to steadfastly walk with you. Please give me strength and grace to prioritize holiness and serve you well. Do not let me get caught up with cares of the world and neglect the need to pursue your kingdom. Empower me through your Holy Spirit to appropriately set my priority so that my name can remain written in the book of life. For in the name of Jesus Christ I make my requests.

Amen.

« DAY 69 »

God's Tremendous Light Will Shine At The End Of Tunnel For Everyone Who Trust Him

Focus Passage: Genesis 43, 44, 45

God's dream became fulfilled in Joseph's life, and he officially introduced himself to his once skeptic and jealous brothers as their God's appointed head. Joseph introduced himself and stated,

> *"...I am Joseph your brother, whom you sold into Egypt. But now, do not therefore be grieved or angry with yourselves because you sold me here; for God sent me before you to preserve life"* **(Genesis 45:4).**

Lesson:
God will honor his promises on his children and he will fulfill his counsels over them. Truly, storms of life may have beat against us (God's children); we may have faced much crises, and the journey of our lives may have appeared to turn downward spiral. Yet, God's tremendous light will eventually shine at the end of our tunnel. Our heavenly father will help make our dreams come true. He will turn our tough situations into many blessings so that we can praise him in the assembly of his people; also, that unbelievers may hear our testimony and turn to pursue his righteousness.

Prayer:
Dear God, I thank you for being my God who is able to beautifully turn situations around for people who love and serve you. Yes, I believe in your transforming power to see my tough situations changing into testimony. I believe your light of grace and goodness will shine at the end of my tunnel. All I'm asking now is grace to keep trusting you! Give me strength to keep exercising my faith in you until all your promises are fully come to pass in my life. Once my story change, let me have all reasons to testify to your goodness in the assembly of your people, so that all people may hear and praise your name. For in the name of Jesus Christ I make my requests.

Amen.

« DAY 70 »

An Earthly Conscious Person Cannot Understand The Concept Of Holy Spirit

Focus Passage: Matthew 22:23-46

A Jewish' Sadducees sect attempted to trick Jesus to stumble on his teaching about "resurrection". The Sadducees, unlike their Pharisees counterpart did not believe in resurrection theory; they confronted Jesus to ask, "If there is resurrection, who would be the husband of a woman who had several previous marriages before she died?" however, Jesus Christ corrected the skeptics and said,

> *"You are mistaken, not knowing the scriptures nor the power of God. For in the resurrection they neither marry nor are given in marriage, but are like angels of God in heaven. but concerning the resurrection of the dead, have you not read what was spoken to you by god, saying, 'i am the god of Abraham, the god of Isaac, and the God of Jacob'? God is not the God of the dead, but of the living." and when the multitudes heard this, they were astonished at his teaching"* **(Matthew 22:29-33).**

Lesson:
It is wrong for anyone to misinterpret the principles of God's kingdom as if they must be earthly relevant only. God's principles are different from human's principles. Many factors with deep spiritual understanding will appear as meaningless to foolishness and insensitive folks who are only earthly conscious. To an earthly conscious person, everything must make a perfect sense before he/she can believe it. He/she must first see cloud formation before he/she believes there can be any rainfall. Unfortunately, the kingdom of God requires that people exercise faith and believe in what are yet to make perfect sense. For example, a believer must believe that Virgin Mary was conceived of the Holy Spirit to give birth to Jesus Christ. Also, the believer must agree that Jesus Christ has no other father than God himself. Another example: a true Christian must walk by faith and not by sight. He/she must confess and believe God for things he/she has yet to physically possess. True believers will call things that are not as though they are (Romans 4:16-18). Hence, the prideful should submit themselves and learn the principles of God's kingdom so that they can qualify to enjoy his peace - both earthly and heavenly. Every true child of God must seek divine wisdom that flow from God's heart in order to keep enjoying his benefits.

Prayer:
Dear God, please keep me humble to learn at your feet so that I can be able to enjoy your full benefits. I understand that earthly wisdom is foolishness when compared with godly wisdom. My goal is to allow your Holy Spirit to teach, lead, and guide me so that I can prosper. Please help me to cooperate with you and continue to learn at your feet so that I can prosper in this earth and in heaven also. For in the name of Jesus Christ I make my requests.

Amen.

« DAY 71 »

Believers Serve Unstoppable God Who Gives And Keeps Unstoppable Promises

Focus Passage: Genesis 46, 47, 48

God's wonders manifested in the life of Joseph as his dreams came true beyond expectations. A once abused and abandoned Joseph turned to become the deliverer of his people. He became a God-sent person to save his father's household from a terrible famine that could have wiped them off from history. King Pharaoh said to Joseph,

> *"I am pharaoh, and without your consent no man may lift his hand or foot in all the land of Egypt...your father and your brothers have come to you. The land of Egypt is before you. Have your father and brothers dwell in the best of the land; let them dwell in the land of Goshen...then Joseph provided his father, his brothers, and all his father's household with bread, according to the number in their families"* **(Genesis 41:44; Genesis 47:6; Genesis 47:12).**

Lesson:

God's greatness is beyond any human comprehension. His greatness surpasses any human thoughts and imaginations! Nothing can stop the creator from doing whatever he has thought of doing. Even when all life circumstances prove otherwise, Jehovah is still strong and capable of doing whatever he's determined. Hence, believers must understand that since we serve an unstoppable God, we must be rest assured on his promises. Any cloud of darkness that we may see today will not be strong enough to stop God's light of salvation from shining. He will save, heal, deliver, and restore as promised. Our God will surely demonstrate his strength to our advantage. He will help us in time of need and bless us - until our cups overflow! Therefore, every son and daughter of God must remain steadfast with him. We must keep walking in obedience and trust him for his promises. Jehovah who neither sleeps nor slumbers will ensure that we have victory and testimony of goodness to share to the honor of his name.

Prayer:

Praise God I serve the one who answers prayers! Praise God I serve a God who neither sleeps nor slumbers! Praise God I have a God who keeps his promises over his children! Hallelujah for I belong to Jesus the Son of God who qualifies me for his father's blessings! All I'm asking now is grace and strength to keep trusting him until all his promises become fulfill in my life. I ask for God's empowerment to keep trusting him even when life circumstances prove otherwise! May the grace of God that surpasses all human understanding be available for me to keep trusting and walking in his will until I have all my expectations met. Let my faith transform into blessing, and let my mouth be filled with testimony of salvation, healing, deliverance, and others - all to the of praises of God's name. For in the name of Jesus Christ I make my requests.

Amen.

« DAY 72 »

Christians Mustn't Be Hypocritical, But Be True Ambassador Of Jesus Christ

Focus Passage: Matthew 23:1-22

Jesus Christ scolded the Pharisees for being inconsistent with the scripture. They preached from the scripture and acted contrarily to the scripture at the same time. They taught and enforced God's laws on others, but themselves acted contrarily to their teachings. However, Jesus knew the Pharisees well and said,

> *"But woe unto you, scribes and Pharisees, hypocrites! For ye shut up the kingdom of heaven against men: for ye neither go in yourselves, neither suffer ye them that are entering to go in. Woe unto you, scribes and Pharisees, hypocrites! For ye devour widows' houses, and for a pretence make long prayer: therefore ye shall receive the greater damnation. Woe unto you, scribes and Pharisees, hypocrites! For ye compass sea and land to make one proselyte, and when he is made, ye make him twofold more the child of hell than yourselves"* **(Matthew 23:13-15 KJV).**

Lesson:
Christians are required to be true representative of Jesus Christ, and not live in pretense. We are commanded to meet God's standard as presented in the bible. We are to preach and teach others to comply with bible standard as we also comply with the same principle. In other words, Christians must practice what they preach! Also, Christian leaders must not be hypocritical but be true ambassadors of Jesus Christ in all ramifications. Jehovah reserves many benefits for people who love and serve him with all honesty; he will bless them beyond their wildest dreams.

Prayer:
Dear God, please make me a true representative of Jesus Christ who live according to bible standard. Help me to be sincere with you in all my approach. Do not let me live a double standard life. Let my "yea be yea and my nay be nay." Keep me honest to sincerely sorry for my sin whenever I commit one, and let me exercise genuine repentance. Please keep me upright with you so that you can see sincerity in me to qualify me for your eternal kingdom. Please keep my feet firm within thy gate o Lord! For in the name of Jesus Christ I make my requests.

Amen.

« DAY 73 »

Life Lessons And Experience Will Cooperate With God's Plans For Those Who Trust Him

Focus Passage: Genesis 49, 50

Joseph's brothers hated him for claiming to have seen a vision indicating that he would one day become a prominent leader that other family members will pay royal respect. To other siblings, Joseph was an arrogant person who despite his low family rank (11th of 12 sons) arrogated himself with honor as their family head. Therefore, the brothers were determined to silence him by all possible means, with the hope that his vision will lay to rest,

> *The brothers sold Joseph to Egypt as a slave and lied to their father that he has died. Unknown to Joseph's brothers, Egypt was part of God's plan to elevate him into materializing his dream to become their family head. One thing led to another, and Joseph eventually became the prime minister of Egypt who later saved his family from famine. Joseph's brothers later learned an important life lesson under intense situations. What they had wanted to prevent eventually came to pass since God ordained it. Tough life lesson forced the brothers to accept and confess Joseph as their family head. They professed him as their leader, and they bowed to him with full royal respect. Record shows that Joseph's brothers bowed to him in (at least) four occasions. In the last occasion, the brothers fell flat before Joseph and stated, "behold, we are your servants!"* **(Genesis 50:18)**

Lesson:

Believers must understand that life has phases, and our life journey may not run smoothly as expected. Challenges will come to stiffen our muscles; Satan also will appear to test our faith in God. However, we must remain steadfast in God and not give in to trials and temptations. We must not curse God when passing through afflictions and learning our life lessons. Surely, afflictions, trials and temptations are all going to subside for the will of God to materialize in our lives. Every life lesson and experience that we undergo will eventually cooperate with God's purpose, since we have his covenant of blessing on us. Every trial will subside and transform into a stepping-stone of greatness; they will work to our advantage so that we can have the name of God to praise.

Prayer:

Dear God, please give me grace to keep serving and trusting you until all your promises are fulfilled in my life. Transform my challenges into a stepping-stone of greatness. Do not let me give in to trials and temptations, but let me continue to faithfully follow your pathway of righteousness so that I can have victory and share the testimony of your goodness in the land of the living. For in the name of Jesus Christ I make my requests.

Amen.

« DAY 74 »

God Expects His People To Acknowledge Their Sins And Repent Rather Than To Rationalize Them

Focus Passage: Matthew 23:23-29

Jesus Christ scolded the Pharisees for their hypocritical behaviors. They pretended to love God and appeared to enforce God's laws, but they had the secret intention of pursuing personal gains. Jesus therefore challenged them to walk straight with God and said,

> "Woe to you, scribes and Pharisees, hypocrites! For you pay tithe of mint and anise and cumin, and have neglected the weightier matters of the law: justice and mercy and faith. These you ought to have done, without leaving the others undone. Blind guides, who strain out a gnat and swallow a camel! "Woe to you, scribes and Pharisees, hypocrites! For you cleanse the outside of the cup and dish, but inside they are full of extortion and self-indulgence. Blind Pharisee, first cleanse the inside of the cup and dish, that the outside of them may be clean also. "Woe to you, scribes and Pharisees, hypocrites! For you are like whitewashed tombs which indeed appear beautiful outwardly, but inside are full of dead men's bones and all uncleanness. Even so you also outwardly appear righteous to men, but inside you are full of hypocrisy and lawlessness. "Woe to you, scribes and Pharisees, hypocrites! Because you build the tombs of the prophets and adorn the monuments of the righteous" **(Matthew 23:23-29)**.

Lesson:
Children of God ought to serve God with plain mind and do their best to satisfy his desires. The creator sees and knows all things; therefore, everyone should walk uprightly before him. Meanwhile, God understands that we humans are far from perfections; we have imperfect nature and we may sometimes fall into sin. He expects us to come humbly before him to confess and repent from our sins. He prefers that we acknowledge our sins and exercise repentance than to rationalize them as if nothing wrong has happened. Sin is a trap that hold-tights its victim; no one can be freed from it except he/she has confessed and repented. People who repent from their sins will receive forgiveness, but pretenders and those who claim self-righteousness will not have a place with God in heaven.

Prayer:
Dear God, please give me grace to walk straight with you and satisfy your desires. Assist me to be pure and plain before you. I do not want to rationalize sin; keep me humble to acknowledge my sins, confess and repent from them. Let me have an open heart to receive the leadership of your holy spirit and walk in your ways so that I can prosper on earth and also enter your heavenly kingdom. For in the name of Jesus Christ I make my requests.

Amen

« DAY 75 »

Jehovah Will Touch And Turn Around Every Needed Situation To Help His Children

Focus Passage: Exodus 1, 2, 3

A pharaoh who did not celebrate the Hebrew (Israelites) heritage was enthroned in Egypt, and he oppressed the Hebrews. He enslaved and forced them to hard labor. Meanwhile, God appointed Moses to speak for his children and lead them out of Egyptians' bondage. God used bush-burning experience to get Moses' attention. The scripture reported,

> *"And God said unto Moses, I Am That I Am: and he said, Thus shalt thou say unto the children of Israel, I Am hath sent me unto you. And God said moreover unto Moses, Thus shalt thou say unto the children of Israel, the Lord God of your fathers, the God of Abraham, the God of Isaac, and the God of Jacob, hath sent me unto you: this is my name for ever, and this is my memorial unto all generations. Go, and gather the elders of Israel together, and say unto them, The Lord God of your fathers, the God of Abraham, of Isaac, and of Jacob, appeared unto me, saying, I have surely visited you, and seen that which is done to you in Egypt: And I have said, I will bring you up out of the affliction of Egypt unto the land of the Canaanites, and the Hittites, and the Amorites, and the Perizzites, and the Hivites, and the Jebusites, unto a land flowing with milk and honey"* **(Exodus 3:14-17 KJV).**

Lesson:
God cares for his people, and he will deliver them from their afflictions. Jehovah knows how to raise help where there appears to be none. He is skilled at performing wonders to show himself strong on behalf of people who dedicate their lives into serving him. He can raise a special deliverer to free his children from oppression. He can tap anyone for his use, and he can also use other factors that someone might consider to be immaterial for the purpose liberating his children. In addition, the creator will not only defend his children from their enemies, but he will punish the enemies also. Hence, all people are encouraged to cast their complete trust on God and serve him well so that they can obtain mercy and find grace in time of needs.

Prayer:
Dear God, please help me to cast my hope and trust on you to obtain mercy and find grace in time of needs. As I continue to serve you, I seize this moment to pray that you deliver me from all my troubles. Set me free from all crises and make my face shine. Silence my enemies and give me upper hands over them, so that I can have complete victory and glorify your name. For in the name of Jesus Christ I make my requests.

Amen.

« DAY 76 »

People Who Have Rejected Jesus' Offer Of Salvation Will Miss Rapture

Focus Passage: Matthew 24:1-28

Jesus Christ mentioned some events that will precede his second coming (notably as rapture). Almost all the events mentioned are now noticed to be happening in our present days. Jesus said prior to his second coming; there shall be false teachers, false prophets, famines, wars, and persecutions of believers. Jesus also stated that some insensitive Christians would compromise their faith and pursue worldly care and deceptive teachers. Jesus said,

> *"Then many false prophets will rise up and deceive many. And because lawlessness will abound, the love of many will grow cold. But he who endures to the end shall be saved"* **(Matthew 24:11-13).**

Lesson:
The second coming of Jesus Christ will only meet the sensitive and devoted Christians. The insensitive Christians and carefree people who have ignored the salvation offer of Jesus Christ will not be rapture to heaven. They will be left behind to suffer affliction from Satan who will later take over the world until God's last Day of Judgment arrives. However, it is advisable that Christians keep focus and serve God well so that they will not be disappointed when Christ returns to rapture his saints. Also, people who have not taken gospel seriously should do so, since there is no other means of obtaining salvation and reaching heaven other than confession of faith in Jesus Christ **(Acts 4:12)**. In other words, all people must confess Jesus Christ as Lord and Savior to enter the kingdom of God.

Prayer:
Dear God, please I do not want to pursue worldly pleasures and miss opportunity of going to heaven. Please count me worthy to be among those who will be raptured on the last day. Do not let me follow multitude to do evil, and do not let me fall victim of deceptive teachers and/or prophet. Lead and guide me through the power of your holy spirit so that I can remain fit for your eternal kingdom. For in the name of Jesus Christ i make my requests.

Amen.

« DAY 77 »

God Will Not Fail His Promises – Believers Must Reserve Their Absolute Faith In Him

Focus Passage: Exodus 4, 5, 6

God instructed Moses to approach King Pharaoh to seek deliverance of Israelites from their slavery; the king become furious as a result of Moses' intrusion, and he multiplied Israelites' oppression. Israelites also reacted to their oppression by getting angry with Moses and God. They accused Moses and God for meddling to complicate their problem. However, while Israelites murmured and remain skeptical about God's promised deliverance, the Creator himself was busy rehearsing on how he would terribly deal with King Pharaoh to liberate them. The scripture explained how Moses' rescue effort sparked rage among Israelites community,

> *"And afterward Moses and Aaron went in, and told Pharaoh, Thus saith the Lord God of Israel, Let my people go, that they may hold a feast unto me in the wilderness. And Pharaoh said, Who is the Lord, that I should obey his voice to let Israel go? I know not the Lord, neither will I let Israel go. And they said, The God of the Hebrews hath met with us: let us go, we pray thee, three days' journey into the desert, and sacrifice unto the Lord our God; lest he fall upon us with pestilence, or with the sword. And the king of Egypt said unto them, Wherefore do ye, Moses and Aaron, let the people from their works? get you unto your burdens. And Pharaoh said, Behold, the people of the land now are many, and ye make them rest from their burdens. And Pharaoh commanded the same day the taskmasters of the people, and their officers, saying, Ye shall no more give the people straw to make brick, as heretofore: let them go and gather straw for themselves. And the tale of the bricks, which they did make heretofore, ye shall lay upon them; ye shall not diminish ought thereof: for they be idle; therefore they cry, saying, Let us go and sacrifice to our God. Let there more work be laid upon the men, that they may labour therein; and let them not regard vain words"* **(Exodus 5:1-9 KJV).**

Lesson:
God has various modes of operations, and he cannot be predicted. However, irrespective of the medium of operation he chooses to adopt in any situation, his prime goal will be to favor his children. Jehovah will do whatever necessary to advocate for his children. He will defend their interest and also silence their foes. Meanwhile, believers must learn how to exercise patience as they wait for the help of God. It is understood that pressures will mount during difficult situations; however God who never sleeps will adequately respond to the needs of his people that faithfully serve and trust him. God will show up during time of need to provide solution. The Creator will ultimately make his children laugh over their challenges so that they can praise his name.

Prayer:
Dear Lord, please teach me how to trust you in all situations so that I can enjoy your benefits in full. Give me grace to be patient and wait for your salvation in all situations of my life. Let your covenant of peace, protection, and prosperity be fulfilled on me. Let me live long to

witness your goodness in the land of the living, so that I can share the testimony of your goodness throughout the world. For in the name of Jesus Christ I make my requests.

Amen.

« DAY 78 »

God Will Soon Establish New Earth And New Heaven For His Saints

Focus Passage: Matthew 24:29-51

Jesus Christ discussed his second coming with his disciples and stated all eyes will see him descending from the sky, but not everyone will be qualified for his rapture. Only few people who have confessed him (Jesus Christ) as Lord and Savior will enter heaven and be crowned with honor. Jesus said,

> *"Then the sign of the son of man will appear in heaven, and then all the tribes of the earth will mourn, and they will see the son of man coming on the clouds of heaven with power and great glory. And he will send his angels with a great sound of a trumpet, and they will gather together his elect from the four winds, from one end of heaven to the other"* **(Matthew 24:30-31).**

Lesson:
The current earth and heaven that humanity see today will not last eternally. They will soon vanish to give way for God's newly created earth and heaven to be established. Meanwhile, one fateful day will mark the beginning of the transition between the old and the new earth - and it will be a specific date and time that Christ appears in the sky to rapture his followers (Christians) to heaven. The unrepentant sinners who have rejected the testimony of Jesus Christ will not be left behind in limbo on earth! Since the old earth will be destroyed by God, the left-behind people will also be destroyed. Unbelievers will find their eternal destination in hell fire - a place reserved for Satan and his evil forces. However, everlasting God who will judge all people has chosen to give everyone an opportunity of repentance. He has delayed the second coming of his Son Jesus Christ till now to offer more grace time for people to exercise repentance. Hence, unbelievers should use every moment they have as an opportunity to become saved. They should confess Jesus Christ as their Lord and personal Savior, so that they can escape God's imminent danger that will soon come over the earth. The process of obtaining Christ' salvation is very easy. One should simply state; "I believe Jesus Christ is the Son of God who died for my sins. I believe he died on the cross for my sins and resurrected to give me eternal life. Therefore, I confess my sins to him and forsake them. I declare Jesus Christ as my personal Lord and Savior, and I will serve him throughout the days of my life. Amen!"

Prayer:
Dear Jesus Christ, please count me worthy to inherit your eternal kingdom. Let me be worthy of your rapture so that I can forever be with you in heaven! I declare you Jesus Christ as my Lord and I confess you as my Savior. You are the Son of God who died for my sins. I give you my complete life today, and I will serve you forevermore! Please write my name in the book of life so that I can eternally rejoice in your presence in the new paradise. Thank you Jesus Christ for your saving grace.

Amen.

« DAY 79 »

It Is A Suicide Mission For Anyone To Attempt To Go Shoulder-To-Shoulder With God

Focus Passage: Exodus 7, 8

King Pharaoh of Egypt attempted to compete with God in performing miracles, but he eventually bowed having realized he has limited strength. The gentile king initially competed with God. He ordered his magicians to perform similar miracles that Moses utilized God's power to perform. Pharaoh's magicians made their fake snakes, blood water, and frogs. However they could not make lice and flies, and neither were they able to compete with God's power any further. Eventually the magicians confronted pharaoh with a bitter truth he hated to hear. The scripture reported,

> *"Now the magicians so worked with their enchantments to bring forth lice, but they could not. so there were lice on man and beast. Then the magicians said to pharaoh, "this is the finger of God..." **(Exodus 8:18-19)**.*

Lesson:

God is different from humans, and no one can successfully compete with him. It is more or less a suicide mission for anyone to go shoulder-to-shoulder with God, because it will backfire. A person who belittles God and attempt to reckon with him as a mere human being is making a big mistake. Such person will have many consequences to pay for his/her action! Jehovah is God and he is our Creator; we must honor him by every standard and offer him our best respect. God specified in his word that he would not allow his glory to be shared with anyone else **(Isaiah 42:8)**, and he will go any extent to keep that promise! Therefore, all people must acknowledge God's sovereignty and pay him due respect. The Creator will definitely make things beautiful for people who honor him, but he will bring down every prideful heart and arrogant look.

Prayer:

Dear God, please help me to recognize your sovereignty over the earth and give you due honor. Help me to be careful not to attempt to share your glory with anyone else, but let my praises come straight from my heart to the glorification of your name. Please empower me through your holy spirit to resist every temptation of self and pride that may want to usurp your authority. Let everything within me lead to the glorification of your name. For in the name of Jesus Christ I make my requests.

Amen.

« DAY 80 »

Rapture Is Imminent And It Will Soon Come; Believers Must Be Prepared

Focus Passage: Matthew 25:1-30

Believers must carefully examine the story of ten virgins that Jesus Christ narrated in the bible to have complete understanding of requirements of God's kingdom. Five out of the ten virgins in Jesus' illustration were declared wise because they made adequate preparation for their expected grooms. Others who missed their opportunity of going with the groom were declared foolish because they lack adequate preparations. Jesus stated,

> *"Then shall the kingdom of heaven be likened unto ten virgins, which took their lamps, and went forth to meet the bridegroom. And five of them were wise, and five were foolish. They that were foolish took their lamps, and took no oil with them: But the wise took oil in their vessels with their lamps. While the bridegroom tarried, they all slumbered and slept. And at midnight there was a cry made, Behold, the bridegroom cometh; go ye out to meet him. Then all those virgins arose, and trimmed their lamps. And the foolish said unto the wise, Give us of your oil; for our lamps are gone out. But the wise answered, saying, Not so; lest there be not enough for us and you: but go ye rather to them that sell, and buy for yourselves. And while they went to buy, the bridegroom came; and they that were ready went in with him to the marriage: and the door was shut"* **(Matthew 25:1-10 KJV).**

Lesson:

Christians must prepare for the second coming of their master, which is Jesus Christ. No believer is expected to be slothful in preparing for the arriving of the master. Believers must do all due diligence to keep fit for the return of Christ; he will raptured those who are well prepared to heaven, but he will abandon the insolent and slothful ones. (What characterizes a wise and a foolish Christian is the amount of relationship that a person keeps with God). Jesus will only transport Christians who prioritize holiness and maintain consistent relationship with him. The Savior has already promised his faithful followers the best part of his kingdom. He has reserved mansions and other amenities for those who faithfully follow him unto the end. Jesus said; *"Let not your heart be troubled; you believe in God, believe also in me. In my father's house are many mansions; if it were not so, I would have told you. I go to prepare a place for you. And if I go and prepare a place for you, I will come again and receive you to myself; that where I am, there you may be also"* **(John 14:1-3).**

Prayer:

Dear Jesus Christ, I want to go to heaven with you on the last day when you shall come to rapture your saints! Let me be consistent with you with my daily thanksgiving and prayers. Also, help me to read and follow your instructions in the bible, and so that I will not deviate from your principles. Let my feet remain firm within your gate, and let me remain rapturable to qualify for your everlasting peace and joy. For in the name of Jesus Christ I make my requests.

Amen.

« DAY 81 »

God's Supernatural Power Is Enough To Break Anyone Free From Satan's Bondage

Focus Passage: Exodus 9, 10, 11

King Pharaoh had no regard for God since he was a powerful earthly king; his arrogance eventually trapped him to have an untimely death. God observed Pharaoh's arrogance and said,

> *"Now if I had stretched out my hand and struck you and your people with pestilence, then you would have been cut off from the earth. But indeed for this purpose I have raised you up, that I may show my power in you, and that my name may be declared in all the earth"* **(Exodus 9:15-16).**

Lesson:

Any form of bondage against God's children can be traced to Satan the enemy of righteousness. The enemy imposes the bondage to afflict God's children. He also aims at harassing them to doubt God's power so that he could rob them of their blessings. Meanwhile, it takes God's supernatural power to deliver anyone from Satan's bondage. Anyone who intends to be freed from the enemy must be ready to exercise his/her authority in Jesus Christ. The person must be ready to declare his/her victory with the use of Jesus' name. Why Jesus name? God has endowed him all authority that humanity need to have deliverance and prosperity. It is written in the scripture,

"Therefore God also has highly exalted him and given him the name which is above every name, that at the name of Jesus every knee should bow, of those in heaven, and of those on earth, and of those under the earth, and that every tongue should confess that Jesus Christ is lord, to the glory of God the father" **(Philippians 2:9-11).** Jesus also confirmed the fact of his authority in Matthew 28:18.

Prayer:

All praises to Jesus Christ for he is the only deity endowed with power and authority to conquer all life battles and award victory. I believe in the name of Jesus Christ, and I align myself with the use of his name. Therefore, I now stand upon the fact of the scripture to challenge devil and overrule all his activities in my life. By the authority in the name of Jesus Christ, I rebuke Satan, and I command him to flee from me. I command every situation that challenges my life to stumble. I break every devil's stronghold, and I command every negative situation to turn positively to my advantage. From now on, my testimony shall stand, and I will sing songs of victory to honor the name of God. For in the name of Jesus Christ I make my declarations.

Amen.

« DAY 82 »

Jesus' Second Coming Will Only Favor Those Who Have Confessed Him As Their Savior

Focus Passage: Matthew 25:31-46

The second coming of Jesus Christ will bring mix reaction to earth inhabitants. He will transport those who have believed his testimony as the true son of God to heaven where they will receive his everlasting joy. Christ will ignore unbelievers and abandon them on earth to face God's wrath that would be released. Satan, the wicked ones, and unrepentant sinners will eventually be hauled to hell fire where there shall be eternal condemnation. The scripture said,

> "And before him shall be gathered all nations: and he shall separate them one from another, as a shepherd divideth his sheep from the goats: And he shall set the sheep on his right hand, but the goats on the left. Then shall the King say unto them on his right hand, Come, ye blessed of my Father, inherit the kingdom prepared for you from the foundation of the world…Then shall he say also unto them on the left hand, Depart from me, ye cursed, into everlasting fire, prepared for the devil and his angels: For I was an hungred, and ye gave me no meat: I was thirsty, and ye gave me no drink: I was a stranger, and ye took me not in: naked, and ye clothed me not: sick, and in prison, and ye visited me not. Then shall they also answer him, saying, Lord, when saw we thee an hungred, or athirst, or a stranger, or naked, or sick, or in prison, and did not minister unto thee? Then shall he answer them, saying, Verily I say unto you, Inasmuch as ye did it not to one of the least of these, ye did it not to me. And these shall go away into everlasting punishment: but the righteous into life eternal" **(Matthew 25:32-46 KJV).**

Lesson:

Jesus' second coming will favor faithful Christians; it won't offer anything good for people who have rejected his testimony. Those who have confessed Jesus Christ as their personal Lord and Savior will rejoice in the heart of God in heaven, while the nonchalant and unrepentant sinners will suffer punishment in hell. Christ' warning should serve as a wakeup call to all people: Those who claimed to believe should renew their relationship with him; those who have not repented should not hesitate to turn a new leaf since Christ will appear when no one expects to rapture his saints. Meanwhile, the fact that Christ will reward his faithful followers in heaven should be enough motivation to challenge everyone to walk rightly with him, and serve him well. Everyone ought to take the important step of salvation by confessing Jesus Christ as his/her personal Lord and Savior.

Prayer:

Dear Jesus Christ, I long to enter your heavenly kingdom therefore I am taking an important step of salvation today. I believe you are the Son of God and the Savior of the world; salvation of soul and repentance of sin can only be obtained through you! Therefore, I confess you (Jesus Christ) as my personal Lord and Savior. I confess and plead for my sins. Please forgive my sins and write my name in the book of life. Let me remain qualified to meet and be raptured with you whenever you return. Please keep my feet firm before you always so that I can make heaven! Thank you Jesus Christ for your saving grace! Amen.

« DAY 83 »

A Person Who Oppresses God's Children Will Face God's Wrath

Focus Passage: Exodus 12, 13

King Pharaoh led his Egyptians citizens to oppress the Hebrews based on accusation that they dominated their land. The Egyptians had fun oppressing the people, but God was infuriated for their actions. Since the Hebrews (Israelites) were God's apple eyes, he was determined to avenge for them. The creator declared his verdict on his children's enemies and stated,

> *"For I will pass through the land of Egypt on that night, and will strike all the firstborn in the land of Egypt, both man and beast; and against all the Gods of Egypt I will execute judgment: I am the lord"* **(Exodus 12:12)**. *God's action against the Egyptians is as reported; "and it came to pass at midnight that the lord struck all the firstborn in the land of Egypt, from the firstborn of pharaoh who sat on his throne to the firstborn of the captive who was in the dungeon, and all the firstborn of livestock"* **(Exodus 12:29)**.

Lesson:
Anyone who oppresses a child of God will not go free but experience God's punishment. The creator will not lightly esteem any act of provocation against his people; he will defend his children against enemies' assaults for the sake of glorifying his name. Meanwhile, God's judgment against the enemies may take a different turn than anyone could imagine. God who is omniscient knows the best way to catch up with wicked people. Since he knows all things, he will corner the wicked ones when they had least expected to award them his judgment. However, the most important lesson here is that everyone be careful to honor God in the lives of God's people. Anyone who is named after God (God's children) must be treated with dignity and honor. Whatever is done to a child of God – whether positively or negatively – is being done to God himself; and the creator will award measurable judgment for every action performed.

Prayer:
Dear God, please help me to be careful to relate with anyone who is called "a child of God!" Do not let me take your children for granted, and do not let me be an obstacle to their progress. Give me strength to support those who belong to you and make positive contributions into their lives. Let me be an agent of light and your true ambassador that makes promote contributions into other people's lives, so that I can qualify for your blessings. For in the name of Jesus Christ I make my requests.

Amen.

« DAY 84 »

God Who Sees All Things Will Reward Every Faithful Service A Person Renders To Him

Focus Passage: Matthew 26:6-13

A woman received special attention from Jesus Christ for doing what others considered to be irrelevant. The woman poured expensive oil on Jesus' head prior to his crucifixion; those who witnessed it took offense and rationalize that the oil could have been converted to money and be donated to charity. However, Jesus gave credit to the woman and expounded on the symbolic representation of what she did. The scripture reported,

> *"Now when Jesus was in Bethany, in the house of Simon the leper, there came unto him a woman having an alabaster box of very precious ointment, and poured it on his head, as he sat at meat. But when his disciples saw it, they had indignation, saying, to what purpose is this waste? For this ointment might have been sold for much, and given to the poor. When Jesus understood it, he said unto them, why trouble ye the woman? For she hath wrought a good work upon me. For ye have the poor always with you; but me ye have not always. For in that she hath poured this ointment on my body, she did it for my burial. Verily I say unto you, Wheresoever this gospel shall be preached in the whole world, there shall also this, that this woman hath done, be told for a memorial of her"* **(Matthew 26:6-13 KJV).**

Lesson:

God will reward any service a person honorably renders to him. He sees hidden things and knows the intention of anyone's heart. God knows if a service rendered to him come from a pure heart or not. He expects all his children to make their presentations with pure heart, without any hidden agenda. However, some Christian loves to rationalize their actions and look for a reason not to offer their best sacrifices to God. They claim God does not spend money and any money or material donated will be spent or used by humans. Also, some Christians accuse their spiritual leaders of living affluent lives; they claim their leaders will convert their charity donations for their personally use. However, whether accusation and rationalization are true or not, it should not be enough reason for anyone to stop supporting God's work. Those who do not give, and those who meagerly give their resources to support God's work will have little return to earn; however, those who give liberally towards gospel will have plentiful benefits to receive from their creator.

Prayer:

Dear God, please give me grace to serve you with a pure heart. Keep me pure and plain to offer my services to you in an acceptable manner. Do not let me rationalize evil deeds, but let my focus always be to serve you well. Give me a heart that liberally offers charity to support your gospel for the sake of expanding your kingdom. Please keep me qualified to receive your benefits. For in the name of Jesus Christ I make my requests.

Amen.

« DAY 85 »

The Same God Of Mercy Is Also God Of Fire And Brimstone; Wicked People Should Be Watchful

Focus Passage: Exodus 14, 15

Israelites found themselves between a rock and a hard place when they exited Egypt. A massive red sea was standing in the front, and a fierce Egyptian army was pursuing them from behind. The descendants of Abraham had no route of escape, but God intervened to set them free. When the Israelites could not lift a finger against their enemies, God miraculously parted red sea for them, and also drown the Egyptian army. The scripture reported how god delivered Israelites from their troubles,

> "And it came to pass, that in the morning watch the Lord looked unto the host of the Egyptians through the pillar of fire and of the cloud, and troubled the host of the Egyptians, And took off their chariot wheels, that they drave them heavily: so that the Egyptians said, Let us flee from the face of Israel; for the Lord fighteth for them against the Egyptians. And the Lord said unto Moses, Stretch out thine hand over the sea, that the waters may come again upon the Egyptians, upon their chariots, and upon their horsemen. And Moses stretched forth his hand over the sea, and the sea returned to his strength when the morning appeared; and the Egyptians fled against it; and the Lord overthrew the Egyptians in the midst of the sea. And the waters returned, and covered the chariots, and the horsemen, and all the host of Pharaoh that came into the sea after them; there remained not so much as one of them. But the children of Israel walked upon dry land in the midst of the sea; and the waters were a wall unto them on their right hand, and on their left" *(Exodus 14: 24-29 KJV).*

Lesson:
God knows how to defend his people from trouble. He will safeguard them from wicked folks who are determined to harm them. There is definitely no condition tough enough to stop God from performing wonders to help his own people. Jehovah can perform any miracle for the sake of his people: as it may apply, he can cause rain to fall in the desert, or cause sun to shine in the arctic. The creator can even use both the living and non-living thing alike for the sake of helping his people. Therefore, those who serve God should be rest assured in him for safety and victory. Once they call on him for help, he will show up to prove himself strong on their behalves. Meanwhile, those who oppress righteous people will have much to account for in the presence of the Creator. God who knows how to catch wicked people will catch up with them and teach them lessons of life. The same God who is merciful towards the meek is also a god of fire and brimstone towards the wicked!

Prayer:
Dear God, I understand that your safety stands sure over people who serve you. You are strong enough to defend those who cry to you for help. Therefore, I cry to you for help today to avenge me of my enemies. Please silence my foes and make them stumble at their words and works. Let those who pursue me mercilessly fall for my sake. Deliver me from wicked people, and give me upper hands over them. Anoint my head with your oil of gladness, and

let my face shine when I sing the songs of victory in the assembly of your people. Let me have a big laughter as I celebrate my victory! For in the name of Jesus Christ I make my requests.

Amen.

« DAY 86 »

Prayer Is The Master-Key Into Addressing All Situations Of Life

Focus Passage: Matthew 26:36-75

Jesus' earthly ministry was about to end, and he knew heavy persecution would mark its end. Therefore, he was heavy in the spirit having known that Satan would seize the moment to mislead people he had come to save. Christ turned to God in prayer to receive strength and courage needed to successfully finish the last lap of his ministry. The scripture reported,

> *"Then Jesus came with them to a place called Gethsemane, and said to the disciples, "sit here while I go and pray over there." and he took with him peter and the two sons of Zebedee, and he began to be sorrowful and deeply distressed. Then he said to them, "my soul is exceedingly sorrowful, even to death. Stay here and watch with me." He went a little farther and fell on his face, and prayed, saying, "o my father, if it is possible, let this cup pass from me; nevertheless, not as I will, but as you will"* **(Matthew 26:36-39).**

Lesson:

Prayer is the master-key into addressing all situations of life. There is nothing beyond the power of prayer. It is an eventual door that grants access to believers to claim their portion of goodness from their creator. Prayer is very efficient when it is done with a pure heart, and faith is exercised. Jehovah will listen to the cries of those who call on him for help, and he will help them. No matter what a life need is - whether light or heavy - God is able to adequately respond to it and grant whatever his children request. Meanwhile, believers must understand that God's ways are different from ours, and his response sometimes may differ from what we requested. He may choose to instantly respond, and he may choose to delay his response. In other words, God may respond to our needs by saying "yes, no, or later." Believers must not be disappointed when things appear differently than what was requested. The Creator knows what is best for us, and he will not allow us to make mistakes despite our sense of urgency. No matter what the situation is, believers must keep serving and trusting God having surely known that our God who has all good things at his disposal will not suffer us life essentials.

Prayer:

Dear God, please teach me how to pray! Help me to commit my life circumstances to you in prayer so that I can live a fulfilled life. Also, teach me how to wait for your promises until they are completely materialized. Do not let me outrun you with my desires and make mistakes, but give me grace to wait for your promises so that I can have a big laughter at the end. Please shower your grace and goodness on me always so that I can testify to your goodness in the assembly of your people. For in the name of Jesus Christ I make my requests.

Amen.

« DAY 87 »

Every Christian Is Expected To Serve God With Unconditional Love

Focus Passage: Exodus 16, 17, 18

Israelites complained against Moses and Aaron soon after they were miraculous delivered from Egypt. They murmured against them for scarcity of food and water, and they argued their lives were better as Egyptians slaves with some food to eat than to be freed in the jungle and starve to death. The Israelites failed to realize that same God who delivered them from Egyptian bondage was strong enough to miraculously feed them in the jungle. The scripture reported the ingrate attitude of the Israelites,

> *"And the children of Israel said to them (Moses and Aaron), "Oh, that we had died by the hand of the Lord in the land of Egypt, when we sat by the pots of meat* and *when we ate bread to the full! For you have brought us out into this wilderness to kill this whole assembly with hunger"* ***(Exodus 16:3).***

Lesson:
Every Christian is expected to serve God with unconditional love. We ought not to serve God with bias mind, neither are we allowed to serve him with any string of selfish attachment. Our motivation for serving God must be to make him happy and nothing more! We are not to chase the Creator for what we intend to get from him only. Also, once we receive his blessings, we mustn't turn our back against him only to return whenever we need other benefits. A true child of God will serve God under whatever circumstance. He/she will serve God during surplus and scarcity. He/she will also serve God in time of good and poor health. In other words, the same God of the good time is still the same God of the bad time, and he will make all things work to our advantage once he could confirm our steadfastness with him. Hence, anyone who intends to receive lasting benefits from his/her Creator should make decisive efforts to stick with him at all times.

Prayer:
Dear God, please teach me how to love you unconditionally. Let me serve you without any selfish or bias mind. Let me be appreciative of your past benefits in my life, and also trust you for those in anticipation. During time of need, give me confidence to keep confessing my trust in you with statement of faith *"My God whom I serve shall supply all my needs."* Enable me with grace to keep trusting you until my joy are full, so that I can continue to serve you more! For in the name of Jesus Christ I make my requests.

Amen.

« DAY 88 »

Christians Are To Mind Their Business And Focus On Self-Improvements

Focus Passage: Matthew 27:1-26

Jesus grew from people's common class to become a significant public figure, and that provoked the Pharisees - His competitors. The opponents could not help people as Christ did, neither could they perform miracles like him. Therefore, they were determined to depose him at all cost. Jesus' opponents wanted to kill him – and they believed their actions would stop him. However, Jesus' opponents failed to realize that crucifixion was his ultimate goal. Christ' mission was to die for the sins of mankind so that he could save them. The bible reported,

> "When morning came, all the chief priests and elders of the people plotted against Jesus to put Him to death. And when they had bound Him, they led Him away and delivered Him to Pontius Pilate the governor"**(Matthew 27:1-26).**

Lesson:
Christianity is not a common race that anyone should run with normal human imagination only. Christianity is a religious exercise that demands spiritual insights. For anyone to adequately run the race and satisfy God, he/she must be spiritually sensitive and understand that nothing can be deemed acceptable to God unless it satisfies bible standard. For example, no Christian should meddle with another person's ministry either to criticize or to condemn it unless God specially charged him/her to do so. (Meanwhile, since the concept of any vision is mainly established between God and the visionary, it is almost impossible for anyone to intrude without making mistakes). Also, a true Christian will take caution in passing accusation against other believers because they have different denomination. Every child of God ought to examine him/herself in God and daily make personal improvement to serve him better. Believer's priority should not be to get into other people's business while theirs lie fallow. God is only interested in people who have personal conviction and are making decisive efforts to improve their relationship with him. Jehovah will strengthen his true children to keep growing in him to perfect his purposes in their lives.

Prayer:
Dear God, please help me to set my priority right and serve you well. Do not let me meddle with other people's business when you have not asked me to do so. Let my focus be to have self-improvement into becoming a better Christian that will be due of your benefits on earth and in heaven. Please empower me through your Holy Spirit to remain sensitive so that I will not sin against you, but remain heavenly worthy! For in the name of Jesus Christ I make my requests.

Amen.

« DAY 89 »

All God's Laws Are compressed Into "Love"

Focus Passage: Exodus 19, 20

God presented his commandments to Israelites as he was leading them through the wilderness to the Promised Land. The Creator required his children to obey his laws so that they can prosper. They would suffer consequences if they dare to disobey. God said,

> *"Now therefore, if you will indeed obey my voice and keep my covenant, then you shall be a special treasure to me above all people; for all the earth is mine. And you shall be to me a kingdom of priests and a holy nation..."* **(Exodus 19:5-6)**. God's commandments given to Israelites are as follows:

- You shall have no other gods before me **(Exodus 20:3)**.
- You shall not make for yourself a carved image – any likeness of anything that is in heaven above, or that is in the earth beneath, or that is in the water under the earth **(Exodus 20:4-6)**.
- You shall not take the name of the LORD your God in vain **(Exodus 20:7)**.
- Remember the Sabbath day, to keep it holy **(Exodus 20:8-10)**.
- Honor your father and your mother **(Exodus 20:12)**.
- You shall not murder **(Exodus 20:13)**.
- You shall not commit adultery **(Exodus 20:14)**.
- You shall not steal **(Exodus 20:15)**.
- You shall not bear false witness against your neighbor **(Exodus 20:16)**.
- You shall not covet your neighbor's house; you shall not covet your neighbor's wife, nor his male servant, nor his female servant, nor his ox, nor his donkey, nor anything that is your neighbor's **(Exodus 20:17)**.

Lesson:
God's laws are considerably light and simple; and they are easy to obey. Thanks to Jesus Christ for he came to even make the laws become simpler to comply with. Christ asks his followers to love God and their neighbors dearly, which will enable them to perfectly satisfy God. That is, if Christ love dwells in us, we will genuinely love God and other people. Genuine love of Christ won't allow us to hurt God with disobedience. Also, it won't allow us to steal, disrespect, kill, fornicate, jealous, or bear false witness. Therefore, everyone who aims at satisfying God's law must adopt Christ' love and be truly committed to it. (It is virtually impossible for anyone to perfectly obey all God's laws without having the love of Christ).

Prayer:
Dear God, I am aware of your commandments and I want to obey them. I am also aware that it is impossible for anyone to successfully obey you without having the love of Jesus Christ; therefore, I humble myself before you today to ask for Christ' love. I open up my heart for Christ to take over. Today, I (*mention your name*) confess Jesus Christ as my personal Lord and Savior. I confess my sins and repent from them. I yield my complete life to Jesus Christ,

and I will serve him forever! I believe that I have become a true child of God from today; I now have the strength of God in me to obey his commandments so that I can prosper. Praise God, I have become a co-sharer of God's kingdom. Hallelujah.

Amen.

« DAY 90 »

Jesus Passed The Most Difficult Test Of Life To Earn Us Salvation

Focus Passage: Matthew 27:27-50

Jesus Christ was assaulted and humiliated by the Roman soldiers: They stripped him naked and mocked him. They also twisted crown of thorn on his head and offered him vinegar. The opponents also hanged Jesus on the cross among two robbers and publicized his accusation for everyone to see, "This is the King of Jews." All people including priests, robbers, and bystanders hauled insults on him chanting, "You have saved others, save yourself now!" The scripture reported Jesus' experience with people who persecuted and crucified him. It is written,

> *"And when they had come to a place called Golgotha, that is to say, Place of a Skull, they gave Him sour wine mingled with gall to drink. But when He had tasted it, He would not drink. Then they crucified Him, and divided His garments, casting lots, that it might be fulfilled which were spoken by the prophet, "They divided my garments among them, and for my clothing they cast lots." Sitting down, they kept watch over Him there. And they put up over His head the accusation written against Him: Then two robbers were crucified with Him, one on the right and another on the left. And those who passed by blasphemed Him, wagging their heads and saying, "You who destroy the temple and build it in three days, save yourself! If you are the Son of God, come down from the cross." Likewise the chief priests also, mocking with the scribes and elders, said, "He saved others; Himself He cannot save. If He is the King of Israel, let Him now come down from the cross, and we will believe Him. He trusted in God; let Him deliver Him now if He will have Him; for He said, 'I am the Son of God.'" Even the robbers who were crucified with Him reviled Him with the same thing"* **(Matthew 27:33-44)**.

Lesson:

Jesus Christ endured the most challenging moments of his life without compromising his mission of saving humanity. Having understood what the ultimate price would be, Christ chose to endure all persecutions and suffered to die on the cross. He shed tears and cried to God for strength to carry through. Jesus prayed; *"My God, My God, why have you forsaken me?"* **(Matthew 27:46)**. Indeed, Jesus terribly suffered from the Pharisees and the Roman soldiers to exchange his innocence for our offenses. We humans deserve punishment, and not Christ. Yet the Son of God chose to suffer punishments on our behalves so that we can be saved. He sacrificed his life on the cross to save our souls! Therefore, everyone who aims at seeing God on the last day must confess Jesus Christ as Lord and accept him as his/her personal Lord and Savior.

Prayer:

I thank you Jesus Christ for enduring all sufferings for the purpose of saving humanity. The only token I can offer to you is to give you my complete life and accept you as my personal Savior. Therefore, I make my declaration in you today that from now on, I *(mention your name)* confess you Jesus Christ as my personal Lord and Savior. I will faithfully serve and obey you till you return to take me to your heavenly kingdom. I thank you one more time for your love and saving grace!
Amen.

« DAY 91 »

God Is Ready To Work With People That Are Willing To Improve On Themselves

Focus Passage: Exodus 21, 22

Israelites were aliens to freedom, and they had tendency of abusing it since they were long-term Egyptians' slaves. Therefore, God handed them some rules to guide them so that they will not sin against him. The Creator simplified his laws to Israelites so that they would find them easy to comprehend and comply with. God extensively analyzed his laws on various subjects which include human justice; violence prevention; livestock management; property protection, and morality. For example, God said,

> "If one man's ox hurts another's, so that it dies, then they shall sell the live ox and divide the money from it; and the dead ox they shall also divide" (Exodus 21:35); "If a man delivers to his neighbor money or articles to keep, and it is stolen out of the man's house, if the thief is found, he shall pay double" **(Exodus 22:7).**

Lesson:
God is the creator of heaven and earth, and he wants all people to maintain good relationship with him. He is ready to work with people until they could comply with his standard. Meanwhile, the Creator is determined to bless those who carefully follow his commandments. He will automatically send blessings into their lives - even when they have not asked for one. However, Jehovah will not entertain those who abuse his rules. He will definitely not honor those who dishonor his commandments, but punish them. Hence, all people must serve God well and carefully obey his commandments so that they can prosper.

Prayer:
Dear God, please give me strength to obey your laws so that I can prosper. Let your Holy Spirit teach and guide me to behave appropriately in a manner that will meet your expectations. Let your blessings follow my obedience, and let me prosper throughout the days of my life. For in the name of Jesus Christ I make my requests.

Amen.

« DAY 92 »

Jesus Death And Resurrection Have Granted Humanity Free Access To God

Focus Passage: Matthew 27:51-66

The death of Jesus Christ on the cross has removed the wall of separation that existed between God and man. The moment Jesus died on the cross, the veil of the temple that demarcated the most holy part of the temple and also separated common people was completely tore apart. Henceforth, all people can gain access to God though Christ' name without consulting any special priest. The scripture reported,

> "...And Jesus cried out again with a loud voice, and yielded up His spirit. Then, behold, the veil of the temple was torn in two from top to bottom; and the earth quake, and the rocks were split" **(Matthew 27:50-51).**

Lesson:
Jesus Christ died to save humanity. He has granted free access to God through his death and resurrection, since temple veil can no more blockade us. Everyone can now talk to God anywhere at any moment. All what people need is to use the name of Jesus Christ whenever they want to consult God in prayer. His name has granted us free access to God to get whatever we need - without any further obligations! Once we have used Jesus name, all things will fall into place for us. Besides opportunity of receiving whatever we desire through Christ' name, believers also have the gift of eternal life to possess. People who have believed in the death and resurrection of Jesus Christ will resurrect on the last day to eternally live with God in heaven. Hallelujah!

Prayer:
Praise God for Jesus Christ died on the cross and resurrected to grant me permanent access to God. Since I have become a child of God through my confession and acceptance of Jesus Christ as Lord, I can now access God to get whatever I want. Also, a crown of righteousness is now awaiting me in heaven and my name is written in the book of life. All I'm now asking is God's grace to keep my confession of faith in Jesus Christ. May God help me to keep serving him until he returns to take me to his heavenly kingdom! I also pray that God grant grace of salvation to those who are yet to believe. Please open their eyes to know and appreciate Christ work of salvation so that they too can qualify for your kingdom. For in the name of Jesus Christ I have made my requests.

Amen!

« DAY 93 »

Sin Irritates God And Give Devil Upper Hands To Operate

Focus Passage: Exodus 23, 24

God warned Israelites not to follow the sinful path of Canaanites (the gentiles); they would suffer if they do so. The Creator emphasized that he was displacing Canaanites and transferring their heritage to Israelites because they serve idols. Israelites must not make the same mistake, or else they suffer similar consequence. God said,

> *"Do not bow down before their gods or worship them or follow their practices. You must demolish them and break their sacred stones to pieces. 25 Worship the Lord your God, and his blessing will be on your food and water. I will take away sickness from among you"* ***(Exodus 23:24-25 NIV).***

Lesson:
Sin irritates God, and it makes a child of God loses his benefits. Despite the Creator's desires to bless his children and care for them, he still finds it difficult to engage them in sin. Meanwhile, devil is the only party that gains upper hand when a sin is committed. The enemy uses a sinful moment to accuse believers before their God. He also seizes a sinful moment to carry out his evil plot. Meanwhile, God still has the greatest strength in every scenario: He has power to forgive and redeem any sinner. He also has power to stop devil's plot. However, to enjoy victory over sin and Satan, believers mustn't be shy to confess any sin committed. Every Christian should consciously make effort to serve God purely, and also genuinely repent from whenever sin he/she realizes has committed. Jehovah who cares will surely redeem his own children and give them grace to keep living victoriously in this sinful world.

Prayer:
Dear Lord, please help me to consciously serve you with purity of mind always. Do not let me yield to the temptations of the enemy. Rescue me whenever I drift into sin; let me confess sins and exercise genuine repentance. Let all Satan's efforts to gain control over my life fail. Give me your grace and empowerment of the Holy Spirit to serve you in humility and full devotion until the very end, so that I can qualify to meet you in heaven. For in the name of Jesus Christ I make my requests.

Amen.

« DAY 94 »

Jesus Christ Is The Only Messiah Who Has Died And Resurrected

Focus Passage: Matthew 28

Jesus Christ rose from the grave to disappoint the Pharisees one more time. Every attempt the opponents made to stop him failed. After Jesus died and was buried, the Pharisees rolled heavy stone to blockade his tomb and also guarded the entire tomb area. However, Jesus still resurrected on the third day against all odds to prove his ultimate triumph. An earthquake rolled off the stone, and guards fainted in fear. Shame to the devil and glory to God! The scripture described the incident,

> *"...And behold, there was a great earthquake; for an angel of the Lord descended from heaven, and came and rolled back the stone from the door, and sat on it. His countenance was like lightning, and his clothing as white as snow. And the guards shook for fear of him, and became like dead* men" **(Matthew 28:2-4).**

Lesson:

Jesus Christ resurrected from death to prove that he is the true Messiah sent by God to save the world. Other people who have sought to claim the messiah title were disproved at their point of death. They died and never resurrected. Jesus Christ was the only Messiah who died and resurrected - which validated gospel. His death and resurrection have furnished the platform needed for humanity to be saved. Whoever believes in Jesus as the true Messiah and confesses him as his/her personal Lord and Savior will be saved. Such person will inherit the gift of eternal life from God. That is, he/she will be granted opportunity to eternally live with Christ in heaven.

Prayer:

Dear Jesus Christ, I believe that you are the true Messiah - the Son of God - sent to save the world. You died and resurrected on the third day to give gift of eternal life to whoever believes in you. Therefore, I declare my faith in you today: I confess you as Lord and accept you as my personal Savior. I also confess my sins and repent from them. From now on, I dedicate my complete life to you and I will serve you forever! Please write my name in the book of life, and keep me ever worthy of your kingdom.

Amen.

« DAY 95 »

God Only Appreciates Willing Offerings From People – He Does Not Arm-Twists Anyone

Focus Passage: Exodus 25, 26

God demanded that his children bring him their offerings from a willing heart. They must bring them willingly without being feel coerced. God said to Moses,

> *"Speak to the children of Israel, that they bring me an offering. From everyone who gives it willingly with his heart you shall take my offering"* **(Exodus 25:2).**

Lesson:
God does not arm-twists people to collect offerings from them, but he expects his children to have grateful mind and offer him their best. Indeed, God is worthy of our appreciations: He has done many remarkable things for us (his children), and we ought to praise him deeply. God has made ways where there were no ways, and he has benefitted us from the sources that we were least expected. Besides, God has done other great things that we could neither see nor quantify. Therefore, our show of appreciation to him must come from a pure heart. Jehovah knows when people hoard their resources from him. He knows when someone pretends to have offered his best while he's not. People who offer their sacrifices to God with liberal mind will definitely receive more benefits from him. Meanwhile, the misers have already limited their future blessings since God only relates with liberal and cheerful givers!

Prayer:
Dear God, you own whatever I have, and I will be willing to offer you plentiful offering in return. Please give me a charitable heart to liberally appreciate your goodness in my life. Let my willing offerings be acceptable in your sight, and let them glorify your name. Please bless me more so that I can continue to sacrifice whatever I have to the glory of your name. For in the name of Jesus Christ I make my requests.

Amen.

« DAY 96 »

Christians Must Be Humble To Receive God's Promotion

Focus Passage: Mark 1:1-22:

The Spirit of God immediately descended on Jesus Christ immediately John baptized him in River Jordan. God's audible voice was heard confirming him stating,

> "You are My beloved Son, in whom I am well pleased" **(Mark 1:11).**

Lesson:
Christians ought to learn humility from Jesus Christ who submitted himself to John for water baptism. Jesus Christ being the Son of God did not consider it an insult to be baptized by a mere prophet. He allowed prophecy to play out for the sake of glorifying his heavenly Father. Therefore, God honored him with an audible affirmation proclaiming that he was pleased with him. We (believers) also must do our best to allow God to manifest his plans in our lives, so that we can have better testimony than any previous time.

Prayer:
Dear God, please give me the spirit of humility that will allow your plans to materialize in my life. Enable me with strength to cooperate with your plans and follow your leadership every day of my life so that I can prosper. Please guide my footsteps to have success! For in the name of Jesus Christ I make my requests.

Amen.

« DAY 97 »

Jesus Simplified And Fine-Tuned Human Relationship With God

Focus Passage: Exodus 27, 28

God required his high priest to prioritize holiness and ensure perfect services before him. Being the only qualified person to enter the most holy part of the temple, the high priest must not make assignment error, or else he dies instantly! God said,

> "...And it shall be upon Aaron when he ministers, and its sound (bell sound) will be heard when he goes into the holy place before the Lord and when he comes out, that he may not die. "You shall also make a plate of pure gold and engrave on it, like the engraving of a signet: HOLINESS TO THE LORD" *(Exodus 28:35-36).*

Lesson:
Casual services were not allowed in God's temple during Old Testament era. The Priest was deemed with perfection, and was not allowed to make mistake. Therefore, serving God was a bit difficult and sensitive. However, Jesus Christ later came to fine-tune our relationship with God. The Son of God simplified the delicacies of priesthood office for everyone to enjoy. He assumed the position of High Priest for himself. That is, Jesus Christ became the Most Holy High Priest through whom all people can offer their services to God. All it takes to have expectations met is for anyone to mention the name of Jesus Christ in his/her prayers. Meanwhile, for any solution to come through Jesus' name, a person must have first confessed him as Lord and accept him as his/her personal Savior.

Prayer:
Dear Jesus Christ, what a wonderful High Priest you are who have helped to overcome human imperfections so that we can have free access to God! Thank you for simplifying the rigid and complex laws with the use of your name. I understand that once I confess you as Lord and mention your name in my prayers, all shall be well with me. Doors of opportunity shall be opened for me to the glorification of your name. I believe your testimony, and I will serve you forever more!

Amen.

« DAY 98 »

Christians Must Learn From Jesus Christ Who Refused Distraction To Successfully Finish His Ministry

Focus Passage: Mark 1:23-45

Jesus Christ made mess of Satan by healing people and casting out demons from those who were possessed. Meanwhile, the Messiah was not carried away with any fame that associated with his good works. He rather instructed people to speak less of him but do their due diligence to the priests. An example of Jesus' reaction to human praises is highlighted below,

> *"And there came a leper to him, beseeching him, and kneeling down to him, and saying unto him, If thou wilt, thou canst make me clean. And Jesus, moved with compassion, put forth his hand, and touched him, and saith unto him, I will; be thou clean. And as soon as he had spoken, immediately the leprosy departed from him, and he was cleansed. And he straitly charged him, and forthwith sent him away; And saith unto him, See thou say nothing to any man: but go thy way, shew thyself to the priest, and offer for thy cleansing those things which Moses commanded, for a testimony unto them. But he went out, and began to publish it much, and to blaze abroad the matter, insomuch that Jesus could no more openly enter into the city, but was without in desert places: and they came to him from every quarter"* **(Mark 1:40-45 KJV).**

Lesson:

Christians should learn from Jesus Christ who followed God's mandate to the letter. While on earth, he avoided human praises to remain focus on his call of leading people to God's kingdom. Jesus was sensitive enough to understand the risk of letting people manipulate him into pride and cares of the world. Instead of throwing party for his fans to celebrate his ministry achievements, he regularly checked-in to the mountains (solitary places) to pray for more strength to keep doing God's will. (Mark 1:23-45). Christians also must practice the same principle so as to have more success in their lives and ministry. A person who gives his/her life to a consistent lifestyle of prayer will have enough strength needed to overcome Satan's temptations, and have victory.

Prayer:

Dear Jesus Christ, please give me grace to keep focus on whatever assignment that you have committed unto my hands. Don't let me get carried away with cares of the world and lose focus of my ministry! Also, do not let me give in to human praises and be distracted from my real commission of serving you and propagating your gospel. Help me to remain focus and be consistent until I finish my earthly race. At the end of earthly journey, let me meet you in heaven to enjoy your eternal benefits. For in the name of Jesus Christ I make my requests.

Amen.

« DAY 99 »

God's Standard Of Righteousness Remain Unchanged Despite The Change Of Testaments

Focus Passage: Exodus 29, 30

God asked Moses to consecrate Aaron and his sons for priesthood office for seven days. The consecration process was rigorous, but Moses must follow God's order to the letter. God said to Moses,

> *"And thou shalt take the ram of the consecration, and seethe his flesh in the holy place. And Aaron and his sons shall eat the flesh of the ram, and the bread that is in the basket by the door of the tabernacle of the congregation. And they shall eat those things wherewith the atonement was made, to consecrate and to sanctify them: but a stranger shall not eat thereof, because they are holy. And if ought of the flesh of the consecrations, or of the bread, remain unto the morning, then thou shalt burn the remainder with fire: it shall not be eaten, because it is holy. And thus shalt thou do unto Aaron, and to his sons, according to all things which I have commanded thee: seven days shalt thou consecrate them..."* ***(Exodus 29:31-35 KJV).***

Lesson:
The process of consecrating God's priests during Old Testament era was cumbersome and overwhelming, but Jesus Christ introduced the New Testament to simplify it. Although the process has become simplified, the principle behind the appointment and consecration of priests remain the same for the two testaments. Every priest must follow God's order: He/she must preach undiluted word of God and endeavor to satisfy God in all his/her officiating activities. Meanwhile, every Christian is now commissioned to serve as God's priest for his/her life and family, since we have all been granted access to reach God through Jesus Christ. Therefore, we must do our best to satisfy God in our spiritual activities.

Prayer:
Dear God, please empower me to faithfully offer my spiritual activities before you always. Do not let me disappoint you with my spiritual practices, so that you can be happy with me. Please guide my ways to remain your consistent Christian throughout the days of my life. For in the name of Jesus Christ I make my requests.

Amen.

« DAY 100 »

Christians Must Ensure Not To Pass Destructive Criticisms On Other People

Focus Passage: Mark 2

Jesus Christ was having fun doing God's work while his opponents (Pharisees) were busy attacking his image character everywhere with the hope that he might cave in and give up his ministry. Jesus continued his ministry by preaching and performing more miracles to populate God's kingdom. However, the Pharisees stalked him and were nitpicking on whatever he said or did. For example, the Pharisees accused him of blasphemy when he healed a paralyzed man,

> *They said, "Why does this Man speak blasphemies like this? Who can forgive sins but God alone?"* **(Mark 2:7)**. *The Pharisees also accused Jesus of paling with sinners (Mark 2:16); they also portrayed him as a weak leader who failed to appropriately teach his disciples how to follow God's law* **(Mark 2:24).**

Lesson:

Children of God must avoid passing destructive criticisms on other people, because the practice is sinful. Our words must be encouraging and be filled with grace. They must also make positive contributions to other people's lives. Meanwhile, an undue criticism mostly generate from the spirit of jealousy - which is a direct violation of God's law. Every believer must ensure to allow God's divine Spirit to rule him/her always to make decisions that are edifying and also glorify God.

Prayer:

Dear God, please make me a channel of blessing to other people's lives. Do not let me be an obstacle to people's progress, but enable me grace to contribute my quota of supports into their lives. Do not let me act in flesh and jealous other people's success but let me encourage and join them to celebrate their victory. I know my day of success will also come, and people will rejoice with me. Please make me a good person Oh Lord! For in the name of Jesus Christ I make my requests.

Amen.

« DAY 101 »

Holy Spirit Brings God's Abiding Presence Into Believers' Lives

Focus Passage: Exodus 31, 32, 33

God desired to have his tabernacle among his people, and he authorized Moses to build one for him. He gave Moses both the master plan and the design specifications that were needed for the tabernacle. In addition, God assured Moses that he had given special talents and capability to some Israelites to make every necessary artistic provision for his tabernacle. God said to Moses,

> *"See, I have called by name Bezaleel the son of Uri, the son of Hur, of the tribe of Judah: And I have filled him with the spirit of God, in wisdom, and in understanding, and in knowledge, and in all manner of workmanship, To devise cunning works, to work in gold, and in silver, and in brass, And in cutting of stones, to set them, and in carving of timber, to work in all manner of workmanship. And I, behold, I have given with him Aholiab, the son of Ahisamach, of the tribe of Dan: and in the hearts of all that are wise hearted I have put wisdom, that they may make all that I have commanded thee" (Exodus 31:2-6 KJV).*

Lesson:
God dwelled in tents and temple among Israelites in the Old Testament, but since the New Testament began, he has made his abiding presence stationed with humans through his divine Holy Spirit. Therefore, all people who crave for God's abiding presence should seek for the Holy Spirit, which can only be obtained through Jesus Christ. Once God's abiding presence is received, a person's life would be transformed for better and excellence. The fellow will live in peace and also operate under God's divine guidance.

Prayer:
Dear God, I understand that your abiding presence is established through the Holy Spirit; therefore, I am asking that you please baptize me with him (Holy Spirit). Let your divine Holy Spirit furnish me an atmosphere of blessing and growth. Let him empower me to maintain a consistent relationship with you so that I can continue to receive and enjoy your benefits. Let your Spirit empower me to serve you well so that I can forever live an overcomer's life. For in the name of Jesus Christ I make my request.

Amen.

« DAY 102 »

Servants Of God Must Endure Persecutions And Remain Focus To Have Successful Ministry

Focus Passage: Mark 3:1-19

Jesus Christ healed a man whose hand was withered, but his action sparked rage and jealousy from his opponents. They conspired to kill him. Meanwhile, despite the dangers that surrounded him, Jesus still continued to heal people and proclaim God's kingdom. The scripture reported,

> *"... And He (Jesus) said to the man who had the withered hand, "Step forward." Then He said to them, "Is it lawful on the Sabbath to do good or to do evil, to save life or to kill?" But they kept silent. And when He had looked around at them with anger, being grieved by the hardness of their hearts, He said to the man, "Stretch out your hand." And he stretched it out, and his hand was restored as whole as the other. Then the Pharisees went out and immediately plotted with the Herodians against Him, how they might destroy Him"* **(Mark 3:3-6).**

Lesson:
God's servants are encouraged to endure persecutions and remain focus in ministry. We must realize that Satan would attempt to raise his ugly head against our gospel activities, and he will make every attempt to discourage us. However, God's servants must not give room for the enemy to win his battle! Every servant of God must diligently pray and pursue his/her ministry as given by God. Surely, Jehovah who calls one to ministry will give the strength needed to overcome devil, and have success.

Prayer:
Dear God, please grant all your servants strength and courage needed to remain focus in their ministries. Help them to resist devil's schemes; empower them with strength to have success. Help your servants throughout the world to keep bearing fruits for your kingdom. For in the name of Jesus Christ I make my requests.

Amen

« DAY 103 »

God Desires Committed Worshipers Who Will Move His Hands Into Performing Signs And Wonders

Focus Passage: Exodus 34, 35

Moses went to a mountain to receive God's Ten Commandments; but he got more benefits than he had wished! Having spent so much time in God's presence, the glory of God befell him and his face became brightened to the extent others could not behold his face. The scripture reported Moses' interaction with Israelites after he had encounter God's glory,

> *"And it came to pass, when Moses came down from mount Sinai with the two tables of testimony in Moses' hand, when he came down from the mount, that Moses wist not that the skin of his face shone while he talked with him. And when Aaron and all the children of Israel saw Moses, behold, the skin of his face shone; and they were afraid to come nigh him. And Moses called unto them; and Aaron and all the rulers of the congregation returned unto him: and Moses talked with them. And afterward all the children of Israel came nigh: and he gave them in commandment all that the Lord had spoken with him in mount Sinai. And till Moses had done speaking with them, he put a vail on his face. But when Moses went in before the Lord to speak with him, he took the vail off, until he came out. And he came out, and spake unto the children of Israel that which he was commanded. And the children of Israel saw the face of Moses, that the skin of Moses' face shone: and Moses put the vail upon his face again, until he went in to speak with him"* ***(Exodus 34:29-35 KJV).***

Lesson:
God descends his glory on anyone who spends quality time in his presence. The amount of time a person spends in his presence will determine the amount of God's glory that will manifest in his/her life. Meanwhile, not only a Christian who stays in God's presence will receive benefits, God himself will enjoy in the adventure. The Almighty God always desire that his children stay long in his presence, and he enjoy the opportunity whenever a deeper worshiper appears in his presence. Hence, since quality time of spiritual fellowship benefit both God and us, believers should create more time to spend time in the presence of their Creator.

Prayer:
Dear God, please give me strength and grace to spend quality time with you always. Help me to rearrange my activities to create more time for you! Let your Holy Spirit take over my life to enjoy every moment I spend with you until my cups are full with your benefits. For in the name of Jesus Christ I make my requests.

Amen.

« DAY 104 »

Christians Should Spread Gospel Without Yielding To Worldly Pressure

Focus Passage: Mark 3:20-35

The family of Jesus Christ did not believe in his ministry; they thought something was wrong with him since he preached some theories that could not be validated with their Jewish traditions. Therefore, they wanted to seize him from public arena and coerce him into following their rules. (Perhaps Jesus' family thought of recommending him for a psychiatric evaluation since his teaching appeared too foreign to them). The scripture reported,

> *"...When his own people heard* about this, *they went out to lay hold of Him, for they said, 'He is out of His mind." "Then His brothers and His mother came, and standing outside they sent to Him, calling Him"* **(Mark 3:21, Mark 3:31).**

Lesson:

Christianity may not mean anything to unbelievers, but it means a lot to believers - and it means so much to God! It is a religion established by God to save mankind from their sin. Therefore, Christians should do their due diligence to spread gospel without yielding to care and pressure of the world. Believers ought not to follow anti gospel opinion (whether it is popular or not). Also, they should not seek for people's approval before they do God's will. Indeed, the people of the world may hate us and be hostile because we serve God, but our choice of serving and obeying him will not go unaccounted for. The Creator will heavily reward our obedience in heaven.

Prayer:

Dear God, please help me to keep focus in serving and propagating your gospel. Help me to ignore whatever pressure the world might be imposing on me to compromise. Also, do not let me seek human praises neither seek their approval before serving you. Let me be bold towards serving you in faithfulness and holiness so that I can reign with you in heaven. For in the name of Jesus Christ I make my request.

Amen.

« DAY 105 »

God Is Only Interested In Freewill Offerings; He Is Does Not Coerce Anyone Into Giving

Focus Passage: Exodus 36, 37, 38

Israelites donated plentiful offerings for building God's tabernacle. They freely gave their material support - and they gave them in excess to deeply please God. Israelites offerings were so plenty to the extent that Moses had to discourage them from further giving because their storages were exhausted. The scripture reported,

> *"The people bring much more than enough for the service of the work which the Lord commanded us to do." So Moses gave a commandment, and they caused it to be proclaimed throughout the camp, saying, "Let neither man nor woman do any more work for the offering of the sanctuary." And the people were restrained from bringing"* **(Exodus 36:5-6).**

Lesson:
God loves cheerful givers, and he will bless them in return. The Creator is interested in seeing people who will give him their freewill offerings; he is not interested to receive any offering from a cocky and reluctant giver. God does not coerce anyone into giving him a gift, and he will not honor a gift from a bias and sneaky giver! Therefore, believers must ensure their offerings come from a pure heart. We must not feel pressured to give our willing offerings! Also, we must not present our gift with the secret intention of bribing God into getting him to meet our heart desires. We must offer our best and quality offerings to God with cheerfulness before they can be acceptable to him! Meanwhile, Jehovah knows how to reciprocate willing offerings. He will bless those who have willingly and cheerfully presented him their offerings, so that they can be motivated to continue their practice.

Prayer:
Dear Jesus Christ, please help me to bring you my best offerings at all times. Let me be a willing and cheerful giver, and let my offerings be genuine. Enable me to freely give my energy, time, money, and other resources to benefit your kingdom. Please let my liberal and charitable heart attract your blessings, and also result to the glorification of your name. For in the name of Jesus Christ I make my requests.

Amen.

« DAY 106 »

True Christianity Requires Deep And Thorough Commitments – Whoever Finishes Well Shall Be Rewarded

Focus Passage: Mark 4:1-20

Jesus Christ narrated the story of a farmer whose seeds encountered different scenarios when they were sown. Jesus said,

> *"Listen! Behold, a sower went out to sow and it happened, as he sowed, that some seed fell by the wayside; and the birds of the air came and devoured it. Some fell on stony ground, where it did not have much earth; and immediately it sprang up because it had no depth of earth. But when the sun was up it was scorched, and because it had no root it withered away. And some seed fell among thorns; and the thorns grew up and choked it, and it yielded no crop. But other seed fell on good ground and yielded a crop that sprang up, increased and produced: some thirtyfold, some sixty, and some a hundred"* **(Mark 4:3-8).**

The Interpretation of each scenario and their applicable lessons are highlighted below:

1. Some seeds fell by the roadside and were eaten by birds.
   - **Interpretation 1***:* This represents people who allowed Satan to steal the effect of God's word from their lives – **Mark 4:15**
   - **Lesson 1:** Anyone who listen to and believes lies will eventually derail from faith.
2. Some seeds fell on the stony ground – they grew quickly but died quickly also.
   - **Interpretation 2***:* This represents people who did not give further thoughts to God's word. The word did not have enough depth in their hearts, and they eventually lost interest in it – **Mark 4:16-17**
   - **Lesson 2***:* Christianity requires personal developments, anyone who fails to personally establish and maintain stable relationship with God will eventually fall away from faith
3. Some seeds fell among thorns and they were shocked.
   - **Interpretation 3***:* This represents people who could not withstand persecutions. They compromised their godly interests for worldly interests – **Mark 4:18-19**
   - **Lesson 3***:* Persecution of saints is bound to happen, therefore every Christian should prepare for it, and be ready to endure faith in Jesus Christ unto the end.
   - Some seeds fell unto good soil and they yielded plentifully.
   - **Interpretation 4***:* This represents few people who took Christianity seriously. They prayed and studied the word of God, and they applied any lesson learned to their daily lives – **Mark 4:20**
   - **Lesson 4***:* Christianity requires seriousness. God will honor people who focus on serving him. He will bless people who prioritize holiness and remain in faith unto the end.

Prayer:

Dear Jesus Christ, please prosper your word in my life. Baptize me with your Holy Spirit, and let him empower me to appropriately respond to the teaching of your word. Give me strength to shun sin and live in holiness. Help me to endure trials and persecutions, so that I can remain steadfast with you unto the end. When my earthly journey is over, let me appear in your presence to enjoy your everlasting benefits. For in the name of Jesus Christ I make my requests.

Amen!

« DAY 107 »

Holiness Has No Substitute As Far As God Is Concerned

Focus Passage: Exodus 39, 40

God ordered Moses to specially decorate his priest in a fashion that would glorify his name. Moses must ensure that the priest's robes legibly have "HOLINESS TO THE LORD" printed on it. The scripture reported,

> *"They made tunics, artistically woven of fine linen, for Aaron and his sons, a turban of fine linen, exquisite hats of fine linen, short trousers of fine woven linen, and a sash of fine woven linen with blue, purple, and scarlet* thread, *made by a weaver, as the Lord had commanded Moses. Then they made the plate of the holy crown of pure gold, and wrote on it an inscription* like *the engraving of a signet: HOLINESS TO THE LORD. And they tied to it a blue cord, to fasten it above on the turban, as the Lord had commanded Moses" **(Exodus 39:27-31).***

Lesson:

God is holy, and he expects his children (and servants) to appear before him in holiness. Our services must be presented in holiness before they can be acceptable in his presence. The Creator will not accept anything short of purity! He will not favorably behold any services rendered to him out of impure mind. Also, he will reject sinful people from entering his kingdom. Everyone must come before him with a pure mind and contrite spirit to be acceptable into his kingdom. Anyone who claims to serve God with impure mind and unrepentant sin is wasting time - Such person will have no place in God's kingdom. Jehovah will only accept pure and upright Christians into his kingdom.

Prayer:

Dear God, please help me to live and serve you in holiness so that I can reach your kingdom. Help me to prioritize holiness; grant me a contrite spirit, and let me always serve you with a pure mind. Please enable me with strength to obey you in all ramifications of life so that I can qualify for your heavenly kingdom. For in the name of Jesus Christ I make my requests.

Amen.

« DAY 108 »

A Person Whose Aim Is To Live Overcomer's Life On Earth Must Be Accustom To Using The Name Of Jesus

Focus Passage: Mark 4:21-41

Jesus Christ demonstrated unprecedented strength among his disciples by rebuking tempest wind; the disciples who had earlier witness him dealing with humans became amazed to also seeing him dealing with nature likewise. Both the living and non-living thing listened to Jesus the same way! The scripture explained how Jesus remarkably saved his distressed disciples on the sea,

> *"And a great windstorm arose, and the waves beat into the boat, so that it was already filling. But He was in the stern, asleep on a pillow. And they awoke Him and said to Him, "Teacher, do you not care that we are perishing?" Then He arose and rebuked the wind, and said to the sea, "Peace, be still!" And the wind ceased and there was a great calm"* **(Mark 4:37-39).**

Lesson:
Jesus Christ has controlling power over all things created. Both the living and non-living things submit to his authority. People who believe in Jesus share the same strength that he has, and they can perform similar miracles. Therefore, anyone who desires to live overcomer's life on earth should summon courage to get accustom to Jesus' name and utilize it accordingly. However, some level of faith must apply before any expected miracle can happen. Impossibility can only become possible when someone exercise his/her faith in God. It is important to emphasize that any miracle outsourced by God will only focus on glorifying his name - and not point to satisfying human ego, or any other self-gratification.

Prayer:
I believe there is power comprised in the name of Jesus Christ. I believe the name carries power to calm life storms and award victory; therefore, I invoke the power of his name over every situation of my life. I decree through Christ name that all Satan's assaults against my life must fail. I claim the strength of Jesus name to triumph over principalities and powers! I proclaim my victory in all ramifications of life - to the glory of God's name. I am now a victor from today, and I will live in Christ' victory forever! For through his name - Jesus Christ - I make my declarations.

Amen!

« DAY 109 »

God Is Not A Beggar, And He Will Only Accept Quality Offerings From Anyone

Focus Passage: Leviticus 1, 2; Psalm 90

God required Israelites to present their costly and valuable items to him as offerings to prove their recognition of his good works in their lives, and also to prove their commitments to him. The scripture reported,

> *" The Lord called to Moses and spoke to him from the tent of meeting. He said, "Speak to the Israelites and say to them: 'When anyone among you brings an offering to the Lord, bring as your offering an animal from either the herd or the flock"***(Leviticus 1:1-2 NIV)***.*

Lesson:

God deserves best and quality offerings from his children. He wants our quality offerings be presented to him in quantity to reflect the depth of our appreciations for all his goodness in our lives. However, God is honorable and he deserves our prestigious gifts; he is not a scavenger who is desperate to collect whatever gift anyone drops into his basket. No Christian should underrate the significance of God's divinity to present him a trash gift. Whatever anyone brings to his presence must have value and be praiseworthy. Indeed, Jehovah will reciprocate any good offering that is presented to him with a blessing. A person who has good attitude towards God will never run out of resources to present before him.

Prayer:

Dear God, Please make me a cheerful giver who presents you good and quality offering from the bottom of my heart. Let my gifts mean something to you! Let whatever gift I bring before you mean something, and let them be presented with dignity and honor. Let my cheerful attitude support my giving so that they can be acceptable to you. Also, let my charitable attitude get your attention to attract more blessings into my life, so that I can be multiplied in riches to bring more gifts for the praises of your holy name. For in the name of Jesus Christ I make my requests.

Amen.

« DAY 110 »

The Name Of Jesus Christ Answers All Questions And Award Victories

Focus Passage: Mark 5:1-20

Jesus Christ demonstrated his omnipotent power over a demon possessed man. The man had been terribly battered by the devil without any help. He was troubled and uncontrollable, and no one could help him - But Jesus Christ came to the scene to set him free. The scripture reported,

> *"...And when He (Jesus) had come out of the boat, immediately there met Him out of the tombs a man with an unclean spirit, who had his dwelling among the tombs; and no one could bind him, not even with chains, because he had often been bound with shackles and chains. And the chains had been pulled apart by him, and the shackles broken in pieces; neither could anyone tame him. And always, night and day, he was in the mountains and in the tombs, crying out and cutting himself with stones. When he saw Jesus from afar, he ran and worshiped Him. And he cried out with a loud voice and said, "What have I to do with You, Jesus, Son of the Most High God? I implore you by God that you do not torment me." For He said to him, "Come out of the man, unclean spirit!"* **(Mark 5:2-8)**.

Lesson:

Jesus Christ - the Son of God - retains all power and authority to deal with the devil and liberate people from his hands. The name of Jesus Christ is strong enough to remove mountains and level valleys. Of course, the power behind Jesus' name come with a special secret - God awarded him the honor! The scripture stated, *"Therefore God also has highly exalted Him and given Him the name which is above every name, that at the name of Jesus every knee should bow, of those in heaven, and of those on earth, and of those under the earth, and that every tongue should confess that Jesus Christ is Lord, to the glory of God the Father"* **(Philippians 2:9-11)**. Hence, since the name of Jesus Christ remains the only solution to all human problems, everyone should gravitate to it and utilize it to their best advantage. All it takes for someone to begin exercising the authority of the name is to first confess Jesus Christ as his/her Lord and personal Savior.

Prayer:

I believe the name of Jesus Christ offers solutions to all human problems - including mine; therefore, I will begin to exercise my authority through the name: I declare Jesus Christ as Lord and I accept him as my personal Savior. Henceforth I am a child of God, and I retain all rights to exercise authority of his name! Therefore, I rebuke devil and I command him to lose his grips from my life. I command all Satan's works to become futile in my life. I destroy all the enemy's manipulations; I command him to stumble in all his schemes, and I proclaim my complete victory over him! From today, I am free from all demonic oppressions, possessions, afflictions, and incursions! I triumph in every aspect of my life to freely serve God and enjoy all his benefits. My victory is now sanctioned with the power contained in the blood of Jesus Christ - and I will live victoriously forever! For in the name of Jesus Christ I exercise my authority and make my declarations!
Amen.

« DAY 111 »

Jesus Lessened The Burden Of Sin Sacrifice By Utilizing Himself As A Sin Sacrifice

Focus Passage: Leviticus 3, 4, 5

God required Israelites to offer animal sacrifice to atone for their sins in the Old Testament. The sin sacrifice which is also known as Trespass Offering has to be done by anyone who has sinned. Something important to note about the sacrifices is that they are not cheap (a sinner has to buy costly animals to sacrifice), and they must be perfectly offered with due procedure. If a sacrifice is not done to the letter, God will reject it, and the sinner involved would have to start all over again. The scripture referenced Trespass Offering,

> *"Now the Lord spoke to Moses, saying, "Speak to the children of Israel, saying: 'If a person sins unintentionally against any of the commandments of the Lord in anything which ought not to be done, and does any of them, if the anointed priest sins, bringing guilt on the people, then let him offer to the Lord for his sin which he has sinned a young bull without blemish as a sin offering"* **(Leviticus 4:1-3).**

Lesson:
The process of seeking God's forgiveness over a sin was neither easy nor cheap in the Old Testament, and the process did not completely remove human sins, but it only appease God to cover them up. However, Jesus Christ the Son of God has helped to lessen the burden of sacrificing animals to appease God. He offered himself as the only one and a lasting sacrifice for human sins. That is, Christ removed the cumbersome and expensive Old Testament sacrifices by exchanging his own life for it. He shed his own blood on the cross for the remission of human sins. Henceforth, humanity can now obtain forgiveness of sin and receive redemption by confessing him (Jesus Christ) as their Lord and Savior. Whoever confesses his/her sins to God - with mentioning of the name of Jesus Christ - will receive forgiveness, and the person will have his/her name written in the book of life.

Prayer:
Dear Jesus Christ, I thank you for sacrificing your life in exchange for rigorous and imperfect sacrifices to make life easy for me. Your blood shed on the cross has replaced any other sacrifices required to receive forgiveness of sins; therefore, I confess you as Lord, and I accept you as my personal Savior. I confess my sins, and I repent from them. From now on, I will do my best to satisfy you, and I will faithfully serve for the rest of my life. Please count me worthy in your kingdom Oh Lord!

Amen.

« DAY 112 »

A Christian Who Exercises Faith In God Over Any Situation Of Life Will Have Expected Testimony

Focus Passage: Mark 5:21-43

A woman who had long-term medical problem obtained an instant healing because she had strong faith in Jesus Christ. While Jesus was on a different mission (to heal a dying daughter of Jairus), the woman with twelve-year-old sickness was determined to violate every protocol to obtain her healing as the scripture reported,

> "So Jesus went with him. A large crowd followed and pressed around him. And a woman was there who had been subject to bleeding for twelve years. She had suffered a great deal under the care of many doctors and had spent all she had, yet instead of getting better she grew worse. When she heard about Jesus, she came up behind him in the crowd and touched his cloak, because she thought, "If I just touch his clothes, I will be healed." Immediately her bleeding stopped and she felt in her body that she was freed from her suffering" **(Mark 5:24-29 NIV)**.

Lesson:

A Christian who exercises faith in God over any situation of life will have his/her expectations met and have testimony. Truly, challenges of life will rise and life storms may beat as if there is no tomorrow, yet God will prove Himself faithful towards those who trust him. Since God never fails, he will come to his children' aid and help them earn victory. Indeed, God still retains power to heal the sick and raise the dead as demonstrated during bible time. Jehovah can also perform other miracles that have not been recorded in history for his children, as the scripture stated, "...*Eye has not seen, nor ear heard, nor have entered into the heart of man the things which God has prepared for those who love Him*" **(1 Corinthians 2:9)**. However, for God to demonstrate his remarkable power in our lives, we must trust him. We must keep confessing our trust in him, even when circumstances are proving otherwise. Jehovah loves to see us trusting him during difficult time so that he can prove himself strong on our behalves.

Prayer:

Dear God, please give me grace to trust you during adversity. Help me to demonstrate remarkable unwavering faith that will put devil to shame, and also glorify your name. Let my faith be so strong to provoke you into disgracing devil and honoring your name! Please let your testimony of your goodness ever fill my mouth from now on, and forever more!

Amen.

« DAY 113 »

Jesus Offered Himself As Perfect Sacrifice; Believers Need Nothing Else To Do Than To Mention His Name

Focus Passage: Leviticus 6, 7

The Peace Offering as well as any other type of offerings mentioned in the Old Testaments were not easy to prepare to satisfy God. The offerings must be perfectly prepared - without any slight room for imperfection. God would reject any imperfect offering, and also punish whoever offered it. In fact, the severity of the punishment may go as far as a death sentence. The scripture stated,

> *"Whoever eats the fat of the animal of which men offer an offering made by fire to the Lord, the person who eats it shall be cut off from his people"* **(Leviticus 7:25).**

Lesson:
Jesus Christ sacrificed his life on the cross to remove various types of offerings that were presented to satisfy God in the Old Testament. Despite the complexity of the requirements of the offerings, they were not strong enough to completely remove human sins and appease God. However, thanks to Jesus Christ who came to rescue humanity from the trap of the sacrifices. Hence, whoever calls on God through his Son's name (Jesus Christ) will receive forgiveness of sins, and be saved. Christ's believers do not need any other form of offerings to appease God - other than to mention the name of Jesus Christ!

Prayer:
Dear Jesus Christ thanks for sacrificing your life on my behalf to save my soul from the pit of hell, and award me the gift of eternal life. From today, I confess you as my personal Lord and Savior, and I dedicate my complete life to you. I will serve you throughout the days of my life. Please give me grace to remain faithful to you unto the end so that I can qualify to dine and wine with you in your eternal kingdom!

Amen.

« DAY 114 »

God Will Honor Those Who Honor His Servants

Focus Passage: Mark 6:1-29

Jesus Christ had difficulty in fulfilling his ministry among his people due to their unbelief. People from his hometown: Neighbors, family and friends underestimated him to the extent that Christ himself was very surprised. They hindered him to perform much miracles; he had to take his ministry to other locations where people appreciated him. The scripture reported Jesus' neighbors stating,

> *"Is this not the carpenter, the Son of Mary, and brother of James, Joses, Judas, and Simon? And are not His sisters here with us? So they were offended at Him"* **(Mark 6:3).**

Lesson:
Familiarity breeds contempt, and believers must be careful not to dishonor God's servants. Believers must not demean gospel ministers but respect them - No matter how familiar they are. We may be familiar with their background and know them from Adam, but that should not be a license to dishonor them. Our condition of relating with any servant of God must not be based on age, gender, class, background, and/or others. We must mainly honor them for the sake of God that they represent! Meanwhile, God who watches people's attitude towards his servant will appropriately reciprocate. He will honor those who specially treat his servants with honor, and dishonor whoever dishonors them!

Prayer:
Dear God, please teach me how to respect people who represent you. Help me to honor your servants so that I can prosper! Do not let me get caught up with pride or ignorance to treat your servants with bias mind. Let me treat them with dignity and honor so that you can favorably behold and bless me. For in the name of Jesus Christ I make my requests.

Amen.

« DAY 115 »

God Seeks Honesty And Humility From His Children In Order To Bless Them

Focus Passage: Leviticus 8, 9, 10

God's wrath busted on priests who mishandled their officiating business among Israelites; his consuming fire killed them instantly. The scripture reported,

> *"Nadab and Abihu, the sons of Aaron, each took his censer and put fire in it, put incense on it, and offered profane fire before the Lord, which He had not commanded them. So fire went out from the Lord and devoured them, and they died before the Lord"* **(Leviticus 10:1-2).**

Lesson:
Believers must carefully serve God and respect him for who he is. We must not take him for granted, but fear and respect him in whatever will do so that he can be pleased with us. Also, Christians are expected to be honest in their services to God; we must not engage in shady business or attempt to manipulate our services to lure him into blessings us. For example, a believer who wears beautiful dress to church and sing beautiful songs but still keep some secret sins cannot be honored in the presence of God. The Creator expects us to avoid pretense but come to him with openness, humility, and genuine repentance so that he can bless us.

Prayer:
Dear God, please make me an honest Christian who seeks to satisfy you with consistent services. Let me be straightforward with you always. Let me genuinely sorry for my sins, and genuinely repent from them. Also, let me take proactive steps into meeting your holiness standard so that I can qualify for your eternal kingdom. Please let your Holy Spirit empower me to satisfy you always! For in the name of Jesus Christ I make my requests.

Amen.

« DAY 116 »

Jesus Cares For Both The Physical And Spiritual Needs Of His Followers

Focus Passage: Mark 6:30-56

Jesus Christ was not only concerned about people's spiritual needs while on earth, but he was also concerned about their physical needs. Record indicates that the Messiah had strong passion for satisfying people's physical needs. Despite his busy schedule and pressure felt to preach instant gospel to the dying sinners, Jesus still cared enough to ask for his audience' welfare. He challenged his disciple to feed them, and when they failed, he performed a food miracle to meet the need. The scripture reported,

> *"He saith unto them, how many loaves have ye? Go and see. And when they knew, they say, five, and two fishes. And he commanded them to make all sit down by companies upon the green grass. And they sat down in ranks, by hundreds, and by fifties. And when he had taken the five loaves and the two fishes, he looked up to heaven, and blessed, and brake the loaves, and gave them to his disciples to set before them; and the two fishes divided he among them all. And they did all eat, and were filled. And they took up twelve baskets full of the fragments, and of the fishes. And they that did eat of the loaves were about five thousand men" (Mark 6:38-44 KJV).*

Lesson:
Christians must know they serve a caring God who is willing to meet all their needs. God will care for both the physical and spiritual needs of his people. Of course, his prime goal is to save sinners and bring them to God's kingdom, but he will do much more! He will feed, cure, protect, and provide for his own people. There is no limit to Jesus' capacity: He will do and undo any situation to meet his people's needs so that they can be happy and praise his name. Therefore, those who have professed Jesus Christ as their Lord should congratulate themselves since they will have unlimited benefits to receive from him. However, those who are yet to confess their faith in Jesus Christ should not hesitate to turn a new leaf and confess him as Lord, so that they too can qualify for his tremendous and unlimited benefits.

Prayer:
Dear Jesus Christ, you are such an awesome God who cares for the needs of people who profess their faith in you. You are able to do all kinds of things for your followers; therefore, I am confessing my faith in you today as God's true Son. I declare you as my Lord and Savior, and I will serve you forever! I am now using this medium to ask for your benefits: Please heal me, protect, and provide for me. Meet all my needs so that I can have full cause to glorify your holy name. Thank you Jesus Christ for you are able to do all things.

Amen.

« DAY 117 »

God Does Not Celebrate Anything Short Of Holiness

Focus Passage: Leviticus 11, 12

Holiness is a no-joke standard for God. He intensified the importance of the standard to Israelites and said,

> *"For I am the Lord who brings you up out of the land of Egypt, to be your God. You shall therefore be holy, for I am holy"* **(Leviticus 11:45).**

Lesson:
People who call on God's name must understand the importance of his "holiness" requirement. Since the Creator is holy, he celebrates nothing short of holiness. Therefore, believers must understand that there is nothing we do that can be substituted for the standard. None of our charity activities can be substituted for God's requirement of holiness. (Our flamboyant donations cannot do the job either). Everyone must fully comply with God's rule of holiness to be acceptable to his kingdom. The scripture rightly expressed this by stating, "Pursue peace with all *people,* and holiness, without which no one will see the Lord" (Hebrews 12:14).

Prayer:
Dear God, please give me grace to live holy life before you. Empower me through your Holy Spirit to purse your kingdom and its righteousness so that I can qualify to inherit your eternal kingdom. For in the name of Jesus Christ I make my requests.

Amen.

« DAY 118 »

Christians Must Only Base Their Standard Of Practice On Bible Doctrine – Not Traditions

Focus Passage: Mark 7:1-13

The Pharisees focused on their religion traditions than God's requirements of holiness; therefore, their wrong orientation caused them to mislead other people. For example, the Pharisees accused Jesus' disciples of not washing hands before meal; they concluded they were sinners. Meanwhile, Jesus who had full knowledge of the scriptures rebuked the Pharisees and stated, "...Well did Isaiah prophesy of you hypocrites, as it is written,

> 'This people honors Me with their lips, But their heart is far from Me. And in vain they worship Me, Teaching as doctrines the commandments of men.'" **(Mark 7:6-7).**

Lesson:
Religion tradition does not directly represent full scriptures; therefore, no Christian should set the basis of his/her faith on any religion traditions. While some traditions may aid us into satisfying God, they still cannot be equated to the full scriptures. Every Christian must consider principles of the bible as the basic standard of which his/her faith must be built. Every believer must study his/her bible well and apply any lesson learned into his/her life. If not for any other reasons, the fact that God will base his Last Day Judgment on bible principles should make us comply with them! Believers must weigh any other principles and bylaws against the bible. Also, any teaching received from any source must be weighed against bible also. Whatever teaching or tradition that fails short of bible standard must be rejected since God will not honor them on his Day of Judgment.

Prayer:
Dear God, please help me to be spiritually sensitive to base my principles and practices on bible standard. Do not let me follow multitude in their sinful practices to sin against you. Let me make bible my best friend, and let me apply every lesson learnt to my life so that I can prosper on earth and in heaven. Please keep my feet firm within your gate so that I will be raptured to your kingdom! For in the name of Jesus Christ I make my requests.

Amen.

« DAY 119 »

Believers Must Constantly Seek The Help Of Holy Spirit To Satisfy God

Focus Passage: Leviticus 13

God specially dealt with leprosy among the Israelites; he required whoever contacted the disease be expelled from the public to live in seclusion - outside the camp. The scripture reported,

> *"And the Lord spake unto Moses and Aaron, saying, When a man shall have in the skin of his flesh a rising, a scab, or bright spot, and it be in the skin of his flesh like the plague of leprosy; then he shall be brought unto Aaron the priest, or unto one of his sons the priests: And the priest shall look on the plague in the skin of the flesh: and when the hair in the plague is turned white, and the plague in sight be deeper than the skin of his flesh, it is a plague of leprosy: and the priest shall look on him, and pronounce him unclean"* **(Leviticus 13:1-3 KJV).**

Lesson:

Sin is irritant to God just as leprosy is irritant to human body. A person who constantly commits sin cannot be in God's good book! The Creator expects anyone who wants to be called his child be conscious of sin, and do his/her best to shun it. Meanwhile, it is absolutely impossible for anyone to live in perfection without the effort of Jesus Christ. Jesus (the Son of God) who was perfect and sinless died for the sinners; therefore whoever confesses his/her faith in him will receive forgiveness of sin and be declared just and acceptable to God. Jesus will also baptize his believers with his Holy Spirit to have power needed to walk in God's ways and comply with his rules. Most importantly, followers of Jesus Christ will qualify for rapture and be taken to heaven to permanently stay with him in heaven.

Prayer:

Dear God, please empower me through your Holy Spirit to live a holy and acceptable life before you so that I can qualify for your kingdom. Plant your fear in my heart so that I can respect your rules and comply with them. Please write my name in the book of life! For in the name of Jesus Christ I make my requests.

Amen.

« DAY 120 »

Believers Must Utilize The Name Of Jesus Christ For Their Faith To Work

Focus Passage: Mark 7:14-37

Jesus Christ preached and healed both deaf and dumb, and he performed other miracles wherever he went. However, not all miracles he performed were based on schedule, some unscheduled miracles also happened through his hands. For example, one Grecian woman whose generation never served God also received a miracle for her child. She crossed her cultural line to persuade Jesus Christ until he granted her request. The scripture reported,

> *And from thence he arose, and went into the borders of Tyre and Sidon, and entered into an house, and would have no man know it: but he could not be hid. For a certain woman, whose young daughter had an unclean spirit, heard of him, and came and fell at his feet: The woman was a Greek, a Syrophenician by nation; and she besought him that he would cast forth the devil out of her daughter. But Jesus said unto her, let the children first be filled: for it is not meet to take the children's bread, and to cast it unto the dogs. And she answered and said unto him, Yes, Lord: yet the dogs under the table eat of the children's crumbs. And he said unto her, For this saying go thy way; the devil is gone out of thy daughter. And when she was come to her house, she found the devil gone out, and her daughter laid upon the bed."* **(Mark 7:24-30 KJV).**

Lesson:
Christianity is faith based, and anyone who hope of receiving something positive from God must exercise his/her faith. There are no limits to God's demonstration of power when faith is applied. Meanwhile, faith cannot stand alone; it has to be anchored with the name of Jesus Christ before it can work. That is, anyone who mentions the name of Jesus Christ during prayers and apply faith will receive whatever he wants. God will not turn down any requests of his children that is asked according to his purpose. Jehovah will perform miracles to favor those who serve him, so that others will be motivated to serve and trust him also.

Prayer:
Dear God, please make me a person of faith, and let me apply it to every necessary situation of my life to have victory. Let my faith in Christ move mountains and level valleys. Let the testimony of your goodness ever fill my mouth, so that I can sing the songs of praises in the land of the living. For in the name of Jesus Christ I make my requests.

Amen.

« DAY 121 »

Only The Blood Of Jesus Christ Can Wash Away Human Sins

Focus Passage: Leviticus 14

Leprosy is a communicable disease, and God detested it among Israelites. To prevent the airborne disease, God commanded his children to isolate all lepers; they must be sent outside the camp to live in isolation. God also commanded a complete destruction of any tent and property that belong to a leper. The scripture reported God's instruction to his priest,

> *"The priest shall come and look; and indeed if the plague has spread in the house, it is an active leprosy in the house. It is unclean. And he shall break down the house, its stones, its timber, and all the plaster of the house, and he shall carry them outside the city to an unclean place"* **(Leviticus 14:44-45)**.

Lesson:

The measure of God's hatred to human sin can be compared to the gravity of his hatred to leprosy disease in the Old Testament. The Creator did not want anything to do with the disease; neither did he encourage his children to come close to it. God hates sin, and he will not favorably look at any sinner unless he/she repents. In addition, sin can also be compared to cloth' stains. Its beauty will remain tainted until the stains are removed. Meanwhile, no form of detergent can wash a sin from anyone's life. The blood of Jesus Christ is the only formidable solution to remit human sin. Christ' blood that was shed on the cross remain strong and powerful to remove every sin. Hence, anyone who comes to God through the name of Jesus Christ will receive forgiveness. The scripture described the importance of Christ redemption as stated, *"And as Moses lifted up the serpent in the wilderness, even so must the Son of Man be lifted up, that whoever believes in Him should not perish but have eternal life. For God so loved the world that He gave His only begotten Son, that whoever believes in Him should not perish but have everlasting life. For God did not send His Son into the world to condemn the world, but that the world through Him might be saved"* **(John 3:14-17)**.

Prayer:

O what the blood of Jesus Christ that was shed to wash my sins away! I believe in the redemption of Jesus Christ. I believe he shed his blood on the cross to wash away my sins. Through the blood of Jesus Christ I receive forgiveness and cleansing. Through the name of Jesus Christ I am saved, and the crown of righteousness is awaiting me in heaven. Praise God I am saved - for Jesus Christ has set me free!

Amen.

« DAY 122 »

Jesus Christ Is Still Alive To Perform Signs And Wonders In The Lives Of Believers

Focus Passage: Mark 8:1-21

Jesus Christ had compassion on his wearied audience who had stayed long to hear his teaching. The people were tired and hungry having stayed all day to listen to him. Therefore, Jesus performed a miracle of food surplus to satisfy their hunger. He miraculously multiplied seven loaves of bread and few fishes to feed about four thousand people; they were all satisfied and still have seven baskets leftovers. The scripture reported,

> *"...So He commanded the multitude to sit down on the ground. And He took the seven loaves and gave thanks, broke them and gave them to His disciples to set before them; and they set them before the multitude. They also had a few small fish; and having blessed them, He said to set them also before them. So they ate and were filled, and they took up seven large baskets of leftover fragments. Now those who had eaten were about four thousand. And He sent them away"* **(Mark 8:1-21)**.

Lesson:

Jesus Christ lived on earth as a miracle-working God to meet people's needs. He was emotionally connected with their circumstances so that he could help them. Meanwhile, the same Jesus that we read about in the bible has never changed. He is still alive, and he currently lives in heaven; however, his Holy Spirit is very much present on earth to help those who believe and call on his name. Anyone who calls on Jesus in faith over an issue of his/her life will not be disappointed. Such person will triumph in all situations to praise God's name. However, even though Jesus Christ is a miracle-working God, believers must still be careful not to mischaracterize him as a magician. His miracles are not only meant to make us feel comfortable on earth, they are meant to motivating us into focusing on God and serve him better.

Prayer:

I believe in the healing power of Jesus Christ, and I obtain my victory through his name. Today, I command every sickness, pain, poverty, disease, failure, and other evil to disappear in my life. I shut every door against devil and all his evil works, and I open the doors of my life to receive God's goodness! I obtain my victory and I declare myself an overcomer through the authority of the name of Jesus Christ - now and forevermore!

Amen.

« DAY 123 »

Animal Sacrifice Was Never Enough To Completely Remove Sin; Jesus Utilized His Life To Solve The Problem

Focus Passage: Leviticus 15,16

God mandated Israelites to sacrifice a scapegoat for their sins. They must present two goats but only sacrificed one of them; the other goat must be set free to wander into the jungle. The goat to be sacrificed would be considered as a scapegoat - with a symbolic meaning. He shall bear consequences of Israelites sins. Meanwhile, prior to the sacrifice God stated,

> *"And Aaron shall lay both his hands upon the head of the live goat, and confess over him all the iniquities of the children of Israel, and all their transgressions in all their sins, putting them upon the head of the goat, and shall send him away by the hand of a fit man into the wilderness: And the goat shall bear upon him all their iniquities unto a land not inhabited: and he shall let go the goat in the wilderness"* **(Leviticus 16:21-22 KJV).**

Lesson:
Animal sacrifices offered during Old Testament were made to appease God for human sins; they were able to cover sins, but not completely remove them. That is, animal sacrifices offered for human sins were not perfect. However, Jesus Christ came to help humans solved the imperfection problem. He sacrificed his own life once and for all to remove animal sacrifices, and also to provide permanent pathway for removing human sins. Henceforth, humanity will receive their soul redemption by confessing and believing Jesus Christ as Lord. Christ' sinless blood shed on the cross will provide permanent removal of sins and offer permanent redemption.

Prayer:
I thank you Jesus Christ for you have offered your life to replace imperfect animal sacrifice. You have granted pathway for people to receive forgiveness of their sins and salvation of their souls through your death and resurrection. I am grateful for your efforts; I confess you as Lord, and I accept you as my personal Savior. Henceforth, I will serve you with my whole life. Please write my name in the book of life.

Amen.

« DAY 124 »

A Good Christian Will Not Base An Action On Feelings, But On Leadership Of The Holy Spirit

Focus Passage: Mark 8:22-38

Peter secretly rebuked Jesus Christ for stating that his opponents would arrest and kill him (but he would resurrect on the third day). The disciple did not want his master undergo suffering; therefore, he wanted to prevent him. However, Jesus rebuked Peter for acting in flesh to satisfy devil's desire. Christ must suffer and died in the hands of wicked people to be able to save the lost souls! The scripture reported the confronting moment that took place between Jesus and Peter,

> *"He then began to teach them that the Son of Man must suffer many things and be rejected by the elders, the chief priests and the teachers of the law, and that he must be killed and after three days rise again. He spoke plainly about this, and Peter took him aside and began to rebuke him. But when Jesus turned and looked at his disciples, he rebuked Peter. "Get behind me, Satan!" he said. "You do not have in mind the concerns of God, but merely human concerns"* **(Mark 8:31-33 NIV).**

Lesson:
Christians are expected to approach and handle life situations spiritually - without being solely depend on human feelings. Unlike unbelievers who may only base their decisions on how they humanly feel about a matter, believers - who are heavenly bound people - are expected to operate in the spirit, and make decisions that satisfy God. We must allow God's Holy Spirit to guide us into making decisions that will give him room to fully manifest his plans in our lives, and in the lives of others.

Prayer:
Dear Jesus Christ, please guide me through your Holy Spirit to base my decisions on the leadership of your Holy Spirit. Do not let me allow flesh to mislead me into carrying out a decision that will hinder your plans for my life. Please let your Holy Spirit direct my thoughts and actions so that you can have all needed rooms to maximize your goodness in my life, and in the lives of others. Let my thoughts and deeds be acceptable to you O Lord. For in the name of Jesus Christ I make my requests.

Amen.

« DAY 125 »

Idol Worship Is Forbidden For A Child Of God

Focus Passage: Leviticus 17, 18

God proved his impartial judgment among earth inhabitants: He was displeased with Canaanites for their idolatry sin, and promised to displace give their land to Israelites who worshiped him. Meanwhile, Jehovah also promised to deal with Israelites the same way he dealt with the Canaanites should they turn away from him. God promised to remove Israelites from any possessed Canaan land if they dare follow the Canaanites footstep to serve their idols. God stated the reasons he was determined to displace Canaanites from their inheritance:

> *Canaanites sacrificed their children to idols **(Lev. 18:21)**; they engaged in homosexual activities **(Lev. 18:22)**, and they had sexual intercourse with animals **(Lev.18:23)**. Jehovah warned Israelites against those evil practices and said, "Do not defile yourselves with any of these things; for by all these the nations are defiled, which I am casting out before you" **(Lev. 18:24)**.*

Lesson:

God requires his children to serve him with purity of mind. They must not worship any idol - no matter how big or small! Every believer must worship and offer his/her sacrifices of thanksgiving to God without any reservation. Some characteristics of God that every Christian must duly observe are highlighted below:

1. God is a jealous God – He will not allow his children to share the glory due to him with any idol.
2. God is pure – He will not celebrate immoral behaviors.
3. God is perfect – He hates to see people attempting to manipulate his creation ingenuity (For example: He respects marriage between a man and a woman only Leviticus.18:23; Romans 1:26-28; Hebrews 13:1-5).
4. God is impartial – He will take benefits from evil people and give them to godly people.

Prayer:

Dear God, please assist me to serve with you with a pure heart so that I can qualify for your benefits. Do not let me serve an idol, and don't let me share glory due you with any other person or deity. Also, do not let me arrogate your glory to myself. Let my services be acceptable before you, so that I can remain fit for your eternal kingdom. For in the name of Jesus Christ I make my requests.

Amen.

« DAY 126 »

Prayer Serves All Purposes For Christians

Focus Passage: Mark 9:1-29

Jesus Christ outperformed his disciples in healing ministry; he healed a deaf and dumb boy after his disciples have tried and failed. The disciples wanted to know the secret behind his power, and he was quick to tell them the fact. Jesus said,

> *"This kind can come out by nothing but prayer and fasting"* **(Mark 9:29).**

Lesson:
Jesus Christ the Son of God utilized power of prayer to have record success in his ministry while on earth. He consistently spent time in the presence of his Father to receive fresh anointing to have more success. Christians should follow the same principle of Jesus to also have success. Through prayer, we can move mountains! Indeed, there will be nothing impossible for us believers to achieve if we can pray. Meanwhile, not only do believers need prayer to receive miracles, but we also need it to receive strength to keep trusting and serving God accordingly. A believer who spends adequate time in the presence of God will receive renewal of strength. The fellow will always have enough grace to keep loving God during moment of joy, sorrow, weakness, persecution, and adversity. Prayer will help believers live overcomers' lives in this sinful and impoverish world.

Prayer:
Dear Jesus Christ, please teach me how to wait on you through prayer. Let prayer be convenient for me! Give me grace to stay in your presence to receive anointing to serve you better and do great exploits. Do not let me cease in praying; let me keep up the practice until I successfully finish my earthly race to meet you in your kingdom. For in the name of Jesus Christ I make my requests.

Amen.

« DAY 127 »

Children Of God Must Have Integrity And Lead By Example

Focus Passage: Leviticus 19, 20

God emphasized the importance of justice to Israelites. He required them to be impartial in their judgment. They must not favor rich people over the poor! God said,

> *"You shall not cheat your neighbor, nor rob him. The wages of him who is hired shall not remain with you all night until morning. You shall not curse the deaf, nor put a stumbling block before the blind, but shall fear your God: I am the Lord. 'You shall do no injustice in judgment. You shall not be partial to the poor, nor honor the person of the mighty. In righteousness you shall judge your neighbor. You shall not go about as a talebearer among your people; nor shall you take a stand against the life of your neighbor: I am the Lord" **(Leviticus 19:13-16).***

Lesson:

Children of God must have integrity, and they must fear God in their judgments. Every Christian must understand that "false balance" is an abomination to God. Jehovah will not lightly esteem a partial person. He will honor those who apply integrity with their positions and powers. However, the Creator will confront people with bias mind and those who practice favoritism. He will catch up with cruel people and deal with them accordingly. Hence, believers must act rightly and do God's will to be blessed.

Prayer:

Dear God, please help me to be a straightforward person who gives impartial judgment. Let me equally treat people with dignity and respect so that you can be happy with me. Enable me not to be partial, but be a channel of blessings to everyone around me - whether they are friends and family, or not. Please let me represent you well on earth so that I can be positively rewarded in your presence on earth and in heaven. For in the name of Jesus Christ I make my requests.

Amen.

« DAY 128 »

Jesus' Teachings Have Spiritual Connotation, Which Can Only Be Interpreted By The Holy Spirit

Focus Passage: Mark 9:30-50

Jesus Christ taught his disciples the principle of self-denial and said,

> *"If your hand causes you to sin, cut it off. It is better for you to enter into life maimed, rather than having two hands, to go to hell, into the fire that shall never be quenched"* **(Mark 9:43)**.

Lesson:
The teaching of Jesus Christ was thorough, but it mustn't be misinterpreted with a literary analogy. For example, Jesus did not ask for body mutation when he stated, *"If your hand causes you to sin, cut it off. It is better for you to enter into life maimed, rather than having two hands, to go to hell, into the fire that shall never be quenched"* **(Mark 9:43)**. Christ simply asked his followers to put pleasures aside and focus on pleasing God – at all cost! Jesus emphasis was based on the fact that a Christian may have to make some uncomfortable decisions for the sake of satisfying God. Anyone worthy of being called a good Christian must make heaven his/her prime target - while every other thing becomes secondary.

Prayer:
Dear Jesus Christ, please help me to love you more than any earthly pleasures. Help me to love you more than silver and gold, so that I will not be disappointed on the last day! Do not let me abuse your grace of salvation in my life and fall into any worldly pleasure that will lead me to eternal condemnation in hell fire. Help me to remain a focus Christian throughout the days of my life, so that I can be accepted to your kingdom. For in your precious name - Jesus Christ - I make my petitions to God.

Amen!

« DAY 129 »

God Does Not Force Hands; He Only Appreciates Willing Offerings

Focus Passage: Leviticus 21, 22

God attached special requirements with an offering that any Israelite must present before him. The offering must be without deformity, and it must be offered freely without grudges. God said,

> *"When you offer a sacrifice of thanksgiving to the Lord, offer it of your own free will"* **(Leviticus 22:29).**

Lesson:
God is not interested in any offering that is offered with grudges. He is not a beggar that takes just anything that is presented to him, but he is God that appreciates thoughtful offerings. He will accept tangible and appropriate offerings that his children bring to him, and he will appreciate them with plentifully rewards.

Prayer:
Dear God, please teach and enable me to bring you tangible offerings that will be acceptable in your sight. Do not let me give you gifts with grudges, but enable me to freely and happily bring you my offerings at all times. For in the name of Jesus Christ I make my requests.

Amen.

« DAY 130 »

God Instituted Marriage For Couples To Be Deeply Committed To Each Other, And To Him

Focus Passage: Mark 10:1-31

Jesus Christ taught people the main reason behind creation of marriage institution. He said,

> *"But from the beginning of the creation God made them male and female. For this cause shall a man leave his father and mother, and cleave to his wife; And they twain shall be one flesh: so then they are no more twain, but one flesh. What therefore God hath joined together, let not man put asunder"* **(Mark 10:6-9 KJV).**

Lesson:
Marriage is God's oldest institution established. He instituted the first marriage between Adam and Eve in the Garden of Eden, and blessed them. Hence, everyone must respect the institution of marriage and ensure that God is glorified in it. All must understand that the institution is not a playground for immature people. It is meant for mature people who are ready to honor it and make each other happy. Some basic facts of marriage must remain unchanged to appease God. For example: Marriage must take place between a man and a woman only. There must be unity, openness, and forgiveness in marriage. Divorce should not be in the radar of any godly marriage; no couple should regard their marriage as a piece of cloth that can be changed at anytime. The twain in marriage must be committed to each other for contributions, corrections, and exhortations for personal development. More importantly, every marriage must centralize on honoring God. Couples must give special room for God for his guidance and leadership in their marriage in order to be successful.

Prayer:
Dear God, please help me to respect marriage institution since it is very sacred to you. Give me strength to act right in my marriage. Help both me and my spouse to behave in a manner that will honor you in our marriage. Help us to be committed into each other, and to you! I also pray the same way for other couples so that your name can be glorified in their marriages. Please bless our homes with every needed fruits so that we can flourish and prosper in the land of the living. For in the name of Jesus Christ I make my requests.

Amen.

« DAY 131 »

God Will Bless Anyone Who Gives Him Special Thanksgiving From A Pure Heart

Focus Passage: Leviticus 23, 24

God required Israelites to establish a special Thanksgiving Season for him. He said,

> *"Also in the fifteenth day of the seventh month, when ye have gathered in the fruit of the land, ye shall keep a feast unto the Lord seven days: on the first day shall be a sabbath, and on the eighth day shall be a sabbath. And ye shall take you on the first day the boughs of goodly trees, branches of palm trees, and the boughs of thick trees, and willows of the brook; and ye shall rejoice before the Lord your God seven days. And ye shall keep it a feast unto the Lord seven days in the year. It shall be a statute for ever in your generations: ye shall celebrate it in the seventh month"* **(Leviticus 23:39-41 KJV).**

Lesson:

God loves thanksgiving offerings, and he also wants his children to bring him quality praises at all times. The Creator will celebrate whoever is thoughtful enough to specially thank him for all his goodness in his/her life. A person who specifically gives God his/her special thanksgiving offering from a pure heart will receive his favor. Also, Jehovah loves to see anyone taking extra steps for the sake of glorifying his name. However, our God is rich in all goodness, and he does not lack anything, but he will gauge our measure of love based on what we give and how we give them. He will reciprocate blessings into the lives of people who genuinely appreciate his efforts in their lives. He will bless people of liberal mind so that they can be motivated to keep their positive practices of thanksgiving.

Prayer:

Dear God, please help me to be thoughtful of your goodness in my life and also appreciate you. Give me a grateful heart to count my blessings and praise your name! Also, help me to give you my best offerings with liberal heart so that they can be acceptable to you. Let my quality offerings be presented to you in quantity to show my sincere appreciation to you, and so that you can bless me more! For in the name of Jesus Christ I make my requests.

Amen.

« DAY 132 »

Believers Must Focus On Leadership Of The Holy Spirit To Offer Acceptable Services To God

Focus Passage: Mark 10:32-52

James and John attempted to lobby with Jesus Christ to get more prominent positions than other disciples in heaven. The scripture reported,

> "Then James and John, the sons of Zebedee, came to him. "Teacher," they said, "we want you to do for us whatever we ask." "What do you want me to do for you?" he asked. They replied, "Let one of us sit at your right and the other at your left in your glory." "You don't know what you are asking," Jesus said. "Can you drink the cup I drink or be baptized with the baptism I am baptized with?" "We can," they answered. Jesus said to them, "You will drink the cup I drink and be baptized with the baptism I am baptized with, but to sit at my right or left is not for me to grant. These places belong to those for whom they have been prepared." When the ten heard about this, they became indignant with James and John. Jesus called them together and said, "You know that those who are regarded as rulers of the Gentiles lord it over them, and their high officials exercise authority over them. Not so with you. Instead, whoever wants to become great among you must be your servant, and whoever wants to be first must be slave of all. For even the Son of Man did not come to be served, but to serve, and to give his life as a ransom for many" **(Mark 10:35-45 NIV).**

Lesson:

God requires people to work out their salvation with fear and trembling to be able to enter into his kingdom (Philippians 2:12). No one can satisfy God in flesh, but we can only please him by living in the Spirit to obeying his laws and commandments. Our physical efforts will not be enough to satisfy God since he weighs every action by his standard of righteousness. Therefore, believers must be careful not to yield to flesh temptations by assuming that any physical effort can satisfy him. In addition, no believer can determine how much benefit he/she will receive for his services. Only the Creator himself can determine what amount of benefits anyone will get. Therefore, instead of gratifying desires of flesh for position, honor, or power, believers should simply submit to the services of God and serve him well. No doubt Jehovah will reward whoever commits him/herself into his righteous service.

Prayer:

Dear God, please keep me humble to pursue things of the spirit and not yield to the satisfaction of flesh. Help me to focus on consistent and righteous services that will promote your kingdom. Let me genuinely devote to you and make you happy so that I can receive your benefits. Also, help me to be satisfied with whatever benefits I receive, so that your name can be glorified in every aspect of my life in this world, and in heaven also. For in the name of Jesus Christ I make my requests.

Amen.

« DAY 133 »

God Will Reciprocate Blessing Into The Lives Of People That Offer Him Special Thanksgiving Offering

Focus Passage: Leviticus 25

God asked Israelites to specially celebrate their Year of Jubilee to his honor. The Jubilee Year (also known as some 50th Year Anniversary) must be celebrated to mark the end of seven Sabbath years in seven multiples places (7 years x 7 years – which is 49 years). The year following which would be 50th year of Sabbath cycles must be specially celebrated as the scripture described,

> *"And thou shalt number seven sabbaths of years unto thee, seven times seven years; and the space of the seven sabbaths of years shall be unto thee forty and nine years. Then shalt thou cause the trumpet of the jubile to sound on the tenth day of the seventh month, in the day of atonement shall ye make the trumpet sound throughout all your land. And ye shall hallow the fiftieth year, and proclaim liberty throughout all the land unto all the inhabitants thereof: it shall be a jubile unto you; and ye shall return every man unto his possession, and ye shall return every man unto his family"* **(Leviticus 25:8-10 KJV).**

During Jubilee celebration, Israelites must apply special discounts to their selling goods, and they must exercise forgiveness of debts and redemption of possessed properties. God emphasized that Israelites must mark every Jubilee Year with dignity and respect among themselves.

Lesson:
God has feelings like us, and he appreciates people who celebrate special events before him. Of course the Creator loves our routine services, but he pays special attentions to those services that are tagged with special honor. Jehovah is also interested in people who provide for needy people while celebrating his goodness in their lives. Surely, the Almighty God will accept any special and honest sacrifices that his children bring before him. He will reciprocate their efforts with more benefits in this life, and in heaven also.

Prayer:
Dear God, please teach me how to honor you with special celebrations. Besides my routine services, let me bring you special sacrifices of praise and thanksgiving for all your goodness in my life. Please make me your grateful child always! Assist and prosper me in all my ways so that I can keep coming back with more special thanksgiving. For in the name of Jesus Christ I made my requests.

Amen.

« DAY 134 »

Believers Are To Focus On Glorifying God, And Not Their Self-Gratifications

Focus Passage: Mark 11:1-18

Jesus sent his disciples to get him a colt (young horse) that he would use for his symbolic ride to Jerusalem. He said to his disciples,

> "...And if anyone says to you, 'Why are you doing this?' say, *'The Lord has need of it,'* and immediately he will send it here" *(Mark 11:3).*

The disciples brought the colt to Jesus, and he made his remarkable royal entry into Jerusalem –The city that meant so much to the nation of Israel.

Lesson:
Bible did not mention the owner of the colt that Jesus Christ rode to Jerusalem; however, the colt owner was not anonymous to God. One could imagine God blessing the secret owner for the prestigious assistance he/she offered to Jesus! Christians should emulate the colt owner (referenced in **Mark Chapter 11**). We should follow the example set by the individual to set our priority on serving God rather than paying much attention to any publicity. Believers ought not to focus on self-gratification, pride, and prestige while serving God. Our focus should rather base on satisfying God by all standard. Jehovah who sees every secret effort knows how to reward it openly, and he will surely do. He will recognize and reward our sacrificial efforts made to promote his glory and populate his kingdom.

Prayer:
Dear God, please teach me how to serve you with humility. Let my priority be only base on satisfying your desires, and not to gratifying fleshly desires. Keep me honest in whatever service I offer before you so that they can be acceptable. Please rule me by your Holy Spirit to pursue righteousness every day of my life! For in the name of Jesus Christ I make my requests.

Amen.

« DAY 135 »

God Can't Be Deceived; His Blessing Will Only Abide With People That Make Him Happy

Focus Passage: Leviticus 26, 27

The deliverance of Israelites from Egyptians' bondage was God's gesture of kindness towards his people. Meanwhile, God set a condition for the deliverance he offered and stated that Israelites would only remain free if they obey his laws. They would suffer punishment if they serve an idol. God said to Israelites,

> *"You shall not make idols for yourselves; neither a carved image nor a sacred pillar shall you rear up for yourselves; nor shall you set up an engraved stone in your land, to bow down to it; for I am the Lord your God"* **(Leviticus 26:1).** Israelites' disobedience to God's instructions would attract his blessings as he stated, *"If you walk in my statutes and keep my commandments, and perform them, then I will give you rain in its season, the land shall yield its produce, and the trees of the field shall yield their fruit. Your threshing shall last till the time of vintage, and the vintage shall last till the time of sowing; you shall eat your bread to the full, and dwell in your land safely. I will give peace in the land, and you shall lie down, and none will make you afraid; I will rid the land of evil beasts, and the sword will not go through your land. You will chase your enemies, and they shall fall by the sword before you. Five of you shall chase a hundred, and a hundred of you shall put ten thousand to flight; your enemies shall fall by the sword before you. For I will look on you favorably and make you fruitful, multiply you and confirm my covenant with you. You shall eat the old harvest, and clear out the old because of the new. I will set my tabernacle among you, and my soul shall not abhor you. I will walk among you and be your God, and you shall be my people"* **(Leviticus 26:3-12).** Israelites would suffer God's punishments if they disobey his laws as stated,
>
> *"And after all this, if you do not obey me, then I will punish you seven times more for your sins. I will break the pride of your power; I will make your heavens like iron and your earth like bronze. And your strength shall be spent in vain; for your land shall not yield its produce, nor shall the trees of the land yield their fruit"* **(Leviticus 26:18-20).**

Lesson:
God cannot be deceived, and his blessings will only stay on people who follow his rules and make him happy. God's measuring yardstick of punishment will remain on his disobedient children; he will not relent in his correction until they repent from their wickedness and turn to him.

Prayer:
Dear God, please plant your fear in my heart so that I might not sin against you. I don't want to take your grace of forgiveness for granted and keep rejoicing in sin; let me genuinely repent from my mistakes and live an acceptable life before you. Also, help me to be conscious of your laws and faithfully observe them so that I can proper. Satisfy me with your goodness in holiness to keep enjoying your grace of salvation. For in the name of Jesus Christ I make my requests.
Amen.

« DAY 136 »

Prayer Is Not Just A Spoken Word, But A Spiritual Exercise

Focus Passage: Mark 11:19-33

Jesus Christ taught his disciples how to apply faith in prayer to get whatever they want. He said,

> *"I say to you, whatever things you ask when you pray, believe that you receive them, and you will have them"* **(Mark 11:24).**

Lesson:
Prayer is not just a spoken word, but it is an exercise of spiritual authority. A person who prays in faith is making spiritual affirmations. He/she will get whatever desires, because God respond to people who cry to him with one mind - without a divided attention. Meanwhile, Jehovah's response to any prayer of faith will be based on his divine Master's plans - which will lead him to either say "Yes, No, or Later!"

Prayer:
Dear God, please help me to use my prayer authority with affirmations. Enable me to apply faith with expectations that you will adequate respond to my requests to my benefits, and to the glory of your name. For in the name of Jesus Christ I make my requests.

Amen.

« DAY 137 »

Precept Upon Precept – God's Promises Will Be Fulfilled On His Children

Focus Passage: Numbers 1, 2

Moses formed an army out of Israelites; he majored them in some battalions as a show of strength to defend their nation. The scripture reported,

> "...*These are the ones who were numbered, whom Moses and Aaron numbered, with the leaders of Israel, twelve men, each one representing his father's house. So all who were numbered of the children of Israel, by their fathers' houses, from twenty years old and above, all who were able to go to war in Israel—all who were numbered were six hundred and three thousand five hundred and fifty*" **(Numbers 1:44-46).**

Lesson:

God proved his faithfulness on the promises he made to Abraham that he would multiply his descendants to flourish the earth. Precept upon precept, and one thing led to another until Israelites grew in numbers, and they witnessed God's covenant coming into fulfillment in their lives. Not only did the Israelites grew in numbers, but they were also able to form an army who could defend their God-given heritage. Since Christians serve the same God that Israelites served, they will also witness God's goodness in their lives. Jehovah's promises will remain intact and materialize in believers' lives - even when any circumstance attempts to prove otherwise. Our God who never fails will honor his promises over us under whatever condition.

Prayer:

Dear God, I am so glad I belong to you, and I know your promises will surely be fulfilled in my life. Although I may face some challenges today but I know that my future is bright! You will not slack in your promises but ensure they are fulfilled in my life. All I'm asking now is grace to keep trusting you. Let me remain confident in you until I have full testimony and sing songs of praises to your holy name. Please do these things and many more. For in the name of Jesus Christ I make my requests.

Amen.

« DAY 138 »

Christians Must Hold Their Grip And Strongly Resist Devil In All His Craftiness

Focus Passage: Mark 12:1-27

The Pharisees attempted to trap Jesus Christ with their usual deceptive schemes; they pretended to be patriotic and questioned Jesus on subject of taxes with the hope that he might stumble at his words. The Pharisees said,

> *"Shall we pay tax, or shall we not?" Jesus responded "Render to Caesar the things that are Caesar's, and to God the things that are God's"* **(Mark 12:17)**.

Lesson:
Satan and his collaborating agents (the losers) often confront and test God's children with the intention of sliding them to compromise their faith. The enemies who are skilled in their deceptive practices are set to derail believers from faith and make them lose their spiritual benefits. Therefore, we (Christians) must be alert! We must remain sensitive not to yield to Satan's temptations. Despite the skills and assets the enemy may have at his disposal, believers still have upper hands over him. We have the unbeatable Holy Spirit of God to help us prevail over him anytime any day! Once we allow God's divine Spirit to keep guiding us, we will flatly beat devil and his followers, and also triumph in every situation of life.

Prayer:
Dear God, please give me strength to act in the Spirit and not in flesh to prevail over Satan and live victoriously. Let me give room for your Holy Spirit to richly dwell in me so that I can triumph in every situation of life! No matter what challenge may come my way, help me to prevail and have testimony of your goodness to share among your people. For in the name of Jesus Christ I make my requests.

Amen.

« DAY 139 »

People Ought To Appreciate God's Servants For They Have Special Commissions From God

Focus Passage: Numbers 3, 4

God desired special attention from Israelites, and he consecrated some of them to become his priests. He ordered Moses to consecrate Levites family to join Aaron in his priesthood office. God said,

> *"Bring the tribe of Levi near, and present them before Aaron the priest, that they may minister unto him. And they shall keep his charge, and the charge of the whole congregation before the tabernacle of the congregation, to do the service of the tabernacle. And they shall keep all the instruments of the tabernacle of the congregation, and the charge of the children of Israel, to do the service of the tabernacle. And thou shalt give the Levites unto Aaron and to his sons: they are wholly given unto him out of the children of Israel"* **(Numbers 3:6-9 KJV).**

Lesson:
God sometimes give special assignments to some people for the purpose of glorifying his name. Those people are called God's servants, and they are expected to have large heart for God, and serve him with deeper commitments than other people. In other words, it is the duty of every servant of God to bring his/her Master quality services that will satisfy him. Meanwhile, since God's servants are representing God himself, every other believer is expected to honor them. We must appreciate God's grace in their lives and offer them every needed support to motivate them into bringing their best services to God.

Prayer:
Dear God, I understand that some people are specially commissioned to carryout your special assignments. I want to honor these people since they have sown their lives into your services. Please give me wisdom, grace, and strength to support them in every capacity. Strengthen me to encourage your servants into satisfying your needs in their lives. At the same time, I am praying for all your servants throughout the world that you will give them strength to operate under the leadership of the Holy Spirit so that they can satisfy you. Help your servants to overcome whatever challenge might be coming their way; give them strength to keep serving to your satisfaction and populate your kingdom. Also, please bless your servants and meet their personal needs. Give them peace and let them remain focus to have all-round success. For in the name of Jesus Christ I make my requests.

Amen.

« DAY 140 »

Anyone Who Is Willing To Enter Heaven Must Allow God's Love To Richly Dwell In Him Or Her

Focus Passage: Mark 12:28-44

Jesus Christ emphasized importance of love, and he asked his followers to ground themselves in it. Jesus said,

> *"The most important one," answered Jesus, "is this: 'Hear, O Israel: The Lord our God, the Lord is one. Love the Lord your God with all your heart and with all your soul and with all your mind and with all your strength.' The second is this: 'Love your neighbor as yourself.' There is no commandment greater than these"* **(Mark 12:29-31 NIV).**

Lesson:
All God's laws are compressed into a simple word "Love." Anyone who is willing to enter heaven must allow God's love to richly dwell in him/her. Also, the person must equally love his neighbors. However, it is virtually impossible for anyone to meet God's criteria of genuine love while operating in flesh. True love can only be demonstrated through the Holy Spirit. Only the divine Spirit of God can empower us into reciprocating God's agape love with true love! Also, only the Holy Spirit can earn us strength needed to love our neighbors without any bias or partial mind. Hence, believers should daily seek for Holy Spirit's empowerment through prayer. We should constantly ask him to fill and guide us into satisfying God's desires so that we can remain fit for his kingdom.

Prayer:
Dear Jesus Christ, please baptize me with your Holy Spirit so that I can demonstrate true and sincere love towards you and towards other people. Do not let me yield to the craving of the flesh and make devil happy. Let your Holy Spirit guide and empower me to do your will so that I can prosper on earth and be acceptable to your kingdom. For in the name of Jesus Chris I make my requests.

Amen.

« DAY 141 »

It Is Advantageous To Receive Spoonful Of God's Blessing Than To Receive His Drum Full Of Punishments

Focus Passage: Number 5, 6

God proclaimed his blessings upon Israelites through Moses his servant. Moses blessed the people and said,

> *"The Lord bless you and keep you; The Lord make His face shine upon you, And be gracious to you; The Lord lift up His countenance upon you, And give you peace."* **(Numbers 6:24-27).**

Lesson:
All children of God are expected to make their best efforts to appease God into earning his blessings. Surely, one spoonful of God's blessing is far better than a drum full of his wrath. We (believers) must make our best efforts into satisfying God in speech and deeds. We must consistently create special time to worship God and make him happy. Also, believers must share gospel! We must spread the word of truth and give other people opportunity to receive Jesus Christ into their lives and be saved. Jehovah will surely reciprocate our efforts with his earthly blessings. More importantly, he will crown our efforts with much heavenly benefits also.

Prayer:
Dear God, I desire to receive your blessing and not curses; therefore, help me to serve according to your expectations. Let me consistently worship and propagate your gospel. Please let my efforts be acceptable in your sight to receive your benefits. For in the name of Jesus Christ I make my requests.

Amen.

« DAY 142 »

Christians Will Suffer Persecution From All Sides, But They Will Be Greatly Rewarded In Heaven

Focus Passage: Mark 13:1-20

Jesus Christ informed his disciples of the End Time suffering they would undergo for the sake of their belief. Jesus said,

> *"But watch out for yourselves, for they will deliver you up to councils, and you will be beaten in the synagogues. You will be brought before rulers and kings for my sake, for a testimony to them"* **(Mark 13:9)**. Christ also said, *"Brother will betray brother to death, and a father his child; and children will rise up against parents and cause them to be put to death. And you will be hated by all for my name's sake. But he who endures to the end shall be saved"* **(Mark 13:12-13)**.

Lesson:
Christianity will not be problem-free; Jesus stated that evil people (antichrist) will persecute believers in reaction to gospel. Christians' opposition will not only come from the outsiders, some family members will also rise to persecute them. However, no matter what form of opposition believers face, Christ has assured them eternal victory in heaven. Therefore, believers must hold firm to their faith and remain focus until they breathe their last breath. Christ will reward his faithful followers in heaven with his crown of righteousness. He will give them gift of eternal life to perpetually live in his Paradise.

Prayer:
Dear God, please help me to remain steadfast in faith and hold on to your testimony until the end. Help me to endure trial, temptation, and persecution to receive your eternal rewards in heaven! Let your Holy Spirit empower me to keep un-compromised faith so that I can meet you in heaven to hear your resounding acknowledgement, "Weldon and welcome my good servant!" for in the name of Jesus Christ I make my requests.

Amen.

« DAY 143 »

God Will Show Himself Strong On Behalf Of His Children To Prove His Covenant Of Faithfulness

Focus Passage: Number 7, 8

Elders of Israel gave their high-priced resources to God with much joy, and the Creator was pleased to accept them. God responded to the offerings and said to Moses,

> *"Accept these from them that they may be used in doing the work of the tabernacle of meeting; and you shall give them to the Levites, to every man according to his service"* **(Numbers 7:5).**

Lesson:
Children of God should have good habit of giving their pleasant offerings to God always. Our God is always pleased to see us responding to his love appropriately - for especially when we make good efforts to support his works. The Creator will surely reciprocate the positive contributions that we are making into his kingdom. He will show himself strong on our behalves to bless us in order to prove the principle of his faithfulness over people who truly serve him.

Prayer:
Dear God, please make me a genuine and cheerful giver who will make you happy always. Give me a charitable heart to liberally give my resources to support your works. Let my efforts benefit your kingdom, and to the glory of your holy name. For in the name of Jesus Christ I make my requests.

Amen.

« DAY 144 »

Christian Must Read Bible And Get Familiar With Signs Of End Time To Better Prepare For Rapture

Focus Passage: Mark 13:21-37

Jesus Christ hinted his disciples to expect some shocking events that will precede his second coming. He stated,

> *"But in those days, after that tribulation, the sun will be darkened, and the moon will not give its light; the stars of heaven will fall, and the powers in the heavens will be shaken"* **(Mark 13:24-25).**

Lesson:
Some uncommon natural events will occur to symbolize End Time - and the period of Jesus second coming. Believers must watch out for those events and interpret them as a symbol of Jesus' fast-approaching second coming. Unfortunately, not all Christians would be sensitive to those signs until Christ himself had appeared in the sky. However, those who recognize the signs have better chance of preparing themselves for the return of Christ. To forewarned is forearmed, every Christian should read his/her bible to get familiar with signs of End Time in order to adequately prepared for Jesus' second coming. The Savior will rapture whoever is well prepared to heaven, but he will leave the insensitive and nonchalant Christian on earth to suffer consequences of his/her actions on earth.

Prayer:
Dear Jesus Christ, please count me worthy for your eternal kingdom. Help me to be sensitive to those signs that will symbolize your second coming, and be prepared. Guide me through your Holy Spirit to wash my cloth in the blood of the Lamb and live acceptable life before you, so that I can qualify for your rapture and go to heaven. Please keep me worthy O Lord for the Feast of the Lamb in heaven. For unto you Jesus Christ I make my requests.

Amen.

« DAY 145 »

Holy Spirit Serves As A Global Positioning System (GPS) For Believers

Focus Passage: Numbers 9, 10, 11

God performed special miracles to direct Israelites' movements in the wilderness. He utilized some unusual visual aids to guide them. Jehovah used cloud to lead during daylight and used a pillar of fire to lead them during the night time. God required Israelites to keep their positions and remain unmoved whenever their guiding objects remain static – under whatever weather condition. The scripture reported how Israelites complied with God in following his guiding rule,

> *"Even when the cloud continued long, many days above the tabernacle, the children of Israel kept the charge of the Lord and did not journey. So it was, when the cloud was above the tabernacle a few days: according to the command of the Lord they would remain encamped, and according to the command of the Lord they would journey. So it was, when the cloud remained only from evening until morning: when the cloud was taken up in the morning, then they would journey; whether by day or by night, whenever the cloud was taken up, they would journey. Whether it was two days, a month, or a year that the cloud remained above the tabernacle, the children of Israel would remain encamped and not journey; but when it was taken up, they would journey. At the command of the Lord they remained encamped, and at the command of the Lord they journeyed; they kept the charge of the Lord, at the command of the Lord by the hand of Moses"* **(Numbers 9:19-23).**

Lesson:
Believers will be in their best performances and yield maximum productivity whenever they operate under God's guidance. Meanwhile, the most effective guidance that every Christian has is Holy Spirit. He represents Christ, and he is in the best position to properly lead us into having success. Therefore, if we (Christians) give room for Holy Spirit to operate, he will become our Global Positioning System (GPS) that will save us from making mistakes, and also lead us into making proper decisions that will honor God and benefit our lives.

Prayer:
Dear God, please guide me through your Holy Spirit to make proper decisions that will honor you and benefit my life. Let me be responsive to the guidance of your Spirit, and not deviate into error so that I can have record success and praise your holy name. For in the name of Jesus Christ I make my requests.

Amen.

« DAY 146 »

Unbelievers May Lack Spiritual Instinct, But Believers Must Prioritize Their Complete Devotion To God

Focus Passage: Mark 14:1-26

A woman who had a flask full of expensive perfume 'spoiled' Jesus with it. She excessively poured it on Jesus – to the extent that everyone around them became jealous. Some of them complained as the scripture reported,

> "...But there were some who were indignant among themselves, and said, "Why was this fragrant oil wasted? For it might have been sold for more than three hundred denarii and given to the poor" (And they criticized her sharply" **(Mark 14:4-5))**. Meanwhile, Jesus Christ rebuked those who murmured as reported, "Jesus said, "Let her alone. Why do you trouble her? She has done a good work for me. For you have the poor with you always, and whenever you wish you may do them good; but me you do not have always. She has done what she could. She has come beforehand to anoint my body for burial. Assuredly, I say to you, wherever this gospel is preached in the whole world, what this woman has done will also be told as a memorial to her" **(Mark 14:6-9)**.

Lesson:
An attitude of giving a precious and costly item to God does not suit worldly people well. To them, giving is considered a waste of resources. Worldly people care less about satisfying God with what they considered as their "hard earned" money; they will rather count their money and invest them into whatever looks promising. However, the worldly people lack spiritual instinct that could have made them realize that earthly resources are temporal! Only whatever a person invests towards God's kingdom will last eternally - every other thing will perish with the world. Therefore, children of God must be careful not to follow world pattern and be obsessive will money or materials that will remain temporal. Believers' resources must be primarily invested towards heaven - where there shall be no corruption. Any Christian's effort (whether money, material, or others) invested towards heaven will yield great rewards, and they will last eternally.

Prayer:
Dear God, please help me to focus on investing my resources into your kingdom by supporting gospel and other charity works. Do not let me be obsessed with any material wealth that will perish with the world. While I am still here on earth to support myself and my loved ones, let my efforts be prioritize to make significant contributions to your kingdom. Please bless my work, and let me reap much rewards in heaven for my efforts. For in the name of Jesus Christ I make my requests.

Amen.

« DAY 147 »

People Who Meddle With God's Business Uninvited Risk God's Punishment

Focus Passage: Numbers 12, 13, 14

Aaron and Miriam ganged up against Moses, and they attempted to usurp his authority. The two siblings argued with their brothers and accused him of marrying an Ethiopian woman against their Jewish tradition. They also accused him of being obsessive with power. However, God defended Moses against Aaron and Miriam, and he was displeased with them. God said to them,

> *"And he said, Hear now my words: If there be a prophet among you, I the Lord will make myself known unto him in a vision, and will speak unto him in a dream. My servant Moses is not so, who is faithful in all mine house. With him will I speak mouth to mouth, even apparently, and not in dark speeches; and the similitude of the Lord shall he behold: wherefore then were ye not afraid to speak against my servant Moses?"* **(Numbers 12:6-8 KJV).**

Lesson:
All people are required to respect God's servants since they are uniquely commissioned for some special assignments. Gospel ministers are God's servants; they are God's mouthpiece, and it is almost impossible for anyone to hurt them and go scot-free. Meanwhile, some unassuming circumstances may erupt around a servant of God, which makes his/her actions unbiblical; however, people should still be careful not to meddle with God's business - uninvited. No one should attempt to help God discipline his servants, because the action will backfire! God is capable of taking care of his own business, and he will do so. He knows the best way to correct any of his servants who fail him morally, or in any other form.

Prayer:
Dear God, please help me to mind my business and not interfere with your business uninvited. Do not let me meddle with your business and sin against you. More importantly, help me to respect your servants and give them due honor, so that you can be happy with me. Let my actions support your servants and motivate them into committing themselves deeper into your services. I also seize this medium to pray for your servants throughout the world to receive grace and strength needed to prosper your kingdom. For in the name of Jesus Christ I make my requests.

Amen.

« DAY 148 »

Children Of God Must Be Careful Not To Rely On Their Natural Ability To Overcome Life Battles

Focus Passage: Mark 14:27-53

The disciples of Jesus Christ who had bragged to defend him against any assault fled during crisis - They all escape to let him face his own challenge and determine his fate. In fact, one of the disciples ran off bare naked when enemies arrived The young man wouldn't wait to pick his cover garment when it dropped **(Mark 14:50-52)**. Meanwhile, the same disciples who abandoned their master during crisis had initially promised him heaven on earth. They promised to stand by him and protect him at all cost. For example, Peter once said to Jesus,

> "'Even if all are made to stumble, yet I will not be.' Jesus said to him, 'Assuredly, I say to you that today, even this night, before the rooster crows twice, you will deny Me three times.' But he spoke more vehemently, 'If I have to die with You, I will not deny you!' And they all said likewise" **(Mark 14:29-31)**.

Lesson:
Children of God must be careful not to rely on their natural ability to overcome life battles. No one can prevail in any situation except God has helped him/her. In addition, it takes Holy Spirit to obtain spiritual strength that is needed to overcome Satan - who orchestrates all evil. The enemy cannot withstand the Spirit of God; he has no choice than to submit to him and pave way for God's children to have their expected victory. Therefore, Christians must be obsessed with Holy Spirit. We must think about him, seek for him, be possessed of him, and also make him our life partner. Once the Spirit of God richly dwells in us, we can soar like an eagle and have perfect victory. Truly, Holy Spirit will never fail anyone who is possessed of him - under whatever condition.

Prayer:
Dear God, please possess me with your Holy Spirit so that I can live victoriously every day of my life. Again, help me to count on the strength of your Spirit to prosper in all ramifications of life! Do not let me rely on any arm of flesh for victory. Let my faith be resolute in you for victory and testimony throughout the days of my life. For in the name of Jesus Christ I make my requests.

Amen.

« DAY 149 »

Meddling With God's Business And Fighting God's Servants Are Two Dangerous Games Everyone Should Avoid

Focus Passage: Numbers 15, 16

A rebel group rose to stir commotion in the camp of Israelites, and they set their eyes on usurping Moses and Aaron leadership positions. The rebel leaders - Korah, Dathan, and Abiram challenged Moses to their faces, and refused to follow their instructions. They said

> *"Is it a small thing that thou hast brought us up out of a land that floweth with milk and honey, to kill us in the wilderness, except thou make thyself altogether a prince over us?"* **(Numbers 16:13 KJV).**

Meanwhile, God took personal offense in the rebels' actions, and he punished them. He did the unspeakable to correct the situation - He made earth open up and swallowed the rebels alive! The scripture reported, *"And the earth opened her mouth, and swallowed them up, and their houses, and all the men that appertained unto Korah, and all their goods. They, and all that appertained to them, went down alive into the pit, and the earth closed upon them: and they perished from among the congregation"* **(Numbers 16:32-33 KJV).**

Lesson:
God does not joke with his kingdom business, and he will terribly deal with anyone who attempts to obstruct it. Also, God considers it as an insult whenever someone harasses his servants; the Creator will be provoked to act to defend his name. Therefore, since meddling with God's business and fighting his servants are two dangerous games, people should be carefully. Everyone should honor God and respect his servants to receive his blessings, and not his wrath. Also, people should make decisive efforts to make their positive contributions into God's business since the efforts will satisfy God into blessing them.

Prayer:
Dear God, please give me humble spirit to give special regard for your servants. Do not let me disrespect them and provoke you to anger; instead, let me honor those who represent you in any capacity so that you can be happy to bless me. Please give me a good spirit towards your kingdom services to receive your blessings! For in the name of Jesus Christ I make my requests.

Amen.

« DAY 150 »

It Wasn't A Failure On God's Part To Allow Enemies To Kill Jesus; It Was His Salvation Work Accomplishment

Focus Passage: Mark 14:54-72

The Pharisees scrambled for false witnesses to validate their crime allegation against Jesus Christ. They were unashamed to publicly interview some liars - all for the sake of their bitterness against Jesus' successful ministry. The scripture reported,

> "But Peter followed Him at a distance, right into the courtyard of the high priest. And he sat with the servants and warmed himself at the fire. Now the chief priests and all the council sought testimony against Jesus to put Him to death, but found none. For many bore false witness against Him, but their testimonies did not agree. Then some rose up and bore false witness against Him, saying, "We heard Him say, 'I will destroy this temple made with hands, and within three days I will build another made without hands.'" But not even then did their testimony agree. And the high priest stood up in the midst and asked Jesus, saying, "Do you answer nothing? What is it these men testify against you?" But He kept silent and answered nothing. Again the high priest asked Him, saying to Him, "Are You the Christ, the Son of the Blessed?" Jesus said, "I am. And you will see the Son of Man sitting at the right hand of the Power, and coming with the clouds of heaven." Then the high priest tore his clothes and said, "What further need do we have of witnesses? You have heard the blasphemy! What do you think?" And they all condemned Him to be deserving of death. Then some began to spit on Him, and to blindfold Him, and to beat Him, and to say to Him, "Prophesy!" And the officers struck Him with the palms of their hands" **(Mark 14:54-65)**.

Lesson:

The enemies of Jesus Christ were able to successfully crucify him; however, it was not a failure on God's part to not defend his only begotten Son! God intentionally allowed him to suffer pain and die on the cross for one important reason! He allowed those odds to happen to him in order to save humanity. Indeed, Christ ultimately paid the penalty of our sins on the cross - and resurrected to award us victory over sin. The Son of God has granted us access to the kingdom of God! Hence, anyone who confesses Jesus Christ as Lord and Savior will be saved. The person will not go to hell fire, but be acceptable to heaven to enjoy God's eternal life (Romans 10:9-10).

Prayer:

Thank you Jesus Christ for you have done it all for me! You endured persecutions and surrendered yourself to die on the cross for the sake of saving my soul. Nothing else remains for me than to reciprocate your love by accepting you as my personal Lord and Savior. Therefore, I declare my faith in you today: I confess you are Jesus Christ the Son of God and the Savior of the world. I yield my complete life to today, and I accept you as my personal Lord and Savior. Please write my name in the book of life, and keep me eternally worthy for your kingdom! Thank you Jesus Christ for your saving grace.
Amen!

« DAY 151 »

God Mandated His Children To Pay Tithes Without Negotiation

Focus Passage: Numbers 17, 18, 19

God required Israelites to pay tenth percent of their income (known as tithe) to the temple treasury; they will take some money out of the treasury to pay the Levites who serve in the temple. Meanwhile, the Levites who receive payment from the treasury must also pay their own tithe like every other person. God insisted that everyone - without exception must pay his/her tithe to him. God stated concerning tithe,

> *"For the tithes of the children of Israel, which they offer up as a heave offering to the Lord, I have given to the Levites as an inheritance; therefore I have said to them, 'Among the children of Israel they shall have no inheritance.' "Then the Lord spoke to Moses, saying, "Speak thus to the Levites, and say to them: 'When you take from the children of Israel the tithes which I have given you from them as your inheritance, then you shall offer up a heave offering of it to the Lord, a tenth of the tithe"* **(Numbers 18:24-26)**.

Lesson:
God instituted the principle of paying tithe, and he requires everyone to comply with it. The Creator left no room for negotiating tithe; he regards it as his own entitlement out of everyone's income. Therefore, it is more or less a sin to violate God's rule of tithing. Believers must equally view the rule as any others. That is, we must consider the rule of paying tithe as carrying the same weight as the rule asking us to love God and our neighbors. As it always applies, Jehovah will favor and bless whoever observes his principle of tithing.

Prayer:
Dear God, please make me a law abiding Christian who truly pays his/her tithe unto you. I know you don't need my money, but you need my faithfulness; therefore, help me to be faithful in paying my dues unto you so that you can be happy to bless me more. For in the name of Jesus Christ I make my requests.

Amen.

« DAY 152 »

People Who Killed Jesus Christ Helped Him Fulfill His Mission Of Saving Humanity

Focus Passage: Mark 15:1-25

Judge Pilate knew the Pharisees who arrested Jesus Christ of wrongdoing had no basis for their action, but were merely jealous. Despite his legal knowledge that justified Jesus' innocence, Pilate still succumbed to the Pharisees' request to condemn him. He granted their wish and handed him over to be crucified. The Pharisees then abused Jesus and crucified him. The scripture reported,

> *"Then the soldiers led Him away into the hall called Praetorium, and they called together the whole garrison. And they clothed Him with purple; and they twisted a crown of thorns, put it on His head, and began to salute Him, "Hail, King of the Jews!" Then they struck Him on the head with a reed and spat on Him; and bowing the knee, they worshiped Him. And when they had mocked Him, they took the purple off Him, put His own clothes on Him, and led Him out to crucify Him"* **(Mark 15:16-20)**

Lesson:
The people who punished and killed Jesus Christ thought they won their battle against him; however, they were not. The opponents had just helped the Messiah fulfill his mission of saving mankind! Christ' death and resurrection have opened pathway of heaven for those who were forbidden due to their sins. Anyone can now access God once he/she confesses his/her faith in Jesus Christ. That is, anyone who believes and confesses Jesus Christ as Lord will be saved. As the scripture stated, *"For God so loved the world that He gave His only begotten Son, that whoever believes in Him should not perish but have everlasting life"* **(John 3:16)**. Also, the scripture stated, *"That if you confess with your mouth the Lord Jesus and believe in your heart that God has raised Him from the dead, you will be saved. For with the heart one believes unto righteousness, and with the mouth confession is made unto salvation"* **(Romans 10:9-10)**.

Prayer:
Praise God Jesus Christ has conquered Satan through his death and resurrection! The Son of God has granted me the key of eternal life through his willing sacrifice to God. Hence, I declare my faith in him. I declare that Jesus Christ is Lord; he is the Savior of the world, and I accept him as my personal Lord and Savior. From now on, my complete life will be dedicated to Jesus Christ, and I will serve him throughout the days of my life. Since I have confessed my faith in Jesus, I believe I have become a child of God, and the crown of righteousness is now awaiting me in heaven. Hallelujah!

Amen.

« DAY 153 »

Period Of Trials Are Bound To Come; Believers Must Be Prepared Not To Succumb To The Will Of Satan

Focus Passage: Numbers 20, 21, 22

Israelites nagged Moses in the wilderness, and they pushed him to sin against God. Since the people could not physically see God to attack him, they logged their complex complaints against his servant Moses. Israelites pressured Moses for lack of food, meat, and water. The man couldn't handle the pressure any longer and he acted in flesh and sin against God. The scripture reported,

> *"And there was no water for the congregation: and they gathered themselves together against Moses and against Aaron. And the people chode with Moses, and spake, saying, Would God that we had died when our brethren died before the Lord! And why have ye brought up the congregation of the Lord into this wilderness, that we and our cattle should die there? And wherefore have ye made us to come up out of Egypt, to bring us in unto this evil place? it is no place of seed, or of figs, or of vines, or of pomegranates; neither is there any water to drink. And Moses and Aaron went from the presence of the assembly unto the door of the tabernacle of the congregation, and they fell upon their faces: and the glory of the Lord appeared unto them. And the Lord spake unto Moses, saying, Take the rod, and gather thou the assembly together, thou, and Aaron thy brother, and speak ye unto the rock before their eyes; and it shall give forth his water, and thou shalt bring forth to them water out of the rock: so thou shalt give the congregation and their beasts drink. And Moses took the rod from before the Lord, as he commanded him. And Moses and Aaron gathered the congregation together before the rock, and he said unto them, Hear now, ye rebels; must we fetch you water out of this rock? And Moses lifted up his hand, and with his rod he smote the rock twice: and the water came out abundantly, and the congregation drank, and their beasts also. And the Lord spake unto Moses and Aaron, Because ye believed me not, to sanctify me in the eyes of the children of Israel, therefore ye shall not bring this congregation into the land which I have given them. This is the water of Meribah; because the children of Israel strove with the Lord, and he was sanctified in them"* **(Numbers 20:2-13 KJV).**

Lesson:

Christians must be sensitive not to handle life pressure in a manner that will cause them to sin against God. Period of trials and temptations are bound come, but believers must be careful not to allow Satan to rejoice over them. To overcome the enemy, believers must pray for guidance of the Holy Spirit and respond to his leadership to make right judgment, and act rightly. God that we (believers) serve is indeed interested in earning us victory in every situation. He won't abandon us to face trials alone, but he will stand by us to have expected victory.

Prayer:
Dear God, please help me to be sensitive in Holy Spirit to overcome Satan's schemes. I know the enemy is a Toothless Bulldog who only appears strong but lacks power! Your divine Holy Spirit has the power needed to overcome Satan always. Therefore, please baptize me with the Holy Spirit for right leadership and guidance. Let him instruct me in all things to live a pure and acceptable life before you so that I can live triumphantly on earth, and also make it to your kingdom. For in the name of Jesus Christ I make my requests.

Amen.

« DAY 154 »

God Ignored Jesus Painful Outcry To Allow Him To Successfully Finish His Mission

Focus Passage: Mark 15:26-47

Jesus Christ (being the Son of God) suffered enemies' persecution like a regular human being. He suffered pains with his terrestrial body; he cried and shed tears. Jesus also craved for some reliefs during his trial moments. However, God refused to help him as the scripture revealed,

> *"...Now when the sixth hour had come, there was darkness over the whole land until the ninth hour. And at the ninth hour Jesus cried out with a loud voice, saying, "Eloi, Eloi, lama sabachthani?" which is translated, "My God, My God, why have you forsaken Me?"* **(Mark 15:33-34).**

Lesson:

Jesus Christ suffered persecution from his enemies to the point of death, and no one helped him. Even God refused to rescue him, but he allowed him to suffer and die. However, Jehovah did not release his Son to suffer and die for nothing! His goal was to make him go through those ordeals for the sake of saving humanity. Indeed, Christ's death and resurrection open door of salvation and granted believers the key of eternal life. Hence, whoever confesses Jesus Christ as Lord, and accept him as his/her savior will be saved. The scripture emphasized,

"And as Moses lifted up the serpent in the wilderness, even so must the Son of Man be lifted up, that whoever believes in Him should not perish but have eternal life. For God so loved the world that He gave His only begotten Son, that whoever believes in Him should not perish but have everlasting life" **(John 3:14-16).**

Prayer:

Dear Jesus Christ, I believe you have suffered enemies' persecutions and died on the cross for the sake of saving my soul. I won't take your salvation efforts for granted, but I will respond to them by submitting my life to you and confess you as Lord. Therefore, I declare you are Christ the Son of God and the Savior of the World. I surrender my life to you today, and I promise to serve you throughout the days of my life. Please help me to keep my promise until the end, so that I can rejoice with you in heaven. So help me God!

Amen.

« DAY 155 »

Christians Operate Under God's Divine Protections; No Weapon Fashioned Against Us Shall Prosper

Focus Passage: Numbers 23, 24, 25

Balaak hired Balaam to curse Israelites, but their plot boomerang. Balaam made three attempts to curse God's children – despite God's warning not to do so. On his third attempt, the man found himself blessing Israelites against his own wish. When on his mission to pronounce curses, Balaam found himself unconsciously stating,

> *"God is not a man, that He should lie, Nor a son of man, that He should repent. Has He said, and will He not do? Or has He spoken, and will He not make it good? Behold, I have received a command to bless; He has blessed, and I cannot reverse it"* **(Numbers 23:19-20).**

Lesson:
Christians are under God's divine protections, and no weapon the enemies fashioned against us that shall prosper. **(Isaiah 54:17)**. God will turn enemies' imaginations into our blessings - so that we can praise his name. People who hate us may devise evil and launch attack, but they will ultimately fail. Even if their schemes appear to be working, God will eventually convert them to our blessings. Since Jehovah that we serve is ever alive, there is no divination or enchantment that anyone attempts against us that will succeed. God will brighten our faces to glorify his name in all situations! Hence, those who associate with God should be encouraged. They should summon courage to keep trusting him during trials since whatever pain they currently suffer will be brief, and they will ultimately triumph to praise God's name.

Prayer:
Dear God, I believe you are God of miracle, and your miracle of provision and protection will never cease in my life. Therefore, I am asking that you rise on my behalf to fight my enemies. Help me to suppress their power and silence them. Give me upper hands over the enemies, and transform their evil counsel into my blessings. Please let my expectations be fulfilled upon my enemies, so that I can live victoriously and praise your name forever! For in the name of Jesus Christ I make my requests.

Amen.

« DAY 156 »

Gospel Propagation Is God's Heartbeat; Every Christian Is Mandated To Evangelize It

Focus Passage: Mark 16

Jesus Christ resurrected from death on the third day, and he celebrated his victory with his disciples. Although his mission to save humanity was accomplished, but he refused to close the chapter. He commanded his disciples to go far and wide to share the good news of his salvation. Everyone must hear gospel and respond to his salvation grace to be acceptable into God's kingdom. Jesus said to his followers,

> *"Go into all the world and preach the gospel to all creation. Whoever believes and is baptized will be saved, but whoever does not believe will be condemned. And these signs will accompany those who believe: In my name they will drive out demons; they will speak in new tongues"* **(Mark 16:15-17 NIV).**

Lesson:

All Christians throughout the world are disciples of Jesus Christ, and we are commanded to share his gospel to people around us and beyond. No believer should consider gospel evangelization as someone else's job. Everyone who claims to be a Christian is also a Christ's evangelist, and must proclaim gospel. Believers must not wait for any convenient time to preach gospel; we must not give any excuse, but utilize every available opportunity to share our faith with others. One soul at a time, believers must reach out to neighbors, family, friends, and coworkers. We must engage our local community with gospel, and also broadcast gospel to distant lands. Christians must use electronics to preach gospel: We must take the advantage of social media, and other new innovations to broadcast gospel of Jesus Christ to the entire world. The more we preach gospel, the more the kingdom of God will be populated, and the less the kingdom of Satan will become. Jehovah will reward his faithful servants in heaven. He will also award them tremendous honor and make them a pacesetter of his indescribable glory on earth.

Prayer:

Dear Jesus Christ, please make me your good evangelist who spread your gospel around. Empower me through your Holy Spirit to not keep silent with my testimony in you! Let me utilize every available medium to talk about your goodness to my local community and the world at large, so that people can be rescued from pathway of hell to heaven. Again, please keep your fire of gospel burning within me so that I can spread the light of your gospel to both the known and unknown world for the sake of populating your kingdom. At the end of it all, count me worthy to enter your kingdom to hear "Weldone my good servant, and welcome home to the joy of you Lord!"

Amen!

« DAY 157 »

All People – Including God's Servants Are Required To Fully Obey God's Commandments To Receive His Full Benefits

Focus Passage: Numbers 26, 27

God disallowed Moses from entering the Promised Land because he disobeyed him in the wilderness. Moses would only take a distant look of the land but he would not enter it. The scripture reported,

> "Now the Lord said to Moses: *"Go up into this Mount Abarim, and see the land which I have given to the children of Israel. And when you have seen it, you also shall be gathered to your people, as Aaron your brother was gathered. For in the Wilderness of Zin, during the strife of the congregation, you rebelled against My command to hallow Me at the waters before their eyes"* **(Numbers 27:12-14).**

Lesson:
All people – including God's servants are required to fully obey God's commandments to receive his full benefits. Jehovah wants our full devotion to his laws; he wants us to be fully committed and observe them. Every believer must understand that the Creator will not partially deal with anyone based on his/her special assignment to him. Inerrant laws of God cannot be manipulated, but must be complied with. However, Jehovah is willing to work with any believer who is struggling with his rules. Therefore, a person who is slack in complying with any of God's laws should not pretend but come humbly before him for confession, and seek help. Such person must willingly take the necessary step of improvement to make God happy. Once a sinner confesses and repents from his/her sins, God will be appeased to forgive and restore his/her joy of salvation.

Prayer:
Dear God, please make me a honest Christian who is not out there to deceive myself. Do not let me tamper with sin and incur your wrath, but let me come clean of my sins and live acceptable life before you. Help me to genuinely repent from my sins and turn a new leaf so that I can be worthy of your eternal kingdom! Please let your Holy Spirit empower me to serve you well throughout the days of my life! For in the name of Jesus Christ I make my requests.

Amen.

« DAY 158 »

Believers Must Understand That God's Faithfulness Last Eternally

Focus Passage: Mark 1:1-20

Priest Zachariah served God with faithfulness despite his wife's barrenness; therefore, an angel of God visited him to announce an answer to his long-time prayer request. God's angel met Zachariah while performing his priesthood business in the temple, and told him that Elizabeth would become a mother! The scripture reported,

> *"So it was, that while he was serving as priest before God in the order of his division, according to the custom of the priesthood, his lot fell to burn incense when he went into the temple of the Lord. And the whole multitude of the people was praying outside at the hour of incense. Then an angel of the Lord appeared to him, standing on the right side of the altar of incense. And when Zacharias saw him, he was troubled, and fear fell upon him. But the angel said to him, "Do not be afraid, Zacharias, for your prayer is heard; and your wife Elizabeth will bear you a son, and you shall call his name John"* **(Luke 1:8-13)**.

Lesson:
Children of God ought to remain consistent in their services to God under whatever circumstance of life. (Believers must not cease in praying also). Our services to God must not be based on moods (either positive or negative). That is, we should not base our attitude of serving God on how we feel. God of the good time is also God of the bad time, and he knows how to turn any wrong situation to a good one. Truly, we (believers) may have some challenging situations that cause sorrow, but they should not restrain us from faithfully serving God. Jehovah has his own schedule that he follows; although he may sometimes appears slow to respond to our requests, but he will surely do so in his right timing. Jehovah will never ignore the outcry of his children; he will respond in due time to shower his goodness into our lives - to brighten our faces and glorify his name.

Prayer:
Dear God, please give me strength to trust you for all my needs at all times. Strengthen my faith to keep faithfully serving you in all situations - whether my expectations are met or not. Let my services to you be unconditional! Help me to faithfully serve you in time of needs and time of surplus! I surely know that you will grant my requests and meet all my expectations as I keep praying and trusting you! Please give me a lasting testimony that will bring glory and honor to your holy name. For in the name of Jesus Christ I make my requests.

Amen.

« DAY 159 »

Christians Must Exercise Their Authority In Godly Manner

Focus Passage: Numbers 28, 29, 30

God explained the conditions that are allowed for a person to override someone else's vow in his presence. He said,

> "If a man makes a vow to the Lord, or swears an oath to bind himself by some agreement, he shall not break his word; he shall do according to all that proceeds out of his mouth. *"Or if a woman makes a vow to the Lord, and binds herself by some agreement while in her father's house in her youth, and her father hears her vow and the agreement by which she has bound herself, and her father holds his peace, then all her vows shall stand, and every agreement with which she has bound herself shall stand. But if her father overrules her on the day that he hears, then none of her vows nor her agreements by which she has bound herself shall stand; and the Lord will release her, because her father overruled her" (Numbers 30:2-5). The same law applies to couples. Husbands have rights to save their wives from inappropriate commitments* **(Numbers 30:6-8).**

Lesson:

God sees authority as a means of protection, and not for oppression; therefore, those who have authority over others should exercise caution, to avoid sinning against God. Every higher authority is expected to protect the lesser ones: Parents are to protect their children, husbands are to protect their wives. In the same manner, employers are to protect their employees, and government leaders are to protect their citizens. Therefore, children of God must be careful to honor God in their positions. No Christian should follow worldly people's example to harass or demean others. God sees everything that humans do, and he will adequately reward everyone according to his/her mode of operations.

Prayer:

Dear God, please help me to appropriately exercise my authority so that I will not sin against you. No matter what power or position I may have, help me to exercise your fear and serve with dignity. Let me be your true ambassador whether in private and in public setting, so that I can bring honor to your holy name. Please let your Holy Spirit guide me at all times! For in the name of Jesus Christ I make my requests.

Amen.

« DAY 160 »

Jesus' Life And Death Story Is A Complete Salvation Package For Mankind

Focus Passage: Luke 1:21-38

Angel Gabriel paid a surprise visit to Mary, and he brought her a huge gift from God. The angel said to Mary,

> *"Behold, you will conceive in your womb and bring forth a Son, and shall call His name Jesus. He will be great, and will be called the Son of the Highest; and the Lord God will give Him the throne of His father David. And He will reign over the house of Jacob forever, and of His kingdom there will be no end"* **(Luke 1:31-33).**

Lesson:

Angel Gabriel paid a surprise visit to Mary to announce that she would give birth to Jesus Christ - the Messiah; however, nothing was a surprise to God. In fact, God himself initiated the visit for the sake of fulfilling his long-time goal of saving humanity from their pathway of hell fire. Since humanity kept sinning and could not change course, God premeditated a plan to send his beloved only Son through a virgin to rescue them. The Son of God would have to sacrifice his own life and use his blood to redeem people from their sinful ways. Anyone who then believes him will be saved. God's plan became fulfilled: Angel visited Virgin Mary to announce the promise; she was conceived of the Holy Spirit, and she gave birth to Jesus Christ. Jesus also lived on earth to sacrifice his life: He died on the cross and shed his blood for the remission of human sins. Hence, anyone who believes in his death and resurrection will be saved and be accepted to heaven.

Prayer:

Hallelujah God sent his Son Jesus Christ to save the world! Hallelujah Jesus came to the world to die for my sins! Hallelujah I can now receive forgiveness of sin and have access to God! I believe in Jesus Christ. I confess him as my Lord, and I accept him as my personal Savior. Hence, the crown of righteousness is waiting for me in heaven. Hallelujah I am now saved!

Amen.

« DAY 161 »

God Hates Idolatry; He Will Neither Bless Nor Accept Idolaters Into His Kingdom

Focus Passage: Numbers 31, 32, 33

God warned Israelites not to make friends with Canaanites because of their sins. If they do, they would become incapacitated to enjoy his awarded blessing of the Promised Land. God said to Israelites,

> "But if ye will not drive out the inhabitants of the land from before you; then it shall come to pass, that those which ye let remain of them shall be pricks in your eyes, and thorns in your sides, and shall vex you in the land wherein ye dwell. Moreover it shall come to pass, that I shall do unto you, as I thought to do unto them" **(Numbers 33:55-56 KJV).**

Lesson:

Sin is detestable to God, and all people are required to detest it also. For example, God passionately hates the sin of idolatry, and whoever worships an idol will be considered his enemy. However, idolatry has taken a new turn in our present days. Unlike olden days, not only a physical object can be regarded as an idol. An idol can now be categorized with both material and immaterial things. Also, a human can now become an idol. For example, an electronic device can be someone's idol. Someone's idol can also be a career, a car, a spouse, or a child. To make this simple: anything - material or immaterial - that takes the place of God in anyone's life is an idol - and it must be shun. Also, a relationship can be amended to take its rightful place without competing with God! Hence, it is important that everyone understands that no idolater will be acceptable into God's kingdom. God will not accept an idol worshipper, but reject him/her from his kingdom!

However, no Christian should presume his/her religion activity will be strong enough to subside God's wrath on his/her idolatry practice! No religion status or activity can appease God from punishing idolaters. Therefore, every believer should assess him/herself and be sure he/she is not an idolater. A Christian who discovers he/she has digressed from serving the true and living God should repent and make amendment, so that God can be appeased to love, redeem, and bless him/her.

Prayer:

Dear God, I will not be unreasonable to replace your position for an idol. I know you hate idolatry, and you will punish idolaters; therefore, please help me to carefully serve you only. Do not let me share any glory due you with any other person, deity, or material. Let my services focus on you, and let them satisfy you to bless me on earth, and qualify me for your eternal kingdom. Please bless me with your Holy Spirit to keep living a holy and acceptable life before you throughout the days of my life! For in the name of Jesus Christ I make my requests.

Amen.

« DAY 162 »

God Blesses People Without Preferential Treatments

Focus Passage: Luke 1:39-56

Moments of joy erupted between Mary and Elizabeth because they were both miraculously pregnant at the same time to give birth to miracle children. The two cousins would both bear miracle children that would make significant contributions to God's kingdom. (Elizabeth became the mother of John Baptist and Mary became the mother of Jesus Christ). Elizabeth said to Mary,

> *"Blessed are you among women, and blessed is the fruit of your womb!" (Luke 1:42) And Mary said: "My soul magnifies the Lord, and my spirit has rejoiced in God my Savior. For He has regarded the lowly state of His maidservant; for behold, henceforth all generations will call me blessed"* **(Luke 1:46-48)**.

Lesson:

God does great things for people in some remarkable ways. He blesses people without giving preferences to people's economic status or cultural backgrounds. Jehovah remembers the poor and he raises them to the positions of honor. For example, out of many virgins that lived in Israel, he handpicked Mary who had no prominent background to become the mother of Jesus Christ that would save the world. Therefore, believers must remain confident in their God, and know that he cares about them. In as much we remain his faithful children, he will recognize and honor us in due time.

Prayer:

Dear God, I know you care about your children and you do not segregate; therefore, I ask you to please remember me in my low estate to glorify your name. Search and find something in me that can be used to showcase your glory, and also to become my blessings. Shower your blessings into my life, and let the abundance of your testimony ever fill my mouth - now and always. For in the name of Jesus Christ I make my requests.

Amen.

« DAY 163 »

God's Laws Are Not Rigid, But It Takes The Help Of Holy Spirit To Comply With Them

Focus Passage: Numbers 34, 35, 36

God required Israelites' authority to execute fair judgment for their citizens. They must not judge people rashly. For example, a manslaughter offense must not be regarded as a murder. God's said,

> "...If he pushes him suddenly without enmity, or throws anything at him without lying in wait, or uses a stone, by which a man could die, throwing it at him without seeing him, so that he dies, while he was not his enemy or seeking his harm, then the congregation shall judge between the manslayer and the avenger of blood according to these judgments. So the congregation shall deliver the manslayer from the hand of the avenger of blood, and the congregation shall return him to the city of refuge where he had fled, and he shall remain there until the death of the high priest who was anointed with the holy oil" **(Numbers 35:22-25)**.

Lesson:

The laws of God presented during Old Testament were not rigid, as some people may have speculated. Despite limited education and resources available at the time, God worked with people to ensure they could comply with his laws. The same God of Israelites is still the same one that reigns today, and he will humanely deal with us to ensure his rules are not intimidating. However, believers in New Testament have better advantage than those who lived during Old Testament, because we have Holy Spirit to guide us. The Holy Spirit also gives us edge advantage over those who do not have him. The Spirit of God earns us insight into God's word for better understanding, and he also grants us strength to comply with God's requirements. Hence, those who lack the Holy Spirit should venture to have him by asking God in prayer through his Son Jesus Christ (John 14:25-26).

Prayer:

Dear God, please baptize me with your Holy Spirit and let him rule me to obey your laws. Let your divine Spirit give me understanding of your word, and let him empower me to fully obey them. Let your Spirit empower me to live a pure and acceptable life before you so that I can prosper throughout the days of my life, and also enter your kingdom! For in the name of Jesus Christ I make my requests.

Amen.

« DAY 164 »

God Does Not Lie; He Will Fulfill Whatever He Has Promised His Children

Focus Passage: Luke 1:57-80

Zachariah prophesied about John the Baptist and said,

> "And you, my child, will be called a prophet of the Most High; for you will go on before the Lord to prepare the way for him, to give his people the knowledge of salvation through the forgiveness of their sins, because of the tender mercy of our God, by which the rising sun will come to us from heaven to shine on those living in darkness and in the shadow of death, to guide our feet into the path of peace" **(Luke 1:76-79 NIV).**

Lesson:
God does not lie; he will fulfill whatever he has promised his people - under whatever circumstances. Since the Creator is not feeble, his words cannot falter but surely come to pass. Hence, we (believers) must have faith in God that we serve! He is God of the bible who has proven record of success - without any failure. Jehovah has proven his repeated faithfulness for his children, and he can still do the same thing again! Therefore, believers must remain hopeful and keep serving him. Our heavenly Father will show himself strong on our behalves in due time, and ensure that his name is glorified in every aspect of our lives.

Prayer:
Song: "What a mighty God we serve; what a might God we serve; what a might God we serve!"

Dear God, you are such a powerful God who does great things for those who serve you! I acknowledge your presence and power in my life, and I know that you will handle everything that concerns me so that I can have victory and praise your name! All I'm asking now is strength to keep focusing on you. Help me to keep trusting you until my joy is full to the glory of your name. For in the name of your Son Jesus Christ I make my requests.

Amen.

« DAY 165 »

Jehovah Will Keep His Promises For His Children, Even When Others Have Failed

Focus Passage: Deuteronomy 1, 2

Prior to Moses death on the mountain, he acknowledged both the success and failures of Israelites in the wilderness. The people largely failed God - with very little success to recount. One out of many failures was Israelites' coward attitude to claim their God's Promised Land by faith. They spied the land and brought back bad report to provoke others into rebelliousness against God and Moses. Moses recounted Israelites refusal to enter the Promised Land and said,

> "And every one of you came near to me and said, *'Let us send men before us, and let them search out the land for us, and bring back word to us of the way by which we should go up, and of the cities into which we shall come.'* "The plan pleased me well; so I took twelve of your men, one man from each tribe. And they departed and went up into the mountains...They also took some of the fruit of the land in their hands and brought it down to us; and they brought back word to us, saying, 'It is a good land which the Lord our God is giving us.' "Nevertheless you would not go up, but rebelled against the command of the Lord your God; and you complained in your tents, and said, 'Because the Lord hates us, He has brought us out of the land of Egypt to deliver us into the hand of the Amorites, to destroy us. Where can we go up? Our brethren have discouraged our hearts, saying, "The people are greater and taller than we; the cities are great and fortified up to heaven; moreover we have seen the sons of the Anakim there."' "Then I said to you, 'Do not be terrified, or afraid of them...Yet, for all that, you did not believe the Lord your God, who went in the way before you to search out a place for you to pitch your tents, to show you the way you should go, in the fire by night and in the cloud by day" **(Deuteronomy 1:22-33)**.

Lesson:
Humans may fail on promises, but God will not fail his promises. Jehovah will keep his promises, even when everyone else has failed. The Creator knows the best way to suit his purpose in every circumstance. He can maneuver any situation for the sake of benefiting his children. In fact, God can make wicked people unconsciously benefit his children! However, believers still have to be careful not to abuse God's eternal promises and live in sin. We cannot take God's grace for granted and expect to live freely! Jehovah cannot be fooled; he will deal with anyone who aims at tempering with his integrity. Truly, God's mercy endures forever, but he still won't let a sinner go unpunished.

Prayer:
Dear God, please plant your fear into my heart so that I will not sin against you! Do not let me take your grace of salvation, provision, protection, and others for granted. I clearly understand your divine promises over me are "Yeah and Amen," therefore help me to keep walking in your will so that I can have all-round success. Let all my expectations be met so that I can praise you forever! For in the name of Jesus Christ I make my requests.
Amen.

« DAY 166 »

"From Cradle To Glory" – Christ Born In The Manger Rose To Become The Savior Of The World

Focus Passage: Luke 2:1-24

Jesus Christ was born during censor when people were much concerned about personal recognition than to pay serious attention to poor people. Public shelter was full, and Joseph and Mary couldn't afford any expensive accommodation; therefore, they checked-in to a manger - And Mary gave birth to Jesus at the manger! The scripture reported,

> *"...And so it was, that, while they were there, the days were accomplished that she should be delivered. And she brought forth her firstborn son, and wrapped him in swaddling clothes, and laid him in a manger; because there was no room for them in the inn." (Luke 2:6-7).*

Lesson:

God mysteriously chose a poor mother and a poor caregiver father for Jesus Christ. He also selected an unpopular birthplace for the Messiah while he has all power to showcase his birth at a luxury hotel or an expensive hospital. God ensured that Christ was born at the lowest place in town of Bethlehem – the manger. Why? God chose a debased background for his Son Jesus Christ for the sake of retaining all honors to Himself! If the Messiah was born to a rich family, his skeptics would have speculated that he bought disciples and paid his audience. However, since Christ was born and raised from a poor background, critics have no option than to scramble around for any other unreasonable excuse to use. Meanwhile, whether some people are skeptic or not, Christ's debased and low birthplace was incomparable to his accomplishments. He rose from the manger to become the most prominent figure of all time. His honor has survived decades, centuries, and generations. Christ's fame and the significance of his earthly mission will also survive this earth, and it will last eternally! Hence, the greatest news ever told will remain forever, "Christ came to earth to set the captives free, and whosoever believes in him will not perish but have everlasting life."

Prayer:

Hallelujah Jesus Christ the Son of God came to earth to seek and save lost sinners like me! I thank you Jesus Christ for submitting yourself to the will of God by accepting to be born in the manger. You being the Son of God did not consider it an insult to be born in a stinking and dirty place - all for the sake of saving my soul! I thank you for accomplishing my salvation work on the cross and you declared "It is finished!" Thanks for I have been redeemed in the blood of the lamb, and my name has been written in the book of life. The crown of righteousness is now waiting for me in heaven, and I will be with you in heaven eternally! Hallelujah, Jesus Christ reigns forever more!

Amen.

« DAY 167 »

God's Measure Of Grace Has Limit, And The Limit Cannot Be Predicted

Focus Passage: Deuteronomy 3, 4

Israelites provoked Moses and caused him to sin against God, which made him missed an opportunity of entering the Promised Land. Moses lamented over his failure and said,

> *"...And I besought the Lord at that time, saying, O Lord God, thou hast begun to shew thy servant thy greatness, and thy mighty hand: for what God is there in heaven or in earth, that can do according to thy works, and according to thy might? I pray thee, let me go over, and see the good land that is beyond Jordan, that goodly mountain, and Lebanon. But the Lord was wroth with me for your sakes, and would not hear me: and the Lord said unto me, Let it suffice thee; speak no more unto me of this matter. Get thee up into the top of Pisgah, and lift up thine eyes westward, and northward, and southward, and eastward, and behold it with thine eyes: for thou shalt not go over this Jordan. But charge Joshua, and encourage him, and strengthen him: for he shall go over before this people, and he shall cause them to inherit the land which thou shalt see..." (Deuteronomy 3:23-29 KJV)*

Lesson:

God rejected Moses' request to pardon his sin and allow him to enter the Promised Land – despite the fact that he was God's best friend. In fact, God told Moses emphatically to stop asking for a pardon for his offense. However, believers should consider a typical lesson to learn from Deuteronomy Chapter 3. We must understand that God's measure of grace has limit, and the limit cannot be predicted. It is wrong for any Christian to assume he could second-guess God on any decision. Also, it is wrong for any Christian to willingly commit a sin with the hope of asking for forgiveness later. God frowns at a premeditated sin, and he will not lightly esteem anyone who attempts to take him for granted. Truly, Jehovah is God of mercy that forgives sins, but he knows how to award measurable consequences. Since he is the one and only perfect judge who searches hearts and weighs actions, he may decide to rain judgment of fire when a person had presumed a pardon for his/her sins.

Prayer:

Dear God, please do not let me abuse your grace, and don't let me take you for granted. Help to carefully observe your laws and serve you well at all times. Let me cherish our Father-to-son/daughter relationship by living a holy and acceptable life before you! Let your Holy Spirit gravitate my feet within your temple so that I can prosper throughout the days of my life. For in the name of Jesus Christ I make my requests.

Amen.

« DAY 168 »

Christians Must Learn From Jesus Christ Who Refused To Be Afraid But Preached Gospel At All Cost

Focus Passage: Luke 2:25-52

Jesus Christ being a miracle child, was not an easy child to raise by any regular parent like Mary and Joseph. Unlike every other child, Jesus grew faster in maturity to the confusion of his parents. He started teaching adults at the age of twelve when he should have stayed home to learn from his parents. At a point, Jesus escaped from his parents' shelter to sit in the temple and teach elders; he fearlessly confronted the elders and taught them the mysteries of God's kingdom. Meanwhile, while Jesus was busy teaching in the temple, his parents were also busy searching for him because they thought he was missing. When Mary and Joseph finally located him and challenged his decision, Jesus could only respond,

> *"Why did you seek me? Did you not know that I must be about my Father's business?"* **(Luke 2:49).**

Lesson:
Jesus Christ is the perfect example that all Christians must follow to adequately serve God. All believers are expected to seriously engage in God's business without fear. Also, we must serve God without seeking for any proper timing. Our main focus must be to satisfy God by all means. Again, believers should not give excuse but preach gospel at all times. Also, we must not give-in to pressure or persecutions; we must not rationalize, but we must preach gospel - whether the action is considered sensible or not. God will be pleased to see us breaking out of routines to propagate his gospel for the sake of populating his kingdom.

Prayer:
Dear God, I understand that your Son Jesus Christ has laid a perfect example for me to follow to populate your kingdom. Please help me to be committed to the propagation of your gospel; also help me to desist from citing excuse for not preaching gospel. Empower me to share the truth of your word whether the time is convenient or not. Anoint me with your Holy Spirit to keep sharing your good news so that your kingdom can be populated. Let me faithfully serve you unto the end so that I can be honored in your kingdom. For in the name of Jesus Christ I make my requests.

Amen.

« DAY 169 »

God Desires His Children To Keep Memory Of His Goodness In Their Lives

Focus Passage: Deuteronomy 5, 6, 7

Moses gave a farewell speech to Israelites prior to his death, and he challenged them to not forget their encounters with God in the wilderness. Israelites must remember the time that God invited them for a dialogue on the mountain, and they were terrified because they couldn't withstand his smoke and fire. Moses quoted Israelites promise at the time. Israelites leaders said,

> "*Surely the Lord our God has shown us His glory and His greatness, and we have heard His voice from the midst of the fire. We have seen this day that God speaks with man; yet he still lives*" **(Deuteronomy 5:24).**

Lesson:

God desires his children to keep the memory of his goodness in their lives. We are to reference his past goodness in our lives and glorify his name. Also, the past memory of God's demonstration of power should become a motivating factor to keep trusting him for our future expectations. Jehovah who has been good to us in time past will not abandon us in the present time. He will help us overcome whatever challenge that may come our way, and help us have victory. Meanwhile, Satan does not want God's children to reflect on any past blessing; all he wants is to keep us focusing on any problem we may have so that we can remain sad. However, believers must be sensitive in every situation to focus on the positive side - which is God. That is, we must focus on God who can help us like previous time. Surely, Jehovah will not disappoint us, but he will keep us afloat in every situation to have astounding victory to the glory of his name.

Prayer:

Dear God, please help me to focus on your goodness in my life; do not let me focus on my problems! Let my spirit be lifted up in every situation to envisage my victory that will come from you. Do not let me give devil a chance to manipulate me into focusing on my problem and be depressed. Rather, let my faith be resolute in you at all times, so that I can have victory that will put devil to shame and also glorify your Name! For in the name of Jesus Christ I make my requests.

Amen.

« DAY 170 »

Holy Spirit Is A Must-Have And An Essential Resource To Qualify Anyone For God's Kingdom

Focus Passage: Luke 3

John Baptized people with water, and also referenced Jesus Christ as a better baptizer who would come to baptize people with the Holy Spirit. John said,

> "I indeed baptize you with water; but One mightier than I is coming, whose sandal strap I am not worthy to lose. He will baptize you with the Holy Spirit and fire. His winnowing fan is in His hand, and He will thoroughly clean out His threshing floor, and gather the wheat into His barn; but the chaff He will burn with unquenchable fire" **(Luke 3:16-17)**.

Lesson:
Both water baptism and Holy Spirit baptisms are important to Christians. However, the baptism of the Holy Spirit is the mostly essential "resource" to have for entering God's kingdom. The functions of the Holy Spirit are endless. His functions range from spirit realm to physical realm. For example, Holy Spirit empowers Christians to live above sin and satisfy God with holiness. He also serves as a comforter for believers; he raises their hope to keep trusting God during difficult time. Not only that, the Spirit of God also gives believers affirmation that they belong to God. It is absolutely impossible for any believer to faithfully serve God and satisfy his desire without the Holy Spirit, since ordinary flesh cannot please God. Hence, every Christian should consider baptism of the Holy Spirit a must-have resource, since he is essential for qualifying anyone for God's kingdom.

Prayer:
Dear God, please baptize me with your Holy Spirit so that I can live acceptable life before you on earth, and also qualify for your eternal kingdom. I understand it is impossible for anyone to satisfy you without the Holy Spirit; therefore please baptize me with him! Let him give me strength to keep living acceptable life before you until you return to rapture me to your eternal kingdom. For in the name of Jesus Christ I make my requests.

Amen.

« DAY 171 »

God Sometimes Allow His Children To Pass Through Difficult Situations For The Purpose Of Strengthening Their Faith

Focus Passage: Deuteronomy 8,9,10

Moses revealed God's motive of making Israelites to travel through a long wilderness journey to the Promised Land, rather than leading them through a bypass route that could have save them time and energy. Moses said,

> *"Remember how the Lord your God led you all the way in the wilderness these forty years, to humble and test you in order to know what was in your heart, whether or not you would keep his commands. He humbled you, causing you to hunger and then feeding you with manna, which neither you nor your ancestors had known, to teach you that man does not live on bread alone but on every word that comes from the mouth of the Lord" (Deuteronomy 8:2-3 NIV).*

Lesson:

God's ways are not mostly our ways, and he may allow his children to pass through some tough situations for the purpose of strengthening their faith. Once every lesson is learnt, Jehovah knows how to turn a difficult situation to a simple one. He knows how to utilize his children's past experience for their benefits, and for glorifying his name. For example, God allowed Israelites to travel through the wilderness to teach them unforgettable lessons of life. The children of God passed through jungles to survive hash weather conditions before they eventually reached their Promised Land. The wilderness experience that Israelites had became their lifetime testimony - which they passed down to their descending generations. Meanwhile, every believer today will also have his/her wilderness experience at one point or the other; the experience will transform into strengthening of faith and glorifying God!

Prayer:

Dear God, please teach me how to trust you during difficult situation. Help me to endure whatever wilderness experience that may come my way, and help me to have victory. Please give me strong faith that will honor you during adversity! As I wait and trust, let my trials transform into testimony so that I can shout the shout of victory and sing songs of praises to your holy name. Please do these things and many more! For in the name of Jesus Christ I make my requests.

Amen.

« DAY 172 »

Children Of God Must Ensure Not To Fear Devil Under Whatever Condition

Focus Passage: Luke 4:1-30

Satan tested Jesus Christ with food immediately after he concluded his 40 days of marathon prayer and fasting. The enemy attempted to trap the Messiah with food since he knew he was hungry and tired. Meanwhile, Satan's ultimate goal was not to subject Jesus to his voice command only, but he also aimed at luring him into worldly cares. The scripture revealed devil's plot, and how Jesus overcame him,

> *"And Jesus being full of the Holy Ghost returned from Jordan, and was led by the Spirit into the wilderness, Being forty days tempted of the devil. And in those days he did eat nothing: and when they were ended, he afterward hungered. And the devil said unto him, If thou be the Son of God, command this stone that it be made bread. And Jesus answered him, saying, It is written, That man shall not live by bread alone, but by every word of God. And the devil, taking him up into an high mountain, shewed unto him all the kingdoms of the world in a moment of time. And the devil said unto him, All this power will I give thee, and the glory of them: for that is delivered unto me; and to whomsoever I will I give it. If thou therefore wilt worship me, all shall be thine. And Jesus answered and said unto him, Get thee behind me, Satan: for it is written, Thou shalt worship the Lord thy God, and him only shalt thou serve. And he brought him to Jerusalem, and set him on a pinnacle of the temple, and said unto him, If thou be the Son of God, cast thyself down from hence: For it is written, He shall give his angels charge over thee, to keep thee: And in their hands they shall bear thee up, lest at any time thou dash thy foot against a stone. And Jesus answering said unto him, It is said, Thou shalt not tempt the Lord thy God"* **(Luke 4:1-12 KJV).**

Lesson:

Children of God have the unbeatable Spirit of God residing in them, and they must not fear devil under whatever condition. Believers are to use the authority of the name of Jesus Christ to rebuke devil and make him flee. Truly, Satan will flee from us if we stand our grounds as true children of God! The enemy cannot withstand the authority residing in the name of Jesus Christ, and he has no choice than to tremble and flee! In fact, the scripture emphasized the importance of Jesus' authority as written, *"Therefore God also has highly exalted Him and given Him the name which is above every name, that at the name of Jesus every knee should bow, of those in heaven, and of those on earth, and of those under the earth, and that every tongue should confess that Jesus Christ is Lord, to the glory of God the Father"* **(Philippians 2:9-11).**

Prayer:

I command Satan to get lost from me in the name of Jesus Christ! I rebuke the enemy, and I command all his works to become futile in my life. I command Satan to get lost from both the physical and spiritual aspects of my life. I destroy his works in my family, health, career, finance, and materials. Through the authority in the name of Jesus Christ, I declare myself an overcomer, for I triumph in every situation to live peaceably on earth and glorify the name of God! For in the name of Jesus Christ I have exercised my authority. Amen.

« DAY 173 »

Christians Serve God Of The Bible; He Will Perform Miracles In Their Lives Also

Focus Passage: Deuteronomy 11, 12, 13

God enlightened Israelites not to mistake Egypt for Canaan Land (the Promised Land), since the two countries were incomparable in values. Egypt symbolized Israelites captivity, but Canaan would only symbolize their freedom. God said,

> *"For the land which you go to possess is not like the land of Egypt from which you have come, where you sowed your seed and watered it by foot, as a vegetable garden; but the land which you cross over to possess is a land of hills and valleys, which drinks water from the rain of heaven, a land for which the Lord your God cares; the eyes of the Lord your God are always on it, from the beginning of the year to the very end of the year"* **(Deuteronomy 11:10-12).**

Lesson:
Christians serve the same God that led Israelites out of Egypt to the Promised Land. The same God of the Old Testament time is still the same one that we serve today; he will commit to his promises and fulfill them in our lives. Nothing whatsoever will be able to limit God's power in believers' lives; he will surely materialize his promises. Therefore, those who call on God should congratulate themselves, since they will not be let down under whatever circumstance. God's sons and daughters will enjoy his safety, grace, and goodness. Their faces will shine for they will forget their past pains to celebrate God's faithfulness in their lives.

Prayer:
Dear God, please take me to the Promised Land that you have preserved for me. I understand you will not fail your promises, but keep and materialize them. Please enable me to maintain good relationship with you so that I can live long to enjoy your benefits and praise your holy name. For in the name of Jesus Christ I make my requests.

Amen.

« DAY 174 »

People Who Have Resolute Faith In God Will Have Their Faces Shine

Focus Passage: Luke 4:31-44

Jesus Christ taught people about the kingdom of God, and performed multiple miracles in one day. Scriptures reported that he cast out demons from those possessed; healed Peter's mother-in-law, and also performed other miracles. It is written,

> *"And came down to Capernaum, a city of Galilee, and taught them on the sabbath days. And they were astonished at his doctrine: for his word was with power. And in the synagogue there was a man, which had a spirit of an unclean devil, and cried out with a loud voice, Saying, Let us alone; what have we to do with thee, thou Jesus of Nazareth? art thou come to destroy us? I know thee who thou art; the Holy One of God. And Jesus rebuked him, saying, Hold thy peace, and come out of him. And when the devil had thrown him in the midst, he came out of him, and hurt him not. And they were all amazed, and spake among themselves, saying, What a word is this! for with authority and power he commandeth the unclean spirits, and they come out. And the fame of him went out into every place of the country round about. And he arose out of the synagogue, and entered into Simon's house. And Simon's wife's mother was taken with a great fever; and they besought him for her. And he stood over her, and rebuked the fever; and it left her: and immediately she arose and ministered unto them. Now when the sun was setting, all they that had any sick with divers diseases brought them unto him; and he laid his hands on every one of them, and healed them. And devils also came out of many, crying out, and saying, Thou art Christ the Son of God. And he rebuking them suffered them not to speak: for they knew that he was Christ"* **(Luke 4:31-41 KJV).**

Lesson:
Jesus Christ is a miracle-working God; he is alive, and he has strong capability to connect with people's needs. Jesus has history of healing the sick, raising the dead, blessing the poor, and performing other wonders. The Son of God has helped people in time past; he is still alive, and he will help again! Christ is still in the business of helping people today. In fact, there is no impossibility with him! People who have expressed their faith in Jesus Christ and accepted him as their Savior will have their expectations met, and their faces will shine in all situations. Let someone who believes shout "Hallelujah!"

Prayer:
I believe in the power of Jesus Christ to overcome all my challenges. I invoke the power of Jesus Christ to overcome my poverty, sickness, family crisis, spiritual challenges, sin, and others. I triumph over every problem of life by the authority in the name of Jesus Christ – and I declare myself a victor. My victory is certain in Jesus Christ forever!

Amen.

« DAY 175 »

God Instituted Principle Of Paying Tithe To Test Believers' Faithfulness

Focus Passage: Deuteronomy 14, 15, 16

God instructed Israelites to understand the principle of paying tithes and said,

> *"You shall truly tithe all the increase of your grain that the field produces year by year"* **(Deuteronomy 14:22).** *God further simplified the principle and stated his children could convert their material tithe into currency, and pay them to him. He said, "But if the journey is too long for you, so that you are not able to carry the tithe, or if the place where the Lord your God chooses to put His name is too far from you, when the Lord your God has blessed you, then you shall exchange it for money, take the money in your hand, and go to the place which the Lord your God chooses"* **(Deuteronomy 14:24-25).**

Lesson:
God required his children to duly pay their tithes to him. They must consider the requirement as a commandment and comply with it. However, believers must understand that our God is not poor, and he does not need our gifts to survive. The basis of his tithe requirement is to test our faithfulness. That is, Jehovah wants to test us and see if we can depend on him for our provision and sustenance after we have paid our tithe. He wants to see if we can share resources and trust him for sustenance at the same time. Also, the Creator wants to check if we are greedy and obsessive of our wealth. Meanwhile, God who established tithing rule will bless whoever complies with it. He will reciprocate every tithe and offering that is presented to him with multiple blessings in return. Hence, a person who adequately gives ten percent (10%) of his income to God will not lack everyday of his/her life.

Prayer:
Dear God, please make me an obedient child who duly pays my tithe unto you. I don't want to be obsessed with money or material wealth, but I want to pay your required tithes, and also add some liberal offerings to it. I want to be consistent in obeying the rule of tithing so that I can prosper. Please reciprocate my faithfulness with your multiple benefits on earth, and let me live in your abundant riches. Also, let my charity efforts be rewarded in heaven. For in the name of Jesus Christ I make my requests.

Amen.

« DAY 176 »

Christians Must Be Sensitive In The Holy Spirit To Enjoy God's Full Benefits

Focus Passage: Luke 5:1-16

Jesus Christ borrowed Peter's boat to preach gospel, and he made him rich afterward. Peter who had suffered scorching sun and terrible sea waves without catching a fish suddenly became rich after he had an encounter with Jesus. The Messiah commanded him to launch his net into the sea to catch fish. Peter was initially reluctant but later obeyed, and his action brought him an unexpected result. The scenario is reported in the scripture, Peter said,

> *"Simon answered, "Master, we've worked hard all night and haven't caught anything. But because you say so, I will let down the nets." When they had done so, they caught such a large number of fish that their nets began to break. So they signaled their partners in the other boat to come and help them, and they came and filled both boats so full that they began to sink"* **(Luke 5:5-7 NIV)**.

Lesson:

God speaks in different ways, and he uses various media to pass his messages across to his children. Unfortunately, not every Christian is sensitive enough to understand God's leading. Also, not all who understand his leading obey. However, those who understand God's leading and obey are bound to prosper on earth. One major reasons while believers experience communication gap with God is because they are too busy to give him his due attention. Some Christians are busy focusing on other things when God is instructing; therefore, they miss opportunity of making appropriate decisions. The party that hears God and fail to obey him are those who have rigid mindset. They have a preconceived notion; therefore, their decisions are either erratic or inadequate. Meanwhile, it takes flexibility in the Holy Spirit for any Christian to prosper on earth. The scripture stated, *"For as many as are led by the Spirit of God, these are sons of God"* **(Romans 8:14)**. Jesus also said, *"The wind blows where it wishes, and you hear the sound of it, but cannot tell where it comes from and where it goes. So is everyone who is born of the Spirit"* **(John 3:8)**.

Prayer:

Dear God, please help me to follow the leadership of your Holy Spirit at all times so that I can prosper in the land of the living. I understand no one can satisfy you in flesh, and it takes the leadership of your divine Holy Spirit to make appropriate decisions. Therefore, please empower me with the Holy Spirit! Let him guide me in all my ways to meet your expectations so that I can prosper throughout the days of my life, and also be qualified for your kingdom. For in the name of Jesus Christ I make my requests.

Amen.

« DAY 177 »

A Christian Who Leads In Any Capacity Is Expected To Represent God Well With Godly Fear

Focus Passage: Deuteronomy 17, 18, 19

God established a standard for any Israelites' future king; he must not imitate any other ruler, but strictly follow God's commandments only. God said,

> *"When thou art come unto the land which the Lord thy God giveth thee, and shalt possess it, and shalt dwell therein, and shalt say, I will set a king over me, like as all the nations that are about me; Thou shalt in any wise set him king over thee, whom the Lord thy God shall choose: one from among thy brethren shalt thou set king over thee: thou mayest not set a stranger over thee, which is not thy brother. But he shall not multiply horses to himself, nor cause the people to return to Egypt, to the end that he should multiply horses: forasmuch as the Lord hath said unto you, Ye shall henceforth return no more that way. Neither shall he multiply wives to himself, that his heart turn not away: neither shall he greatly multiply to himself silver and gold. And it shall be, when he sitteth upon the throne of his kingdom, that he shall write him a copy of this law in a book out of that which is before the priests the Levites"* **(Deuteronomy 17:14-18 KJV).**

Lesson:
Any Christian who leads in any capacity is expected to operate in God's fear and lead by example. Whether a position is based on appointment or election, every Christian leader is expected to exercise godly fear and manage the position well. No leader who expects God's blessing should be unfair or be partial in his/her operations. In other words, no godly leader should be bias or practice preferential treatment. God who is the greatest leader of all people sees everything that any leader does; he will appropriately measure performances and award his perfect judgment on every leader.

Prayer:
Dear God, please make me a God-fearing leader who leads to honor you. Help me to lead by example; do not let me be bias, and neither let me exercise partial judgment. Let my operations be in compliance with your word, so that your name can be honored among people. Help me to operate with grace to the honor of your name! For in the name of Jesus Christ I made my requests.

Amen.

« DAY 178 »

Hypocritical Christians Are Nothing But Pharisees!

Focus Passage: Luke 5:17-39

The Pharisees criticized Jesus Christ for attending a party that was organized by Matthew the chief tax collector. Everyone - including Jesus and Matthew's colleagues was enjoying the moment, but the Pharisees showed up to express their rage against Jesus. The Pharisees labeled Jesus an immoral teacher who spends time with sinners. However, Jesus corrected the Pharisees and said,

> *"Those who are well have no need of a physician, but those who are sick. I have not come to call the righteous, but sinners, to repentance." **(Luke 5:31-32)**.*

Lesson:
Inconsistent Christians could be labeled as Pharisees, since Jesus' era Pharisees were not consistent with God. "Pharisee Christians" shifts their focus from serving God to something else, and they always find an excuse to justify their action. For examples, Pharisee Christians worship their church denomination, and some worship their spiritual leaders instead of worshipping the true God of heaven. Also, some Pharisees Christians come up with hand-made rules to make God's laws become stricter with the hope the action will make them receive better positions in heaven. In addition, Pharisee Christians elevate their customized practices and are quick to condemn other Christian sects who do not comply with them. However, God expects the Pharisee Christians to change their beliefs and mode of operations in order to consider them "justified" in his presence. God requires that all people - whether they claim Christianity or not - to become genuinely born-again so that they can be acceptable to his kingdom. Only those who follow bible standard and faithfully serve God will be acceptable to heaven on the last day.

Prayer:
Dear God, please make me a true Christian who focuses on the bible principles to appease you. Please save me from self-righteous acts that cannot lead anywhere near your kingdom! Give me the spirit of humility to focus on improving my relationship with you, and not to get busy in condemning others! Let me be less critical of others, but enable me with grace to focus on activities and actions that will motivate people into moving closer to you. Let my operations result into populating your kingdom, and not to depopulate it. After my earthly race is over, please count me worthy to enter your kingdom to hear your favorable acceptance statement, "Weldon and welcome my good servant." For in the name of Jesus Christ I make my requests.

Amen.

« DAY 179 »

Christians Are To Reference Their Past Successes To Motivate Them Into Receiving Future Benefits

Focus Passage: Deuteronomy 20, 21, 22

God asked Israelites to demonstrate courage and maintain their confidence in him during war, even when their enemies outnumber them. The people must reference their past experience of God's faithfulness to boost their faith to receive future victory. The same God who has helped them in time past is still alive to demonstrate similar strength again. God said to Israelites,

> *"When you go out to battle against your enemies, and see horses and chariots and people more numerous than you, do not be afraid of them; for the Lord your God is with you, who brought you up from the land of Egypt"* **(Deuteronomy 20:1)**

Lesson:
Christians are to always have confident in God and believe in his power of safety and provision. No matter the gravity and intensity of a situation, Jehovah will turn it around for the benefit of his children. He is well and alive to make difficult situation become an easy one! Meanwhile, Satan may make some challenges appear more difficult than they are to test people into compromising their faith in God. Believers should not yield to the enemy's temptation; we must always remember that God has controlling power over all situations. He cares, and he will ensure difficult situation does linger beyond what we can handle. He will make problem subside to pave way for our deliverance, so that they can have victory and testify to the goodness of his name.

Prayer:
Dear God, I believe you are God of miracle, and you will surely help me to overcome my problems. Please help me to continue to maintain my confidence in you until I have my expected victory. Let my faith remain resolute in you during adversity to put devil to shame and glorify your name! When things become positively turn around to my advantage, let me return with joy to testify to your goodness in the assembly of your people. For in the name of Jesus Christ I make my requests.

Amen.

« DAY 180 »

Believers Must Explore Jesus' Success Examples To Prevail Over Satan

Focus Passage: Luke 6:1-26

The Pharisees were bitter critics of Jesus Christ, and they disguised under their religion to express their rage against him. The critics were eager to stalk Jesus and attempted to trick him with their questions with hope they might find any legitimate reason to trap him. The scripture reported some of Pharisees' actions,

> *"Now it happened on the second Sabbath after the first that He (Jesus) went through the grainfields. And His disciples plucked the heads of grain and ate them, rubbing them in their hands. And some of the Pharisees said to them, "Why are you doing what is not lawful to do on the Sabbath?" The scripture also reported, "Now it happened on another Sabbath, also, that He entered the synagogue and taught. And a man was there whose right hand was withered. So the scribes and Pharisees watched Him closely, whether He would heal on the Sabbath, that they might find an accusation against Him"* **(Luke 6:6-7) (Luke 6:1-2).**

Lesson:

Satan and his agents are forces of darkness that are prone to attacking children of light – which are Christians. The enemies are quick to seek loopholes with the hope of stealing believers' confidence and make them lose their salvation **(John 10:10)**. The enemy would attempt to castigate believers by all possible means by throwing every available stone at them. Believers must be spiritually sensitive (be watchful) through bible study with prayer and fasting to counteract and overcome the enemy. They must yield to the leadership of the Holy Spirit to prevail in all situations. Also, Christians must endeavor to follow Jesus' examples to appropriately react during temptations. When Satan instigated the Pharisees to waylay Jesus, he reacted as follows:

- He ignored the Pharisees – *Believers should largely ignore their critics.*
- He remained persistent in God's business – *Believers should never stop engaging in God's work.*
- He often withdrew unto mountain to pray – *Believers must constantly pray for renewal of strength.*
- He changed locations to avoid enemies' distractions – *Believers should diversify in ministry to outsmart their enemies.*

Prayer:

Dear God, please give me strength to overcome Satan and live triumphant life on earth to the glorification of your holy name! Help me not to pay attention to devil's manipulations, but be alert in the Holy Spirit to remain immovable in faith. Also, help me to maintain consistent lifestyle of prayer and fasting so that I can have enough strength to live triumphant life on earth, and be worthy of your eternal kingdom. Let me finish my race well to hear your favorable voice "Weldon and welcome my good servant!" For in the name of Jesus Christ I make my requests.
Amen.

« DAY 181 »

God Expects His Children To Timely Fulfill Their Pledges To Receive His Blessings
Focus Passage: Deuteronomy 23, 24, 25

God required Israelites to honor and redeem their pledges before him in timely manner to receive his blessings. God promised to force the people into compliance with their promises if they fail to appropriately redeem them. Basically, God insisted on Israelites pledges as his portion of entitlement that must not be compromised. God said,

> *"If you make a vow to the Lord your God, do not be slow to pay it, for the Lord your God will certainly demand it of you and you will be guilty of sin. But if you refrain from making a vow, you will not be guilty. Whatever your lips utter you must be sure to do, because you made your vow freely to the Lord your God with your own mouth"* **(Deuteronomy 23:21-23 NIV).**

Lesson:
God appreciates redemption of pledges, and he expects his children to return with appreciable hearts to redeem their pledges before him. People who have promised God for one thing or the other during moments of joy and/or sorrow should not hesitate to honor their promises. It is unfortunate that some believers underrate the importance of their promises made before God. They are quick to say anything they want to receive God's blessing and deliverance, however they do not consider the gravity of the promises that are attached with their requests. Meanwhile, God does not have faulty memory, and he won't forget whatever vows his children have made before him. Some consequences are attached with failed promises; it could cause a believer to either experience delay blessing, or completely lose the blessing! Meanwhile, God will bless any of his children that honor his/her pledges and redeem them in timely fashion. Those individuals will always have testimony of God's goodness to share with others.

Prayer:
Dear God, please make me a person of integrity who honors his/her pledges before you. Let me have good attitude of honoring my pledges in timely fashion also. Let my good attitude of appropriately redeeming pledges open door of opportunity for me so that I can be more blessed. Please forgive my sin of empty promises; let me start to make necessary restitution to activate my passive blessings. Please make me a beacon of praise and honor to your holy name from now on and always. For in the name of Jesus Christ I make my requests.

Amen.

« DAY 182 »

A Person Who Aims God's Kingdom Must Be Ready To Go Out Of His Or Her Ways To Satisfy God

Focus Passage: Luke 6:27-49

Jesus Christ taught his disciples some fundamental truth about God's kingdom that other religion teachers of his time were afraid to confront. The teachings are uncomfortable and violate humans' conventional wisdom, but they are required to be observed for anyone to inherit God's kingdom. Jesus instructed his disciples and said:

1. Bless those who curse you **(Luke 6:28)**
2. Give to everyone who asks you something **(Luke 6:30)**
3. Do as you want other people to do to you **(Luke 6:31)**
4. Love your enemies **(Luke 6:35)**
5. Do not judge others **(Luke 6:37)**
6. Give abundant charity to other people **(Luke 6:38)**

Lesson:
The teachings of Jesus Christ remain consistent throughout the scriptures, and they are fundamental principles of God that must be observed to inherit his kingdom. Those requirements can be summarized as "holiness standard of God," and no one can comply with them without the help of the Holy Spirit. Therefore, believers are encouraged to daily seek God and ask for the divine guidance of his Spirit (Holy Spirit) to comply with them. People that operate under guidance of the Holy Spirit will prosper in this life, and they will also make it to God's kingdom!

Prayer:
Dear Jesus Christ, please help me to run my Christian race with seriousness, so that I can qualify for your eternal kingdom. I don't want to waste time by living a compromised lifestyle that won't earn me your kingdom! My prayer is to comply with your standard of righteousness both in speech and practice so that I can remain qualified. Please guide me through your Holy Spirit to meet your expectations so that I can be counted among people that will forever rejoice in your presence in heaven. For in the name of Jesus Christ I make my requests.

Amen.

« DAY 183 »

The Rule Of Tithe Established In The Bible Is Mandated For All Christians

Focus Passage: Deuteronomy 26, 27:

God emphasized importance of tithe payment, and he charged Israelites to observe the laws once they reach the Promised Land. God said,

> *"When you have finished laying aside all the tithe of your increase in the third year—the year of tithing—and have given it to the Levite, the stranger, the fatherless, and the widow, so that they may eat within your gates and be filled, then you shall say before the Lord your God: 'I have removed the holy tithe from my house, and also have given them to the Levite, the stranger, the fatherless, and the widow, according to all Your commandments which You have commanded me; I have not transgressed Your commandments, nor have I forgotten them'"* **(Deuteronomy 26:12-13).**

Lesson:

God's tithing rule established for Israelites during Old Testament remains relevant during New Testament. That is, the present days Christians are required to observe the rule. The rule is non negotiable; God claims ownership of ten percent (10%) of every income his children earn. This means whoever fails to appropriately pay his/her tithes is technically stealing from God, and such person will incur some punishments in return. The consequences which may include delayed blessings and missed opportunity. Meanwhile, people who adequately observe God's rule of tithing will not live in lack. The person may not be notable as a millionaire, but he or she will live a fulfilled life on earth.

Prayer:

Dear God, please help me to obey your rule of tithe payment as required in the scriptures so that I can prosper. Forgive my past failures, and let me start to act faithfully and trust you for my prosperity. Let my obedience open doors of opportunity for me so that I can prosper in this very earth before I meet you in heaven. For in the name of Jesus Christ I make my requests.

Amen.

« DAY 184 »

Christians Must Learn From Jesus Christ To Minister To Both Physical And Spiritual Needs Of People

Focus Passage: Luke 7:1-30

Jesus Christ showed compassion on a widow whose only son had died, and he brought him back to life. The scripture reported,

> *"And when He (Jesus) came near the gate of the city, behold, a dead man was being carried out, the only son of his mother; and she was a widow. And a large crowd from the city was with her. When the Lord saw her, He had compassion on her and said to her, "Do not weep." Then He came and touched the open coffin, and those who carried him stood still. And He said, "Young man, I say to you, arise." So he who was dead sat up and began to speak. And He presented him to his mother" (Luke 7:12-15).*

Lesson:

Jesus Christ who is the Savior and the spiritual mentor for all Christians did not focus his earthly ministry on people's spiritual needs only. He attended to people's physical needs also. Christ showed compassion on people, and helped them overcome their natural challenges. For example, Christ multiplied few breads and fishes to feed thousands of people because he had compassion on them (Mark 6:30-44). Also, he raised a dead man to life because he had compassion on his mother (Luke 7:12-15). Christians must follow Jesus' examples to help needy people as well. Our spiritual exercise must include feeding hungry people; clothing naked people, and assisting the orphans. The list of the charitable activities that we can conduct is endless. Our positive contributions to people's lives will help gospel spread further, which of course will motivate more people towards God's kingdom.

Prayer:

Dear Jesus Christ, please give me a charitable heart that cares for people's needs. Help me to be your true ambassador by loving others. Let me contribute my quota of support for those who are in need, and let my activities motivate them into moving closer to receive your free offer of salvation. Again, please let your light shine through me so that your gospel can prosper in people's lives! For in the name of Jesus Christ I make my requests.

Amen.

« DAY 185 »

All People Are To Comply With God's Irrevocable Standard Of Holiness To Receive His Blessings

Focus Passage: Deuteronomy 28, 29

God gave Israelites his commandments with promises of blessing if they comply. He also itemized the punishments that are attached with disobedience to his laws. The Creator used 14 verses of Deuteronomy Chapter 28 to itemize the blessings that associated with obedience to his laws; he used the remaining 54 verses of the chapter to itemize the severe punishments that Israelites would receive if they disobey him. God itemize Israelites' rewards of obedience and said,

> *"And it shall come to pass, if thou shalt hearken diligently unto the voice of the Lord thy God, to observe and to do all his commandments which I command thee this day, that the Lord thy God will set thee on high above all nations of the earth: And all these blessings shall come on thee...Blessed shalt thou be in the city, and blessed shalt thou be in the field. Blessed shall be the fruit of thy body, and the fruit of thy ground, and the fruit of thy cattle, the increase of thy kine, and the flocks of thy sheep. Blessed shall be thy basket and thy store. Blessed shalt thou be when thou comest in, and blessed shalt thou be when thou goest out. The Lord shall cause thine enemies that rise up against thee to be smitten before thy face: they shall come out against thee one way, and flee before thee seven ways"* **(Deuteronomy 28:1-7 KJV).**

God also itemize Israelites' rewards of disobedience and said, *"But it shall come to pass, if thou wilt not hearken unto the voice of the Lord thy God, to observe to do all his commandments and his statutes which I command thee this day; that all these curses shall come upon the... Cursed shalt thou be when thou comest in, and cursed shalt thou be when thou goest out. The Lord shall send upon thee cursing, vexation, and rebuke, in all that thou settest thine hand unto for to do, until thou be destroyed, and until thou perish quickly; because of the wickedness of thy doings, whereby thou hast forsaken me"* **(Deuteronomy 28:15-20 KJV).**

Lesson:
God has irrevocable standard of righteousness that he uses to relate with his children. Besides his universal grace for humanity, his nature cannot bless anyone that goes against his will. His automatic blessing will abide with people that serve him with integrity and honor; he will make their faces radiate beauty of his goodness. In contrast, some automatic limitations will apply to people that are resistant to God's laws. Jehovah will keep a distance from them until they can appease him with compliance to his laws. Hence, a person who expects God's lasting benefits should prioritize holiness by complying with his laws, and serve him with deep devotion.

Prayer:
Dear God, please help me to carefully obey your laws so that I will not sin against you. Empower me to serve you with integrity, and let your divine Holy Spirit guide me to serve you pleasantly so that I can prosper! For in the name of Jesus Christ I make my requests. Amen.

« DAY 186 »

Christians Must Be Spiritually Sensitive And Operate Under Holy Spirit Guidance To Make Good Judgment

Focus Passage: Luke 7:31-50

The Pharisees criticized Jesus Christ for permitting a woman to anoint him with expensive oil. The scripture reported,

> "And one of the Pharisees desired him that he would eat with him. And he went into the Pharisee's house, and sat down to meat. And, behold, a woman in the city, which was a sinner, when she knew that Jesus sat at meat in the Pharisee's house, brought an alabaster box of ointment, And stood at his feet behind him weeping, and began to wash his feet with tears, and did wipe them with the hairs of her head, nd kissed his feet, and anointed them with the ointment. Now when the Pharisee which had bidden him saw it, he spake within himself, saying, This man, if he were a prophet, would have known who and what manner of woman this is that toucheth him: for she is a sinner. And Jesus answering said unto him, Simon, I have somewhat to say unto thee. And he saith, Master, say on. There was a certain creditor which had two debtors: the one owed five hundred pence, and the other fifty. And when they had nothing to pay, he frankly forgave them both. Tell me therefore, which of them will love him most? Simon answered and said, I suppose that he, to whom he forgave most. And he said unto him, Thou hast rightly judged. And he turned to the woman, and said unto Simon, Seest thou this woman? I entered into thine house, thou gavest me no water for my feet: but she hath washed my feet with tears, and wiped them with the hairs of her head. Thou gavest me no kiss: but this woman since the time I came in hath not ceased to kiss my feet. My head with oil thou didst not anoint: but this woman hath anointed my feet with ointment" (Luke 7:36-46 KJV).

Lesson:
People must understand that Christianity is a spiritual religion that is established to satisfy God; it must not be mistaken for any institution that get things done mechanically. Believers must operate under the guidance of the Holy Spirit at all times before we can meet God's expectations. We must be sensitive enough to understand the move of the Holy Spirit, and not base our activities on human understanding only. That is, we cannot attempt to only physically judge matters and expect God to be satisfied! As God's children, our decisions and activities must be carefully considered under the guidance of the Holy Spirit before we carry them out.

Prayer:
Dear God, please help me to be spiritually inclined and not operate in flesh so that I will not make mistakes. Help me to operate under the guidance of your Holy Spirit so that I can prosper! Again, do not let me get carried away with mood and physical circumstances. Help me to critically consider matters under the leadership of the Holy Spirit so that I can prosper always. For in the name of Jesus Christ I make my requests.
Amen.

« DAY 187 »

God Will Accept And Forgive Anyone That Comes To Him With Genuine Repentance

Focus Passage: Deuteronomy 30, 31

God promised to chase Israelites out of the Promised Land and scatter them abroad if they serve Canaanites' idols. Jehovah also gave a conditional statement of blessing and said he would reinstate the people if they repent from their evil practices. God said,

> *"And it shall come to pass, when all these things are come upon thee, the blessing and the curse, which I have set before thee, and thou shalt call them to mind among all the nations, whither the Lord thy God hath driven thee, And shalt return unto the Lord thy God, and shalt obey his voice according to all that I command thee this day, thou and thy children, with all thine heart, and with all thy soul; That then the Lord thy God will turn thy captivity, and have compassion upon thee, and will return and gather thee from all the nations, whither the Lord thy God hath scattered thee. If any of thine be driven out unto the outmost parts of heaven, from thence will the Lord thy God gather thee, and from thence will he fetch thee: And the Lord thy God will bring thee into the land which thy fathers possessed, and thou shalt possess it; and he will do thee good, and multiply thee above thy fathers. And the Lord thy God will circumcise thine heart, and the heart of thy seed, to love the Lord thy God with all thine heart, and with all thy soul, that thou mayest live"* **(Deuteronomy 30:1-6 KJV).**

Lesson:
God is merciful and forgiving; he forgives sins and save sinners. The Creator will forgive anyone who comes to him with a repentant heart, and he will reaffirm his unconditional love with him/her. All people are to take advantage of God's love and return to him to receive his forgiveness and restoration. Anyone who comes to God should do so by confessing his Son Jesus Christ as his/her personal Lord and Savior. The process will make the person become a "Child of God." Whoever takes the step will not only prosper on earth but will also qualify to inherit God's kingdom. Meanwhile, a person who rejects Jesus' offer of salvation until the end will have his/her portion in everlasting lake of fire called Hell Fire – where there shall be everlasting torment.

Prayer:
Dear God, please save my soul from the pit of hell! I declare your Son Jesus Christ as Lord, and accept him as my personal Savior. From now on, my complete life will be devoted to Jesus, and I will serve him for the rest of my life. So help me God! For in the name of Jesus Christ I make my requests.

Amen.

« DAY 188 »

The Authority Of Jesus Christ Has No Restriction; Believers Ought To Utilize It To Their Best Advantage

Focus Passage: Luke 8:1-25

Jesus Christ performed many healing miracles to aid people into believing in the demonstrative power of God. His miracles include familiar healing of the sick and raising the dead. However, Jesus also performed some unfamiliar miracles, which include speaking into wind and storms to alleviate people's problems. An example of Jesus' rare miracles is quoted as follows:

> *"Now it happened, on a certain day, that He got into a boat with His disciples. And He said to them, "Let us cross over to the other side of the lake." And they launched out. But as they sailed He fell asleep. And a windstorm came down on the lake, and they were filling with water, and were in jeopardy. And they came to Him and awoke Him, saying, "Master, Master, we are perishing!" Then He arose and rebuked the wind and the raging of the water. And they ceased, and there was a calm. But He said to them, "Where is your faith?" And they were afraid, and marveled, saying to one another, "Who can this be? For He commands even the winds and water, and they obey Him!"* **(Luke 8:22-25)**.

Lesson:

Jesus Christ has an unchallenged authority that brings all creations to their knees! His authority is forceful, powerful, and undefeatable. The authority invested in Jesus Christ put Satan in disarray and subdues his power. However, the good news is that the Son of God has gracefully shared his unbeatable authority with Christians for their benefits! Christ said, *"Assuredly, I say to you, whatever you bind on earth will be bound in heaven, and whatever you loose on earth will be loosed in heaven"* **(Matthew 18:18)**.

Hence, believers must utilize their heritage in Jesus Christ! We must utilize the authority embedded in the name of Jesus to our advantage. Believers should mention the name of Jesus Christ to overcome whatever crisis may come their way. With faith applied, there shall be no limitation to the amount of success that would be recorded.

Prayer:

I believe in the authority of the name of Jesus Christ. I declare my "Right of Use" of the name of Jesus! Therefore, I proclaim and declare that all satanic influences in my life must collapse! I destroy all devil's strongholds in my life, and I break myself free to enjoy all God's benefits reserved for me. I will enjoy God's beauty and benefits, and I will prosper in the land of the living - Forevermore! For in the name of Jesus Christ I exercise my authority!

Amen.

« DAY 189 »

People Who Faithfully Serve God Will Have Much Benefits To Share With Their Descendants

Focus Passage: Deuteronomy 32, 33, 34

Moses, the servant of God, wrapped-up his leadership duties among Israelites, and he bided them farewell with counseling and prayers. Moses advised Israelites to faithfully walk with God as he called out tribe by tribe to pronounce blessing on them. Moses blessed each Israel's tribe and said,

> "Let Reuben live, and not die, Nor let his men be few." And this he said of Judah: "Hear, Lord, the voice of Judah, and bring him to his people; Let his hands be sufficient for him, and may you be a help against his enemies." And of Levi he said: "Let Your Thummim and Your Urim be with Your holy one, Whom You tested at Massah, And with whom You contended at the waters of Meribah, Who says of his father and mother, 'I have not seen them'; Nor did he acknowledge his brothers, Or know his own children; For they have observed Your word And kept Your covenant... Of Benjamin he said: "The beloved of the Lord shall dwell in safety by Him, Who shelters him all the day long; and he shall dwell between His shoulders." And of Joseph he said: "Blessed of the Lord is his land, With the precious things of heaven, with the dew, And the deep lying beneath, With the precious fruits of the sun, With the precious produce of the months, With the best things of the ancient mountains, With the precious things of the everlasting hills, With the precious things of the earth and its fullness, And the favor of Him who dwelt in the bush. Let the blessing come 'on the head of Joseph, And on the crown of the head of him who was separate from his brothers..." **(Deuteronomy 33:6-29).**

Lesson:
God's blessing will rest and abide with people that faithfully serve God. Their prosperity will outlast them and extend to their descending generations. However, believers must understand that some challenges may still confront them despite God's blessing proclaimed on them. Those challenges will eventually turn around to cooperate with God's plans and yield them more testimonies. Hence, it is wise for anyone to gravitate to God and serve him well since much benefit are bound to follow. In other words, believers ought to intensify their services before God, and unbelievers should seriously consider serving God to receive his tremendous benefits.

Prayer:
Dear God, I understand that your blessing will abide with people that faithfully serve you. You will not forsake your faithful servants, but you will bless them. People who serve you will enjoy your benefits, and their descendants will enjoy benefits also. Therefore, I ask that you give me grace and strength to faithfully serve you throughout the days of my life. Help me to remain committed to your services so that I can forever prosper as your child! For in the name of your Son Jesus Christ I make my requests.
Amen.

« DAY 190 »

Anyone Who Demonstrates Strong Faith In God Will Have His Or Her Expectations Met

Focus Passage: Luke 8:26-56

A woman with 12-year-old sickness decided to violate cultural barrier to touch Jesus' garment to receive her healing, and she was healed instantly. The scripture reported,

> "Now when Jesus returned, a crowd welcomed him, for they were all expecting him. Then a man named Jairus, a synagogue leader, came and fell at Jesus' feet, pleading with him to come to his house because his only daughter, a girl of about twelve, was dying. As Jesus was on his way, the crowds almost crushed him. And a woman was there who had been subject to bleeding for twelve years,[a] but no one could heal her. She came up behind him and touched the edge of his cloak, and immediately her bleeding stopped" (Luke 8:40-44 NIV).

Lesson:
Any sick person that trust God for healing miracle will receive it! Everyone can be an architect of his/her own healing by exercising faith in Jesus Christ. For any miracle to happen, it must have been conceived in faith and be physically demonstrated. Christians are challenged to put their faith into practice to experience signs and wonders in their lives. Believers must confess faith and take steps of faith to experience breakthrough! That is, we must be ready to quote God's promises in the scriptures against any uncomfortable situation that may come our way. Whether sensible or not, a believer must be able to declare God's promises on negative doctor's reports and economic challenges. Testimony is bound to follow declarations of faith that proceed from a child of God!

Prayer:
Dear God, I have learnt that "Faith is the substance of things hoped for, the evidence of things not seen" **(Hebrews 11:1)**; therefore, I ask you to help me to conceive and exercise faith to have my expected victory! Help me to demonstrate steps of faith that will earn me victory over all my challenges. Give me reasons to rejoice and testify to your goodness in the assembly of your people. For in the name of Jesus Christ I demonstrate my authority.

Amen.

« DAY 191 »

A Person That Consistently Studies His Or Her Bible Shall Prosper

Focus Passage: Joshua 1, 2, 3

God appointed Joshua as a new leader for the Israelites, and he encouraged him to carry out his tasks with confidence. The Creator assured Joshua of victory wherever he turns to serve his purpose. God said to Joshua,

> *"Every place that the sole of your foot will tread upon I have given you, as I said to Moses. From the wilderness and this Lebanon as far as the great river, the River Euphrates, all the land of the Hittites, and to the Great Sea toward the going down of the sun, shall be your territory. No man shall be able to stand before you all the days of your life; as I was with Moses, so I will be with you. I will not leave you nor forsake you"* (Joshua 1:3-5).
>
> God also challenged Joshua to maintain consistent relationship with him so that his prosperity can be secured. God said,
>
> *"Only be strong and very courageous, that you may observe to do according to all the law which Moses My servant commanded you; do not turn from it to the right hand or to the left, that you may prosper wherever you go. This Book of the Law shall not depart from your mouth, but you shall meditate in it day and night, that you may observe to do according to all that is written in it. For then you will make your way prosperous, and then you will have good success"* **(Joshua 1:7-9).**

Lesson:
Daily meditation of God's word is the key to achieving lasting success. A person who consistently studies his/her bible to learn more about God will prosper. Bible which is God's "Book of Law" inspires people to develop godly principles that are necessary for inheriting his kingdom. Also, a habit of consistent bible study opens doors of opportunity for people. That is, a person who consistently study his/her bible and apply lessons learnt to his/her life will receive God's automatic blessing. Christians are therefore challenged to make daily bible devotion their constant practice.

Prayer:
Dear God, please help me to consistently study my bible and apply any lesson learn to my life so that I can prosper. Also, give me grace to consistently interact with you in prayers, and through fellowshipping with other brethren. Let my devotions open doors of opportunity for me, and let my face radiate your glory as I enjoy your earthly prosperity – and much more in heaven! For in the name of Jesus Christ I make my requests.

Amen.

« DAY 192 »

Jesus' Authority Has Been Endowed On His Disciples To Have Prosperity

Focus Passage: Luke 9:1-17

Jesus Christ sent out his disciples to preach gospel with accompany authority to perform signs and wonders. The scripture reported,

> *"Then He called His twelve disciples together and gave them power and authority over all demons, and to cure diseases. He sent them to preach the kingdom of God and to heal the sick"* **(Luke 9:1-3).**

Lesson:

Jesus Christ retains the highest authority anyone needs to prosper for God's kingdom, and also to live triumphantly on earth. The magnitude of the power of Jesus Christ is declared in the bible stating, *"Therefore God also has highly exalted Him and given Him the name which is above every name, that at the name of Jesus every knee should bow, of those in heaven, and of those on earth, and of those under the earth, and that every tongue should confess that Jesus Christ is Lord, to the glory of God the Father"* **(Philippians 2:9-11).**
Meanwhile, Jesus - the Son of God - has shared his most valuable authority with his followers (Christians); hence believers can demonstrate God's power in every situation to live better lives and profit for God's kingdom. Every Christian is therefore expected to stand to his/her feet to utilize Christ's invested authority and prosper! Christ has already stated, *"Go therefore and make disciples of all the nations, baptizing them in the name of the Father and of the Son and of the Holy Spirit, teaching them to observe all things that I have commanded you; and lo, I am with you always, even to the end of the age." Amen!* **(Matthew 28:19-20).**

Prayer:

Dear Jesus Christ, what a wonderful privilege to know that I am not an ordinary person since I have become your follower! I understand that you have shared your valuable authority with me to proclaim gospel, and also to prosper on earth. Therefore, I immediately request for strength to stand on my feet to exercise my rights. Give me boldness needed to fearlessly preach undiluted gospel that will promote your kingdom. Let your Holy Spirit empower me to perform signs and wonders that will convict unbelievers and challenge them to become your children. Please bless me as I venture to satisfy your desire on earth! For unto you "Jesus Christ" I tender my requests.

Amen.

« DAY 193 »

Anyone Who Follows God's Leading Can't Lose But Win Every Battle

Focus Passage: Joshua 4, 5, 6

God instructed Israelites to use rare tactic to defeat the City of Jericho that served as an obstacle to their possession of the Promised Land. God asked Israelites to daily march around the fortified wall of Jericho City for six days, and march around it seven times on the seventh day. The people must make a loud noise and blow trumpets at the completion of their seventh march – and they would have victory. God said to Joshua,

> *"See! I have given Jericho into your hand, its king, and the mighty men of valor. You shall march around the city, all you men of war; you shall go all around the city once. This you shall do six days. And seven priests shall bear seven trumpets of rams' horns before the ark. But the seventh day you shall march around the city seven times, and the priests shall blow the trumpets. It shall come to pass, when they make a long blast with the ram's horn, and when you hear the sound of the trumpet, that all the people shall shout with a great shout; then the wall of the city will fall down flat. And the people shall go up every man straight before him"* **(Joshua 6:2-5)**. *Israelites carried out the tactic as instructed, and it worked. The walls of Jericho fell, and they were able to defeat its dwellers* **(Joshua 6:20-21)**

Lesson:

Jehovah is God, and he has power over all things. His ways are not always our ways, and it is difficult to predict him. He can sometimes act against the natural laws to perform miracles for his children. Meanwhile, The Creator expects us (his children) to cooperate with him in whatever miracle the he intends to perform. He expects us to follow his instructions and not question them. Since he sees and knows the end from the beginning, he understands the price at stake as he instructs; he won't lead us beyond his watch! Therefore, believers are expected to trust and obey as he leads – even when his leadership violates our conventional wisdom. Obedience to God's instructions will always yield us his blessing. We are bound to have testimony as we are flexible under his leadership!

Prayer:

Dear God, please help me to be spiritually sensitive and operate under your leadership. Help me to cooperate with your leadership so that I can have record success. Again all I am saying is "Give me grace to follow the leadership of your Holy Spirit so that I can prosper!" Please let it be well with me throughout the days of my life. For in the name of Jesus Christ I make my requests.

Amen.

« DAY 194 »

Anyone Who Expects To Meet God In Heaven Must Have Discipline And Integrity

Focus Passage: Luke 9:18-36

Jesus Christ explained the need of disciplined to his disciples as the basis of inheriting God's kingdom. Jesus said,

> *"...If anyone desires to come after me, let him deny himself, and take up his cross daily, and follow me. For whoever desires to save his life will lose it, but whoever loses his life for my sake will save it. For what profit is it to a man if he gains the whole world, and is himself destroyed or lost? For whoever is ashamed of me and my words, of him the Son of Man will be ashamed when He comes in His own glory, and in His Father's, and of the holy angels"* **(Luke 9:23-26).**

Lesson:

Christians are disciples of Jesus Christ, and we must have self-discipline and follow his teachings to the letter. Some characteristics of true Christianity are given below:

1. A true Christian must maintain consistent relationship with God
   (*If anyone desires to come after me, let him deny himself, and take up his cross daily, and follow me* - **Luke 9:23**).

2. A true Christian must be proud of gospel and consistently preach it to all people
   (*Whoever desires to save his life will lose it, but whoever loses his life for my sake will save it* – **Luke 9:24**).

3. A true Christian must have integrity and live a righteous life

   (*What profit is it to a man if he gains the whole world, and is himself destroyed or lost?* – **Luke 9:25**).

4. A true Christian must identify and support bible views – even when it violates the worldview

   (*Whoever is ashamed of me and my words, of him the Son of Man will be ashamed when He comes in His own glory, and in His Father's, and of the holy angels* – **Luke 9:26**).

Prayer:

Dear Jesus Christ, please help me to be an active Christian who live a bible-principled lifestyle. Help me to have self-discipline and live a life that is consistent with your teachings. Let your Holy Spirit empower me to live in compliance with your laws so that I can prosper! Anoint me to preach gospel and prosper your kingdom! Let your light shine through me so that unbelievers can know you and be saved. For in your precious name – Jesus Christ – I made my requests.
Amen.

« DAY 195 »

Sin Irritates God, And It Can Cause Him To Turn His Back Against His Children

Focus Passage: Joshua 7, 8, 9

A man called Achan sinned against God, and his action caused the Israelites to lose battle to a significantly smaller city. A small City of Ai defeated Israelites in a battle because God abandoned them as a result of Achan's sin. The scripture reported God said to Joshua,

> *"Get up! Why do you lie thus on your face? Israel has sinned, and they have also transgressed my covenant which I commanded them. For they have even taken some of the accursed things, and have both stolen and deceived; and they have also put it among their own stuff. Therefore the children of Israel could not stand before their enemies, but turned their backs before their enemies, because they have become doomed to destruction. Neither will I be with you anymore, unless you destroy the accursed from among you." **(Joshua 7:10-12)***

Lesson:
Holiness is God's uncompromised standard that all people must observed before they can receive his blessing. Children of God must live in compliance to God's laws to enjoy his full benefits. That is, believers cannot live in sin and expect God's grace to abide! The same God that made the rule of holiness cannot violate it. He will relate with people base on amount of respect they have for his laws. Therefore, children of God must make every effort to satisfy him to receive his benefits. However, it takes the empowerment of the Holy Spirit for anyone to adequately comply with God's standard. The Spirit guides people and makes God's laws easily complied. Hence, believers must consistently seek God's face to receive the empowerment of the Holy Spirit at all times.

Prayer:
Dear God, please help me to live a life that is not complacent with sin. Let your Holy Spirit empower me to act rightly and comply with your laws always. Help me to live a life that is acceptable to your kingdom, and also worthy of your earthly blessing. For in the name of Jesus Christ I make my requests.

Amen.

« DAY 196 »

Believers Must Be Full Of Holy Ghost To Comply With God's Laws

Focus Passage: Luke 9:37-62

Jesus Christ informed his disciples about the dangers that lied ahead of his salvation mission: A friend would betray him, and anti-gospel people would persecute him to the point of death. Jesus said,

> *"Let these words sink down into your ears, for the Son of Man is about to be betrayed into the hands of men. "But they did not understand this saying, and it was hidden from them so that they did not perceive it; and they were afraid to ask Him about this saying"* **(Luke 9:44-45).**
>
> Meanwhile, the disciples' actions immediately they received Jesus' warning proved they did not understand him. They argued and competed on matters that were not relevant. The scripture stated,
>
> *"Then a dispute arose among them as to which of them would be greatest. And Jesus, perceiving the thought of their heart, took a little child and set him by Him, and said to them, "Whoever receives this little child in my name receives me; and whoever receives me receives Him who sent me. For he who is least among you all will be great"* **(Luke 9:46-47).**

Lesson:
Christians are to walk by faith – and not only walk by sight in order to please God. We are spiritual people, and our activities must reflect that we understand the principle of God's kingdom. That is, we must give in-depth thoughts to situations and prayerfully consider matters so that we can act appropriately. Also, we must make it a practice to seek God's face in prayer and fasting to understand his mind. Once we receive his direction, we must act accordingly and properly follow his instructions so that we can have an expected result. Surely, there shall be no regret when believers know God's mind and appropriately operate under his leadership. The more we know and follow his leadership, the better chance we have to enjoy his benefits and prosper!

Prayer:
Dear God, please help me to be a person of the Spirit, and not someone that operates in flesh! Help me to be sensitive to your leadership so that I can make decisions that are edifying and profitable. Let my motivations be to satisfy you by all standards, and live a life that deserves your benefits. For in the name of Jesus Christ I make my requests.

Amen.

« DAY 197 »

God Can't Be Restricted; He Will Do Whatever He Determines

Focus Passage: Joshua 10, 11, 12

God remarkably delivered Israelites from their enemies that had upper hands over them. The enemies outnumbered the Israelites who were few in numbers with primitive tools to defend themselves, yet God fought for them and they had victory. The scripture reported,

> *"And it happened, as they (the enemies) fled before Israel and were on the descent of Beth Horon, that the Lord cast down large hailstones from heaven on them as far as Azekah, and they died. There were more who died from the hailstones than the children of Israel killed with the sword"* **(Joshua 10:11).**

Lesson:
God has power to defend his children under whatever circumstance. He has enough power to change any situation and make it cooperate with his mandate for his children. No skill, weapon, or influence can confront God's omnipotent power, they will all submit to him! The Almighty God can dry up an ocean for the sake of leading his children to safety! Therefore, those who reserve their trust in God should remain steadfast and not compromise. Jehovah who remains alive will respond to the needs of his children and help them. He will solve people's problems to glorify his name. People who remain confident in God will not be ashamed – under whatever condition!

Prayer:
Dear God, please give me strength to reserve my absolute trust in you always. Help me to have strong faith that will put devil to shame and glorify your name. Give me grace and strength to keep my positive confession of your goodness until I experience full joy! For in the name of Jesus Christ I make my requests.

Amen.

« DAY 198 »

Christians Have Jesus' Invested Authority To Preach Gospel And Perform Miracles

Focus Passage: Luke 10:1-24

Jesus Christ sent 70 disciples to preach gospel and demonstrate his power to free people from Satan's bondages. The disciples later returned to share testimony of their successful ministries. Jesus launched his disciples into the world and said,

> *"Behold, I give you the authority to trample on serpents and scorpions, and over all the power of the enemy, and nothing shall by any means hurt you"* **(Luke 10:19).**

Lesson:
Christians possess Jesus' invested power to preach gospel and set the captives free from Satan's strongholds. Therefore, believers are to engage in ministry activities with guaranteed assurance to succeed. In other words, no Christian should complain of any inadequacy. We have all been given grace and anointing to prosper for God's kingdom. Every Christian – without exception – is equipped through the Holy Spirit to preach gospel and have success! We must preach from the bible and direct people to serve God. Also, we must demonstrate God's power as true ambassadors of Jesus Christ; we must pray to heal people's sicknesses, and meet other needs. Indeed believers shall prosper through the help of the Holy Spirit! Jesus has reserved best honor for us in his kingdom as we serve him faithfully. The reward of believers' faithfulness shall forever abide in heaven.

Prayer:
Dear Jesus Christ, I understand that you have endowed your power and authority on Christians to preach gospel and perform signs and wonders to benefit your kingdom. Therefore since I am a Christian, I stand to exercise my right to use your authority! By faith I receive your anointing to preach gospel, and perform signs and wonders to benefit your kingdom! By faith I receive the baptism of the Holy Spirit to go into places to proclaim God's kingdom. With Holy Spirit on my side, I shall yield multiple benefits for God's kingdom, and I shall rejoice with Christ in heaven when my earthly race is over! For I have made my proclamation of faith through Jesus Christ my Lord!

Amen.

« DAY 199 »

Jehovah Will Reward A Person That Demonstrate Irresistible Faith To Honor Him

Focus Passage: Joshua 13, 14, 15

Caleb claimed his heritage from Israelites in fulfillment to God's promise made for him in the wilderness. God had promised to give Caleb a heritage of the Promised Land since he demonstrated great courage to honor him in the presence of others. When 12 spies were sent to spy Canaan Land, only Caleb and Joshua returned to positively confess their willingness to claim it. The remaining 10 spies compared themselves to "Grasshoppers against Giants;" they disputed God's ability to help them possess the land. Therefore, God promised to honor Caleb for his steadfastness **(Numbers 14:24)**. Meanwhile, Caleb did not only demonstrate strong faith to honor God in the wilderness, but he also proved his faith at an old age. The scripture testified that Caleb approached Joshua at age 85 years to request for the land of giants as his own portion of inheritance. He believed the same God who has helped his nation possessed Canaan Land against all odds was still alive to help him drive out the giants that lived on his apportioned land. Caleb said to Joshua,

> "Forty years old was I when Moses the servant of the Lord sent me from Kadeshbarnea to espy out the land; and I brought him word again as it was in mine heart. Nevertheless my brethren that went up with me made the heart of the people melt: but I wholly followed the Lord my God. And Moses sware on that day, saying, Surely the land whereon thy feet have trodden shall be thine inheritance, and thy children's for ever, because thou hast wholly followed the Lord my God. And now, behold, the Lord hath kept me alive, as he said, these forty and five years, even since the Lord spake this word unto Moses, while the children of Israel wandered in the wilderness: and now, lo, I am this day fourscore and five years old. As yet I am as strong this day as I was in the day that Moses sent me: as my strength was then, even so is my strength now, for war, both to go out, and to come in. Now therefore give me this mountain, whereof the Lord spake in that day; for thou heardest in that day how the Anakims were there, and that the cities were great and fenced: if so be the Lord will be with me, then I shall be able to drive them out, as the Lord said. And Joshua blessed him, and gave unto Caleb the son of Jephunneh Hebron for an inheritance. Hebron therefore became the inheritance of Caleb the son of Jephunneh the Kenezite unto this day, because that he wholly followed the Lord God of Israel. And the name of Hebron before was Kirjatharba; which Arba was a great man among the Anakims. And the land had rest from war" **(Joshua 14:7-15 KJV).**

Lesson:

God will stand by the sides of people that exercise strong faith to honor him. Irrespective of circumstances, Jehovah will prove his faithfulness towards his children that exercise their faith to honor him. No limitation applies; God will pay bills, heal the sick, and solve other problems. Hence, it is advantageous that Christians walk in faith of the Lord to claim their blessings. However, when a condition becomes unbearable to exercise faith, believers should not succumb to faithlessness, we should keep praying and making positive confessions – even if our minds refuse to accept it. Also, believers should also consult other Christians to support them in prayers. Our God remains alive, and he will show up in time of need to grant petition and solve our problems.

Prayer:

Dear God, please make me a person of faith that keeps making positive confessions until I have my expected victory. I understand that all things submit to you, and you will make any difficult situation work to my advantage! Therefore, I ask that you give me strength to trust you during time of challenges. Let me demonstrate courage and prove irresistible faith that will put devil to shame and glorify your name. Help me to remain steadfast in you until I have full joy and testify to your goodness. Let my life be filled with the abundance of your joy, love, peace, and prosperity. For in the name of Jesus Christ I desire to have resolute faith in you.

Amen!

« DAY 200 »

Christians Should Be Christ's Ambassador With True Love

Focus Passage: Luke 10:25-42

One lawyer attempted to trick Jesus Christ into agreeing with his selfish idea. He asked, "Teacher, what shall I do to inherit eternal life?" **(Luke 10:25)**. Jesus responded,

> *'Thou shalt love the Lord thy God with all thy heart, and with all thy soul, and with all thy strength, and with all thy mind; and thy neighbour as thyself. And he said unto him, Thou hast answered right: this do, and thou shalt live. But he, willing to justify himself, said unto Jesus, And who is my neighbour? And Jesus answering said, A certain man went down from Jerusalem to Jericho, and fell among thieves, which stripped him of his raiment, and wounded him, and departed, leaving him half dead. And by chance there came down a certain priest that way: and when he saw him, he passed by on the other side. And likewise a Levite, when he was at the place, came and looked on him, and passed by on the other side. But a certain Samaritan, as he journeyed, came where he was: and when he saw him, he had compassion on him, And went to him, and bound up his wounds, pouring in oil and wine, and set him on his own beast, and brought him to an inn, and took care of him. And on the morrow when he departed, he took out two pence, and gave them to the host, and said unto him, Take care of him; and whatsoever thou spendest more, when I come again, I will repay thee. Which now of these three, thinkest thou, was neighbour unto him that fell among the thieves? And he said, He that shewed mercy on him. Then said Jesus unto him, Go, and do thou likewise"* **(Luke 10:27-37 KJV)**.

Lesson:
People should understand the true meaning of Christianity and practice it accordingly. Jesus explained what the religion meant by citing an example of a "Good Samarian." According to Jesus' story, anyone to be regarded as a good Christian ought to be a good neighbor **(Luke 10:27-37)**. Who then is a good neighbor? Definitely not an acclaimed spiritual person that lives down the street! A good Christian is someone that connects with feelings of others, and he/she is willing to offer any assistance within capacity to alleviate their suffering. A good Christian is not selfish, but genuinely pursues good welfare of other people so that they can live happy and fulfilled life.

Prayer:
Dear God, please help me to be a Christian that truly represents you on earth. Help me to truly love you and love my neighbors as you required. Let me be selfless in my thought and practices to genuinely seek peace and prosperity of others. Enable me with ability to make positive contributions to people's lives so that they can have sense of hope and reasons for living. Bless my friends, family, and neighbors! For in the name of Jesus Christ I make my requests.

Amen.

« DAY 201 »

Every Believer Ought To Improve His Or Her God's-Given Ability To Have Full Success

Focus Passage: Joshua 16, 17, 18

Some Israelites were dissatisfied with their land allocations in Canaan Land and they murmured against Joshua. The Israelite leader then challenged the individuals to depose more Canaanites and acquire more lands to their satisfactions. The scripture reported,

> *"Then the children of Joseph spoke to Joshua, saying, "Why have you given us only one lot and one share to inherit, since we are a great people, inasmuch as the Lord has blessed us until now?" So Joshua answered them, "If you are a great people, then go up to the forest country and clear a place for yourself there in the land of the Perizzites and the giants, since the mountains of Ephraim are too confined for you." But the children of Joseph said, "The mountain country is not enough for us; and all the Canaanites who dwell in the land of the valley have chariots of iron, both those who are of Beth Shean and its towns and those who are of the Valley of Jezreel." And Joshua spoke to the house of Joseph—to Ephraim and Manasseh—saying, "You are a great people and have great power; you shall not have only one lot, but the mountain country shall be yours. Although it is wooded, you shall cut it down, and its farthest extent shall be yours; for you shall drive out the Canaanites, though they have iron chariots and are strong"* **(Joshua 17:14-18).**

Lesson:
God's tremendous blessings are reserved for his children to use, but they may not all be readily available for immediate use. Believers may still have to make extra efforts to improve and develop their God-given resources before they can fully manifest. For examples, a person who has natural gift of art still needs to practice and make personal improvements to fine-tune it, or else he/she may end up living below God's expectations for his/her life!

Prayer:
Dear God, please empower me to take the necessary steps needed to fully manifest my gifts and talents. Let my professions of faith and actions cooperate with your plans until your resources invested in me had fully manifested to become an embodiment of testimony to your holy name. For in the name of Jesus Christ I make my requests.

Amen.

« DAY 202 »

Christians Are To Tender Their Requests To God With Faith Expectation

Focus Passage: Luke 11:1-28

Jesus Christ taught his disciples how to pray in Luke 11:2-4, and he further explained that God is ever willing to grant petitions of his children. Jesus said,

> *"If you then, being evil, know how to give good gifts to your children, how much more will your heavenly Father give the Holy Spirit to those who ask Him!"* **(Luke 11:13).**

Lesson:
Christians are to tender their requests to God in faith with an expectation that he would respond to meet their needs. Jehovah owns worldwide resources, and he won't deprive his children their due benefits as they act in faith. Therefore, believers should learn not to act as unbelievers that would prefer to consult other media than God to receive solution. Believers' consultation must be towards God who never fails. That is, our attitude during difficult situation must be to pray and ask for God's guidance and solution. Once we get him on board, things will come under control and whatever appears as insurmountable problem will subside to pave way for our victory.

Prayer:
Dear God, I believe you are still alive to solve people's problem, and you will surely solve my problems! Please teach me how to consult you in prayer over my situations, and also teach me how to trust you for solution. Let my prayers of faith pave way for my healing, deliverance, and obtaining other solutions so that I can continue to praise you. For in the name of Jesus Christ I make my requests.

Amen.

« DAY 203 »

God Honors True Believers, And He Will Make Their Faces Shine

Focus Passage: Joshua 19, 20, 21

Joshua who led Israelites to possess the Promised Land received his portion of inheritance to mark fulfillment of God's promises on his life. Indeed Joshua had done great things for God and his people, and he deserved to be rewarded. He joined Caleb to resist other ten spies that wanted to change Israelites mind from pursuing possession of the Promised Land. Also, Joshua was very supportive to Moses throughout his tenure, and he remained faithful to God after Moses died. (Joshua led Israelites to the Promised Land). The scripture reported how Joshua was rewarded,

> *"When they (Israelites) had made an end of dividing the land as an inheritance according to their borders, the children of Israel gave an inheritance among them to Joshua the son of Nun. According to the word of the Lord they gave him the city which he asked for, Timnath Serah in the mountains of Ephraim; and he built the city and dwelt in it"* ***(Joshua 19:49-50).***

Lesson:
People that faithfully serve God deserve his benefits, and they shall be blessed. Jehovah will reward his faithful children in this life, and in heaven also. Therefore, Christians ought to evaluate their activities before God, and ensure they are up to the standard to qualify for his blessing. No Christian should be slothful in doing God's work, but ensure quality inputs are made to generate great result. Also, believers must have stable relationship with God and obey his laws to the letter. Again, we must serve God with our best ability to honor God! Once the Creator sees our faithfulness, he will reciprocate his blessing into our lives. He will open doors of opportunity for us so that we can be motivated to keep offering him our best services.

Prayer:
Dear God, please give me strength to offer you my best services always. Let my consistency honor you and lead to my prosperity! As I serve you with faithfulness, let doors of opportunity be opened for me for growth, expansion, and prosperity so that my life can continue to be an embodiment of testimony to your holy name. For in the name of Jesus Christ I make my requests.

Amen.

« DAY 204 »

Christians Must Prioritize Gospel Evangelization To Grant Unbelievers Salvation Opportunity

Focus Passage: Luke 11:29-54

Jesus Christ could not accommodate hypocritical behaviors of the Pharisees, and he rebuked them. Jesus said,

> *"Now then, you Pharisees clean the outside of the cup and dish, but inside you are full of greed and wickedness. You foolish people! Did not the one who made the outside make the inside also? But now as for what is inside you—be generous to the poor, and everything will be clean for you. "Woe to you Pharisees, because you give God a tenth of your mint, rue and all other kinds of garden herbs, but you neglect justice and the love of God. You should have practiced the latter without leaving the former undone. "Woe to you Pharisees, because you love the most important seats in the synagogues and respectful greetings in the marketplaces. "Woe to you, because you are like unmarked graves, which people walk over without knowing it""* **(Luke 11:39-44 NIV).**

Lesson:
Gospel message is not meant to satisfy people but to convict everyone into compliance to God's laws so that we can qualify for God's kingdom. Therefore, Christians must make every effort to preach gospel at all times. We must keep focus to preach unbiased and fearless gospel without seeking personal gain or gratuity. We must preach as the Holy Spirit gives us utterances to convict sinners and propel them into repentance and acceptance of Jesus Christ as their Lord and Savior. The Creator who knows how to reward people's faithfulness will surely reward us for prioritizing the matter of his kingdom.

Prayer:
Dear God, please give me grace to be a true Christian that proclaims gospel to win people for your kingdom. Let your Holy Spirit empower me to fearlessly preach unbiased gospel that can convict sinners into repentance, and qualify them for your kingdom. Please keep me faithful to you unto the end so that I can be worthy of your special honor in your kingdom. For in the name of Jesus Christ I make my requests.

Amen.

« DAY 205 »

A Believer Who Stays Within God's Plan Will Have Success

Focus Passage: Joshua 22, 23, 24

Joshua at age 110 years recounted some of God's faithfulness that he witnessed among the Israelites. God demonstrated supernatural power to deliver Israelites from Egyptian bondage and parted Red Sea. God suspended some natural laws to lead his children through wilderness to the Promised Land. Joshua counseled Israelites to be grateful to God and obey his commandments to keep receiving more blessing. Joshua said,

> *"Be very strong; be careful to obey all that is written in the Book of the Law of Moses, without turning aside to the right or to the left. Do not associate with these nations that remain among you; do not invoke the names of their gods or swear by them. You must not serve them or bow down to them. But you are to hold fast to the Lord your God, as you have until now. "The Lord has driven out before you great and powerful nations; to this day no one has been able to withstand you. 10 One of you routs a thousand, because the Lord your God fights for you, just as he promised"* **(Joshua 23:6-10 NIV).**

Joshua explained the consequences that Israelites would suffer if they disobey God. He said, *"But just as all the good things the Lord your God has promised you have come to you, so he will bring on you all the evil things he has threatened, until the Lord your God has destroyed you from this good land he has given you. If you violate the covenant of the Lord your God, which he commanded you, and go and serve other gods and bow down to them, the Lord's anger will burn against you, and you will quickly perish from the good land he has given you"* **(Joshua 23:15-16 NIV).**

Lesson:
God is ever faithful and strong to minister to the needs of his people. He will provide and meet the interest of his children so that unbelievers can witness it and be motivated to serve him. However, children of God must ensure they continue to walk in his wills, and live in compliance with his laws. This will prevent losing God's protections, which can open door for Satan to rob them of their benefits. (A believer who takes God's laws for granted runs the risk of loosing God protection, which may eventually grant Satan an access to launch his ugly attacks against him/her). God's guaranteed security will only abide with people that prioritize holiness, and faithfully serve him.

Prayer:
Dear God, please help me to operate under your guidance, and let me obey your laws so that I can continue to enjoy your security and blessing. Give me grace to prioritize holiness and consciously walk before you with integrity so that I can prosper throughout the days of my life. For in the name of Jesus Christ I make my requests.

Amen.

« DAY 206 »

Anyone Forgiven of His Or Her Sins Should No Longer Live In Condemnation

Focus Passage: Rom 8:1-21

No Christian is expected to live in condemnation after Jesus Christ has set him or her free. The scripture stated,

> "There is *therefore now no condemnation to those who are in Christ Jesus, who do not walk according to the flesh, but according to the Spirit. For the law of the Spirit of life in Christ Jesus has made me free from the law of sin and death. For what the law could not do in that it was weak through the flesh, God* did *by sending His own Son in the likeness of sinful flesh, on account of sin: He condemned sin in the flesh, that the righteous requirement of the law might be fulfilled in us who do not walk according to the flesh but according to the Spirit"* **(Romans 8:1-4).**

Lesson:
Believers in Jesus Christ are not under bondage of sin and condemnation, but we have been freed to enjoy salvation of the Lord Jesus Christ. We are no more expected to live in condemnation after we have been saved and received forgiveness of sin. We are now bona fide Christians qualified to receive God's benefits through Jesus Christ! However, Satan the enemy of righteousness has custom of tempting God's children into unjust condemnation. He may remind a Christian of his/her past sins after forgiveness. Meanwhile, if Christ has set us free, we are free indeed! Since we have been born-again in Jesus, we must claim his justification. Having said all, any Christian who is tempted to remain sad in a forgiven sin must resist the enemy out rightly. He or she must affirm his/her stand in God by saying *"There is therefore now no condemnation to those who are in Christ Jesus, who do not walk according to the flesh, but according to the Spirit. For the law of the Spirit of life in Christ Jesus has made me free from the law of sin and death..."* **(Romans 8:1-4).**

Prayer:
In the name of Jesus Christ I am free from sin and condemnation of sin. Jesus Christ has paid the penalty of my sins on the cross. He has washed me clean and made me fit for his kingdom. Since I have confessed and repented from my sins, I am no more under bondage of sin, and neither does condemnation of sin have power over me. Jesus Christ has made me free today, tomorrow, and forever! Hallelujah, I am heavenly bound, and Christ will be my king forever.

Amen!

« DAY 207 »

God Reigns Supremely Over All; He Reigns Specially For His Children

Focus Passage: Isaiah 45, 46

God declared his sovereignty over earth and said,

> *"For thus saith the Lord that created the heavens; God himself that formed the earth and made it; he hath established it, he created it not in vain, he formed it to be inhabited: I am the Lord; and there is none else. I have not spoken in secret, in a dark place of the earth: I said not unto the seed of Jacob, Seek ye me in vain: I the Lord speak righteousness, I declare things that are right"* **(Isaiah 45:18-19 KJV).**

Lesson:
God is the best of all beings in existence; he is the only deity that never fails. He retains autonomous power to do whatever pleases him. He is an omnipresent God– the one that is present everywhere. He is also an omniscient God – the one that is most powerful. Meanwhile, despite his unquestionable ability and authority, the Creator still chooses to act rightly to benefit mankind. He will not hurt anyone, but rather bless people. Therefore, since Jehovah is such a wonderful deity, all people should honor him and serve him well. If we make him feel special through our righteous services, he will make things turn beautiful for us, and our lives will never be the same again!

Prayer:
Dear God, I know that you are the Almighty God, and there is no one to be compared with you. Therefore, I ask you to become the king of my life. I commit my total life to you, and I beg you to take absolute control. Please teach me how to satisfy you, and empower me to faithfully serve you always so that I can qualify for your benefits. For in the name of Jesus Christ I make my requests.

Amen.

« DAY 208 »

Holy Spirit Is The Backbone Of Christianity

Focus Passage: Rom 8:22-39

God supremely manifests his power in people's lives through his divine Holy Spirit. The Holy Spirit performs variety of tasks, and he does them well. He (Holy Spirit) understands our feelings and knows perfect solution to our problems. The Holy Spirit also guides our prayers to fit God's standard, so that he can answer them. The divine Spirit translates our muddled up speeches during prayers into clear and distinct languages that God can reckon with. This is rightly explained in the scripture,

> *"Likewise the Spirit also helps in our weaknesses. For we do not know what we should pray for as we ought, but the Spirit Himself makes intercession for us with groaning which cannot be uttered. Now He who searches the hearts knows what the mind of the Spirit is, because He makes intercession for the saints according to the will of God"* **(Romans 8:26-27).**

Lesson:
Holy Spirit is the backbone of Christianity; we cannot satisfy God without him. The divine Holy Spirit governs our actions; teaches us about God, and strengthens us to comply with God's standard. Also, God's Holy Spirit comforts us to stay happy during difficult period. In fact, the works of Holy Spirit are many! Therefore, any Christian who desires to live happily and triumphantly on earth must not hesitate to specially seek God's face through prayer and fasting to receive baptism of the Holy Spirit.

Prayer:
Dear God, I desire the baptism of your Holy Spirit, please baptize me with him today. Let the Holy Spirit possess me so that I can be a good Christian who will live triumphantly on earth and also qualify for your kingdom. Let the Holy Spirit strengthen me, conform me, and encourage me. Also, let him change me from inside out so that I can remain rapturable! Through your Holy Spirit, let me be fit to receive your royal welcome in heaven on the last day. For in the name of Jesus Christ I make my requests.

Amen.

« DAY 209 »

There Is No Substitute For Obedience

Focus Passage: Isaiah 47, 48, 49

Wicked people have no place with God, unless they repent. Jehovah promised to punish wicked people. He said,

> "There is *no peace,*" says the Lord, *"for the wicked"* (Isaiah 48:22). *However, the Creator explained what he considered as acceptable practice from his people. He said, "Thus says the Lord, your Redeemer, The Holy One of Israel: "I am the Lord your God, Who teaches you to profit, who leads you by the way you should go. Oh, that you had heeded my commandments! Then your peace would have been like a river, And your righteousness like the waves of the sea. Your descendants also would have been like the sand, and the offspring of your body like the grains of sand; His name would not have been cut off nor destroyed from before me"* **(Isaiah 48:17-19).**

Lesson:
There are many profits in doing God's will and obeying his commandments. The efforts will earn us peace and prosperity. In fact, our acts of obedience could be termed as a "Win Win Situation," since there is nothing to lose in the process. Meanwhile, disobedient acts incur God's wrath; they create disaster and lead to painful experience. The best thing a person can do on earth to live happily is to faithfully serve God and obey his commandments, since the condition of guaranteed security and blessing is relative to it. All people should consider it "a must" to comply with God's laws.

Prayer:
Dear God, I submit at your feet to ask for grace to obey your instructions. I repent from my sins, and I promise to make things right with you from today. Please give me grace to faithfully obey your laws, so that I can enjoy your benefits. For in the name of Jesus Christ I make my requests.

Amen.

« DAY 210 »

God Will Have Mercy On The Lost Sheep; He Will Find And Save Them

Focus Passage: Rom 9:1-15

Jesus Christ originated from Israel, but the Israelites rejected him. They rejected his claim as the true messiah ordained by God to save the world. Meanwhile, Paul lamented for Jews as stated,

> *"I tell the truth in Christ, I am not lying, my conscience also bearing me witness in the Holy Spirit, that I have great sorrow and continual grief in my heart. For I could wish that I myself were accursed from Christ for my brethren, my countrymen according to the flesh, who are Israelites, to whom* pertain *the adoption, the glory, the covenants, the giving of the law, the service* of God, *and the promises; of whom* are *the fathers and from whom, according to the flesh, Christ* came, *who is over all,* the *eternally blessed God. Amen" **(Romans 9:1-5).***
>
> However, despite loss of opportunity for Israelites due to their unbelief, there is still a silver lining in the sky; God will show mercy on Israel and save them. They will eventually believe Christ and be saved! The scripture stated,
>
> *"I will have mercy on whomever I will have mercy, and I will have compassion on whomever I will have compassion" **(Romans 9:15).***

Lesson:
People who practice Judaism find it difficult to accept Jesus Christ as the true Messiah. Judaism which is mostly practiced by Jews has its root established in the Law of Moses. It promotes traditional mode of worship practiced in the Old Testament. Judaism supports a theory that Messiah (Christ) would come from God to save the world. However, the religion observers rejected Jesus as the true Messiah. (Meanwhile, "faith in Jesus" is very important to "salvation"). However, despite Israelites' unbelief, God will still grant them grace of salvation. Jehovah will open their minds to understand Jesus' ministry in order to accept him as true Messiah - since his salvation is meant for both Jews and gentiles. Hence, those who have already believed in Jesus Christ should not be silent about gospel. We must preach and pray for the unbelievers so that they can exercise change of mind, and be saved.

Prayer:
Dear God, please extend your grace of salvation to people who find it difficult to believe your Son Jesus Christ. Grant salvation opportunity to people who have lost it in the past. Help the skeptics understand the length and depth of Christ love, so that they accept him as their savior and be saved. Save people from sin and unbelief, and let those who are weak in faith become strong. Let all people enjoy your grace of salvation on earth to be qualified for heaven. For in the name of Jesus Christ I make my requests.

Amen.

« DAY 211 »

God Cares For His Children, And He Will Stand By Them Always

Focus Passage: Isaiah 50, 51, 52

Prophet Isaiah was confident in God; he believed God would take care of his business if he continues to trust him. Isaiah said,

> *"For the Lord God will help me; therefore I will not be disgraced; therefore I have set my face like a flint, and I know that I will not be ashamed. He is near who justifies me; who will contend with Me? Let us stand together. Who is my adversary? Let him come near Me. Surely the Lord God will help me; who is he who will condemn Me? Indeed they will all grow old like a garment; the moth will eat them up"* **(Isaiah 50:7-9).**

Lesson:
God is ever faithful towards his children. He will fulfill his promises over us. Our needs are not beyond his capacity; he will meet them if we can trust him. God who is the ultimate provider will not allow us to suffer. Also, he is ever strong, and he will protect us. Indeed, challenges of life may rise against us, but they will exist for a short moment. God who keeps his children does not sleep, neither does he slumber. He will help us overcome! Meanwhile, despite his guaranteed safety and provisions, the Creator still expects us to trust him. He also wants our attention through committed services. Jehovah must be regarded as All-In-All in our lives before we can enjoy his prime benefits. Therefore, we children of God must endeavor to allow him to take complete leadership of our lives.

Prayer:
Dear God, I appreciate the fact that you are All-In-All. You have power to take control of all situations, and I really want you to take control of my life, so that I can qualify for your full benefits. Therefore, I am asking for special grace to trust you. Teach me how to completely trust you! Help me to be closer to you and maintain consistent relationship with you, so that I can be fit to live a victorious life on earth. For in the name of Jesus Christ I make my requests.

Amen.

« DAY 212 »

Christ Will Save Whoever Comes In Submission Before Him

Focus Passage: Rom 9:16-33

God will not cast off people who have rebelled against him, but he will show them mercy and grant them grace of salvation. God stated through Prophet Hosea,

> *"I will call them my people, who were not my people, and her beloved, who was not beloved." "And it shall come to pass in the place where it was said to them, 'You are not my people,' There they shall be called sons of the living God"* **(Romans 9:25-26).**

Lesson:
People who have distant themselves from the salvation grace of Jesus Christ still have chance of getting saved. God will patiently wait for unbelievers to exercise change of heart, so that he can save them. However, the door of salvation will not indefinitely open for sinners, but it will be shut at God's appointed time. Once the last trumpet blasts, unbelievers will be hurled to hell fire while believers are sent to heaven **(Revelation 20:8).** Therefore, since "faith in Jesus Christ" remains the only formidable access to God's kingdom, all people must exercise it. Everyone must confess Jesus Christ as Lord and accept him as his or her personal Savior to be saved.

Prayer:
Dear Jesus Christ, I understand that there is no any other way through which a person can be saved other than you. Therefore, I confess you as my Lord and personal Savior. I believe you are the Son of God who was sent to save sinners. I confess my sins to you, and I repent from them. I will serve you from now on, and forever! Please write my name in your book of life, and count me worthy for your kingdom. I believe I am now saved through faith since I have confessed you as my Lord. Glory be to God.

Amen.

« DAY 213 »

Christ Suffered And Paid For Our Sins; We Ought Not To Pay Again

Focus Passage: Isaiah 53, 54, 55

Isaiah prophesied about the person of Jesus Christ the Messiah (Yeshua Ha-Mashiach) to be born. Prophet Isaiah said,

> *"...For He shall grow up before Him as a tender plant, And as a root out of dry ground. He has no form or comeliness; and when we see Him, There is no beauty that we should desire Him. He is despised and rejected by men, A Man of sorrows and acquainted with grief. And we hid, as it were, our faces from Him; He was despised, and we did not esteem Him. Surely He has borne our grieves and carried our sorrows; yet we esteemed Him stricken, Smitten by God, and afflicted. But He was wounded for our transgressions, He was bruised for our iniquities; the chastisement for our peace was upon Him, and by His stripes we are healed"* **(Isaiah 53:2-5).**

Lesson:
Jesus Christ was persecuted to the point of death by his own people. He was beaten, tortured, and killed for some unfounded accusations. Meanwhile, it was Jesus' will to suffer for sins of mankind. While the Messiah had chance to denounce his mission for a lesser penalty, he refused. He insisted on his purpose and maintained his position as the true Son of God sent to save the world. Christ volunteered himself to suffer and die! However, his death and resurrection became our most valuable asset. The scripture explained this, *"Surely He has borne our griefs and carried our sorrows; yet we esteemed Him stricken, Smitten by God, and afflicted. But He was wounded for our transgressions, He was bruised for our iniquities; the chastisement for our peace was upon Him, and by His stripes we are healed"* **(Isaiah 53:4-5).**

Since Jesus Christ has suffered and died for our sins, we ought not to experience similar predicament anymore. No need to suffer for remission of sin again! Christ has paid for it! Meanwhile, Christ' effort on the cross will remain unaccomplished over us - until we have willingly surrendered our lives to him. We must confess Jesus Christ as Lord, and we must dedicate our lives for his worship. The Savior reserves eternal rewards for us in heaven if we faithfully follow him. He will honor us for making his crucifixion experience a worthwhile effort.

Prayer:
Dear God, I believe that Jesus Christ is your true Son who has suffered and died for my sins. Therefore, I confess my sins and forsake them. I declare Jesus Christ as my Lord and personal Savior. As from today, I dedicate my life to Jesus Christ, and I will serve him throughout the days of my life. Please give me grace to keep following you, and let me remain worthy to inherit your eternal kingdom. For I have made my requests and declaration of faith through the name of your beloved Son Jesus Christ.

Amen.

« DAY 214 »

Salvation Of Jesus Is The Most Precious Gift Anyone Can Ever Have

Focus Passage: Rom 10

Christianity is simple, and the requirement of becoming born again is simple also. The scripture stated,

> "...That if you confess with your mouth the Lord Jesus and believe in your heart that God has raised Him from the dead, you will be saved. For with the heart one believes unto righteousness, and with the mouth confession is made unto salvation" **(Romans 10:9-10)**.

Lesson:
Salvation offer of Jesus Christ is simple, and it is easily obtained. Anyone can become saved within a short moment. The process of obtaining Christ's salvation can be categorized into two:

(1) Profession of faith.
(2) Confession of faith.

Meanwhile, it is expedient that people of all status align themselves with Jesus Christ by confessing him as their Lord. Christ is the only sure way that leads to heaven. He guaranteed assurance of eternal life for people who follow him.

Prayer:
Dear Jesus, I believe in you; I am sure that you are Christ the Son of God. You are the only pathway that leads to God, and there is no other way besides you. Therefore, I confess you Jesus Christ as my personal Lord and Savior. I promise to commit my total life unto you from today, and I will serve you throughout the days of my life. Please keep me fit for your eternal kingdom. Thank you Jesus Christ for your saving grace.

Amen.

« DAY 215 »

Christianity Can Not Be Equated For Human Pride

Focus Passage: Isaiah 56, 57, 58

God requires all his children to shun insensitive religion dogma, but sincerely serve him according to expectations. Jehovah prefers that we exercise our religion activities before him in good faith. He wants us to offer our services plainly without being hypocritical. God stated in the scripture,

> *"Is it such a fast that I have chosen? a day for a man to afflict his soul? is it to bow down his head as a bulrush, and to spread sackcloth and ashes under him? wilt thou call this a fast, and an acceptable day to the Lord? Is not this the fast that I have chosen? to loose the bands of wickedness, to undo the heavy burdens, and to let the oppressed go free, and that ye break every yoke? Is it not to deal thy bread to the hungry, and that thou bring the poor that are cast out to thy house? when thou seest the naked, that thou cover him; and that thou hide not thyself from thine own flesh? Then shall thy light break forth as the morning, and thine health shall spring forth speedily: and thy righteousness shall go before thee; the glory of the Lord shall be thy reward. Then shalt thou call, and the Lord shall answer; thou shalt cry, and he shall say, Here I am. If thou take away from the midst of thee the yoke, the putting forth of the finger, and speaking vanity; And if thou draw out thy soul to the hungry, and satisfy the afflicted soul; then shall thy light rise in obscurity, and thy darkness be as the noon day: And the Lord shall guide thee continually, and satisfy thy soul in drought, and make fat thy bones: and thou shalt be like a watered garden, and like a spring of water, whose waters fail not. And they that shall be of thee shall build the old waste places: thou shalt raise up the foundations of many generations; and thou shalt be called, The repairer of the breach, The restorer of paths to dwell in"* **(Isaiah 58:5-12 KJV).**

Lesson:
God will honor us if we humbly and faithfully serve him. He considers charity as an acceptable service, and he expects us to really get into business of helping others. The Creator promised to make us experience peace and prosperity if we are not obsessed with mundane things, but freely share our resources with others. Contrarily to popular opinion, our religion activities such as fasting and prayers are not only the necessary key factors into receiving blessing. Those spiritual activities will only earn us fruits if we can apply God's principles of sowing positive seeds into the lives of other people.

Prayer:
Dear God, please make me a faithful Christian. Help me to faithfully serve you and care for other people around me. Help me to be sensitive and support people who may be going through one type of difficulty or the other. Enable me with grace to be your faithful ambassador who makes positive contributions into other people's lives. Also, please bless me and let me have testimony of your goodness to share with others. For in the name of Jesus Christ I make my requests.

Amen.

« DAY 216 »

Jesus Will Gravitate Whoever Believes Him To God

Focus Passage: Rom 11:1-18

Jews who denied Jesus Christ as the true messiah may still have opportunity to receive his salvation again. The fact that they initially rejected Christ have successfully opened door of salvation for non-Jews who would believe. Hostility and persecutions that early Christians suffered from Jews forced them out of comfort zones to preach to the gentiles. They extended their gospel evangelization to people who were not traditional Jews. However, God would not cast off Jews forever, Paul said,

> "If by any means I may provoke to jealousy those who are my flesh and save some of them. For if their being cast away is the reconciling of the world, what will their acceptance be but life from the dead? For if the first fruit is holy, the lump is also holy; and if the root is holy, so are the branches. And if some of the branches were broken off, and you, being a wild olive tree, were grafted in among them, and with them became a partaker of the root and fatness of the olive tree, do not boast against the branches. But if you do boast, remember that you do not support the root, but the root supports you. You will say then, "Branches were broken off that I might be grafted in." Well said. Because of unbelief they were broken off, and you stand by faith. Do not be haughty, but fear. For if God did not spare the natural branches, He may not spare you either" **(Romans 11: 14-21).**

Lesson:
God loves Jews; he raised them from a few people, and turned them to a great nation. Meanwhile, not only Jews are God's children, Christians are his children also. Both Jews and Christians are like branches of the same tree grafted to God. However, Jews cannot survive in isolation, they need salvation of Jesus Christ to offer acceptable service to God. The scripture stated that God would not give up on Israel, but he would enlighten their mind to accept Jesus Christ as the true Messiah of God (Yeshua Ha-Mashiach). With faith in Jesus Christ, both Jews and Christians will partake in the Lord's Passover in heaven. Hence, since Jesus Christ is so important to salvation, all people - Jews and non-Jews should consider it necessary to believe in him.

Prayer:
Dear God, I pray for Jews and all people who have not believed Jesus Christ as the true messiah to do so. Please enlighten their minds to understand the sacrifice that Jesus Christ made on their behalf. Let them understand that Jesus Christ died and resurrected to give them eternal life, so that they can inherit your kingdom. For in the name of Jesus Christ I make my requests.

Amen.

« DAY 217 »

God Loves Honest People; He Will Forgive And Bless Them

Focus Passage: Isaiah 59, 60, 61

The scripture explained one major reason behind Israelites' unanswered prayers as quoted,

> "Behold, the Lord's hand is not shortened, that it cannot save; nor His ear heavy, that it cannot hear. But your iniquities have separated you from your God; and your sins have hidden His face from you, So that He will not hear. For your hands are defiled with blood, and your fingers with iniquity; your lips have spoken lies, your tongue has muttered perversity" **(Isaiah 59:1-3).**

Lesson:
God loves righteousness but hates sin. He will not operate where sin reigns, but he will demonstrate his power where righteousness is promoted. The Creator always has good intention of blessing all people; however since he cannot break his own rule, he will not entertain sinfulness. Therefore, we must yield to God's instructions to receive his blessing. If we in deed obey him, the Creator will do whatever necessary to furnish us with his benefits - so that his name can be praised among all people.

Prayer:
Dear God, I do not want to experience delay and unanswered prayers anymore! I want to enjoy your benefits as your true child; therefore, please keep me pure in your presence. My desire is to be in your good book of people that are due for your blessings, please keep me fit! I am determined to turn a new leaf today, and I will faithfully serve you forever! For in the name of Jesus Christ I made my requests.

Amen.

« DAY 218 »

God Can Not Bypass His Standard To Bless A Disobedient Child

Focus Passage: Rom 11:19-36

The scripture admonished us to take salvation of the Lord Jesus Christ serious, and not handle it with levity. It is written,

> *"Therefore consider the goodness and severity of God: on those who fell, severity; but toward you, goodness, if you continue in His goodness. Otherwise you also will be cut off"* **(Romans 11:22).**

Lesson:
God's children are expected to listen and obey his voice. Since we are the clay and he is the portal, our actions are subject to his review. He will honor and bless us if we faithfully follow his instructions. However, Jehovah reserves his measurable corrections for any of his children that abuse his/her salvation grace.

Prayer:
Dear God, I desire to satisfy you always through holy and acceptable services. Therefore, please give me grace to serve you well. Help me to meet up with your expectations so that I can be worthy to receive your blessing. For in the name of Jesus Christ I make my requests.

Amen.

« DAY 219 »

God Will Work With Anyone Who Is Humble Enough To Admit His/Her Sins

Focus Passage: Isaiah 62, 63, 64

Redemption will come on people who repent from their sins and faithfully serve God. The scripture stated,

> *"The Lord has sworn by His right hand and by the arm of His strength: "Surely I will no longer give your grain as food for your enemies; and the sons of the foreigner shall not drink your new wine, For which you have labored. But those who have gathered it shall eat it, and praise the Lord; those who have brought it together shall drink it in my holy courts"* **(Isaiah 62:8-9).**

Lesson:
God will forgive our sins if we can humble ourselves and serve him faithfully. Jehovah understands that we are humans made out of dust, and flesh cast heavy weight of sin on us. He will not forsake us forever, but he will show us mercy if we can forsake our sins and repent from them. However, despite God's enduring grace of forgiveness, he will turn eye brown on any stubborn sinner who refuses to repent. He will severe defiant sinners with fire of hell. Therefore, no one should take God for granted, but we must all honor him with holiness and acceptable services,

Prayer:
Dear God, I understand that you are a forgiving God who shows mercy on repentant sinners, therefore I choose to humbly come before you today. I open my heart to you for holiness and faithful service. I confess my past sins and repent from them. I completely yield my life to you today, and I will serve you for the rest of my life. Please give me your grace to remain consistent with you. For in the name of your Son Jesus Christ I make my requests.

Amen.

« DAY 220 »

God Desires Holiness; Christians Must Prioritize It

Focus Passage: Rom 12

Apostle Paul explained what God considers as an acceptable service rendered by his children. Paul stated,

> *"I beseech you therefore, brethren, by the mercies of God, that you present your bodies a living sacrifice, holy, acceptable to God, which is your reasonable service. And do not be conformed to this world, but be transformed by the renewing of your mind, that you may prove what is that good and acceptable and perfect will of God"* **(Romans 12:1-2).**

Lesson:
Holiness takes priority with God. He appreciates no other language than holiness! For us (Christians) to fully satisfy God, we must strife against sin with sincerity. At the same time, we must be conscious of our Christian activities and ensure they are void of ritual and other ungodliness. We must perform our activities with consciousness to make God happy, and we must follow scriptures to the letter. Self-righteousness and selfishness must not be on our plate for God to delight in our services. If we duly obey God, he will shine his light of gospel through us, and he will make our lives become his center of excellence. God's tremendous rewards will overflow his faithful children!

Prayer:
Dear God, I desire to satisfy you wholly and purely. I have nothing more important in my life than you; therefore, help me to work before you with sanctity of life. Enable me with grace through your Holy Spirit to honor you in whatever I do so that your glory can shine through me. Please anoint me with grace to consciously work before you with honesty, so that I can prosper throughout the days of my life. For in the name of Jesus Christ I make my requests.

Amen.

« DAY 221 »

Heaven Has Indescribable Resorts Reserved For The Saints

Focus Passage: Isaiah 65; 66

God promised to gather his children from all walks of life to a restful habitation where they will see and taste his goodness forever! The scripture stated,

> *"For I know their works and their thoughts. It shall be that I will gather all nations and tongues; and they shall come and see my glory"* **(Isaiah 66:18).**

Lesson:
God has reserved heaven for us - his children. We will gather to fellowship and enjoy his eternal benefits. Saints will share common playground with God in heaven; we will play with him as a familiar friend. We will also eat from the same table with Jesus Christ and share similar cups. Heaven will be pleasant for people who believe in Jesus Christ and faithfully serve him! In heaven, we shall sing songs of melody and dance with Jesus Christ. Heaven will remain God's permanent resort preserved for his children. Only those who have received salvation of Jesus Christ will qualify to enter heaven. Everyone who desires to go to heaven must make a decisive decision of confessing Jesus Christ as his/her Lord.

Prayer:
Dear God, I love heaven, and I want to be there when I die. My prayer is to make heaven, please let me make it! I confess your son Jesus as my Lord, and I receive him into my life as my true Savior. With faith, I receive your Holy Spirit to leave a life worthy of inheriting your kingdom. Please overflow me with grace to keep serving you throughout my life, so that I can meet you in heaven. For in the name of Jesus Christ I make my requests.

Amen.

« DAY 222 »

Human Laws Are Subject To God's Laws

Focus Passage: Rom 13

Christians must obey the laws of their land, but not at the detriment of violating God's laws. World governments are not above God's authority. They must appease God with submission in order to receive his blessing. The scripture emphasized,

> *"Let every soul be subject to the governing authorities. For there is no authority except from God, and the authorities that exist are appointed by God. Therefore whoever resists the authority resists the ordinance of God, and those who resist will bring judgment on themselves. For rulers are not terrors to good works, but to evil. Do you want to be unafraid of the authority? Do what is good and you will have praise from the same"* **(Romans 13:1-3).**

Lesson:
God recognizes various world government as legitimate establishments fit to cater for their citizens; however, they are not above his authority. Leaders of various governments are expected to rule with fairness. In fact, the scripture addressed world leaders as stated, *"For rulers are not a terror to good works, but to evil"* **(Romans 13:3a)**. Therefore, any leader who terrorizes his/her people has violated God's law. Such ruler will not go scot-free on God's last Day of Judgment, but he/she will stand trial to be condemned to the lowest part of hell fire. Therefore, leaders of all capacity should be careful not to abuse their positions, since nemesis will hunt them on God's last Day of Judgment. Any ruler who realizes his/her mistakes and turn a new leave will receive God's forgiveness.

Prayer:
Dear God, please make our government and their rulers operate with fairness. Do not let them be power drunk and abuse their positions. Let our leaders serve with humble spirit and promote godliness. Let selfishness and pride be removed from our leaders' circle. Let both government leaders and citizens apply godly fear to whatever they do, so that you can prosper them. Please let righteousness reign in our lands, and let the light of your gospel shine in every coast of our countries. Please keep us fit for your coming so that we can forever enjoy your forthcoming paradise. For in the name of Jesus Christ I make my requests.

Amen.

« DAY 223 »

Sin Exposes Anyone To Satan's Assault

Focus Passage: Hosea 1, 2, 3, 4

Israelites abandoned God to pursue sin, and the action led to their destruction. God said about Israelites,

> *"My people are destroyed for lack of knowledge. Because you have rejected knowledge, I also will reject you from being priest for me; because you have forgotten the law of your God, I also will forget your children. "The more they increased, the more they sinned against me; I will change their glory into shame""* **(Hosea 4:6-7)**.

Lesson:
God is not responsible for any action that leads us to sin; we are to be responsible for our own actions - and their consequences. Our suffering may be relative to the consequences of our actions. Sin is evil; it makes anyone vulnerable to Satan's assault. The enemy loves to gain advantage of sinful moment to tempt and attack God's children. To avoid falling victim of the enemy, a believer must walk well with God and carefully observe his instructions. However, if we are tempted and fall into sin, we should repent to receive God restoration and his blessing. The Scripture stated, *"No temptation has overtaken you except such as is common to man; but God is faithful, who will not allow you to be tempted beyond what you are able, but with the temptation will also make the way of escape, that you may be able to bear it"* **(1 Corinthians 10:13)**. A repentant believer will surely receive God's blessing and experience victory.

Prayer:
Dear God, I am sorry if I have neglected you; sorry for all my mistakes. I will not distant myself from you anymore; I am fully ready to establish a consistent relationship with you from today. I will prioritize your interest above mine, and I will faithfully serve you. Please give me grace to meet all your expectations so that I can be fit enough to receive your blessing. For in the name of Jesus Christ I make my requests.

Amen.

« DAY 224 »

Disunity Among Christians Favors No One Other Than Satan!

Focus Passage: Rom 14

Christians must understand importance of unity and act together as one. The scripture admonished us to shun segregations, and avoid unhealthy rivalries which are detrimental to propagation of gospel. No Christian sect should assume superiority over others; rather, we should serve God with humble spirit and consider others to be more important. The scripture emphasized,

> *"Whoever regards one day as special does so to the Lord. Whoever eats meat does so to the Lord, for they give thanks to God; and whoever abstains does so to the Lord and gives thanks to God. For none of us lives for ourselves alone, and none of us dies for ourselves alone. If we live, we live for the Lord; and if we die, we die for the Lord. So, whether we live or die, we belong to the Lord"* **(Romans 14:6-8)**.

Lesson:
Unity will promote Christianity, but disunity will halt its expansion. Unfortunately, Satan has tricked Christians to arrogantly compete with each other; Factions claim rivalry and pursue mundane things that contribute little or nothing to God's kingdom. Meanwhile, God expects his children to serve him with purity and liberty of the spirit - without entertaining hot argument and rat races. According to **Romans 14:6-8**, God allows true worship with liberty of the spirit. If a person is adept in Mosaic Laws to only worship God on Saturday, let him do so! If he refuses to eat pork, do not dishonor him! Also, a vegetarian who believes on eating vegetable in conjunction with his Christian services has not sinned! Meanwhile, God did not state that human tradition will lead to our salvation - they are relevant to this earth only! Salvation offer of Jesus Christ is the only God approved passage that leads to heaven. Anyone who believes in Jesus Christ will be saved - irrespective of his/her culture and background. Christians should serve God humbly, plainly, and truthfully - and avoid all forms of self-righteousness that can affect gospel expansion.

Prayer:
Dear God, please save Christian community from plague of disunity. Let brethren stop condemning one another, but let us focus on gospel expansion. Let Christian denominations be tolerant and work in unity so that anti gospel forces can be subdued. Let the church invest their resources and energy on activities that can motivate unbelievers to repent and convert to Christianity. Please strengthen the body of Christ throughout the world to pursue righteousness so that your name can be praised in the land of the living. For in the name of Jesus Christ I make my requests.

Amen.

« DAY 225 »

God Can't Be Manipulated To Change His Standard Of Holiness

Focus Passage: Hosea 5, 6, 7, 8

God was furious with his disobedient children and he charged his prophet to announce what calamity would befall them. God said to Prophet Hosea,

> *"Set the trumpet to your mouth! He shall come like an eagle against the house of the Lord, because they have transgressed my covenant and rebelled against my law. Israel will cry to me, 'My God, we know you!' Israel has rejected the good; the enemy will pursue him"* ***(Hosea 8:1-3).***

Lesson:
God cannot be bribed. There is no amount of manipulations that can make him lessen his standard of holiness. God has established his position over all matters once and for all: He asked all people to work uprightly before him so that they can prosper. Anyone who fails to obey God's instruction would be questioned and be punished on God's last Day of Judgment. Therefore, it is important that we make God happy in everything we do, so he can prosper us.

Prayer:
Dear God, please help me to fear you and faithfully serve you so that I can prosper. I desire to enjoy your benefits through obedience, and not incur your wrath through disobedience. Please give me strength to observe your laws, and let me serve you with honesty. Qualify me for both your earthly blessings and your eternal heavenly rewards. For in the name of Jesus Christ I make my requests.

Amen.

« DAY 226 »

Believers Need Holy Spirit To Run A Successful Ministry For Christ

Focus Passage: Rom 15:1-13

Paul prayed for Christians to have spirit of unity so that they can serve God together with one mind. Paul prayed,

> *"Now may the God of patience and comfort grant you to be like-minded toward one another, according to Christ Jesus, that you may with one mind* and *one mouth glorify the God and Father of our Lord Jesus Christ"* **(Romans 15:5-6).**

Lesson:
Christians need to operate in unity to promote gospel and expand God's kingdom. However, it is almost impossible to achieve this goal among brethren without the help of the Holy Spirit. Believers need the Holy Spirit more than anything else! The Holy Spirit will help brethren to pursue ultimate goal of satisfying God's desires - than satisfying world pressure and craving of flesh. Therefore, it is important that Christian body devote tangible time to seek God's face to receive empowerment of the Holy Spirit, and operate under his divine guidance.

Prayer:
Dear God, please baptize Christian community with your Holy Spirit. Let brethren lay down self and pride to submit to each other in love. Let genuine love reign among brethren, so that your light of gospel can radiate through them to the world, and unbelievers become saved. For in the name of your Son Jesus Christ I make my requests.

Amen.

« DAY 227 »

An Unrepentant Sinner Risks God's Heavy Punishment

Focus Passage: Hosea 9, 10, 11

God warned that he would punish Israelites for there sins unless they repent. The Creator promised to avert evil if his disobedient children could repent and pursue righteousness. God said,

> "Sow for yourselves righteousness; Reap in mercy; Break up your fallow ground, For it is time to seek the Lord, Till He comes and rains righteousness on you" **(Hosea 10:12).**

Lesson:
There are God's punishments to apply for human sinful actions. His righteous standard would grant positive rewards for people who pursue righteousness and faithfully serve him. However, God will pursue and overtake wicked people; he will overpower them and consume them with his judgment. The Creator desires that all people repent from their wickedness so that he can bless and award them with his immeasurable peace and prosperity.

Prayer:
Dear God, I know that you have established a standard to prosper righteous people and surfer wicked people. Therefore, I want to be your righteous child so that I can prosper. Please empower me to repent from my sins, and let me faithfully serve you so that I can enjoy your blessing here on earth and in heaven also. For in the name of Jesus Christ I make my requests.

Amen.

« DAY 228 »

Relentless Evangelism Yield Much Fruits For God's Kingdom

Focus Passage: Rom 15:14-33

Paul's primary objective was to preach gospel of Jesus Christ throughout the world. His set his eyes on preaching to gentiles in the distant lands where gospel has not been heard. The apostle referenced Isaiah's prophecy to validate his mission. He said,

> "Those who were not told about him will see, and those who have not heard will understand" (**Romans 15:21 NIV**).

Lesson:
Paul was a true follower of Jesus Christ who went everywhere to talk about his Master. For gospel's sake, he risked many assassination attempts as he preached to his reluctant audience. Despite many challenges that he faced, the apostle never showed any sign of discouragement; his relentless efforts paid off for Christ. Through his dynamic evangelism, the Asian, Greek, and Roman Empires heard gospel. In fact, Paul's letters to the gentiles become so significant that they were later canonized as part of the bible. Meanwhile, today's Christians should emulate relentless attitude of Paul to propagate gospel also. Believers must preach gospel of Jesus Christ to everyone around to help populate God's kingdom. All Christians must understand that we do not have any other primary assignment than evangelism. We must preach Christ so that unbelievers can hear and be saved.

Prayer:
Dear God, I do not want to be a Christian who bears no fruit for your kingdom. Please help me to prioritize evangelism, and preached your gospel with full devotion. Empower me to share gospel of Jesus Christ to my neighbors, friends, and family. Also, help me to support other efforts that promote your gospel– whether they come from my local church or other places. Let the light of your gospel shine through me to both local places and distant lands for the sake of populating your kingdom. For in the name of your Son Jesus Christ I make all my requests.

Amen.

« DAY 229 »

God Can Not Be Fooled; Whatever A Man Sows He Shall Receive

Focus Passage: Hosea 12, 13, 14

God accused Israelites of keeping manipulative relationship with him. They appeased God to receive his benefits, but to later return to idolatry to satisfy their devilish desires. Therefore, the Creator promised to punish the deceptive Israelites for their inconsistency. God said,

> *"When Ephraim spake trembling, he exalted himself in Israel; but when he offended in Baal, he died. And now they sin more and more, and have made them molten images of their silver, and idols according to their own understanding, all of it the work of the craftsmen: they say of them, Let the men that sacrifice kiss the calves. Therefore they shall be as the morning cloud and as the early dew that passeth away, as the chaff that is driven with the whirlwind out of the floor, and as the smoke out of the chimney. Yet I am the Lord thy God from the land of Egypt, and thou shalt know no god but me: for there is no saviour beside me. I did know thee in the wilderness, in the land of great drought. According to their pasture, so were they filled; they were filled, and their heart was exalted; therefore have they forgotten me. Therefore I will be unto them as a lion: as a leopard by the way will I observe them: I will meet them as a bear that is bereaved of her whelps, and will rend the caul of their heart, and there will I devour them like a lion: the wild beast shall tear them"* **(Hosea 13:1-8 KJV)**.

Lessons:
God's children are not allowed to play double games with him. We are not allowed to be benefit driven. We must not aim at serving God to receive his benefits only, but we must serve him to enjoy father-to-son/daughter relationship. Whatever blessing will have received from him should motivate us to serve him more; they should not prompt us to be self-satisfied and turn our back against him. The Creator desires our consistent relationship, and he will prosper us if we meet his desires

Prayer:
Dear God, please help me to keep a consistent relationship with you. Let my motivation be to satisfy you in all I do. Do not let me be tempted to live a deceptive life and play double games with you! Help me to remain honest so that you can be challenged to bless me more. Ultimately, please count me worthy to receive your imperishable rewards in heaven. For in the name of Jesus Christ I make my requests.

Amen.

« DAY 230 »

True Symbol Of Christianity Is To Care For Others

Focus Passage: Rom 16

A lady called Phoebe caught Paul's special attention with her exceptional servant heart. Paul recognized her efforts as she ministered to people's needs. Paul mentioned in his letter,

> *"I commend to you Phoebe our sister, who is a servant of the church in Cenchrea, that you may receive her in the Lord in a manner worthy of the saints, and assist her in whatever business she has need of you; for indeed she has been a helper of many and of myself also"* **(Romans 16:1-2).**

Lesson:
Christians' efforts are not limited to Sunday worship services. We are required to demonstrate Christ' love within and without the church. It is important that we minister to others and help meet their needs. Some fellow Christians are in dire need of what we can afford. Some do not need extra material, but need moral support. Each believer must be sensitive to the needs of others and make significant effort to assist them. Whether money and material are needed or not, brethren must operate as a team and share common love as Christ would expect them. No brother or sister in Christ should be left unattended to. Each Christian is a member of God's kingdom; everyone must be treated with respect, since we are co-sharers of God's benefits. However, the fact that God is watching our attitude towards other brethren should be resonating in our heart! Whatever we do to a brother or sister in Christ is what we are technically doing to God himself. God is watching us!

Prayer:
Dear God, please help me to be a relevant Christian who offers supports and make positive contributions to other brethren's lives. Please help me to be relevant in your kingdom! Again, I want to faithfully serve you and support others. Give me resources needed to take care of my brothers and sisters in Christ. Empower me to stand upright and support your gospel, and all that associate with it. Give me understanding and energy to do whatever necessary to promote your name in the lives of others, so that your name can be glorified always. At the end of it all, let me qualify to hear "Weldone and welcome my good servant in heaven!" For in the name of Jesus Christ I make my requests.

Amen.

« DAY 231 »

God Hates Wickedness; He Will Distance Himself From Wicked People

Focus Passage: Micah 1,2,3

God hates wickedness, and he mandated wicked people to repent from their evil ways. Jehovah will bless those who repent, but the end game will be rough and tough for wicked people who persist in evil. God said,

> *"Woe to those who plan iniquity, to those who plot evil on their beds! At morning's light they carry it out because it is in their power to do it. They covet fields and seize them, and houses, and take them. They defraud people of their homes, they rob them of their inheritance"* **(Micah 2:1-2 NIV).**

Lesson:
God does not walk in the same direction with wicked people. He hates wickedness! People who oppress others and abuse their positions will remain at the mercy of God's judgment unless they repent. As far as wickedness is concern, repentance should be the only option. Since Jehovah knows all things and sees all things, he will exert his righteous judgment on wicked people in due time. However, some pleasant actions that God desires - which will incur blessings - include fairness, justice, and compassion. Anyone who expects God's blessing should care for others and treat them with respect. Also, the fellow must be in right standing with God.

Prayer:
Dear God, please help me to treat other people with fairness and respect. Do not let me be obsessed with any position or power that I may have, but help me to be an agent of positive influence. Please forgive my past sins, and restore me in your love. Empower me to have compassion and demonstrate your grace on others, so that your name can be glorified in every situation. For in the name of Jesus Christ I make my requests.

Amen.

« DAY 232 »

God Is Seeking Faithful Christians Who Will Launch End Time Gospel Crusades

Focus Passage: Acts 21:1-17

God's prophets advised Paul not to extend his evangelistic campaign to Jerusalem. They warned that he may be persecuted and die in the adventure. However, Paul insisted on his mission despite warning of imminent danger,

> "Paul responded to his counselors, "What do you mean by weeping and breaking my heart? For I am ready not only to be bound, but also to die at Jerusalem for the name of the Lord Jesus." So when he would not be persuaded, we (fellow brethren) ceased, saying, "The will of the Lord be done" **(Acts 21:13-14).**

Lesson:
God seeks dedicated preachers who will prioritize propagation of gospel above any influencing factor. Servants of God – with various talents and abilities – should summon courage to step out of their comfort zones and adequately preach gospel. God has invested so much grace to the lives of men and women who can break forth into mainstream to launch end time gospel crusades. We are mandated to use our available resources to elevate the name of Jesus Christ. We must use both primitive and sophisticated tools to evangelize gospel. We must ensure that someone in Africa hear gospel. It is our duty to ensure that a person currently located in Asia become born-again. People in South America, North America, Europe, and Australia must give their lives to Jesus Christ. We servants of God must not keep silent; we must influence all people to accept Jesus Christ as their Lord and Savior so that they can enter the kingdom of God.

Prayer:
God I want to be a fearless Christian who preaches gospel by all means. I am determined and ready to preach gospel; I will do this as much as I have your grace. I want to use my talents and resources to lead others to Jesus Christ - without complaining. Help me to use my existing abilities for your sake, and give me the new ones! Enable me to use my skill of drama presentations, music, communication, technology, and others to influence people for your kingdom. At the end of it all, let me enter heaven and hear your word "Weldone my good servant!" For in the name of Jesus Christ my Lord I make my requests.

Amen.

« DAY 233 »

Crisis Will Soon End For Believers, And They Will Permanently Be With God

Focus Passage: Micah 4,5

The scripture raises sure hope for believers; they will live permanently with God in his kingdom once their world crises are over. It is written,

> *"He will judge between many peoples and will settle disputes for strong nations far and wide. They will beat their swords into plowshares and their spears into pruning hooks. Nation will not take up sword against nation, nor will they train for war anymore. Everyone will sit under their own vine and under their own fig tree, and no one will make them afraid, for the Lord Almighty has spoken"* **(Micah 4:3-4 NIV).**

Lesson:
Whatever suffering that a child of God undergoes will not last eternally, but it will come to an end one day. All children of God will soon escape these terrible world crises to permanently be with God in heaven. In heaven, Jesus Christ will be our life president, and we shall suffer no more! There will be perfect peace that has no traces of sadness. In fact, saints will drink from peaceful river that flows from the heart of God himself. Therefore, since high price of victory awaits believers, all Christians should remain steadfast with God. We should endure whatever temptation and affliction that enemy may throw at us - having knowing fully that God's eternal rewards are waiting for us in heaven.

Prayer:
Dear God, I love you more than silver and gold. I love you more than persecution and afflictions. My goal is to reach heaven at the end of my earthly journey; therefore, I commit my complete life to you today. I accept Jesus Christ as my true Savior, and I accept him as my Lord. Please keep me consistent with you and let me wholeheartedly serve you throughout the days of my life, so that I can qualify to enjoy everlasting life with you in heaven. For in the name of Jesus Christ I make my requests.

Amen.

« DAY 234 »

Human Traditions Cannot Be Substituted For Christ's Salvation

Focus Passage: Acts 21:18-40

The church at Jerusalem made a judgment call on whether to exempt non-Jewish believers from Jewish traditions. They concluded that it was essential for brethren to serve God in the liberty of their spirit – without giving room for human traditions that could inhibit gospel expansion. Church elders wrote Paul and said,

> *"...But concerning the Gentiles who believe, we have written and decided that they should observe no such thing, except that they should keep themselves from things offered to idols, from blood, from things strangled, and from sexual immorality"* **(Acts 21:25).**

Lesson:
Many polls indicate that non-Jewish Christians outnumber the Jewish Christians. Meanwhile, whether a Christian was born Jewish or not, we are all required to obey God's laws; we must engage in praiseworthy activities that glorify God's name. Although tradition may challenge us into moral behaviors, but they must not be mistaken for God's laws. Human traditions are not God's laws! Therefore, we must duly study scriptures to understand God's requirements. Our success can only abide if we know and do the truth. God will forever glorify his name in the lives of people that honorably follow him.

Prayer:
Dear God, I have learnt that human tradition is different from God's standard of holiness. Therefore, I ask you to please save me from any tradition that may pose threat to your standard of holiness. Enable me with grace to commit myself into studying the scriptures so that I can live the life expected of me. Please save my soul from error, so that I will not be disappointed on final Day of Judgment! For in the name of Jesus Christ I make my requests.

Amen.

« DAY 235 »

Repentance Is A Symbol Of Integrity And Honesty To God

Focus Passage: Micah 6,7

An act of repentance is not a symbol of cowardice; it is a symbol of honesty to the living God. True and humble people are not ashamed to repent from their sins. They refuse to rejoice in sin, but repent from them. Repentant people are also hopeful in God to have strength needed to overcome future temptations. One prophet confessed his progressive standing with God, and declared his hope of a victorious future. The prophet stated,

> *"Do not rejoice over me, my enemy; when I fall, I will arise; when I sit in darkness, The Lord will be a light to me. I will bear the indignation of the Lord, because I have sinned against Him, Until He pleads my case and executes justice for me. He will bring me forth to the light; I will see His righteousness"* **(Micah 7:8-9).**

Lesson:
God loves people who are humble enough to repent from their sins. He appreciates them for their act of courage to shun evil and pursue righteousness. The scripture emphasized, "God resists the proud, but gives grace to the humble" (James 4:6). Therefore, children of God must place high emphasis on repentance of sin. Any child of God who is drifted and fell into sin should repent, so that he/she can obtain God's forgiveness. The Creator is a loving Father, and he will forgive and restore a sinner who repents.

Prayer:
Dear God, I am a sinner, and I am very sorry for my sins. I understand that you are a loving and forgiving God; therefore, I ask you to please forgive my past sins. Please restore unto me the joy of my salvation! Let your Holy Spirit give me strength to overcome enemy's temptations. Please help me to be strong towards righteousness, and let me be more sensitive to your laws. Please keep me fit to receive your blessings on earth and in heaven also. For in the name of Jesus Christ I make my requests.

Amen.

« DAY 236 »

Anyone Can Become A Christian Irrespective Of Background

Focus Passage: Acts 22

Paul transformed from being a church persecutor to become a church-goer and leader. He had an encounter with God and converted to Christianity. Paul recounted his story and said,

> *"I persecuted this Way (Christianity) to the death, binding and delivering into prisons both men and women, as also the high priest bears me witness, and all the council of the elders, from whom I also received letters to the brethren, and went to Damascus to bring in chains even those who were there to Jerusalem to be punished.*
>
> *"Now it happened, as I journeyed and came near Damascus at about noon, suddenly a great light from heaven shone around me. And I fell to the ground and heard a voice saying to me, 'Saul, Saul, why are you persecuting me?' So I answered, 'Who are You, Lord?' And He said to me, 'I am Jesus of Nazareth, whom you are persecuting'"* **(Acts 22:4-8).**

Lesson:
God is always willing to see a sinner repents from his/her sin and accept the salvation offer of his Son Jesus Christ. Christ's salvation is available to everyone. It is precious but free! Christ will accept anyone who comes to him. No matter how filthy someone's life is, Christ will clean him/her up. He will repair damaged life and restore beautiful future for anyone that comes to him. No religion is restricted; people of other faith can also come to Jesus Christ. He will accept everyone that comes to him - whether, Muslim, Buddhist, Hindu, traditionalist, or other. There is no other alternative means of obtaining eternal salvation than through Jesus Christ. People who currently practice other religions are expected to change their courses and become followers of Jesus Christ. All people must confess Jesus Christ as Lord to be saved. Jesus Christ said, *"I am the way, the truth, and the life. No one comes to the Father except through me"* **(John 14:6).**

Prayer:
Song:
"I have decided to follow Jesus; I have decided to follow Jesus; I have decided to follow Jesus. No turning back; no turning back!"

Today, I *(mention your name)* declare Jesus Christ as my Lord; I confess my sins and repent from them. I dedicate my complete life to Jesus Christ, and I will serve him for the rest of my life. No more sin! No more playing devil's games! My life belong to Jesus Christ from today, and forever more!

Amen.

« DAY 237 »

God Desires Steadfast Relationship From His Children

Focus Passage: Nahum 1, 2, 3

Christians are required to give due honor to God; we must not take him for granted, but we must give all it takes to make him happy with our faithful living. The Creator reserves measurable punishments for any of his children that deviate from the truth. It is written,

> *"God is jealous, and the Lord revengeth; the Lord revengeth, and is furious; the Lord will take vengeance on his adversaries, and he reserveth wrath for his enemies. The Lord is slow to anger, and great in power, and will not at all acquit the wicked: the Lord hath his way in the whirlwind and in the storm, and the clouds are the dust of his feet. He rebuketh the sea, and maketh it dry, and drieth up all the rivers: Bashan languisheth, and Carmel, and the flower of Lebanon languisheth. The mountains quake at him, and the hills melt, and the earth is burned at his presence, yea, the world, and all that dwell therein. Who can stand before his indignation? and who can abide in the fierceness of his anger? his fury is poured out like fire, and the rocks are thrown down by him. The Lord is good, a strong hold in the day of trouble; and he knoweth them that trust in him. But with an overrunning flood he will make an utter end of the place thereof, and darkness shall pursue his enemies"* **(Nahum 1:2-8 KJV).**

Lesson:
God's goodness is ever available to overflow his children. He will go extra miles to defend his names in their lives. However, the scriptures warn us to be careful in how we deal with God. We are not allowed to misuse his benefits; we must make every effort to appreciate him with godly living. If we do things right and serve him well, the Creator will increase his goodness in our lives, and he will decorate us with more honor.

Prayer:
Dear God, please give me grace to walk in your ways always. Do not let me take your benefits for granted, but help me to be appreciative of them. Empower me to live acceptable life before you always, and please multiply your benefits in my life, so that I can share the testimony of your goodness every day of my life. For in the name of Jesus Christ I make my requests.

Amen.

« DAY 238 »

Every Christian Has All It Takes To Preach Gospel

Focus Passage: Acts 23:1-15

Paul intelligently defeated his opponents by referencing scriptures to support his arguments. Two organized Jewish sects (Pharisees and Sadducees) that collaborated to persecute him for his ministerial activities became confused when Paul argued they were just harassing him based on subject matter that some of them believed. (Pharisees believed in resurrection but Sadducees did not). Paul – a lawyer turned preacher – demonstrated his skills as the scripture reported,

> *"When Paul perceived that one part (of the opposing sects) were Sadducees and the other Pharisees, he cried out in the council, "Men and brethren, I am a Pharisee, the son of a Pharisee; concerning the hope and resurrection of the dead I am being judged!" And when he had said this, a dissension arose between the Pharisees and the Sadducees; and the assembly was divided. For Sadducees say that there is no resurrection—and no angel or spirit; but the Pharisees confess both. Then there arose a loud outcry. And the scribes of the Pharisees' party arose and protested, saying, "We find no evil in this man; but if a spirit or an angel has spoken to him, let us not fight against God"* **(Acts 23:6-9).**

Lesson:
Christians are not naive, but we are intelligent people showcasing the glory of God. Believers have natural abilities and inbuilt skills to preach gospel wherever we go. Our skills must manifest to motivate other people to be in touch with God. The Creator has raised and trained us under different circumstances. He has dispersed us into various disciplines to develop skills and strength needed to propagate gospel. Every Christian has one ability or the other needed to aid gospel and help populate God's kingdom! Therefore, no Christian should complain of lack of resources as an excuse for not preaching gospel. Christians of every profession are expected to bring out their best for God. People of special expertise should propagate gospel - whether lawyer, doctor, engineer, architect, nurse, pharmacist, journalist, carpenter, mechanic, accountant, housekeeper, janitor, cashier, clerk, secretary, politician, and others. All people must rise up to the task of preaching gospel of Jesus Christ. Without reservations, we must preach gospel to people of various culture and backgrounds. If we obey God, devil's kingdom will suffer losses and God's kingdom will be populated.

Prayer:
Dear God, please make me a useful vessel for you. Give me strength to use my natural ability (my gifts and my talents) to preach your gospel. Please use me to lead as many people as possible to your kingdom. I also pray for my fellow believers throughout the world that you grant them courage to keep preaching your gospel. Let brethren keep preaching about you so that people can escape punishment of hell and be qualified for heaven. Let devil be put to shame and glory be given to your name through our effective evangelism! For in the name of Jesus Christ I make my requests.
Amen.

« DAY 239 »

God Desires Repentance of Every Sinner

Focus Passage: 2 Chronicles 33:5-9

King Manasseh of Judah cared less about God, but focus on serving idols. He promoted idolatry to a great extent. He sacrificed his own children to idol (as human sacrifice). He also sponsored other evil practices such as witchcraft, sorcery, and spiritism. The scripture recorded about King Manasseh,

> *"And he built altars for all the host of heaven in the two courts of the house of the Lord. And he caused his children to pass through the fire in the valley of the son of Hinnom: also he observed times, and used enchantments, and used witchcraft, and dealt with a familiar spirit, and with wizards: he wrought much evil in the sight of the Lord, to provoke him to anger. And he set a carved image, the idol which he had made, in the house of God, of which God had said to David and to Solomon his son, In this house, and in Jerusalem, which I have chosen before all the tribes of Israel, will I put my name for ever: Neither will I any more remove the foot of Israel from out of the land which I have appointed for your fathers; so that they will take heed to do all that I have commanded them, according to the whole law and the statutes and the ordinances by the hand of Moses. So Manasseh made Judah and the inhabitants of Jerusalem to err, and to do worse than the heathen, whom the Lord had destroyed before the children of Israel"* **(2 Chronicles 33:5-9 KJV)**. God punished King Manasseh for his evil deeds: Invaders captured and transported him to Babylon as a prisoner of war. However, the king later repented, and God forgave him of his sins It is reported, *"And when he was in affliction, he besought the Lord his God, and humbled himself greatly before the God of his fathers"* **(2 Chronicles 33:12 KJV)**. God restored Manasseh and gave him another opportunity to do damage control.

Lesson:
God will forgive our sins if we repent from them. There is no sin too big for him to forgive. Once we show true humility and genuine repentance, he will forgive us. Meanwhile, the Creator expects us to make definite improvements after repentance. He wants us to disengage from our old and sinful ways. He wants us to work on a new and just path that is fit for his kingdom. The scripture emphasized, *"Therefore, if anyone is in Christ, he is a new creation; old things have passed away; behold, all things have become new"* **(2 Corinthians 5:17)**.

Prayer:
Dear Jesus Christ, you have done enough job to save my life. You sacrificed your life and die for my sins on the cross. I repent from my sins today. I confess them and forsake them. I accept you Jesus Christ as my personal Lord and Savior. From now on, I am determined to start working newly with you - and I forsake my old way of life. My total life is committed to you from today, and forever!
Amen.

« DAY 240 »

God Will Bless Those Who Make Positive Contributions Towards Gospel Success

Focus Passage: Acts 23:16-35

Anti gospel people planned to kill Paul in an attempt to silence his campaign, but God frustrated their efforts. The scripture reported,

> *"Then the commander took him by the hand, went aside, and asked privately, "What is it that you have to tell me?" And he said, "The Jews have agreed to ask that you bring Paul down to the council tomorrow, as though they were going to inquire more fully about him. But do not yield to them, for more than forty of them lie in wait for him, men who have bound themselves by an oath that they will neither eat nor drink till they have killed him; and now they are ready, waiting for the promise from you." So the commander let the young man depart, and commanded him, "Tell no one that you have revealed these things to me"* **(Acts 23:19-22).**

Lesson:

People who aim at attacking God's servants in an attempt to stop gospel expansion are just wasting their time, because gospel cannot be stopped since God himself established it. The gospel will remain effective until Christ returns to rapture his saints to heaven. Meanwhile, those who persecute God's servants are hurting God, and they will pay for their mistakes unless they repent. Instead of hurting God's servants, we can choose to support and encourage them in their good works. We can pray for God's servants and offer them needed resources to continue to promote God's interests in this world. God's divine blessings will reign in the lives of people who motivate his ministers into serving him.

Prayer:

Dear God, I understand that your servants deserve honor, and I want to start honoring them. Please forgive me of any improper way that I have handled your servants in the past. Help me to start to do things rightly. I will start to pray for your servants and offer them every needed help, so that they can continue to promote your interest in whatever capacity that you have positioned them. Please give me a loyal heart to keep supporting your gospel, so that your good works can be promoted in people's lives locally and globally, and for your kingdom to be populated. For in the name of Jesus Christ I make my requests.

Amen.

« DAY 241 »

The Present Earth Will Soon Vanish And Be Replaced With A New One

Focus Passage: Zephaniah 1, 2, 3

God designed the present earth to exist temporarily. He will remove it from existence at the appointed time as the scripture stated,

> *"I will utterly consume everything from the face of the land," Says the Lord; "I will consume man and beast; I will consume the birds of the heavens, the fish of the sea, and the stumbling blocks along with the wicked. I will cut off man from the face of the land," Says the Lord"* ***(Zephaniah 1:2-3).*** However, Jehovah promised to replace our corrupt earth with a better one that would be a perfect habitation for his saints. Only God's saints will qualify to enjoy the new earth! God said, *"Then I will purify the lips of the peoples, that all of them may call on the name of the Lord and serve him shoulder to shoulder. From beyond the rivers of Cush my worshipers, my scattered people, will bring me offerings. On that day you, Jerusalem, will not be put to shame for all the wrongs you have done to me, because I will remove from you your arrogant boasters. Never again will you be haughty on my holy hill. But I will leave within you the meek and humble. The remnant of Israel will trust in the name of the Lord. They will do no wrong; they will tell no lies. A deceitful tongue will not be found in their mouths. They will eat and lie down and no one will make them afraid."* ***(Zephaniah 3:9-13).***

Lesson:
The present earth will not last eternally, but it will come to an end at God's appointed time. Jehovah will establish a new earth that is void of wickedness and corruption. Only those who have faithfully served God and believed in the testimony of the Lord Jesus Christ will qualify to enter the new earth and new heaven to be established. All workers of iniquity will not qualify to partake in the paradise (new earth). Wicked people will be shut out of it, but they will have their portions in the lake of fire **(Revelation 21:1-3).**

Prayer:
Dear God, please make me qualify for your kingdom. Keep my feet firm within your gate by living a lifestyle that meet your standard. Let your Holy Spirit guide me into all righteousness, so that my name can be written in the book of life. For in the name of Jesus Christ I make my requests.

Amen.

« DAY 242 »

Believers Must Ensure To Keep Their Evangelism Fire Burning

Focus Passage: Acts 24

Mr. Tertullus, a lawyer hired by Paul's opponents lashed out against Paul and Christianity. He said,

> *"We have found this man to be a troublemaker, stirring up riots among the Jews all over the world. He is a ringleader of the Nazarene sect and even tried to desecrate the temple; so we seized him"* **(Acts 24:5-7).** Paul shunned Tertullus, but tactically defended his faith in the court. Paul articulated his speech and said to the judge, *"...But this I confess to you, that according to the Way which they call a sect, so I worship the God of my fathers, believing all things which are written in the Law and in the Prophets. I have hope in God, which they themselves also accept, that there will be a resurrection of the dead, both of the just and the unjust. This being so, I myself always strive to have a conscience without offense toward God and men"* **(Acts 24:14-16).**

Lesson:
Christianity has always faced opposition from unbelievers (and it will continue to face it). God is well and able to defend us if we are challenged. Inasmuch there is God on the throne, there is no force of any kind that can overpower us. We Christians are children of light, and no darkness can prevail over us. We are not ordinary people; we are God's servants, and we have been anointed by Jesus Christ to proclaim his good news to the ends of the earth.
Meanwhile, believers cannot afford to sit around unreasonable opponents and waste precious time needed to further gospel evangelization. Christians should avoid wasting time with people who are adamant in their old way of thinking and would not consider the benefits of gospel. Believers should concentrate their efforts on sharing gospel with people, and pay due attention to their willing audience. Also, we must follow up with people and ensure they remain consistent in their faith with the Lord. Our Christian efforts must be productive in all ramifications. As it is necessary, we must be prayerful to receive God's grace and strength to keep standing in faith at all times.

Prayer:
In the name of Jesus Christ I receive power and grace to continue preaching irresistible gospel. I receive Christ' anointing to share his gospel to every land, nation, and tongue. I receive the power of the Holy Spirit to stand firm in faith and be resilient in my confession of Jesus Christ. In the name of Jesus Christ I reaffirm my authority over devil and all his agents and instrument: I command them to bow in the name of Jesus Christ! I frustrate every power of the enemy that is set out to silence me. I command Satan to get lost from every aspect of my life, so that I can continue to shine gospel light to the ends of the earth. For in the name of Jesus Christ I exercise my authority!

Amen!

« DAY 243 »

God Expects His Children To Love Him Unconditionally

Focus Passage: 2 Chronicles 35; Habakkuk 1,2,3

God desires unconditional love from his children. He wants us to serve him without hidden agenda. He will bless us if we serve him well, but our services must not be solely based on any favor we intend to get. Christians' motive of service should be similar to what Prophet Habakkuk stated in the scripture,

> *"Although the fig tree shall not blossom, neither shall fruit be in the vines; the labour of the olive shall fail, and the fields shall yield no meat; the flock shall be cut off from the fold, and there shall be no herd in the stalls: Yet I will rejoice in the Lord, I will joy in the God of my salvation. The Lord God is my strength, and he will make my feet like hinds' feet, and he will make me to walk upon mine high places..."* **(Habakkuk 3:17-19 KJV).**

Lesson:

Christians are not different from other people; we have our own past (sweet and sour) experience. Meanwhile, Christ found us, cleaned us, and saved us. Of course we may still lack one thing or the other, but our motive behind serving God must be unconditional. Some circumstances might have drawn us closer to God, but those circumstances have become secondary. Our primary motive is to serve God unconditionally! Christians must serve God whether it rains or shines. We must beautifully serve God - whether our surrounding factors are good or bad. Children of God cannot afford to become obsessed with their problems and allow them to mar their relationship with God. A child of God must remain committed to God - whether his/her expectations are met or not! However, our heavenly Father is ever able and strong to cater for us. He will meet our needs and satisfy us if we can prove an unwavering and unconditional love for him.

Prayer:

Dear God, enough of playing games with you! I am determined to get serious in my relationship with you. I will not serve you for what I intend to get only, but I will serve you unconditionally. I will devote my time and energy to sing beautiful songs and sincerely pray to your holy name. I will serve you: share your gospel and support those who share it. I will allow your Holy Spirit to teach and lead me into the truth of the scripture. Again, I declare that I have sold out my total heart for you Jesus! My loyalty and unconditional love shall remain for you, and you only! My declarations remain valid today, tomorrow, and forever! For in the name of Jesus Christ I make my affirmations.

Amen!

« DAY 244 »

Believers May Face Persecutions On Earth But Their Rewards Will Be Great In Heaven

Focus Passage: Acts 25

Government authority persecuted Paul for his self-discipline and roles in gospel propagation. Corrupt political leaders like Governor Festus and Felix failed to exercise justice, and they kept Paul in bondage to satisfy their greed. The scripture reported,

> "...But Festus, wanting to do the Jews a favor, answered Paul and said, "Are you willing to go up to Jerusalem and there be judged before me concerning these things?" So Paul said, "I stand at Caesar's judgment seat, where I ought to be judged. To the Jews I have done no wrong, as you very well know" **(Acts 25: 9-10).**

Lesson:
Christians live in an imperfect world filled with leaders that terrorize their citizens with oppression and imbalance justice. The world sinful system will cause Christians to suffer many persecutions for the sake of their faith. Meanwhile, believers sufferings will not last a eternally. Believers will have new experience once Christ rapture them to heaven. The Son of God will wipe tears off the faces of his saints, and he will decorate them with beauty and honor. Therefore, believers are encouraged to endure whatever persecution is coming their ways since the price of their endurance will ever be refreshing in heaven.

Prayer:
Dear God, I understand that the world system will refute gospel light and persecute your saints; they will accuse believers and make them suffer, but all to contribute to believers' huge rewards in heaven. Therefore, I want to be a Christian that will endure persecution and promote the light of your gospel. Help me to remain resolute and be immovable in my confession of faith in Jesus Christ so that I can qualify for your eternal rewards in heaven. For in the name of Jesus Christ I make my requests.

Amen.

« DAY 245 »

God Reserves Huge Rewards For People Who Faithfully Serve Him On Earth

Focus Passage: Jeremiah 1, 2

God asked Jeremiah to speak out against the nation of Israel for turning their back against him. He assured Jeremiah that his selection to be his mouthpiece was predetermined before his inception. God said to Jeremiah,

> "The word of the Lord came to me, saying, "Before I formed you in the womb I knew you, before you were born I set you apart; I appointed you as a prophet to the nations." "Alas, Sovereign Lord," I said, "I do not know how to speak; I am too young." But the Lord said to me, "Do not say, 'I am too young.' You must go to everyone I send you to and say whatever I command you. Do not be afraid of them, for I am with you and will rescue you," declares the Lord" **(Jeremiah 1:4-8 NIV).**

Lesson:
It is a good thing to serve God, and the effort has no regret. God's servants have the backing of their commander - Almighty God, and they are bound to succeed. The rewards of people that have special commission for God's service are not limited to this world only, but they will last eternally in heaven. Therefore, people who take one special assignment or the other in God's vineyard should be courageous to do their best and satisfy God to the fullness, since their rewards will abide on earth and in heaven.

Prayer:
Dear God, I receive your grace and boldness to continue in your service. Please help me to keep focus, and let me serve to your satisfaction. Let my rewards be enriching and profitable for your kingdom. Let my labor of love not be in vain; count me worthy in your kingdom, and let my rewards abide. For in the name of Jesus Christ I have made my requests.

Amen.

« DAY 246 »

Whoever Comes To Jesus Christ Will Receive Gift of Eternal Life

Focus Passage: Acts 26

Paul made a public confession about his mistakes as a persecutor of Christianity, and he condemned his actions. Paul recounted,

> *"Why should it be thought incredible by you that God raises the dead? "Indeed, I myself thought I must do many things contrary to the name of Jesus of Nazareth. This I also did in Jerusalem and many of the saints I shut up in prison, having received authority from the chief priests; and when they were put to death, I cast my vote against them. And I punished them often in every synagogue and compelled them to blaspheme; and being exceedingly enraged against them, I persecuted them even to foreign cities"* **(Acts 26:8-11).**
>
> Paul further explained his transforming experience with Christ and said, *"At midday, O king, along the road I saw a light from heaven, brighter than the sun, shining around me and those who journeyed with me. And when we all had fallen to the ground, I heard a voice speaking to me and saying in the Hebrew language, 'Saul, Saul, why are you persecuting me? It is hard for you to kick against the goads.' So I said, 'Who are You, Lord?' And He said, 'I am Jesus, whom you are persecuting. But rise and stand on your feet; for I have appeared to you for this purpose, to make you a minister and a witness both of the things which you have seen and of the things which I will yet reveal to you"* **(Acts 26:13-16).**

Lesson:
Jesus Christ accepts people who turn to him for salvation - he never rejects anyone. Irrespective of past failures, he will forgive repentant sinners and overlook their mistakes. He will call repentant sinners "saints," and decorate them with beauty and honor in heaven. All what it takes for anyone to enjoy God's eternal benefits are confession of sin; repentance of sin, and acceptance of Jesus Christ as Lord. Whoever confesses Jesus Christ as his personal Lord and Savior will not be ashamed but be honored with gift of everlasting life in heaven.

Prayer:
I was once lost in sin, but now I am saved in Jesus Christ since I have confessed him as my personal Lord and Savior! Christ the Son of God has changed my life: He found me, forgave my sins, and redeemed my soul from condemnation of hell fire. My life is now transformed in Jesus Christ, and I am now saved! Praise God, my name is now written in the book of life, and the kingdom of God is meant for me to enjoy! Praise Jesus Christ for saving a poor sinner like me. I ask my Lord Jesus Christ to give me grace to remain heavenly worthy.

Amen

« DAY 247 »

God Is Willing To Save Repentant Sinners Than To Send Them To Hell Fire

Focus Passage: Jeremiah 3, 4, 5

God is more interested in blessing people than punishing them. He is willing to see a sinner repent from his/her sin and be blessed than to remain adamant in sin to receive eternal condemnation in hell. Also, God wants repentance of backslidden Christians; he will accept them with open arms if they could turn a new leaf. In his statement to the nation of Israel, God said,

> *"'Return, backsliding Israel,' says the Lord; 'I will not cause my anger to fall on you. For I am merciful,' says the Lord; 'I will not remain angry forever. Only acknowledge your iniquity, that you have transgressed against the Lord your God, and have scattered your charms to alien deities under every green tree, and you have not obeyed my voice,' says the Lord. "Return, O backsliding children," says the Lord; "for I am married to you. I will take you, one from a city and two from a family, and I will bring you to Zion"* **(Jeremiah 3:12-14).**

Lesson:

God loves humanity, and he is willing to save us all. He will save anyone who comes to him to seek refuge and salvation. However, it is painful for the Creator to see that some people are adamant in their sins, and refuse repentance option. Also, some Christians that have fallen away from faith are causing God enormous pain with their decisions. Jehovah expects his children to be in good term with him, so that he can bless them. Therefore, God's arms remain widely open to receive backslidden Christians and other sinners. He will transform their lives and make them fit for his eternal blessing - if they can sincerely return to him.

Prayer:

Dear God, I am sorry for all my wrongdoing, and I am ready to repent and return to you again. I want to stop hurting you with my actions; I want to start satisfying your desires. I consider myself a prodigal child who has rebelled and lost everything; please I have returned to you today. I will start working in your ways, and I will faithfully serve you for the rest of my life so that I can prosper in all my ways. Please give me grace to do so. For in the name of Jesus Christ I make my requests.

Amen.

« DAY 248 »

God Will Take Control Of Any Situation That Relates To His Children

Focus Passage: Acts 27: 1-26

Paul (a gospel minister held as a prisoner) alongside others suffered shipwreck. None would have survived the accident due to its severity, but God spared them all - since his servant was involved. Paul described the encounter he had with God on the ship in order to assure other prisoners of God's safety. Paul said,

> *"But now I urge you to keep up your courage, because not one of you will be lost; only the ship will be destroyed. Last night an angel of the God to whom I belong and whom I serve stood beside me and said, 'Do not be afraid, Paul. You must stand trial before Caesar; and God has graciously given you the lives of all who sail with you'"* **(Acts 27:22-24 NIV).**

Lesson:
Any situation that appears as a tempest wind cannot endure long in believers' lives, it will subside. Challenges may come, but they will soon vanish. No situation is difficult for God, he will overcome them all. Jehovah has control over air, land, and sea. All situations listen to him, and they submit to his authority. Since Christians are God's apple eyes, we can be guaranteed of safety and victory at all times. Therefore, we believers must be full of faith and assurance that God will glorify himself in our lives under whatever circumstance.

Prayer:
Dear God, I understand that I am not alone, but you are with me. You will help me overcome all my challenges, and you will give me victory. Please, give me faith and make me strong to live a victorious life throughout the days of my life. Let me raise my head above waters, and let my mouth be full of victory songs. Please do these things and many more. For in the name of Jesus Christ I make my requests.

Amen.

« DAY 249 »

There Are God's Promises Of Blessing For Whoever Obeys Him

Focus Passage: Jeremiah 6, 11, 12

God considered Israelites' rebellion acts as serious crime, and he promised to make them suffer dire consequence if they refuse to repent. God spoke through Jeremiah, "'Thus says the Lord God of Israel,

> *"... Cursed be the man that obeyeth not the words of this covenant, Which I commanded your fathers in the day that I brought them forth out of the land of Egypt, from the iron furnace, saying, Obey my voice, and do them, according to all which I command you: so shall ye be my people, and I will be your God: That I may perform the oath which I have sworn unto your fathers, to give them a land flowing with milk and honey, as it is this day. Then answered I, and said, So be it, O Lord"* **(Jeremiah 11:3-5 KJV)**.

Lesson:
God has fundamental rules which cannot be bent. The rules are fundamental, but simple. God affirmed that people must stay away from sin and act honorably. We must love him and also love our neighbors. The Creator added a condition of blessing to our obedience; he promised to bless whoever follows his commandments, so that other people can be motivated to follow the same example.

Prayer:
Dear God, please give me grace to duly follow your instructions. Give me grace to love you and my neighbors. Let your blessing overflow my life so that unbelievers can be motivated to serve you also. Please do these, and many more. For in the name of Jesus Christ I make my requests.

Amen.

« DAY 250 »

Believers Must Keep Positive Confessions Until Their Expectations Are Met

Focus Passage: Acts 27:27-44

Paul rose above challenges of shipwreck and turbulence, and he encouraged others to follow his footsteps. Paul encouraged others to eat food after 14 days of their sailing crisis. He openly ate his meal as reported,

> *"And as day was about to dawn, Paul implored them all to take food, saying, "Today is the fourteenth day you have waited and continued without food, and eaten nothing. Therefore I urge you to take nourishment, for this is for your survival, since not a hair will fall from the head of any of you." And when he had said these things, he took bread and gave thanks to God in the presence of them all; and when he had broken it he began to eat"* **(Acts 27:33-35).**

Lesson:
Children of God are expected to make positive confessions at all times; however, we sometimes face tough situations that may tempt us to act otherwise. Believers should not fall for temptations and deny their insurmountable faith in God. We must not cease in making positive confession with expectations. Our heavenly Father will not withdraw his promises from us, but fulfill them.

Prayer:
Dear God, please teach me how to have faith and make positive confession during adversity. I know that you are ever faithful, and you will keep your promises over me. Please help me to keep trusting you until all my expectations are met. Let your songs of victory ever be in my mouth. For in the name of Jesus Christ I make my requests.

Amen.

« DAY 251 »

Humility And Integrity Are Great Virtues

Focus Passage: Jeremiah 7, 8, 26

Jeremiah ran into trouble for prophesying the mind of God. The government and religion leaders of Judah arrested him for cautioning them to desist from evil or face consequences. The scripture reported,

> *"Now it came to pass, when Jeremiah had made an end of speaking all that the Lord had commanded him to speak unto all the people, that the priests and the prophets and all the people took him, saying, Thou shalt surely die. Why hast thou prophesied in the name of the Lord, saying, This house shall be like Shiloh, and this city shall be desolate without an inhabitant? And all the people were gathered against Jeremiah in the house of the Lord"* **(Jeremiah 26:8-9 KJV).**

Lesson:
Dishonest people hate confrontation, but honest people like it. People who hate confrontation and would not budge for correction are more or less proud. They see things in their own eyes only, and they would rationalize sin to suit their selfish interest. God hates the proud. He dislikes people who would not give a second thought to correction, and make necessary improvement. Children of God must be careful not to fall into this category. We must not be rigid towards sin, but be correctable, and be willing to change whenever we are confronted with our sins. We must yield to God's corrections and instructions in the bible. We must also yield whenever we are challenged through other medium - whether through preaching or direct confrontation. Jehovah will honor us if we are flexible in his hands. His divine blessings will abide with people who behave like sheep in the hands of their master!

Prayer:
Dear God, please make me a honest and a humble person who is bendable in your hands. Let me be correctable! Mortify my flesh to respond to your instructions in the bible. Also, enable me to yield to your instructions which may be passed through other media, so that I can prosper on earth and make it to heaven. Please give me grace to keep serving you according to your expectations. For in the name of Jesus Christ I make my requests.

Amen.

« DAY 252 »

God's Promises Of Blessing For His Children Are Irrevocable !

Focus Passage: Acts 28

Paul was confronted from every side for the sake of gospel, but God preserved his life to keep thriving in his kingdom business. God helped Paul to survive Jewish persecutions and shipwreck. He also saved him from an attack of a venomous snake. The scripture reported,

> *"...But when Paul had gathered a bundle of sticks and laid them on the fire, a viper came out because of the heat, and fastened on his hand. So when the natives saw the creature hanging from his hand, they said to one another, "No doubt this man is a murderer, whom, though he has escaped the sea, yet justice does not allow to live." But he shook off the creature into the fire and suffered no harm. However, they were expecting that he would swell up or suddenly fall down dead. But after they had looked for a long time and saw no harm come to him, they changed their minds and said that he was a god" (Acts 28:3-6).*

Lesson:
The promises of God stand sure over his children. He will fulfill his promises over us, and help us have victory. Truly, we might face uncomfortable situations in this world, which may tempt us to doubt God's saving strength. However, we Christians must be encouraged to remain resolute in faith. Our God who made all things is the one who is in control of our lives; he will not let us down but earn us victory! God's promises will be fulfilled over us - and there is nothing that devil can do to stop him! Let every child of God say "I believe in God's strength for my safety, provision, and sustenance."

Prayer:
Dear God, please help me to remain strong in faith at all times. Empower me to keep confessing positively until all my problems are solved. Whether a situation is comfortable or not, help me to always affirm my boldness and make positive confession in you. Let my confession always be "I know my God whom I serve. He will not leave me alone in any situation, but he will rescue me and provide for all my needs." For in the name of Jesus Christ I make my requests.

Amen.

« DAY 253 »

Believers Must Not Be Boastful Of Their Success, But Be Appreciative To God

Focus Passage: Jeremiah 9, 10, 14

God expects us to be appreciative of him for our achievements, and not to boast in flesh. The Creator does not want us to boast on our human abilities and/or material wealth as if we acquired them by our self-efforts. Our achievements are obtained by God's help, and we must be humble to glorify his name. The scripture taught us to wisely handle our achievements as it is written,

> *"Thus says the Lord: "Let not the wise man glory in his wisdom, Let not the mighty man glory in his might, Nor let the rich man glory in his riches; But let him who glories glory in this, That he understands and knows Me, That I am the Lord, exercising lovingkindness, judgment, and righteousness in the earth. For in these I delight," says the Lord" **(Jeremiah 9:23-24).***

Lesson:
Believers must understand how to glorify God with their achievements. A child of God must be able to say, "I am what I am by the grace of God." We Christians must understand that God is the brain behind our success. He has brought us this far by his saving strength, and not by our human efforts. Therefore, we must remain grateful to him always. Of course, we can still reference our achievements and be proud of our success, but we ought to always add a phrase that honor God.

Prayer:
Dear God, I thank you for all my achievements. You are the brain behind my success, and without you I would not be where I am today. You have given me all I have, and without you I would have acquired nothing! Therefore, I will praise you throughout the days of my life. Please give me grace to ever be appreciative of your goodness; do not let me be full of myself to arrogate your glory to my human ability. Let my testimony ever lead to the glorification of your name. For in the name of Jesus Christ I make my requests.

Amen.

« DAY 254 »

Jesus Christ Is The Clear Mirror Of God; Through Him We Shall See God

Focus Passage: Colossians 1

Paul explained the person of Jesus Christ and his remarkable strength that became our blessing. Paul said,

> *"He (God) has delivered us from the power of darkness and conveyed us into the kingdom of the Son of His love (Jesus Christ), in whom we have redemption through His blood, the forgiveness of sins. He is the image of the invisible God, the firstborn over all creation. For by Him all things were created that are in heaven and that are on earth, visible and invisible, whether thrones or dominions or principalities or powers. All things were created through Him and for Him. And He is before all things, and in Him all things consist. And He is the head of the body, the church, who is the beginning, the firstborn from the dead, that in all things He may have the preeminence"* **(Colossians 1:13-18).**

Lesson:
The invisible God has made all things about him visible through his Son Jesus Christ; hence, it becomes simple for anyone to understand God's attributes. Jesus Christ is the clear mirror of God; through him all humanity will receive forgiveness of their sins. Also, through Jesus Christ all people will have access to God. (Jesus Christ is the gift of eternal life for everyone who choose to believe in him). It is important that everyone establishes good relationship with him, and confess him as Lord and Savior.

Prayer:
Dear Jesus, I know who you are, and I understand your status. You are the Christ - the Savior of the world. I confess you as Lord and I accept you as my personal Savior. I give you my complete life, and I promise to faithfully serve you for the rest of my life. Please keep my name in the book of life, so that I can receive the gift of eternal life in heaven. For in the name of Jesus Christ I make my requests.

Amen.

« DAY 255 »

Christians Should Reserve Their Absolute Trust In God Since He Never Fails

Focus Passage: Jeremiah 15, 16, 17

The scriptures warned us not to trust arms of flesh - for they will fail. We are challenged to reserve our trust in God who never fails. It is written,

> *"Thus says the Lord: "Cursed is the man who trusts in man and makes flesh his strength, whose heart departs from the Lord. For he shall be like a shrub in the desert, And shall not see when good comes, But shall inhabit the parched places in the wilderness, In a salt land which is not inhabited. "Blessed is the man who trusts in the Lord, and whose hope is the Lord. For he shall be like a tree planted by the waters, Which spreads out its roots by the river, And will not fear when heat comes; But its leaf will be green, And will not be anxious in the year of drought, Nor will cease from yielding fruit"* **(Jeremiah 17:5-8).**

Lesson:

Humans are not perfect, but God is perfect; therefore, children of God are encouraged to place their absolute trust in God only. God has no fallible nature, but human has. A person may change his mind at any time; he/she may simply fail. Worse still, a person trusted may die. However, God keeps promises, and he lives forever. He has final authority over all things. His words are absolute, and no one dares to challenge him. He has the scriptures full of his promises for his children. His promising voice can even be heard in Jeremiah 29:11 (For I know the thoughts that I think toward you, says the Lord, thoughts of peace and not of evil, to give you a future and a hope). Therefore, believers should affirm their trust in God. We should be bold towards his promises and claim them to our lives - for having peace, prosperity, and the rest!

Prayer:

Dear God, you are the only being in existence that never fails. Any other person on earth may fail; therefore, my complete trust will be placed in you only. I swear my allegiance into serving you, and trusting you over all my needs. Let my faith align with my confession always, and let it be easy for me to declare, "I know my God whom I serve, and he shall deliver me from all troubles and meet my needs!" Please satisfy all my needs, and let me have testimony of your goodness to share with others. For in the name of Jesus Christ I make my requests.

Amen.

« DAY 256 »

Believers Must Not Live On Fantasy But Be Sound With Biblical Doctrine

Focus Passage: Colossians 2

Paul advised Christians to stand by true faith and be careful not to get trapped with mere traditions that contribute little or nothing to God's kingdom. Paul said,

> *"Therefore do not let anyone judge you by what you eat or drink, or with regard to a religious festival, a New Moon celebration or a Sabbath day. These are a shadow of the things that were to come; the reality, however, is found in Christ. Do not let anyone who delights in false humility and the worship of angels disqualify you. Such a person also goes into great detail about what they have seen; they are puffed up with idle notions by their unspiritual mind. They have lost connection with the head, from whom the whole body, supported and held together by its ligaments and sinews, grows as God causes it to grow. Since you died with Christ to the elemental spiritual forces of this world, why, as though you still belonged to the world, do you submit to its rules: "Do not handle! Do not taste! Do not touch!?"* **(Colossians 2:16-21 NIV).**

Lesson:
Christians are to be careful not to live on fantasy, but to stand firm with biblical principles. We must have clear standing with God, and reject teachings that lack basis in the scripture. Also, we must be careful not to allow Satan to manipulate us into believing in spiritual fantasy. We ought not to entertain any revelation, teaching, or instruction which contradict bible. However, we must cooperate with God's Holy Spirit to guide us into all truth. We must allow him (the Holy Spirit) to prepare and keep us fit for God's rich rewards in this life, and in heaven also.

Prayer:
Dear God, please let me be a sensitive Christian who dance to the tune of the Holy Spirit always. Guide me not to fall victim of erratic teachings that contradict bible, but help me to cherish principles that have their root grounded in the Bible. Let me remain fit for your blessings in this world, and in heaven also. For in the name of Jesus Christ I made my requests.

Amen.

« DAY 257 »

God Is Greater Than Humans – By All Standards

Focus Passage: Jeremiah 18, 19

All people are nothing but breakable clay in the hands of their potter. God is the potter and we are the clay. He has autonomous power over us; he is the maker of the universe, and all things submit to him. God stated in the scripture,

> *"O house of Israel, can I not do with you as this potter?" says the Lord. "Look, as the clay is in the potter's hand, so are you in my hand, O house of Israel!"* ***(Jeremiah 18:6).***

Lesson:
We human beings are not All-In-All, but God is. We are subject to him, and he has the final authority over us. We are not allowed to do whatever we like, unless they satisfy the Creator. We are required to revere him with honor and obey his commandments, so that we can prosper.

Prayer:
Dear God, please keep me humble before you, and let me reverence you with dignity and honor. Do not let me be full of myself and disrespect you in anyway. Since you are the porter and I am the clay, let me yield to your instructions so that I can prosper in all my ways. For in the name of Jesus Christ I make my requests.

Amen.

« DAY 258 »

The Present Earth Will Remain A Temporal Home For Believers

Focus Passage: Colossians 3

The scripture encouraged Christians to focus on eternal joy that is awaiting them in heaven. We must focus on Jesus Christ and not be carried away with any earthly simulating activity that is temporal. It is written,

> *"If then you were raised with Christ, seek those things which are above, where Christ is, sitting at the right hand of God. Set your mind on things above, not on things on the earth. For you died, and your life is hidden with Christ in God"* **(Colossians 3:1-3).**

Lesson:
Our present earth is nothing but a market full of distracting activities; believers must be careful not to be trapped by them! We Christians must not lose sense of spiritual understanding to adequately deal with this world. We must be in the spirit to resist devil and all his temptations. Also, we must mortify our flesh to resist sins. The scripture encouraged us to take proactive steps towards holiness as written in **Colossians 3:5** *"Therefore put to death your members which are on the earth: fornication, uncleanness, passion, evil desire, and covetousness, which are idolatry."*

In addition, the scripture emphasized the need for moral values and heavenly worthy activities as mentioned in **Colossians 3:12-14** *"Therefore, as the elect of God, holy and beloved, put on tender mercies, kindness, humility, meekness, longsuffering; bearing with one another, and forgiving one another, if anyone has a complaint against another; even as Christ forgave you, so you also must do. But above all these things put on love, which is the bond of perfection."*

Prayer:
Dear God, I understand that Christianity involves committed activities than becoming a mere nominal Christian. You require more sacrifices from me than lip service; In fact, my faith will not be measured base on numbers of bibles I have or amount of religion activities I perform. You required a committed heart with contrite spirit. Therefore, I am ready to give you what you required! I am ready to live a committed life unto you. I will follow the scripture and walk in holiness. Please empower me with your Holy Spirit to meet your expectations, so that I can qualify for your kingdom. For in the name of Jesus Christ I make my requests.

Amen.

« DAY 259 »

Christians Are To Speak The Truth And Live In The Truth To Glorify God

Focus Passage: Jeremiah 20, 35, 36

People of Judah persecuted Prophet Jeremiah for speaking out the mind of God. Their abusive characters forced the prophet to have an inner battle and considered a possibility of changing course of action. He thought of stop speaking the truth, but God's Spirit would not let him to do so. Jeremiah's expressions were quoted as reported,

> *"O Lord, thou hast deceived me, and I was deceived; thou art stronger than I, and hast prevailed: I am in derision daily, every one mocketh me. For since I spake, I cried out, I cried violence and spoil; because the word of the Lord was made a reproach unto me, and a derision, daily. Then I said, I will not make mention of him, nor speak any more in his name. But his word was in mine heart as a burning fire shut up in my bones, and I was weary with forbearing, and I could not stay"* **(Jeremiah 20:7-9 KJV).**

Lesson:

Christians are required to stand up for the truth and speak out the mind of God at all times. We are expected to say the truth, even when it is not convenient. Of course, persecution will rise against us for doing God's will, but God has promised us victory! We must not allow pressure and intimidation of others to persuade us into disobeying God. We Christians are God's children, and we must obey God always. Our righteous efforts will promote God's name and make more people become thoughtful of him. (People will serve God more when they are thoughtful of him). Also, our acts of obedience will lead to our blessings, since God has promised
"... For those who honor me I will honor, and those who despise Me shall be lightly esteemed" **(1 Samuel 2:30).**

Prayer:

Dear God, Please help me to stand up with you and do your will at all times. Help me to stand up for righteousness and obey you! Please do not let me give in for the pressure of this world and disobey you. Let me truthfully do all that is required of me so that you can be pleased. Let my yea be yea, and let my nay be nay. Also, let me speak out the truth of the scripture to others; do not let me follow popular opinions that are erratic. Let me live according to the bible, so that you can bless me on this earth and in heaven. For in the name of Jesus Christ I make my requests.

Amen.

« DAY 260 »

Prayer Is A Necessity Tool For Every Believer

Focus Passage: Colossians 4

Paul asked his fellow Christians to support him in prayers, so that he could have strength to keep propagating gospel. Paul requested,

> *"Continue earnestly in prayer, being vigilant in it with thanksgiving; meanwhile praying also for us, that God would open to us a door for the word, to speak the mystery of Christ, for which I am also in chains, that I may make it manifest, as I ought to speak"* **(Colossians 4:2-4).**

Lesson:
Prayer is effective to obtaining victories. Believers should pray always to live happily and triumphantly. Meanwhile, our prayers should not only focus on personal needs, but we should also cultivate a habit of praying for God's strength to keep serving him faithfully. Indeed, we need God's strength to continuously serving God! When we pray, Holy Spirit will occupy our mind and boost our energy to stand uprightly before God. Also, prayer will strengthen our faith to confidently preach gospel. We would be able to withstand temptations, and we would be empowered to be doing justly. In addition, prayer is needed to aid gospel evangelization, so that unbelievers can be convinced to accept the lordship of Jesus Christ.

Prayer:
Dear God, please teach me how to pray! Help me to pray acceptable prayers in your sight. Let my prayers generate positive results. Help me to daily pray for strength and stability in faith. Let my prayers result to my edification, and the edification of my brethren. Also, let prayer strengthens me to be a soul winner and preach irresistible gospel to populate your kingdom. For in the name of Jesus Christ I make my requests.

Amen.

« DAY 261 »

God's Mercy Has limit

Focus Passage: Jeremiah 25, 45, 46

God finalized his judgments over Judah and Israel after he had given them enough rope to pull. Despite all warnings, God's children persistent in sins; therefore, the Creator declared his verdict on them as said,

> *"...Turn ye again now every one from his evil way, and from the evil of your doings, and dwell in the land that the Lord hath given unto you and to your fathers for ever and ever: And go not after other gods to serve them, and to worship them, and provoke me not to anger with the works of your hands; and I will do you no hurt. Yet ye have not hearkened unto me, saith the Lord; that ye might provoke me to anger with the works of your hands to your own hurt. Therefore thus saith the Lord of hosts; Because ye have not heard my words, Behold, I will send and take all the families of the north, saith the Lord, and Nebuchadrezzar the king of Babylon, my servant, and will bring them against this land, and against the inhabitants thereof, and against all these nations round about, and will utterly destroy them, and make them an astonishment, and an hissing, and perpetual desolations"* **(Jeremiah 25:5-9 KJV)**.

Lesson:
God's mercy has limit; the Creator has a final line to draw if a sinner refuses to repent. If a sinner persists in sin, he/she would face ultimate consequence of eternal punishment in hell. Therefore, all people should take God's warning seriously, and yield to his corrections. All nations and tongues must confess the Lordship of Jesus Christ to inherit eternal life. There would be grace, peace, and prosperity for any person who repents from his/her sins. God will rejoice over anyone who repents and confesses Jesus Christ as his/her Lord and Savior.

Prayer:
"All to Jesus I surrender; All to Him I freely give; I will ever love and trust Him, In His presence daily live. I surrender all, I surrender all; All to Thee, my blessed Savior, I surrender all."

Dear Jesus Christ, I give my complete life to you today. I confess you as my personal Lord and Savior. I confess my sins, and repent from them. From today, I will serve you with all my strength, and I will follow you unto the end. Please give me grace to remain consistent with you throughout the days of my life, so that I can inherit eternal life in your presence in heaven. For in your name Jesus Christ I tender my requests.

Amen!

« DAY 262 »

Jesus Christ Is The Foundation Of Faith And Rooftop Of Salvation

Focus Passage: Hebrew 1

The scripture revealed the lordship identity of Jesus Christ: He was not an ordinary human being as some may have presumed. He was God in human form when he came to earth - and he still retains the same identity today. It is written,

> *"But to the Son He says: "Your throne, O God, is forever and ever; a scepter of righteousness is the scepter of your kingdom. You have loved righteousness and hated lawlessness; Therefore God, Your God, has anointed you with the oil of gladness more than your companions." And: "You, Lord, in the beginning laid the foundation of the earth, and the heavens are the work of your hands. They will perish, but you remain; and they will all grow old like a garment; like a cloak you will fold them up, and they will be changed. But you are the same, and your years will not fail"* **(Hebrews 1:8-12).**

Lesson:
Jesus Christ is the foundation of faith and the rooftop of salvation. Also, he is the perfection of God's love. He simplified God's law and presented it to us to reckon with. The Savior laid a royal carpet for us to step on; hence, anyone who confesses him as the Son of God and accept him as his/her personal Savior will be saved! People of all status should come humbly before Jesus Christ and accept him as Lord. Whoever comes to Jesus Christ will not regret, but will have everlasting life in heaven.

Prayer:
Dear Jesus, I understand that you are Christ - the Son of God - who died for sinners. You sacrificed your life for a poor sinner like me so that I can inherit the gift of eternal life. Since you are so kind to me, I offer my complete life to you: I confess you as my Lord and Savior, and I will serve you for the rest of my life. From now on, I will share the testimony of your goodness to my friends and neighbors. I will proclaim your gospel so that other people can become saved also. Please help me to stay with my conviction, and keep my promise to you!

Amen!

« DAY 263 »

God Will Bless Those Who Satisfy His Desires, But Punish Adamant Sinners

Focus Passage: Jeremiah 47, 48

God spoke through Prophet Jeremiah that he would destroy an arrogant nation which exalted itself above his interest. God said,

> *"And Moab shall be destroyed as a people, because he exalted himself against the Lord"* **(Jeremiah 48:42).**

Lesson:
All people are made by God, and everyone is accountable to him. Christians or no Christian, we are all accountable to God! Meanwhile, the Creator is not partial; he will exercise righteous judgment on all. He will bless anyone that satisfies his desires, but punish sluggish and adamant sinner. Therefore, all people are encouraged to serve God with consistent relationship. However, no one can adequately satisfied God's desires except he has relationship with Jesus Christ. (He is the true and only way that leads to God - John 14:6).

Prayer:
Dear God, I humble myself before you so that I can be saved! I repent from my sins, and I confess you as my Lord and personal Savior. As from today, I submit my desires to you. I will obey your commandments, and I will faithfully serve you for the rest of my life. Please count me worthy for your eternal kingdom. For in the name of Jesus Christ I make my requests.

Amen.

« DAY 264 »

Salvation Wasn't Cheap – Jesus Died For It; Everyone Should Appreciate It

Focus Passage: Hebrew 2

Believers are challenged to understand the real motivation behind the salvation of their souls received through Jesus Christ. No one should take his salvation for granted, but deeply appreciate it. The scripture stated,

> *"How shall we escape if we neglect so great a salvation, which at the first began to be spoken by the Lord, and was confirmed to us by those who heard* Him, *God also bearing witness both with signs and wonders, with various miracles, and gifts of the Holy Spirit, according to His own will?"* **(Hebrews 2:3-4).**

Lesson:
The process of obtaining salvation for humankind was never cheap for Jesus Christ. He had to vacate heaven (with all its comforts) to come to earth; he had to suffer persecution from his enemies. Ultimately, Christ had to die to on the cross to obtain salvation for humankind. Hence, no child of God should take his/her grace of salvation for granted! We are to humbly come to the feet of Jesus Christ and accept him as our Lord and Savior. Also, to appreciate Christ's work of salvation, we must truthfully serve God with a devoted mind.

Prayer:
"I have decided to follow Jesus; I have decided to follow Jesus; I have decided to follow Jesus: No turning back; No turning back." I (*mention your name*), I give my life to Jesus Christ. I believe he is the Son of God; he has paid for my sins, and I receive my forgiveness of sin through him. Therefore, I declare him (Jesus Christ) to be the Lord of my life. I give my complete life to him, and I will faithfully serve him with all my strength and might. I will follow Jesus Christ for the rest of my life! Please Lord; give me grace to serve you unto the end! For in Jesus Christ' name alone I pray.

Amen!

« DAY 265 »

Christians Must Live Jesus' Lifestyle – With Integrity

Focus Passage: Jeremiah 13, 22, 49

God challenged Judah inhabitants to stand up for righteousness and stop abusing the weak and the less privileged people. Judah would be blessed if they care for others, but they would suffer terrible consequence if they act otherwise. Jeremiah prophesied,

> *"Thus saith the Lord; Execute ye judgment and righteousness, and deliver the spoiled out of the hand of the oppressor: and do no wrong, do no violence to the stranger, the fatherless, nor the widow, neither shed innocent blood in this place. For if ye do this thing indeed, then shall there enter in by the gates of this house kings sitting upon the throne of David, riding in chariots and on horses, he, and his servants, and his people. But if ye will not hear these words, I swear by myself, saith the Lord, that this house shall become a desolation"* **(Jeremiah 22:3-5 KJV)**.

Lesson:
Children of God are required to fairly treat others - with respect, and without prejudice. To demonstrate that we are truly God's children, we must not violate the right of others. We must not take advantage of other people, and we must abstain from selfish ambitions. However, our behavior (as God's true children) must be to care for the less privileged people. We must consider the needs of others. We must provide for orphans, widows, and other people in position of need. Jehovah will delight in us if we carefully observe these things. Once he is satisfied, we should be expecting him to bless us - he will lift us above our limitations. Jehovah will ensure that we do not suffer lack!

Prayer:
Dear God, please help me to care for others. I do not want to be a selfish individual who is only obsessed with his personal needs. Help me to have empathy for others, and help me to do my best in meeting their needs. Please fill me with your divine Holy Spirit to do what is just; empower me with grace to demonstrate good heart towards others. Let me be your true ambassador on earth, so that people can be happy and praise your holy name. After all these things, please bless me, and meet me in every area of my needs. For in the name of Jesus Christ I make my requests.

Amen.

« DAY 266 »

Christians Must Live Bible-Principled Lifestyle

Focus Passage: Hebrews 3

Every Christian is challenged to daily monitor his/her life, and ensure not to fall victim of erratic practices that have perpetrated our society. The scripture stated,

> *"But exhort one another daily, while it is called "Today," lest any of you be hardened through the deceitfulness of sin. For we have become partakers of Christ if we hold the beginning of our confidence steadfast to the end"* **(Hebrews 3:13-14).**

Lesson:
Christianity is a seasoned religion based on the lifestyle of Jesus Christ; Christians must practice the religion with full devotion. We must follow the scriptures to the letter, and we must live according to God's standard. Since Christianity is a pilgrimage process that leads to God, believers must be careful to observe it with care. We cannot be loose in faith and compromise bible principles; we must stand up for righteousness. Also, we must not give in to any temptation and/or persecution. We must be sensitive and be prayerful to confront and overcome any circumstance that may challenge our faith in Jesus Christ. It is important that we Christians rely on God's power to overcome our challenges! We must be prayerful and daily ask for the infilling of the Holy Spirit.

Prayer:
Dear God, I am a Christian, and it is my choice to stand upright and meet bible requirements. It is my desire to live a devoted life to you. I do not want to compromise my faith under whatever circumstance. I do not want to follow popular opinions that are contradictory to the bible, but I want to stand up for righteousness and do whatever you required of me. Please give me strength through your Holy Spirit to be a true Christian! Anoint me with grace to meet your heavenly mandates, so that I can rejoice with you on the last day. Please prosper my ways on earth also, so that I can be motivated to serve you more. For in the name of Jesus Christ I make my requests.

Amen.

« DAY 267 »

God Will Destroy The Present Earth, And Establish A New One For His Saints

Focus Passage: Jeremiah 23, 24

God has designed a permanent solution for the current world crises. He has commissioned his Son Jesus Christ to establish a perfect kingdom that will be void of all evil. The scripture stated,

> *""Behold, the days are coming," says the Lord, "That I will raise to David a branch of righteousness; a King shall reign and prosper, and execute judgment and righteousness in the earth. In His days Judah will be saved, and Israel will dwell safely; now this is His name by which He will be called: THE LORD OUR RIGHTEOUSNESS"* **(Jeremiah 23:5-6)**.

Lesson:

Jesus Christ has the perfect solution for the current world crises. He will save the world by establishing a new earth, and allow this present one to go into extinction. The new earth will be void of any evil. Christ himself will be its ruler, and his government will ascertain peace and prosperity for its citizens. The scripture revealed thus: *"Now I saw a new heaven and a new earth, for the first heaven and the first earth had passed away. Also there was no more sea. Then I, John, saw the holy city, New Jerusalem, coming down out of heaven from God, prepared as a bride adorned for her husband. And I heard a loud voice from heaven saying, "Behold, the tabernacle of God is with men, and He will dwell with them, and they shall be His people. God Himself will be with them and be their God. And God will wipe away every tear from their eyes; there shall be no more death, nor sorrow, nor crying. There shall be no more pain, for the former things have passed away"* **(Revelation rev 20:1-5)**.

"Meanwhile, not everyone who currently lives in this earth will partake in the new one to come. Some people will be disallowed to enter it! Only those who have confessed Jesus Christ as their Lord and Savior will be accepted in the new earth to come. Unbelievers would be shut out of heaven. Their portion would be lake of fire called "Hell Fire". Unbelievers will pay bitter price for their failure to confess Jesus Christ as Lord as the scripture emphasized, *"But the cowardly, unbelieving, abominable, murderers, sexually immoral, sorcerers, idolaters, and all liars shall have their part in the lake which burns with fire and brimstone, which is the second death"* **(Revelation 21:8)**.

Therefore, everyone - without exception - should take a step of faith to confess Jesus Christ as his Lord and Savior in order to be saved!

Prayer:

Dear Jesus Christ, I believe that you are the Son of God that was sent to save the world, and I confess you as my personal Lord and Savior. I confess my sins and forsake them, and I promise to serve you throughout the days of my life. Please write my name in the book of life, and count me worthy to inherit your kingdom. For in your true name - Jesus Christ - I made my confession and declarations.

Amen!

« DAY 268 »

Jesus Is The Greatest High Priest That Sacrificed His Own Life For Mankind

Focus Passage: Hebrews 4

God's priests are people of high standard that play honorable roles on behalf of God in people's lives. All God's priest should be respected, but there is one priest that is greater than every other priest in rank. His name is Jesus Christ; through him people receive remission of their sins, and they obtain permanent solutions to their problems. The scripture analyzed,

> *"Therefore, since we have a great high priest who has ascended into heaven, Jesus the Son of God, let us hold firmly to the faith we profess. For we do not have a high priest who is unable to empathize with our weaknesses, but we have one who has been tempted in every way, just as we are—yet he did not sin. Let us then approach God's throne of grace with confidence, so that we may receive mercy and find grace to help us in our time of need"* **(Hebrews 4:14-16 NIV).**

Lesson:
Jesus Christ is the most high priest of all time. His priesthood roles are greater than any other. He offered himself as the sacrificial lamb for our sins; he pleaded for our sins, and reconciled us back to God. (Indeed our sins have turned us to fugitive, but Christ reconciled us back to God). Christ did not only work on redemption of our souls, he also took the responsibility of establishing a new earth and a new heaven to host us after the present one stop to exist. Since Jesus Christ owns all it takes to live a complete and a fulfill life now and in future, all people should consider accepting his salvation invitation. Everyone should confess him as God's only Son sent to save the world **(John 3:16)**. Everyone must confess Jesus Christ as Lord in order to be saved!

Prayer:
Dear Jesus Christ, I know that you are the most high priest of God who can best reconcile anyone to God. You sacrificed your life for humanity so that they can be saved. I believe that you are the Savior of the world, and I personally confess you as my Lord and Savior. I yield my complete life to you today, and I will continue to serve you throughout the days of my life. Please give me all it takes to faithfully serve you unto the end. For in your name Jesus Christ I make my confession of salvation.

Amen.

« DAY 269 »

God Is Smarter Than Humans By All Standards

Focus Passage: Jeremiah 27, 28, 29

God vouch to send the nations of Israel and Judah to captivity for the sake of their sins. Both nations would suffer under foreign invaders, and many of their citizens would be transported to suffer in a distant land - for about 70 years. Meanwhile, God promised to restore Israel and Judah back to their soil if they repent. God stated,

> *"I have made the earth, the man and the beast that are upon the ground, by my great power and by my outstretched arm, and have given it unto whom it seemed meet unto me. And now have I given all these lands into the hand of Nebuchadnezzar the king of Babylon, my servant; and the beasts of the field have I given him also to serve him"* ***(Jeremiah 27:5-6 KJV).***

Lesson:
It is more or less a suicide mission for anyone to attempt to take God for granted. God has clear understanding of all matter and he has strong capability to do whatever he desires. God has power to give anything, and he has power to take anything away! Therefore, we humans must understand that we cannot play God; neither can we usurp his power. He is the Father of creation, and whatever he says is the final. Hence, humanity ought to tremble before God, and carefully follow his instructions. He will prosper us if we obey him, but he will punish us if we disobey his rules.

Prayer:
Dear God, please give me grace to serve you with fear and trembling. Do not let me take you for granted, so that I will not be punished. Let me carefully follow your instructions, so that I can prosper in all my ways. Please let it be well with me as I endeavor to faithfully serve you every day. For in the name of Jesus Christ I make my requests.

Amen.

« DAY 270 »

Christianity Requires Consistent Relationship With God

Focus Passage: Hebrews 5

The scripture challenged all Christians to fully comply with God's laws. Believers must live consistent lifestyles with the bible, and we must be matured in our approach to physical and spiritual matters. It is emphasized in the scripture,

> *"For though by this time you ought to be teachers, you need someone to teach you again the first principles of the oracles of God; and you have come to need milk and not solid food. For everyone who partakes only of milk is unskilled in the word of righteousness, for he is a babe. But solid food belongs to those who are of full age,* that is, *those who by reason of use have their senses exercised to discern both good and evil"* **(Hebrews 5:12-14).**

Lesson:
God is interested in seeing his children (Christians) growing in closer relationship with him. Christians should grow in faith, and not remain in the same position. We are expected to grow and improve in our prayer lives. We must study bible more, and practice our faith. As Christ' followers, we are expected to get stronger in faith and become more mature. We must daily interact with God and live a consistent life with him. If we remain consistent, our heavenly Father will reward us with his benefits in this life, and in heaven also.

Prayer:
Dear God, I understand that you want me to have an improved relationship with you, and I am now ready. I have made up my mind to serve you better. I am willing to study your word more and live a devoted life before you. Please baptize me with your Holy Spirit to have enough strength to meet your expectations. Please let my services be acceptable before you, and let me qualify for your blessings in this life, and in heaven also. For in the name of Jesus Christ I make my requests.

Amen.

« DAY 271 »

God Is God Of Love And Mercy; He Will Forgive Any Sinner Who Repents From His or Her Sins

Focus Passage: Jeremiah 50

God allowed Babylonians to subdue the nations of Israel and Judah due to their sins; however, the Creator promised to restore the two nations because they repented. God stated he would restore Israel and Judah, but punish the Babylonians that have taken their advantage. God said through Jeremiah,

> " In those days, and in that time, saith the Lord, the children of Israel shall come, they and the children of Judah together, going and weeping: they shall go, and seek the Lord their God. They shall ask the way to Zion with their faces thitherward, saying, Come, and let us join ourselves to the Lord in a perpetual covenant that shall not be forgotten. My people hath been lost sheep: their shepherds have caused them to go astray, they have turned them away on the mountains: they have gone from mountain to hill, they have forgotten their resting place. All that found them have devoured them: and their adversaries said, We offend not, because they have sinned against the Lord, the habitation of justice, even the Lord, the hope of their fathers. Remove out of the midst of Babylon, and go forth out of the land of the Chaldeans, and be as the he goats before the flocks. For, lo, I will raise and cause to come up against Babylon an assembly of great nations from the north country: and they shall set themselves in array against her; from thence she shall be taken: their arrows shall be as of a mighty expert man; none shall return in vain" **(Jeremiah 50:4-9 KJV).**

Lesson:
God is God of love and mercy; he will forgive any sinner who repents from his sins. Indeed, sin opens doors for enemies to oppress God's children, but once they exercise repentance, those doors would be shut. God will restore his children who return to him in good term. He will cleanse a sinner with the blood of his Son Jesus Christ. God will reward a repentant sinner the gift of eternal life in heaven! Meanwhile, an unrepentant sinner has missed opportunity of forgiveness and restoration; he cannot see God at the end of his life journey. (A person who rejects salvation of Jesus Christ is regarded as a sinner, and he will not enter heaven). Only those who have confessed their sins, and declared Jesus Christ as their Lord and Savior will meet God in heaven. Hence, all people are encouraged to repent from their sins, and confess Jesus Christ as their Lord and Savior, so that they can be saved.

Prayer:
Dear God, I confess that I am a sinner; I have sinned before you, and I am not worthy to be called your child. However, today, I repent from my sins. I confess them, and I repent from them. From now on, I will give you my complete life, and I will serve you throughout the days of my life. Please write my name in the book of life, and count me worthy to reign with you in heaven. For in the name of your only Son Jesus Christ I make my requests.
Amen.

« DAY 272 »

Christianity Requires Firmness Of Godly Characters

Focus Passage: Hebrew 6

Christians are challenged to improve their relationship with God. No Christian should be complacent with elementary aspect of Christianity, but everyone should make decisive efforts to meet God's standard and satisfy him. It is written in the scripture,

> *"Therefore, leaving the discussion of the elementary principles of Christ, let us go on to perfection, not laying again the foundation of repentance from dead works and of faith toward God, of the doctrine of baptisms, of laying on of hands, of resurrection of the dead, and of eternal judgment. And this we will do if God permits. For it is impossible for those who were once enlightened, and have tasted the heavenly gift, and have become partakers of the Holy Spirit, and have tasted the good word of God and the powers of the age to come, if they fall away, to renew them again to repentance, since they crucify again for themselves the Son of God, and put Him to an open shame"* **(Hebrews 6:1-6).**

Lesson:
Christianity is a religion with specific characteristics. The religion presents us the requirements that we must meet in order to go to heaven. Hence, every Christian should practice Christianity at best. We cannot afford to dilly-dally in faith and/or compromise our precious salvation. Every Christian should endeavor to make God happy in whatever he/she does. Much reward awaits Christians with contrite spirits that satisfy God at their best. Heaven will honor faithful Christians in this life and in heaven also.

Prayer:
Dear God, please give me grace to love and serve you with full devotion. Give me strength to serve you with contrite heart; empower me through your Holy Spirit to meet all your expectations so that I can prosper on earth and in heaven also. For in the name of Jesus Christ I make my requests.

Amen.

« DAY 273 »

God Will Help Whoever Identifies Himself Or Herself With Him

Focus Passage: Jeremiah 30, 51

Nation of Babylon has oppressed Israel for long, but God said he has determined to stop them. God stated through Jeremiah,

> *"'For it shall come to pass in that day, saith the Lord of hosts, that I will break his yoke from off thy neck, and will burst thy bonds, and strangers shall no more serve themselves of him: But they shall serve the Lord their God, and David their king, whom I will raise up unto them"* **(Jeremiah 30:8-9 KJV).**

Lesson:
God will ever keep his children in mind; he will remember his love for them, and he will forgive their sins. The Creator will deliver his children from any form of affliction that Satan might have imposed on them. Since his name is Jehovah Nissi, he will do whatever necessary to defend his children. Hence, it makes sense for anyone to associate himself with God and become his child. All it takes to become a child of God is very simple: A person must confess Jesus Christ as the true Son of God, and must accept him as his Lord and personal Savior. Once Christ takes over such person's life, he/she will automatically become a child of God - that deserves his overwhelming protection and blessings!

Prayer:
Dear God, I know that you are the Almighty God who has power to do all things. You will do whatever necessary to protect the interest of your children. Therefore, I give my life to you today; I dedicate my life to become your child. I confess that Jesus Christ is your true and only Son sent to save the world, and I accept him to my life as my personal Lord and Savior. Please write my name in the book of life, and let me start to enjoy your benefits of provision and protections from now on! For in the name of Jesus Christ - your Son - I have made my requests.

Amen.

« DAY 274 »

Principle Of Tithing Was Established By God, And Has Long Time History

Focus Passage: Hebrew 7

Children of God are required to pay their tithes and offerings to God. The principle has history that is dated to the period of Abraham in Old Testament. The patriarch paid his tithe to Priest Melchizedek has illustrated in the scripture,

> *"For this Melchizedek, king of Salem, priest of the Most High God, who met Abraham returning from the slaughter of the kings and blessed him, to whom also Abraham gave a tenth part of all, first being translated "king of righteousness," and then also king of Salem, meaning "king of peace"* **(Hebrews 7:1-2; Genesis 14:18-20).**

Lesson:
God established a rule which required all his children to pay their tithes into his own house (Malachi 3:10). We must obey this rule to please God. We must bring our tithes and offerings to our home churches where we worship God. Once we obey God, multiple blessings will overtake our lives, and we will not remain the same again. However, any attempt to disobey the requirement of paying tithe and offering may lead to negative consequence. God may withhold our due benefits - which would cause us significant loss. Therefore, every Christian should prioritize paying his tithe and offering to his primary place of worship. Jehovah who reserves the bank of blessings will surely multiply his riches in the lives of people that honor him.

Prayer:
Dear God, I understand that it is mandatory for me to pay my tithe and offering in my church; I am determined to start doing so. I am sorry for my past failures, but as from now, things will change, and I will pay my tithe consistently! I will pay your dues, so that you can pay my due benefits also! Please give me grace to stay consistent, and teach me how to trust you for my provisions. Please meet me at every area of my need. For in the name of Jesus Christ I make my requests.

Amen.

« DAY 275 »

God Will Forgive And Restore Humble People Who Repent From Their Sins

Focus Passage: Jeremiah 31, 32

Israelites that survived war-time will also enjoy peace of the Lord. God promised to reinstate his lost children into their heritage - with guaranteed rest and safety. It is written in the scripture,

> *"At the same time, saith the Lord, will I be the God of all the families of Israel, and they shall be my people. Thus saith the Lord, The people which were left of the sword found grace in the wilderness; even Israel, when I went to cause him to rest. The Lord hath appeared of old unto me, saying, Yea, I have loved thee with an everlasting love: therefore with lovingkindness have I drawn thee"* **(Jeremiah 31:1-3 KJV).**

Lesson:

God is an everlasting Lord of love and mercy, and he will forever show mercy on his own children. He will not cast off his children forever, but he will show them mercy. Jehovah will restore his children from their pitfalls, and save them in time of crisis. However, the compassionate God still expects his children to exercise repentance; he wants us to have renewed mind and change of attitude prior to our restoration. It is important that a child of God submit to God with humble heart, and genuinely repents from his/her sins. Any individual who humbly comes before God will be redeemed. It is written

"Come to Me, all you who labor and are heavy laden, and I will give you rest" **(Matthew 11:28).**

God will stretch his forgiving arms towards any person or a group of people who are humble enough to repent from their sins. He will erase their sins and reverse his punishments on them. Jehovah will care for repentant sinners, and give them peaceful habitations.

Prayer:

Dear God, I am sorry for all my sins! Today, I repent from all my wrong doings, and I return to you in good faith. Please wipe off my sins and redeem my soul. Give me a godly heart to carefully obey your instructions and faithfully serve you. From now on, I yield my complete life to you, and I will faithfully serve you for the rest of my life. Please restore the joy of your salvation back to me. Write my name in the book of life, and forever keep me fit to inherit your kingdom. For in the name of Jesus Christ I make my requests.

Amen.

« DAY 276 »

God Reserves His Best Creativity For His Saints To Enjoy In Heaven

Focus Passage: Hebrews 8

God promised a new and better covenant with his children, as they reserve their trust in him. The scripture said, "...For if that first *covenant* had been faultless, then no place would have been sought for a second. Because finding fault with them, He says,

> *"For if that first covenant had been faultless, then should no place have been sought for the second. For finding fault with them, he saith, Behold, the days come, saith the Lord, when I will make a new covenant with the house of Israel and with the house of Judah: Not according to the covenant that I made with their fathers in the day when I took them by the hand to lead them out of the land of Egypt; because they continued not in my covenant, and I regarded them not, saith the Lord. For this is the covenant that I will make with the house of Israel after those days, saith the Lord; I will put my laws into their mind, and write them in their hearts: and I will be to them a God, and they shall be to me a people: And they shall not teach every man his neighbour, and every man his brother, saying, Know the Lord: for all shall know me, from the least to the greatest. For I will be merciful to their unrighteousness, and their sins and their iniquities will I remember no more"* **(Hebrews 8:7-12 KJV).**

Lesson:
God has made inhabitants of this earth witness his signs and wonders in so many ways. We have seen amazing wonder works of God - The beautiful creations and nature. Meanwhile, none of the creative works of God ever witnessed can be compared with those that are still kept in reserve. Some superb and most amazing works of God will be displayed in heaven (and in the forthcoming earth) for Christians to enjoy. Believers in Jesus Christ - Christians - will receive free passes to enjoy God's hilarious display of his creative works in heaven! In fact, the saints will not only witness their demonstrations, but they will also benefit in their actuality! Christians will live to enjoy God's goodness in heaven perpetually. Therefore, Christians should congratulate themselves for God has reserved his best for them. Meanwhile, a non-Christian should endeavor to become a Christian so that he/she can be qualified to enjoy the tremendous works of the Creator in heaven, and on earth.

Prayer:
Dear God, I want to go to heaven, please count me worthy! Please qualify me for your kingdom so that I can enjoy benefits than I ever had! Please make me a good Christian who follows you to the end. To play my part: I am re-dedicating my life to your Son Jesus Christ, and I give my complete life to him. I honor him and I accept him as my Lord and personal Savior. Please write my name in the book of life and keep me ever worthy for your eternal home. For in the name of Jesus Christ I make my requests.

Amen.

« DAY 277 »

Christians Are Co-Sharers Of God's Blessings Proclaimed On Abraham

Focus Passage: Jeremiah 21, 33

God affirmed his promises over Israelites his children; he would favor them and restore their losses. God declared,

> *""Thus says the Lord: 'If My covenant is not with day and night, and if I have not appointed the ordinances of heaven and earth, then I will cast away the descendants of Jacob and David My servant, so that I will not take any of his descendants to be rulers over the descendants of Abraham, Isaac, and Jacob. For I will cause their captives to return, and will have mercy on them'"* **(Jeremiah 33:25-26)**.

Lesson:
God is merciful and gracious, and he will not permanently cast off his children. The Creator of heaven and earth will remember the covenants that he has made with Abraham, Isaac, and Jacob. He will also remember their descendants and bless them. Christians share equal rights with any descendant of Abraham (They have been gravitated to the same covenant through Jesus Christ). Therefore, people who have confessed their faith in Jesus Christ should congratulate themselves. Those who have not taken step of faith should do so by confessing Jesus Christ as their Lord and Savior.

Prayer:
I am so glad that I have confessed Jesus Christ as my Lord and Savior. Hence, the covenant of Abraham is bound to apply to my life. I pray that God should keep my feet firm in the courtyard of his blessings, so that I can enjoy his benefits forever! For in the name of Jesus Christ I make my requests.

Amen.

« DAY 278 »

Old Testament Priests Offered Animal Sacrifice, But Jesus Christ Offered Himself As The Living Sacrifice

Focus Passage: Hebrews 9

The high priests of Old Testament period offered animal sacrifices to cleanse human sins, but those sacrifices were never perfect since the high priests themselves were not perfect. To help stop human dilemma, God sent his own Son as the perfect High Priest to sacrifice his life for their sins. The Son of God would not slaughter animal for sacrifice, but he would use his own life! Christ surrendered his life for all humanity, and he resurrected again as the scripture attested,

> "...*Christ came as High Priest of the good things to come, with the greater and more perfect tabernacle not made with hands, that is, not of this creation. Not with the blood of goats and calves, but with His own blood He entered the Most Holy Place once for all, having obtained eternal redemption. For if the blood of bulls and goats and the ashes of a heifer, sprinkling the unclean, sanctifies for the purifying of the flesh, how much more shall the blood of Christ, who through the eternal Spirit offered Himself without spot to God, cleanse your conscience from dead works to serve the living God? And for this reason He is the Mediator of the new covenant, by means of death, for the redemption of the transgressions under the first covenant, that those who are called may receive the promise of the eternal inheritance*" **(Hebrews 9:11-15).**

Lesson:
Jesus Christ is the Savior of the world, and he is the Most High Priest with strong capability to perfect redemptive work of human souls. He came to earth, died for human sins, and resurrected to give life to people who follow him. Anyone who confesses Jesus Christ as his or her Lord and Savior will automatically partake in his redemptive grace. The scripture analyzed,

"*For Christ did not enter a sanctuary made with human hands that was only a copy of the true one; he entered heaven itself, now to appear for us in God's presence. Nor did he enter heaven to offer himself again and again, the way the high priest enters the Most Holy Place every year with blood that is not his own. Otherwise Christ would have had to suffer many times since the creation of the world. But he has appeared once for all at the culmination of the ages to do away with sin by the sacrifice of himself. Just as people are destined to die once, and after that to face judgment, so Christ was sacrificed once to take away the sins of many; and he will appear a second time, not to bear sin, but to bring salvation to those who are waiting for him*" **(Hebrews 9:24-28 NIV).**

Prayer:
Hallelujah Christ sacrificed his life for me so that I will not need any other sacrifice again. Praise God, I am a partaker of Christ' grace. Henceforth, my name has been written in the book of life, and crown of righteousness is waiting for me in heaven. Praise God, I am saved and heaven is my home!
Amen.

« DAY 279 »

God's Servants Deserve Respect Since They Represent The Most High God

Focus Passage: Hebrews: 34, 37, 38

Judah authority punished Jeremiah for speaking out God's mind. They threw him into a pit with the hope of starving him to death. The scripture reported,

> "So they took Jeremiah and cast him into the dungeon of Malchiah the king's son, which was *in the court of the prison, and they let Jeremiah down with ropes. And in the dungeon* there was *no water, but mire. So Jeremiah sank in the mire*" **(Jeremiah 38:6).**

Lesson:
We live in a world where people show little respect for God, and they would abuse God's servants to hurt God. God's servants are often abused; misunderstood, and misrepresented. Meanwhile, Jehovah cannot be happy with those who abuse his servants. Since they are his oracles, God will defend his servants! People who abuse them will have so much consequence to pay for! Instead of irrational behaviors towards God's servants, people can choose to understand their tasks and honor them.

God's servants are God's oracles; they speak God's mind. God's servants are expected to tell truth of the scripture always, and people are expected to follow their lead. God's servants are answerable to God, they are not answerable to us - and we should not take them for granted! We should not harass God's servants for performing their roles; instead, we should follow their instructions. It is important that we honor God's servants since they represent God; whatsoever we do to them is what we have technically done to God himself. A person who expects some benefits from God should not attempt to dishonor his servants!

Prayer:
Dear God, I understand that it is disastrous to dishonor your servants. You will punish anyone who abuses people that you have commissioned with special assignments. Therefore, I am determined to start honoring your servants. I am sorry for how I have mishandled your servants in the past. From now on, I will honor your servants. I will support them in any capacity so that they can be motivated to keep serving you in good spirit. Please give me grace to start doing things rightly! At the same time, I am seizing this opportunity to pray for your servants throughout the world, that you will anoint them with grace to keep serving you. Give them energy to keep obeying you, and prosper them in all their ways - so that your name can be praised in their lives. For in the name of Jesus Christ I make my requests.

Amen.

« DAY 280 »

Jesus Saved Humanity From Routine Sacrifices That Only Result To Limited Sin Remission

Focus Passage: Hebrews 10:1-18

A clear distinction exists between Old Testament priesthood and the priesthood of Jesus Christ. Old Testament priests were bound to periodically sacrifice animals to atone human sins, but Jesus Christ atoned human sins once and for all! The scripture explained,

> *"For it is not possible that the blood of bulls and goats could take away sins"* **(Hebrews 10:4).** It is also written, *"Every priest stands ministering daily and offering repeatedly the same sacrifices, which can never take away sins"* **(Hebrews 10:11).**
>
> However, Jesus Christ being God in human flesh provided lasting solution as stated, *"But this Man, after He had offered one sacrifice for sins forever, sat down at the right hand of God, from that time waiting till His enemies are made His footstool. For by one offering He has perfected forever those who are being sanctified"* **(Hebrews 10:12-14).**

Lesson:
Jesus Christ saved humanity from routine sacrifices that have trapped humanity into achieving limited sin remission. The Son of God sacrificed his own life to permanently remit sins of humanity, and reconcile them back to God. (In the past, priests have sacrificed goats and sheep to atone human sins, but those efforts did not give permanent solution - since blood of animals could not remove sins. Jesus' blood - full of life - was utilized to permanently atone sins and bring eternal redemption.) Hence, people who have confided in Jesus Christ and accepted him as their Savior would not need to sacrifice animals anymore; Christ has sacrificed himself for them! Anyone who confesses Jesus Christ as his/her Lord and Savior will receive forgiveness of sins, and have his/her name written in the book of life.

Prayer:
Praise God, Christ has sacrificed his life for my sins. The Son of God has removed the need to sacrifice goats and sheep for remission of my sins! Since I am a believer in Jesus Christ, my sins have been washed away, and the crown of righteousness is waiting for me in heaven! Praise God, my name is written in the book of life; I am a child of God, and heaven is my home. Thank you Jesus Christ for saving my soul. My heart desire is to serve you throughout the days of my life, and this will I do as long as I have grace - so help me God!

Amen.

« DAY 281 »

God Cannot Be Predicted; It Is Dangerous For Anyone To Take Him For Granted

Focus Passage: Jeremiah 39, 40, 52

God's day of reckoning caught Israelites unaware. Since God had removed his protection from them due to their sins, foreign invaders were able to storm their cities and looted their treasures. The Babylonians (invaders) ripped the nation of Israel and Judah apart, and they transported their citizens to Babylon as captives. Unfortunately for Israelites that rebelled against their creator, they would live and die in Babylon - unless the Creator's wrath is appeased! The scripture reported invasion of Jerusalem,

> *"Now in the fifth month, in the tenth day of the month, which was the nineteenth year of Nebuchadrezzar king of Babylon, came Nebuzaradan, captain of the guard, which served the king of Babylon, into Jerusalem, And burned the house of the Lord, and the king's house; and all the houses of Jerusalem, and all the houses of the great men, burned he with fire: And all the army of the Chaldeans, that were with the captain of the guard, brake down all the walls of Jerusalem round about"* **(Jeremiah 52:12-14 KJV).**

Lesson:
Children of God are called to honor God; we are to respect God, and dare not to take him for granted. The fact that we have son/daughter-to-father relationship with God does not mean that we should take him for granted. Indeed he is our father, but he is a heavenly Father also, and we cannot compare him to any earthly father. He is a supreme God who has an affirmed standard. He is nice towards his children, but brutal towards his enemies. More importantly, God hates sin, and he does not tolerate people who attempt to take him for granted. Meanwhile, God appreciates people with contrite spirit. He will honor those who faithfully serve him and carefully follow his instructions. Hence, we believers should walk in integrity before God, so that he can multiply his goodness in our lives.

Prayer:
Dear God, please instill your fear in my heart so that I will not sin against you. Help me not to take your grace of salvation for granted so that I will not be punished; empower me through your Holy Spirit to walk carefully and faithfully in your presence. Anoint me to serve you with beauty of my heart, and let my services be considered honorable before you so that I can be qualified to receive your blessings. For in the name of Jesus Christ I make my requests.

Amen.

« DAY 282 »

Believers To Endure And Patiently Wait For The Return Of Jesus Christ

Focus Passage: Hebrews 10:19-39

A Christian who endures in faith unto the end will receive eternal rewards from God. It is written,

> *"For you have need of endurance, so that after you have done the will of God, you may receive the promise, "For yet a little while, and He who is coming will come and will not tarry. Now the just shall live by faith; but if anyone draws back, my soul has no pleasure in him." But we are not of those who draw back to perdition, but of those who believe to the saving of the soul"* **(Hebrews 10:36-39).**

Lesson:
"Endurance and patience" are important virtues that everyone must have to run a successful Christian race on earth. If we patiently and carefully run our Christian race, we shall see God on the last day. We Christians are to endure any suffering that might associate with our faith. Whatever hash circumstance that may come our way today will disappear one day. Pains and suffering of persecution will not last eternally; Christ will bring an ultimate end to all suffering. Christ will wipe tears off the face of his saints; he will give us new names, and award us royal honor. Followers of Jesus Christ will enjoy everlasting peace and joy in heaven - and all senses of sorry will vanish for forever!

Prayer:
Dear God, please give me enduring heart to stand in faith unto the end. Assist me to have resolute faith that cannot be overcome by any wave of persecution and/or suffering. Let my confession of Jesus Christ remain resolute, and grant me grace to steadfastly serve you in the beauty of your holiness. Please keep my feet firm within your gate, and let me remain qualified to partake in joy of your kingdom. Please give me grace to faithfully serve you unto the end! For in the name of Jesus Christ I make my requests.

Amen.

« DAY 283 »

God Required His Children To Accept Corrections In Good Faith

Focus Passage: Jeremiah 41, 42

God warned remnant of Judah who remained in their land not to seek refuge in Egypt; they would be punished if they do so. They would prosper if they remain in the land of Judah. God spoke through Jeremiah and said,

> *"'If ye will still abide in this land, then will I build you, and not pull you down, and I will plant you, and not pluck you up: for I repent me of the evil that I have done unto you. Be not afraid of the king of Babylon, of whom ye are afraid; be not afraid of him, saith the Lord: for I am with you to save you, and to deliver you from his hand. And I will shew mercies unto you, that he may have mercy upon you, and cause you to return to your own land. But if ye say, We will not dwell in this land, neither obey the voice of the Lord your God, Saying, No; but we will go into the land of Egypt, where we shall see no war, nor hear the sound of the trumpet, nor have hunger of bread; and there will we dwell: And now therefore hear the word of the Lord, ye remnant of Judah; Thus saith the Lord of hosts, the God of Israel; If ye wholly set your faces to enter into Egypt, and go to sojourn there; Then it shall come to pass, that the sword, which ye feared, shall overtake you there in the land of Egypt, and the famine, whereof ye were afraid, shall follow close after you there in Egypt; and there ye shall die"* **(Jeremiah 42:10-16 KJV).**

Lesson:
God required his children to be humble and accept correction in good faith. We are expected to follow instructions; respond to corrections whenever we make mistake, and make necessary amendment. Children of God are not expected to be boastful of their wrongdoing, but be remorseful and turn a new leaf. Our ever-gracious God is interested in our repentance; he loves to see us walking within his plans so that he can shower his goodness on us. If we meet the Creator's expectations, he will bless us in due time, and raise our banner in honor.

Prayer:
Dear God, please give me a humble heart to admit mistakes and make necessary corrections. Give me strength to be submissive to your instructions and duly follow them, so that I can prosper in the land of the living. Let me remain under your watchful eyes, and make me ever qualify for your blessings. For in the name of Jesus Christ I make my requests.

Amen.

« DAY 284 »

Faith Is The Major Rod That Connects Us With God

Focus Passage: Hebrews 11:1-19

Faith is important to humans and God. It is the connecting rod between the two. A person without faith cannot relate with God, even if he attempted it, God would not respond. The scripture stated,

> *"Now faith is the substance of things hoped for, the evidence of things not seen. For by it the elders obtained a good testimony. By faith we understand that the worlds were framed by the word of God, so that the things which are seen were not made of things which are visible"* **(Hebrews 11:1-3).**

Lesson:
Faith is the anchor of creation. God created all things through faith. The Creator had trust in Himself by creating all things out of nothing. With word of command he created the earth, and everything in it. God said, *"Let there be..."* **(Genesis 1).** Whatever he said came into existence. Meanwhile, since God trusted himself, his creation must also trust him to live a properly functioned life. Creation must have faith in God that created it. Humanity must believe in existence of God; they must trust his power, and they must profess their expectations in him - as though they will irrevocably manifest. A person who expects the manifestation of God's supernatural power must believe that God can do all things, and the fellow must declare his/her committed faith in him.

Prayer:
Dear God, please help me to have faith in you; give me strength to be able to declare my confidence in you over every area of my life. Let your Holy Spirit empower me to be able to declare bible promises and claim them into my life. Let my confessions be positive, and let me ever live a triumphant life on earth. Please let me reap fruits of faith, and let my testimony ever abide. For in the name of Jesus Christ I make my requests.

Amen.

« DAY 285 »

God Deserves Our Honor – With Full Reverence

Focus Passage: Jeremiah 43, 44

Israelites despised God's warning not to run to Egypt for refuge; they confronted Jeremiah and claimed the Creator has failed them, therefore they would do whatever they please, and no one could stop them. The scripture reported Israelites' actions,

> *"Then all the men which knew that their wives had burned incense unto other gods, and all the women that stood by, a great multitude, even all the people that dwelt in the land of Egypt, in Pathros, answered Jeremiah, saying, As for the word that thou hast spoken unto us in the name of the Lord, we will not hearken unto thee. But we will certainly do whatsoever thing goeth forth out of our own mouth, to burn incense unto the queen of heaven, and to pour out drink offerings unto her, as we have done, we, and our fathers, our kings, and our princes, in the cities of Judah, and in the streets of Jerusalem: for then had we plenty of victuals, and were well, and saw no evil* **(Jeremiah 44:15-19 KJV).**

Since Israelites disrespected God and refused to obey his instruction, God was determined to punish them beyond their expectations. He promised to humiliate them as they chose to exile to Egypt. God said,

> *"Thus saith the Lord of hosts, the God of Israel, saying; Ye and your wives have both spoken with your mouths, and fulfilled with your hand, saying, We will surely perform our vows that we have vowed, to burn incense to the queen of heaven, and to pour out drink offerings unto her: ye will surely accomplish your vows, and surely perform your vows. Therefore hear ye the word of the Lord, all Judah that dwell in the land of Egypt; Behold, I have sworn by my great name, saith the Lord, that my name shall no more be named in the mouth of any man of Judah in all the land of Egypt, saying, The Lord God liveth. Behold, I will watch over them for evil, and not for good: and all the men of Judah that are in the land of Egypt shall be consumed by the sword and by the famine, until there be an end of them"* **(Jeremiah 44:25-27 KJV).**

Lesson:

God is greater than humans; he is not our age-mate, and we should reverence and honor him. No human is in position to be compared with God. As far as heaven is greater than the earth, so is God greater and stronger than us. Jehovah has the attributes that cannot be compared with humans. He is the highest authority in existence; whatever he commands stays, and no one can question him. The fact that the Creator has decorated humanity with beauty and honor does not equate us with him. God will remain God, and we will remain humans. Therefore, since we are the creative works of God, everyone should adore him, and give him due honor.

Prayer:
Dear God, please give me a heart that honors you always. Do not let me disrespect you in any way. Never let me take your grace for granted, but help me to diligently serve and obey your instructions. No matter what I become in life, let me ever remain humble to you. Let me ever regard you as my All-in-All. Please glorify yourself in my life as I choose to follow you with a loyal heart. For in the name of Jesus Christ I make my requests.

Amen.

« DAY 286 »

"Faith" Is What Makes Christianity Meaningful

Focus Passage: Hebrews 11:20-40

Many bible patriarchs made unpopular decisions through faith, yet they were not ashamed. God backed and honored them, and he made them become uncommon champions. For instance,

> *"By faith Moses, when he became of age, refused to be called the son of Pharaoh's daughter, choosing rather to suffer affliction with the people of God than to enjoy the passing pleasures of sin, esteeming the reproach of Christ greater riches than the treasures in Egypt; for he looked to the reward. By faith he forsook Egypt, not fearing the wrath of the king; for he endured as seeing Him who is invisible. By faith he kept the Passover and the sprinkling of blood, lest he who destroyed the firstborn should touch them. By faith they passed through the Red Sea as by dry land, whereas the Egyptians, attempting to do so, were drowned"* **(Hebrews 11:24-29).**

Lesson:

"Faith" is what makes Christianity meaningful. If we believers in Jesus Christ lack faith, we are not different from the unbelievers. We the followers of Jesus Christ must conceive faith and profess faith. More importantly, we must operate in faith and take dominion over every situation of our lives. God is not a coward, and we children of God must not be afraid to take charge over any circumstance that arises in our lives. The exercises of our faith count a lot! Faith will make us different from the unbelievers – in terms of earthly prosperities and holiness living.

Prayer:

Dear God, "Faith" is all I need! Give me extra ordinary grace to exercise my faith over all circumstances that surround me. Let me declare my authority as a child of God over all matters, and let me live as an overcomer throughout the days of my life. In fact, I am putting my faith into action right now. I command all problems in my life to become solved in the name of Jesus Christ. I command all my success and prosperities to materialize in the name of Jesus Christ. As from today, I declare that I am an overcomer! I am more than a conqueror and I shall prosper in the land of the living. For I have made all my declarations of faith by the authority in the name of Jesus Christ.

Amen!

« DAY 287 »

God Still Awards Consequences For Human Sins; People Should Fear Him

Focus Passage: Lamentations 1, 2

Jeremiah lamented for Israelites having witnessed the consequences of their rebellion acts against God. Jeremiah cried,

> *"How lonely sits the city that was full of people! How like a widow is she, who was great among the nations! The princess among the provinces has become a slave! She weeps bitterly in the night, her tears are on her cheeks; among all her lovers she has none to comfort her. All her friends have dealt treacherously with her; they have become her enemies. Judah has gone into captivity, under affliction and hard servitude; She dwells among the nations, she finds no rest; all her persecutors overtake her in dire straits"* **(Lamentation 1:1-3).**

Lesson:
God awards a few consequences for human actions. Everyone - without exemption - is in danger of paying terrible consequences for his/her actions committed against him. God's penalty for sin may beat our imaginations, since his action cannot be underestimated. However, the Creator will be willing to work with any sinner, and see him/her repent to avoid penalty. Jehovah gives a window of opportunity for repentance, and expects a sinner to take necessary repentant action. However, the Creator will not leave his door of grace open indefinitely; he will award punishment for sins and make unrepentant sinners pay dire consequences for their actions. Hence, it is profitable for every disobedient child to turn a new leaf and return to God with a repentant heart. God will honor those who submit and serve him with humility. He will respect repentant sinner; forgive their sins, and restore them into his divine purposes for their lives.

Prayer:
Dear God, please give me a humble heart to repent from my sins and make necessary amendment, so that I can remain your true child. I do not want to be a stubborn child who refuses to repent and get punished. I want to follow you wholeheartedly! Help me not to rationalize sin, but let me be honest in all I do in your presence so that I can be blessed. Please prosper and perfect all that concerns me. For in the name of Jesus Christ I make my requests.

Amen.

« DAY 288 »

Christians Must Run Their Spiritual Race With Seriousness

Focus Passage: Hebrews 12

Christians are encouraged not to focus on challenges but focus on God. We can resemble Jesus Christ and take after his approach to situations of life. Christ fixed his eyes on God to have a successful redemptive work. The scripture stated,

> *"Therefore we also, since we are surrounded by so great a cloud of witnesses, let us lay aside every weight, and the sin which so easily ensnares us, and let us run with endurance the race that is set before us, looking unto Jesus, the author and finisher of our faith, who for the joy that was set before Him endured the cross, despising the shame, and has sat down at the right hand of the throne of God"* **(Hebrews 12:1-2).**

Lesson:
Christians have mandate to run their spiritual race with seriousness in order to finish well. We cannot afford to allow petty situations and circumstances to blow us away from our prestigious pilgrimage. We must be dead to flesh and be alive in the Spirit. We must serve God with sincerity; genuinely confess our sins, and exercise true repentance. A heavenly bound Christian must refute temptations, and stand up for righteousness. A genuine born-again Christian must daily serve God, and proclaim gospel in whatever capacity that he/she has. Also, Christians must be filled with the Holy Spirit, be prayerful, and worship God in beauty of his holiness. God's rewards await us in heaven if we duly serve him, and make him proud. Those who remain committed to their Creator will enjoy peace and prosperity in heaven.

Prayer:
"Jerusalem on high; My song and city is; My home whene'er I die; The centre of my bliss. O happy place! When shall I be, My GOD, with Thee, To see Thy Face?"

Dear God, I want to go to heaven; I do not want anything to keep me away from your kingdom. Please teach me how to be your true child and serve you with complete trust. Give me grace to be steadfast in my relationship with you. Do not let me cave in to trials and temptations. Help me to serve you in beauty of your holiness, and let my services remain acceptable in your sight. Please prosper me in this life, and the next one to come. For in the name of Jesus Christ I make my requests.

Amen.

« DAY 289 »

Children Of God Should Cultivate The Habit Of Praising God Always

Focus Passage: Lamentations 3, 4, 5

Evil befell the City of Jerusalem, but Jeremiah still found some reasons to praise God. The prophet praised God for sparing a few remnants of Israel in their land to honor his promise made for their forefathers. Jeremiah praised God and said,

> "Through *the Lord's mercies we are not consumed, because His compassions fail not.* They are *new every morning; great is your faithfulness*" **(Lamentations 3:22-23).**

Lesson:
Children of God should cultivate a habit of praising God in whatever circumstance they found themselves. Indeed, some uncomfortable wind may blow towards our shore, but we still have God who has control of all situations. God who has saved us from terrible situations in the past can still save us again. He can deliver us from troubles; heal our diseases, and meet other needs. Yes, God of the good time is the God of the bad time! He has power to make whatever wrong become right again! Jehovah will not forget his children, but he will do whatever necessary to lift our heads above waters and make us smile again. Our heavenly Father who never sleeps will surely take care of us - to his best satisfactions! Therefore, no child of God should slumber to depression; every believer should have hope declaration and say "My God whom I serve daily shall supply all my needs!"

Prayer:
I am a child of God, and I believe in his power to meet all my needs! God has power over all situations; he will triumph over any circumstance that may come my way. Jehovah will subdue mountains and level valleys for my sake. With God on my side, I will prevail over every adversity; I will triumph in all situations. Yes, I can do all things through Christ who strengthens me. I am a winner, and God's songs of testimony will never elude my mouth. Victory of the Lord is my portion, and God's testimony is my heritage in the land of the living - forever! For in the name of Jesus Christ I make my declarations!

Amen.

« DAY 290 »

Christians Must Love God And Other People

Focus Passage: Hebrews 13

Children of God must demonstrate true love towards other people; they must also love unbelievers as the scripture required,

> *"Let brotherly love continue. Do not forget to entertain strangers, for by so doing some has unwittingly entertained angels. Remember the prisoners as if chained with them—those who are mistreated—since you yourselves are in the body also"* **(Hebrews 13:1-3).**

Lesson:
A Christian who claims to truly love God must not nurse hatred in his/her heart. Every child of God is required to act like Jesus Christ in speech and indeed! Believers must seek the welfare of others. We must pray and take proactive steps towards the betterment of other people's lives! Meanwhile, our loving and charity activities are not to be limited to fellow believers only. We must love the unbelievers, and be true representative of Jesus Christ in their lives, so that they can be challenged to become Christians. Truly, it may be difficult to love the enemies, but Christ requires that we love them also! We are challenged to pray for those who spitefully deal with us. Therefore, we must seek God's strength to do our due diligence. Believers must pray for the empowerment of the Holy Spirit to meet God's expectations in all ramifications. With God's strength at our disposal, we can do all things! We can love our friends and enemies; we can pray for those who despise us. When we seek God's face for strength, we can stand uprightly and be true soldiers of Christ who will not fail the heavenly Master.

Prayer:
Dear Jesus Christ, please teach me how to be a good Christian. Empower me to run my Christian race according to the bible. Let your Holy Spirit give me strength to love you wholeheartedly; empower me to love my fellow believers, and give me grace to love unbelievers also. Let your true love reign supremely in my heart, so that your name can be glorified always. Please let the light of your gospel so shine in this dark age, so that all people can come to your true love and be saved. Please do these things and many more for the sake of your name. For I make all my requests in your precious name Jesus Christ.

Amen.

« DAY 291 »

God Is Searching For People That Will Prove Their Faith And Stand Up For Him

Focus Passage: Daniel 1, 2; 2-Chronicles 36

Daniel and his fellow three Hebrew boys (popularly known as Shadrach, Meshach, and Abednego) decided not to defy themselves with Nebuchadnezzar's foods that violated their faith and practices. They chose to obey God than to lavish their stomach with Babylonian choice diet. Daniel, on behalf of others said to the king's servant,

> *"Prove thy servants, I beseech thee, ten days; and let them give us pulse to eat, and water to drink. Then let our countenances be looked upon before thee, and the countenance of the children that eat of the portion of the king's meat: and as thou seest, deal with thy servants. So he consented to them in this matter, and proved them ten days"* **(Daniel 1:12-14 KJV).** Since Daniel and his fellows honored God with their faith, God blessed them in return. The scripture stated, *"As for these four children, God gave them knowledge and skill in all learning and wisdom: and Daniel had understanding in all visions and dreams. Now at the end of the days that the king had said he should bring them in, then the prince of the eunuchs brought them in before Nebuchadnezzar. And the king communed with them; and among them all was found none like Daniel, Hananiah, Mishael, and Azariah: therefore stood they before the king. And in all matters of wisdom and understanding, that the king enquired of them, he found them ten times better than all the magicians and astrologers that were in all his realm"* **(Daniel 1:17-20 KJV).**

Lesson:
God honors people of faith; he will stand by them and ensure they are not put to shame. In this time and age, acts of steadfast faith are becoming unpopular; however, God is seeking for people who would make him proud in their decisions. Jehovah is searching for people who would stand up against opinions that are contradictory to his will. People who stand up for God will be honored; they will be favored above their peers, and their names will ever be affixed to God's good book! Therefore, children of God must be close to their bible. We must search the scriptures to know God's true requirements. Our lifestyle must be consistent with the bible, and we must consider satisfying God our top priority. Yes, our godly decisions may draw fire from other folks; they may attempt to abuse, oppress, and persecute us. Yet, crowns of righteousness will be waiting for us in heaven! The host of heaven will rate us high if we are resolute in our faith, and remain contrite Christians.

Prayer:
Dear God, please make me a confident Christian who will not settle for anything other than your requirements. Please make me a person of faith, and let me have resilient and unshifted bible principles. Let my professions and lifestyle meet your standard, so that your name can be glorified in this corrupt and evil world. Let me be your agent of light in this world of darkness, and let your testimony of victory ever remain in my mouth. Please keep me consistent with you so that I can be celebrated in heaven. For in the name of Jesus Christ I make my requests.
Amen.

« DAY 292 »

Christian Leaders Are To Lead By Example

Focus Passage: Titus 1

Paul explained the qualities that make a person fit for church leadership appointments. Paul said,

> *"An elder must be blameless, faithful to his wife, a man whose children believe and are not open to the charge of being wild and disobedient. Since an overseer manages God's household, he must be blameless—not overbearing, not quick-tempered, not given to drunkenness, not violent, not pursuing dishonest gain. Rather, he must be hospitable, one who loves what is good, who is self-controlled, upright, holy and disciplined. 9 He must hold firmly to the trustworthy message as it has been taught, so that he can encourage others by sound doctrine and refute those who oppose it"* **(Titus 1:6-9 NIV)**.

Lesson:
All Christians leader are expected to lead by example. They must demonstrate good characters that other people can emulate. Since church leaders are appointed to represent God, they must be careful not to act in any manner or fashion that can mislead people. All activities of Christian leaders are expected to make people move closer to God.

Prayer:
Dear God, I pray for all Christian leaders that you will help them to lead by example. Please help them to overcome any challenges that may be confronting them. Please fill them with your Holy Spirit so that they can lead your people according to your will. For in the name of Jesus Christ I make my requests.

Amen.

« DAY 293 »

God Remains Alive To Rescue His People From Dangers

Focus Passage: Daniel 3, 4

Three Hebrew men (Shadrach, Meshach, and Abednego) fearlessly rejected King Nebuchadnezzar's command to bow for his idol. The people were defiant to the king's order since it contradicted God's supreme order. (God commanded that people must not serve an idol). The men said to king Nebuchadnezzar,

> *"O Nebuchadnezzar, we have no need to answer you in this matter. If that is the case, our God whom we serve is able to deliver us from the burning fiery furnace, and He will deliver us from your hand, O king. But if not, let it be known to you, O king, that we do not serve your gods, nor will we worship the gold image which you have set up"* **(Daniel 3:16-18).**

God remarkably rescued Shadrach, Meshach, and Abednego from King Nebuchadnezzar's furnace – and the incident turn the heart of the gentile king to honor the living God. The scripture reported,

> *"Then King Nebuchadnezzar was astonished; and he rose in haste and spoke, saying to his counselors, "Did we not cast three men bound into the midst of the fire?" They answered and said to the king, "True, O king." "Look!" he answered, "I see four men loose, walking in the midst of the fire; and they are not hurt, and the form of the fourth is like the Son of God." Then Nebuchadnezzar went near the mouth of the burning fiery furnace and spoke, saying, "Shadrach, Meshach, and Abednego, servants of the Most High God, come out, and come here." Then Shadrach, Meshach, and Abednego came from the midst of the fire"* **(Daniel 3:24-26).**

Lesson:
Christians are encouraged to trust God during adversity to honor his name and have victory. In as much we are human beings, challenges are bound to happen but we must allow God to take control. Christians must make decisions that glorify God – even when undergoing challenging moment. The Creator utilizes time of adversity to strengthen the faith of his children and also glorifies his name. That is, adversity often yield God's children groundbreaking victory when it is handled honorably. Therefore, we must try our best to demonstrate strong faith during adversity to give God an opportunity to step in to demonstrate his power. Any miracle that God performs when faith is demonstrated will challenge unbelievers to fear him and be receptive of his gospel. God's miracle melts people of stony heart to submit to gospel message and become born again Christians.

Prayer:
Dear God, please give courage to demonstrate strong faith during adversity to glorify your name. Let my profession and actions create an atmosphere that will allow you to demonstrate your wonders! Let the miracle that you will perform about my case send a special message to unbelievers to become humble and accept you as Lord. Let the miracle that you will perform concerning my situation melt unbelievers hearts to confess Jesus Christ as Lord and be saved! For in the name of Jesus Christ I make my requests.

Amen.

« DAY 294 »

Christians Are To Maintain Bible Standard Even When The World Standard Keep Degrading

Focus Passage: Titus 2

Gospel ministers are directed to teach and lead people to be good stewards of Jesus Christ. The scripture stated,

> *"You, however, must teach what is appropriate to sound doctrine. Teach the older men to be temperate, worthy of respect, self-controlled, and sound in faith, in love and in endurance. Likewise, teach the older women to be reverent in the way they live, not to be slanderers or addicted to much wine, but to teach what is good. Then they can urge the younger women to love their husbands and children, to be self-controlled and pure, to be busy at home, to be kind, and to be subject to their husbands, so that no one will malign the word of God. Similarly, encourage the young men to be self-controlled. In everything set them an example by doing what is good. In your teaching show integrity, seriousness 8 and soundness of speech that cannot be condemned, so that those who oppose you may be ashamed because they have nothing bad to say about us"* **(Titus 2:1-8 NIV)**.

Lesson:

Christians are to live according to bible standard - and nothing more or less! Believers are required to stand clear of ungodly cultural practices as they surface and re-surface. As it is today, world culture and practices will not cease from changing, but believers must not be caught up in the same syndrome. People will demoralize God's laws to suit their selfish desires; believers must not be part of that! Thank God we have bible, and its standard does not change! Therefore, we believers must adopt our culture from it! Since we are heavenly bound people, we must observe God's law to the letter, and we must ensure that we reference our practices from it. Heavenly God is a serious kind, and he would not change is mind as men do. Men may change, but God's requirement for heaven will not change! Therefore, anyone who desires to go to heaven on the last day must stand to his/her feet to comply with God's law.

Prayer:

Dear God, I am definitely not there yet! I am still unfit for your kingdom! I have compromised your requirements for heaven. I have followed multitude to sin against you! However, I have decided to turn a new leaf: I repent from my errors; I ask you to forgive my failures and cleanse me. Please make me fit for your kingdom. I believe in your Son Jesus Christ, and I accept him as my Lord and Savior. From now on, please give me strength to stand up for righteousness and do your will wholeheartedly - even when it would not make me popular. Please equip me with your Holy Spirit to stay fit for the second coming of your Son Jesus Christ. Count me worthy for heaven! For in the name of Jesus Christ I make my requests.

Amen.

« DAY 295 »

Jehovah Will Honor Any Christian That Demonstrate Unwavering Faith In Him

Focus Passage: Daniel 5, 6, 7

Daniel chose to give undivided attention to God, and his action infuriated his enemies. Therefore, they plotted to kill him. The scripture reported,

> "So the governors and satraps sought to find some charge against Daniel concerning the kingdom; but they could find no charge or fault, because he was faithful; nor was there any error or fault found in him. Then these men said, "We shall not find any charge against this Daniel unless we find it against him concerning the law of his God" **(Daniel 6 4-5).** Daniel's enemies were able to successfully cast him to the lion's den, but God defended his servant. God shut the lions' mouths, and they could not hurt him. Consequentially, Daniel's opponents landed in the lions' den, and the animals feasted on them. It is reported, "(The king said) I make a decree that in every dominion of my kingdom men must tremble and fear before the God of Daniel. For He is the living God, and steadfast forever; His kingdom is the one which shall not be destroyed, and His dominion shall endure to the end. He delivers and rescues, And He works signs and wonders in heaven and on earth, who has delivered Daniel from the power of the lions" **(Daniel 6:26-27).**

Lesson:

God will defend his people, and he will not allow the enemies to mock his name in their lives. When we (believers) act in faith, God is glorified! Therefore, we must stay with our confession of faith, and practice Christianity in a way that will glorify Christ. Once we make God happy by demonstrating unwavering faith, he will honor us in return. However, common fact about Christianity remains the same: Believers would face challenges in this present world. Satan and his forces will attempt anything to stop a believer from trusting God. However, faithful sons and daughters of God must remain committed to Christ - the Savior. The mixture of good and evil that we may face in this world are temporal. They would soon become things of the past. Believers in Jesus Christ must be courageous always, since we know that our present afflictions are just for a short time. Time of redemption is on the way, and Christ will move us from this evil world to a perfect one - where no form of evil will exist. Believers must expect the second coming of Jesus Christ, and be prepared always!

Prayer:

Dear God, please give me strength to remain committed to my confession of faith in you. Help me to stand strong against any opposition that may challenge my belief. Let your Holy Spirit empower me to stand firm in faith so that devil can be put to shame, and your name be glorified. Assist me to remain fit for your second coming, so that I can be partaker of your benefits in heaven. Please keep me fit now and always! For in the name of Jesus Christ I make my requests.

Amen.

« DAY 296 »

Believers Must Uphold God's Standard Of Righteousness

Focus Passage: Titus 3

Scripture required God's children to walk with dignity and honor. We are to practice plain Christianity and avoid irrelevant arguments that have little or no contribution to our spiritual growth. The scripture stated,

> *"Avoid foolish disputes, genealogies, contentions, and strivings about the law; for they are unprofitable and useless. Reject a divisive man after the first and second admonition, knowing that such a person is warped and sinning, being self-condemned"* **(Titus 3:9-11).**

Lesson:
Followers of Jesus Christ are to resemble Jesus Christ. Believers must have discipline and demonstrate honorable posture, since God himself has discipline. Our speech and actions must prove that Christ indeed dwells in us. Our lives must be consistent with the bible, and we must be firm to uphold God's standard of righteousness. We Christians must be consistent with our professions of faith! Heaven requires that we avoid unnecessary arguments, but celebrate sound bible doctrines. However, followers of Jesus Christ must understand the importance of demonstrating Christianity with grace! Believers must operate in love and grace; we must be loving, and we must accommodate other people (without compromising bible standard). God expects his children to glorify his name in every aspect of their lives, and we must do so!

Prayer:
Dear God, please let my life be consistent with your standard. Help me to practice true Christianity so that your name can be glorified in all situations! Empower me through your Holy Spirit to walk in righteousness. Let my yea be yea, and my nay be nay - according to bible standard. Please shine your light into my life, and enable me to extend the same light to other people. Please make me your true ambassador on earth, so that I will be qualified for your heavenly rewards. For in the name of Jesus Christ I make my requests.

Amen.

« DAY 297 »

Christians Are Expected To Be Patriotic To Their Respective Earthly Countries
Focus Passage: Daniel 8, 9, 10

Daniel researched record to avert the tribulation that has befallen his country. From research, the Man of God realized past prophecy that explained future deliverance of Israel. Israelites that were held captive in Babylon would be released after a period of 70 years. Israelites would return to rebuild their homeland, and they would live in peace again. Having uncovered the fact about the destiny of his people, Daniel began praying and fasting to remind God of his promises. The scripture reported,

> *"In the first year of his reign I, Daniel, understood by the books the number of the years specified by the word of the Lord through Jeremiah the prophet, that He would accomplish seventy years in the desolation of Jerusalem. Then I set my face toward the Lord God to make request by prayer and supplications, with fasting, sackcloth, and ashes. And I prayed to the Lord my God, and made confession, and said, "O Lord, great and awesome God, who keeps His covenant and mercy with those who love Him, and with those who keep His commandments, we have sinned and committed iniquity, we have done wickedly and rebelled, even by departing from Your precepts and Your judgments **(Daniel 9:2-5)** ...O my God, incline Your ear and hear; open Your eyes and see our desolations, and the city which is called by Your name; for we do not present our supplications before You because of our righteous deeds, but because of Your great mercies. O Lord, hear! O Lord, forgive! O Lord, listen and act! Do not delay for your own sake, my God, for your city and your people are called by your name"* **(18-19)**

Lesson:
Children of God are expected to be patriotic to their respective country. Indeed heaven is our homeland, but we still live in this world; we must do our best to support the interest of our earthly home. We must pray for the peace of our country where we hold right of citizenship. We must contribute our quota of efforts that will aid our society to be peaceful and habitable. Christians must make efforts to promote unity and integrity of their society! Since, we are god's children, we must influence people around us to be responsible and create positive impact. The same God who has utilized the efforts of his children in time past to positively transform people's destiny can still do the same thing again. God will honor the efforts of his children again, and he will visit our lands!

Prayer:
Dear God, please help me to be patriotic to my homeland. Give me grace to make every necessary contribution within my capacity to help make my country strong and be successful. Please, enable my fellow Christians to make positive contributions to their society, so that your name can be glorified among the people. Please remember our political leaders to properly govern us. Weed out selfishness and corruption from our government; let morality reign, so that the citizens of our land can enjoy their right benefits and live peacefully. Please do this and many more! For in the name of Jesus Christ I make my requests.
Amen.

« DAY 298 »

Christians Must Be Good Stewards And Be Good Examples For Others

Focus Passage: Philemon 1

Paul called Philemon a brother, and he appreciated him for being a good steward of Jesus Christ. Paul said,

> *"I thank my God, making mention of you always in my prayers, hearing of your love and faith which you have toward the Lord Jesus and toward all the saints, that the sharing of your faith may become effective by the acknowledgment of every good thing which is in you in Christ Jesus. For we have great joy and consolation in your love, because the hearts of the saints have been refreshed by you, brother"* **(Philemon 1:4-7)**.

Lesson:
Christians are to be good stewards of Jesus Christ. We are to live exemplary lifestyle that will challenge unbelievers to venture into becoming Christians also. Christians must be full of faith; we must be reflective of Jesus characters in all aspects of life. As Christ's ambassador on earth, selfishness, prideful heart, immorality, and all other ungodly acts must not be found with us. Our lives must be full of grace, and we must ensure that God's name is praised in every circumstance of our lives.

Prayer:
Dear God, please help me to be a Christian that live exemplary lifestyle for other people to emulate. Help me to be your good steward; let me be reflective of you in speech and in deed. Empower me through your Holy Spirit to live acceptable lifestyle before you always, so that I can be qualified to receive your eternal rewards in heaven. For in the name of Jesus Christ I make my requests.

Amen.

« DAY 299 »

The Present Earth Will Become Obsolete; New One Will Be Established

Focus Passage: Daniel 11, 12

God showed Prophet Daniel the end game for existence of the present earth. The earth will become extinct, and wicked people who have lived in it will go into everlasting punishment of hell. At the same time, people who have lived godly lives on earth will be rewarded with the gift of eternal life. Daniel explained God's vision,

> *"And at that time shall Michael stand up, the great prince which standeth for the children of thy people: and there shall be a time of trouble, such as never was since there was a nation even to that same time: and at that time thy people shall be delivered, every one that shall be found written in the book. And many of them that sleep in the dust of the earth shall awake, some to everlasting life, and some to shame and everlasting contempt. And they that be wise shall shine as the brightness of the firmament; and they that turn many to righteousness as the stars forever and ever" (Daniel 12:1-3 KJV).*

Lesson:

The present earth and heaven will soon become obsolete; God will bring them to a complete end. Jehovah will destroy the present earth alongside the wicked people who ever lived in it. (The present heaven will be removed also). Meanwhile, the Creator will create a new earth and a new heaven with an established righteous government. People who ever served God well on earth and believed Jesus Christ as God's Son will partake in the new earth (and new heaven). Jehovah will provide everlasting peace for his newly created universe, and all his saints will have eternal satisfactions. Hence, since the present universe has a destructive end, all people should venture to partake in the new one to come. Every soul on earth should accept Jesus Christ as God's true Son, and confess him as his/her personal Lord and Savior.

Prayer:

Dear God, please count me worthy to inherit your eternal kingdom. Forgive my sins, and cleanse me from all my unrighteousness. I confess Jesus Christ as your Son and accept him as my personal Lord and Savior. Please write my name in the book of life, and let me qualify to partake in your new earth and new heaven to come. For in the name of Jesus Christ I make my requests.

Amen.

« DAY 300 »

God's Children Must Have Unconditional True And Thorough Love

Focus Passage: 1 Timothy 1

The scripture explained the essential requirement for faithful Christian living. LOVE! It is written,

> *"Now the purpose of the commandment is love from a pure heart, from a good conscience, and from sincere faith, from which some, having strayed, have turned aside to idle talk"* **(1 Timothy 1:5-6).**

Lesson:
Love is a key factor that makes Christianity relevant in the world. The whole thing about love started with God: He loved the world and sent his Son Jesus Christ to save it from destruction (John 3:16). Christ came to earth for the sake of love: He preached love and died for love! Therefore, anyone who has hope of going to heaven must have love! However, love must not be misinterpreted for it to be relevant. Love must be void of evil. Since God's love for humanity is pure and perfect (agape), whatever we call love must be undefiled also. Anyone who claims to have love must demonstrate it to glorify God. God's children must have unconditional true and thorough love. Our love for fellow humans must be void of selfishness. Once we satisfy God with desired demonstration of love, he will shower his blessings on us beyond what anyone can imagine!

Prayer:
Dear God, I understand that love is a very important factor that leads to godliness and holiness. No one will inherit your kingdom without true love. Therefore, I humbly seek your Spirit of true love. Please give me your Holy Spirit to truly love you and love other people around me! Let my love for you be unconditional, and let me serve you whole-heartedly. Empower me to love my friends and neighbors, and sincerely seek their peace and prosperity. Please, keep my heart pure, so that I will live an acceptable life to be fit to inherit your kingdom. For in the name of Jesus Christ I make my requests.

Amen.

« DAY 301 »

Satan May Have Brief Joy Over Believers, But He Will Eternally Suffer In Hell

Focus Passage: Psalm 137; Ezekiel 1, 2

Enemies mocked Israelites, and they asked them to sing their melodious Zion songs in the foreign land, but Israelites refused. Instead, Israelites lamented in protest as reported,

> *"By the rivers of Babylon, there we sat down, yea, we wept, when we remembered Zion. We hanged our harps upon the willows in the midst thereof. For there they that carried us away captive required of us a song; and they that wasted us required of us mirth, saying, Sing us one of the songs of Zion. How shall we sing the Lord's song in a strange land?" (Psalm 137:1-4 KJV).*

Lesson:

Satan and his forces love to mock God's children during distress. The enemies have field day when a Christian falls to their traps, and they would be quick to persecute, condemn, and ridicule him/her. However, God cares for his children, and he will not allow Satan (and his evil elements) to prevail over them. God will help his children rise above their challenges; he will restore them from their pitfalls, and help them to come to a renewed relationship with him. The Creator will forgive and restore his children to his true love. However, God's children are not losers, but Satan and his forces are! While the enemies might enjoy brief victory over a Christian who fell from grace, they have eternal condemnation to suffer. Satan (who has no repentance and forgiveness opportunity) will spend his eternal life in hell fire - and his attaché will follow suit to the same location. Jesus' followers will remain in heaven to enjoy his everlasting benefits!

Prayer:

Praise God I am a child of God! Praise God, I am a redeemed person of the Lord! It is my choice to sing God's songs, and his praises shall ever remain in my mouth. Satan has lost his battle over my life. I will neither sing nor dance before him again. My total life is committed to God, and his praises shall ever remain in my mouth. I will praise God from now and ever more. Thanks to Jesus Christ who turned me to God!

Amen.

« DAY 302 »

Believers Should Pray For Their Government Officials

Focus Passage: 1 Timothy 2

Christians are required to pray for one another, and also pray for the government leaders. It is written,

> *"Therefore I exhort first of all that supplications, prayers, intercessions, and giving of thanks be made for all men, for kings and all who are in authority, that we may lead a quiet and peaceable life in all godliness and reverence. For this is good and acceptable in the sight of God our Savior, who desires all men to be saved and to come to the knowledge of the truth"* ***(1 Timothy 2:1-4).***

Lesson:

Christians are to pray for government officials since they make decisions that affect our lives. We should pray for them to have contrite heart to make good decisions that will positively impact our society. More importantly, we should pray for our political leaders to believe God and serve him - since godly fear leads to wisdom **(Proverbs 9:10)**, Believers should pray that our leaders prioritize citizens' interests above their political ambitions. The spirit of selfishness and corruption must be subdued in the lives of our leaders - through prayers! God still answer prayers, and he will answer us. God will use our prayers to initiate a change that will stir our society in the right direction. With God on our sides, our streets can be saved again, and God's righteous standard can be upheld in the city halls.

Prayer:

Dear God, please I pray for our leaders to have your fear so that they can make decisions that will positively impact our lives. Let our leaders have peace, clarity of mind, and ability to govern us appropriately. Let our leaders have integrity and pursue righteousness, so that our society can have progress. Please remove the spirit of self-centeredness, arrogance, and corruption from our leaders. Let them have godly conscience and integrity to lead our land into having abundant prosperity. For in the name of Jesus Christ I make my requests.

Amen.

« DAY 303 »

God's Servants Are Not Allowed To Serve At Will, But Always

Focus Passage: Ezekiel 3, 4

Servants of God are to be firm with their bible interpretations. They must call a spade a spade, and ensure the truth is told from the altar. Whether convenient or not, God's servants must tell the truth so that people can know what God requires from them. God warned Prophet Ezekiel of the danger looming over him and his people if he refused to speak God's mind appropriately. God warned Ezekiel and said,

> *"Son of man, I have made thee a watchman unto the house of Israel: therefore hear the word at my mouth, and give them warning from me. When I say unto the wicked, Thou shalt surely die; and thou givest him not warning, nor speakest to warn the wicked from his wicked way, to save his life; the same wicked man shall die in his iniquity; but his blood will I require at thine hand. Yet if thou warn the wicked, and he turn not from his wickedness, nor from his wicked way, he shall die in his iniquity; but thou hast delivered thy soul. Again, When a righteous man doth turn from his righteousness, and commit iniquity, and I lay a stumbling-block before him, he shall die: because thou hast not given him warning, he shall die in his sin, and his righteousness which he hath done shall not be remembered; but his blood will I require at thine hand. Nevertheless if thou warn the righteous man, that the righteous sin not, and he doth not sin, he shall surely live, because he is warned; also thou hast delivered thy soul"* **(Ezekiel 3:17-21 KJV)**.

Lesson:
God's servants are his treasured instruments, and he expects nothing but discipline from them. God holds his servants with high esteem; they must appropriately speak his mind and ensure to safeguard people from pitfalls. God's servants are not allowed to serve God at will, but they are mandated to meet God's standard at all times! Honor belongs to a servant who does his/her job well, but God's punishments loom over a servant who fails his Master! Since the Creator is counting on his servants to represent him well, they should not hesitate to honorably carry out their due diligence. By so doing, heavy rod of punishments will be averted, and huge positive rewards will be obtained (by God's servants, and their people). Congratulations to those servants who faithfully serve God, for their rewards will be obtained on earth, and in heaven!

Prayer:
Dear God, please make me a true and thorough servant who will faithfully serve you. Let me be consistent with your word, and let me serve you wholeheartedly. Give me strength to speak the truth at all times - whether convenient or not. Let my speech and deed glorify you, so that other people can be motivated to serve you also. Please anoint me with fresh ointment to faithfully serve you unto the end! At the same time, I pray for all your ministers throughout the world: Please give them strength to faithfully serve you. Let your ministers lead by example so that your name can be glorified among their people. For in the name of Jesus Christ I make my requests.
Amen.

« DAY 304 »

Gospel Ministers Must Have Personal Integrity To Adequately Fit Their Positions

Focus Passage: 1 Timothy 3

Anyone who desires to be a church leader must first of all be responsible at home. His/her life must be relevant to his family, before considering leading any church office. The scripture stated,

> "This is a faithful saying: If a man desires the position of a bishop, he desires a good work. A bishop then must be blameless, the husband of one wife, temperate, sober-minded, of good behavior, hospitable, able to teach; not given to wine, not violent, not greedy for money, but gentle, not quarrelsome, not covetous; one who rules his own house well, having his children in submission with all reverence (for if a man does not know how to rule his own house, how will he take care of the church of God?); not a novice, lest being puffed up with pride he fall into the same condemnation as the devil. Moreover he must have a good testimony among those who are outside, lest he fall into reproach and the snare of the devil" **(1 Timothy 3:1-7).**

Lesson:
Christian leaders must be responsible and lead by example. Since charity begins at home, a gospel minister must first be responsible in his/her personal life: He must be a responsible spouse and parent. He must be held with high esteem in his family. Anyone who considers the honor of a church leader must have reputation among his peers, and he must lead by example. Besides, a church leader must understand the concept of the bible, and be ready to give it a clear and contrite interpretation. He must be ready to share gospel in truth and walk in the integrity of his heart. It is understood that some people mistakenly follow their church leaders more than they follow Jesus Christ himself; hence, the challenge of such leader leading by godly example is paramount! Church members must not derail into pitfall of hell fire! Therefore, every church leader and those who minister in other capacity must ensure to make decisive effort that will positively influence their members/followers/protégé, so that God's name can be glorified in their lives.

Prayer:
Dear God, please help our church leaders to lead by example, so that members can be faithful to you. Help our leaders to lead by example! Let them be people of integrity that sincerely promote your interest in people's lives. Please help your servants to be strong from home, so that they can have enough momentum to positively impact others. Anoint your servants with grace to promote undiluted gospel in this corrupted world! Let them be filled with the Holy Spirit to have power and boldness to preach fundamental truth of the bible, so that your name can be praised, and for people to make it to heaven. Please do these things and many more. For in the name of Jesus Christ I make my requests.

Amen.

« DAY 305 »

God Will Restore Any Sinner That Comes To Him - No Matter The Gravity Of A Sin

Focus Passage: Ezekiel 5, 6, 7

God was disappointed to see Israelites persisted in their rebellion acts, despite his warning. Therefore, he promised to severely punish them until they exercise repentance. (Israelites would have to suffer from their enemies who will dissolve their nation). God said to Ezekiel,

> *"...Thou son of man, thus saith the Lord God unto the land of Israel; An end, the end is come upon the four corners of the land. Now is the end come upon thee, and I will send mine anger upon thee, and will judge thee according to thy ways, and will recompense upon thee all thine abominations. And mine eye shall not spare thee, neither will I have pity: but I will recompense thy ways upon thee, and thine abominations shall be in the midst of thee: and ye shall know that I am the Lord. Thus saith the Lord God; An evil, an only evil, behold, is come. An end is come, the end is come: it watcheth for thee; behold, it is come. The morning is come unto thee, O thou that dwellest in the land: the time is come, the day of trouble is near, and not the sounding again of the mountains. Now will I shortly pour out my fury upon thee, and accomplish mine anger upon thee: and I will judge thee according to thy ways, and will recompense thee for all thine abominations"* **(Ezekiel 7:1-8 KJV).**

Lesson:

God hates sin as a detestable disease. Sin forces his hands to withdraw his benefits from his own people. Devil rejoices when a Christian commits sin, because he would have opportunity to strike against him/her - for especially when repentance is not exercised. However, consequences of sin are not easily predictable, since one does not know how God would respond. In most cases, the punishments awarded for sinful actions appear outrageous! However, God who exercises judgment of punishment is mostly interested in repentance of his people. He expects a sinner to repent and return to his/her true love of Christ, so that devil can be put to shame. Jehovah will restore any sinner who comes to him - no matter the gravity of his/her sin. Hence, every child of God should consider serving God in the beauty of his holiness. Any believer who falls into sin should consider it a must to repent and turn a new leave so that devil can be ashamed, and God be glorified. A person who walks carefully before his Maker will enjoy his divine benefits, but a rebellion child will incur his Maker's rod of punishment.

Prayer:

Dear God, what advantage do I have in an act of rebelliousness? What would be my gain if I sin or I refuse to repent from my sins? Wouldn't devil be glorified in my sin? Therefore, I am determined to walk before you in the beauty of holiness. I will do whatever you ask me to do, and I will obey you in all aspects of my life. In as much as I have your grace, I will faithfully serve you and obey your instructions, so that I can prosper. Please give me a simple and sincere heart to walk before you in godly fear. Enable me to be humble to repent from my sins, and give me grace to do your will throughout the days of my life. For in the name of Jesus Christ I make my requests. Amen.

« DAY 306 »

Believers Must Be Watchful Of False Doctrine And Not Derail

Focus Passage: 1 Timothy 4

Christians are to be careful of false doctrines, and avoid them. The scripture warned,

> *"The Spirit clearly says that in later times some will abandon the faith and follow deceiving spirits and things taught by demons. Such teachings come through hypocritical liars, whose consciences have been seared as with a hot iron. They forbid people to marry and order them to abstain from certain foods, which God created to be received with thanksgiving by those who believe and who know the truth"* **(1 Timothy 4:1-3).**

Lesson:
This generation has witnessed many events and practices which the scripture have predicated to be signs of End Time. "False Doctrine" is one of the signs **(Matthew 24).** Believers are warned to be sensitive to bible teachers, and ensure they are not derailed. While it is important to appreciate God's servants, we must still be careful of the teachings that we receive. Believers must be sensitive to comply with the bible always. Our degraded society has proven that some preachers, teachers, prophet, and/or others would appear to use subtle approach to deceive their audience. In fact, bible warned that some ministers would even perform miracles to manipulate people for their selfish gains, and haul people to hell fire. However, Christians must ensure to avoid pitfalls; they must be students of the bible themselves. Believers must read their bible on consistent basis, and allow the Holy Spirit to give them godly interpretations. A good Christian must validate any teaching that he/she receives with the bible! All believers must ensure to be on the right track and stand uprightly with God in order to make it to heaven.

Prayer:
Dear God, please help me to be careful not to entertain false teachings. Help me to only entertain teachings that comply with bible standard. Do not let me become a victim of false teaching and miss opportunity of going to heaven. Give me grace to daily study my bible to establish all truth, so that I can meet you in heaven on the last day. Please keep my feet firm in faith, and count my worthy for your eternal kingdom! For in the name of Jesus Christ I make my requests.

Amen.

« DAY 307 »

God Requires Honesty From His Children

Focus Passage: Ezekiel 8, 9, 10

God scolded Israelites for their hypocritical behaviors. Israelites pretended to love God, but they meant the opposite. God exposed them to Ezekiel and said,

> *"Then said he unto me, Hast thou seen this, O son of man? turn thee yet again, and thou shalt see greater abominations than these. And he brought me into the inner court of the Lord's house, and, behold, at the door of the temple of the Lord, between the porch and the altar, were about five and twenty men, with their backs toward the temple of the Lord, and their faces toward the east; and they worshipped the sun toward the east. Then he said unto me, Hast thou seen this, O son of man? Is it a light thing to the house of Judah that they commit the abominations which they commit here? for they have filled the land with violence, and have returned to provoke me to anger: and, lo, they put the branch to their nose. Therefore will I also deal in fury: mine eye shall not spare, neither will I have pity: and though they cry in mine ears with a loud voice, yet will I not hear them"* **(Ezekiel 8:15-18 KJV).**

Lesson:

God is too big to be played, and he cannot be fooled. He understands people well, and he knows those who serve him sincerely. He also knows those who give lip-service and eye-service. While it is easy for anyone to claim that he/she is a Christian and religious, a good Christian must serve God with all sincerity. A good Christian must not portray godly appearance and still keep secret sins. A true Christian must not be manipulative; he must neither be obsessive nor possessive of evil. A true Christian must be candid in his/her approach to all things. Anyone who aims at being a true child of God must faithfully serve God, and care for other people also. Jehovah, who knows people who faithfully serve Him will surely bless them in this life, and in heaven also!

Prayer:

Dear God, please help me to be a straightforward Christian who does things rightly. Help me to live a straightforward lifestyle before you! Help me to admit my mistakes and take every necessary step of repentance. Please let me serve you well on earth so that I can qualify to receive your benefits in this life, and in heaven also. For in the name of Jesus Christ I make my requests.

Amen.

« DAY 308 »

The Rule "Charity Begins At Home" Applies To Christians Equally

Focus Passage: 1 Timothy 5

The common sense rule that states, "Charity begins at home" applies to all Christians. The scripture stated,

> *"But if anyone does not provide for his own, and especially for those of his household, he has denied the faith and is worse than an unbeliever"* ***(1 Timothy 5:8).***

Lesson:
Indeed, charity begins at home! We Christians are required to be responsible for our immediate family before we should attempt to extend the same sense of responsibility to the outside world. A good Christian must be a reasonable and a responsible father, mother, husband, wife, son, or daughter. Better sermons are preached through our family - How we take care of them and lead them into serving God. No Christian should neglect his/her family in the name of religion! The responsibility of being a good Christian must start from home, and then be extended to the outside world. Let us learn from Jesus: He took care of Mary (his earthly mother) to the point of his death. He was also a good example for his siblings - which made his skeptical brothers (James and Jude) eventually turned to become Christians and gospel ministers. Therefore, since Jesus Christ remains our perfect example, all Christians must endeavor to take up their responsibilities in their respective family.

Prayer:
Dear God, please help me to be a responsible Christian who adequately takes care of his/her family. Help me to be your true ambassador to my family! Let my words and activities be seasoned with grace to motivate them into serving you! Also, please empower me to extend the same love to my friends and neighbors and to the outside world so that your name can be glorified always. For in the name of Jesus Christ I make my requests.

Amen.

« DAY 309 »

God Created Redemptive Pathway For Humanity Through Jesus Christ

Focus Passage: Ezekiel 11, 12, 13

God expressed his fatherly love towards the outcast Israelites - which have heavily paid for their disobedience. The Creator would lighten Israelites burdens and restore them from captivity to their homeland. God said to Ezekiel about Israelites,

> *"Therefore say, Thus saith the Lord God; Although I have cast them far off among the heathen, and although I have scattered them among the countries, yet will I be to them as a little sanctuary in the countries where they shall come. Therefore say, Thus saith the Lord God; I will even gather you from the people, and assemble you out of the countries where ye have been scattered, and I will give you the land of Israel. And they shall come thither, and they shall take away all the detestable things thereof and all the abominations thereof from thence. And I will give them one heart, and I will put a new spirit within you; and I will take the stony heart out of their flesh, and will give them an heart of flesh"* **(Ezekiel 11:16-19 KJV).**

Lesson:
God is gracious and merciful; he will not cast off sinners forever, but he will restore them back into his true love. Despite the magnitude of evil that humans have committed, Jehovah still chose to create a redemptive pathway for us! God understands that we are humans made out of dust and we are far from perfection; therefore, he will work with us until we are fully redeemed. Jehovah will forgive our sins and restore us into his perfect love. To achieve this, he sent his only begotten Son Jesus Christ to earth to save the world. Christ would die for sins of humanity and reconcile us to our Creator! Indeed, Christ achieved this purpose; hence, humanity must express their faith in him to be saved. Anyone seeking redemption from sins must confess Jesus Christ as God's only divine Son, and accept him as his/her personal Lord and Savior.

Prayer:
Dear God, I understand that I am a stinking sinner who does not deserve anything good from you! However, I humbly come before you today to ask for forgiveness. Please forgive my sins, and cleanse me from my unrighteousness. Grant me redemption and restoration through my faith in your Son Jesus Christ. I declare my faith in Jesus Christ, and I accept him as my personal Lord and Savior. Please write my name in the book of life, and count me worthy to partake in your eternal kingdom. For in the name of Jesus Christ I have made my requests.

Amen.

« DAY 310 »

A Good Christian Must Have Clear Understanding Of The Bible, And Practice It

Focus Passage: 1 Timothy 6

God's words are instant and exacts; they must be accurately interpreted to perform their intended purposes in believers' lives; therefore, Christians must ensure to only relate with (or listen to) gospel ministers who share facts of the scriptures. Bible can neither be over-simplified nor under-simplified; it must be simple, exact, and purposeful to glorify God, and bless people. It is written,

> *"If anyone teaches otherwise and does not agree to the sound instruction of our Lord Jesus Christ and to godly teaching, they are conceited and understand nothing. They have an unhealthy interest in controversies and quarrels about words that result in envy, strife, malicious talk, evil suspicions and constant friction between people of corrupt mind, who have been robbed of the truth and who think that godliness is a means to financial gain"* **(1 Timothy 6:3-5 NIV).**

Lesson:
A serious Christian is expected to celebrate the truth of the scripture. He/she is expected to adequately interpret scripture without rationalization! A good Christian must understand and celebrate God's view of charity, morality, and holiness. More importantly, a good Christian should know how to select a godly spiritual leader! No serious Christian should settle for callous spiritual leader who waters down the scripture! A good Christian should not follow the multitude to practice whatever society dictate for him/her. A good Christian should personally study the scripture on consistent basis to ensure that he/she is doing what is right in the presence of God. To cap it all, a good Christian must be prayerful, and be full of Holy Spirit to have clear understanding of the scripture, and to adequately satisfy the will of God. Jehovah will honor faithful Christians in this life, and in heaven also.

Prayer:
Dear God, please make me a serious Christian who serves you wholeheartedly. Give me grace to only celebrate whatever makes you happy! Do not let me follow multitude to do evil, but let me live a life of integrity that is worthy of your blessing. Help me to be sensitive to any teaching that I receive, and empower me through your Holy Spirit to only celebrate your approved righteous standard. Please let my walk with you be pure, so that I can inherit your eternal kingdom. For in the name of Jesus Christ I make my requests.

Amen.

« DAY 311 »

God Can't Stand Sin, He Will Make Whoever Persists In Sin Pay For It

Focus Passage: Ezekiel 14, 15

Israelites' persistent sins infuriated God, and he promised to severe them with heavy punishments. God said to Ezekiel,

> *"Son of man, when the land sinneth against me by trespassing grievously, then will I stretch out mine hand upon it, and will break the staff of the bread thereof, and will send famine upon it, and will cut off man and beast from it: Though these three men, Noah, Daniel, and Job, were in it, they should deliver but their own souls by their righteousness, saith the Lord God. If I cause noisome beasts to pass through the land, and they spoil it, so that it be desolate, that no man may pass through because of the beasts: Though these three men were in it, as I live, saith the Lord God, they shall deliver neither sons nor daughters; they only shall be delivered, but the land shall be desolate"* **(Ezekiel 14:13-16 KJV).**

Lesson:

God cannot stand sin, and he will make anyone who persist in it pay for his/her action. A person who refuses repentance and die in sin will not meet God in heaven. Such person will face the danger of hell fire. It is written *"The soul that sinned shall die* **(Ezekiel 18:20)."** However, a person who humbly confesses his/her sins, and repents from it will receive forgiveness. Meanwhile, forgiveness of sin can only be obtained through the name of Jesus Christ. Christ will advocate for any sinner who seeks forgiveness through his name! The Savior will plead on his behalf to God to receive forgiveness and restoration. Hence, anyone who aims at inheriting God's kingdom must submit to the feet of Christ and confess him as Lord.

Prayer:

Dear Jesus, I understand that no one can inherit God's kingdom without first accepting you as Christ and confesses you as Lord. Therefore, I declare you as my Lord today! I confess my sins and forsake them. From now on, I am determined to faithfully follow you and serve you with all my heart, so that I can inherit God's kingdom. Please keep my feet standing at your gate, and make me forever fit to partake in your everlasting peace and joy in heaven. For in the name of Jesus Christ I make my requests.

Amen.

« DAY 312 »

Christ Will Advocate For People That Confess Him As Lord On The Day Of Judgment

Focus Passage: 2 Timothy 1

A child of God must maintain his confidence in God, and remain steadfast with his/her confession of faith in Jesus Christ. The scripture stated,

> *"For God has not given us a spirit of fear, but of power and of love and of a sound mind. Therefore do not be ashamed of the testimony of our Lord, nor of me His prisoner, but share with me in the sufferings for the gospel according to the power of God"* ***(2 Timothy 1:7-8).***

Lesson:
Christians are the most fortunate people on earth, and they should remain confident with their faith conviction in Jesus Christ. Christians are heavenly bound people; Christ will advocate for them on God's last Day of Judgment since they have confessed Jesus Christ as their personal Lord and Savior. Christ will plead on behalf of his followers and ask God to forgive their sins for the sake of his blood that he has shed on their behalves. Since Christ was sinless but died for sinners, God will honor his request and exonerate Christians! Therefore, it is prestigious for anyone to be a Christian! A person who has not turned to Jesus Christ should do so - without wasting time - since Christ is the only formidable advocate that can withstand God's Judgment. Congratulations to anyone who has taken the wise decision of confessing Jesus Christ as his/her personal Lord and Savior - for heavenly home shall be his/her permanent resort!

Prayer:
"O the Blood of Jesus washes me. O the Blood of Jesus shed for me. What a sacrifice that saved my life. Yes the blood it is my victory"
Thank you Jesus Christ for the good works that you have finished on the cross me! You died to save my soul from condemnation and judgment of hell. Therefore, I yield my complete life to you today! I declare you Jesus Christ as the Lord of my life, and I confess you as my personal Savior. Please wash my sins away, and declare me as your bona-fide child that will inherit your everlasting kingdom.Thank you Jesus Christ for your saving grace.

Amen.

« DAY 313 »

Believers' Attitude Of Gratitude Will Provoke God's Blessings

Focus Passage: Ezekiel 16, 17

God promised to grant Israelites an unmerited favor despite their rebellious activities. Jehovah would embarrass Israelites with love instead of judgments and condemnations. The Creator said,

> *"Nevertheless I will remember my covenant with thee in the days of thy youth, and I will establish unto thee an everlasting covenant. Then thou shalt remember thy ways, and be ashamed, when thou shalt receive thy sisters, thine elder and thy younger: and I will give them unto thee for daughters, but not by thy covenant. And I will establish my covenant with thee; and thou shalt know that I am the Lord: That thou mayest remember, and be confounded, and never open thy mouth any more because of thy shame, when I am pacified toward thee for all that thou hast done, saith the Lord God" (Ezekiel 16:60-63 KJV).*

Lesson:
All people ought to reverence God for his goodness towards humanity. Out of all creations, God shows special interest in human race; he cares about us like a father cares for his children. Jehovah cares, provides, and protects humans beyond other creatures! He specially fashioned us to dominate other species. We have grace to flex our muscles and do whatever we want. Indeed God has given special preference to humanity! Therefore, we should forever be grateful to him. We should appreciate God's love and cares over us. To really show our appreciations to the Creator, we should serve him. We should do our best to give him faithful services and make him proud. Nothing will turn Jehovah on to bless us more than our attitude of gratitude, and the lives of holiness that we live before him.

Prayer:
Dear God, what a wonderful Father of all nations you are! You are so great in power and marvelous in deed! By your power you created the earth, and by your power you chose humanity to dominate it. Humanity is fortunate to have you chose our race as your favorites. All I need from you is grace to live appreciative life before you. Help me to give you my best efforts into serving you! Let me faithfully serve you throughout the days of my life, so that I can qualify for more blessing on earth, and also to inherit your eternal kingdom. For in the name of Jesus Christ I make my requests.

Amen.

« DAY 314 »

Christianity Requires Sense Of Seriousness From Its Observers

Focus Passage: 2 Timothy 2

Bible is God's approved guide-book that all Christians must study and follow. The scripture emphasized,

> *"Be diligent to present yourself approved to God, a worker who does not need to be ashamed, rightly dividing the word of truth. But shun profane and idle babblings, for they will increase to more ungodliness"* **(2 Timothy 2:15-16).**

Lesson:
Christianity is a disciplined religion that requires anyone who practice it to do so with all seriousness. Anyone who claims to be a Christian must constantly read his/her bible; the fellow must pray and apply any lesson learnt to his/her life. Also, it is important that a Christian have integrity in speech and indeed. No child of God should engage in cheap talks that promote devil and his evil works. His/her words must be seasoned with grace to glorify God at all times. In addition, despite the mandate that Christians must share gospel with other people, we must ensure that we do not entrap ourselves with conversation that may lead to irrelevant argument, promiscuity, and/or other ungodliness. Heaven will clap for any Christian who follows bible principles, and maintain integrity of heart.

Prayer:
Dear God, please let me be a Christian who practice bible to the letter. Let me be committed into studying your word, and let me apply your godly lessons into my life. Let my words and deeds be seasoned with grace to glorify your name. Lead and teach me to behave appropriately, so that I can become a beacon of praise to your holy name. Please let your Holy Spirit empower me to demonstrate true Christianity that will receive your divine endorsement in heaven! For in the name of Jesus Christ I make my requests.

Amen.

« DAY 315 »

Jesus Christ Is The Only Sure Way That Leads To Eternal Life In Heaven

Focus Passage: Ezekiel 18, 19

God will judge earth inhabitants based on his unbiased rule. He will bring earth inhabitants to justice, and all people will be accountable for their past sins. God emphasized,

> *"The soul that sinneth, it shall die. The son shall not bear the iniquity of the father, neither shall the father bear the iniquity of the son: the righteousness of the righteous shall be upon him, and the wickedness of the wicked shall be upon him. But if the wicked will turn from all his sins that he hath committed, and keep all my statutes, and do that which is lawful and right, he shall surely live, he shall not die. All his transgressions that he hath committed, they shall not be mentioned unto him: in his righteousness that he hath done he shall live. Have I any pleasure at all that the wicked should die? saith the Lord God: and not that he should return from his ways, and live? But when the righteous turneth away from his righteousness, and committeth iniquity, and doeth according to all the abominations that the wicked man doeth, shall he live? All his righteousness that he hath done shall not be mentioned: in his trespass that he hath trespassed, and in his sin that he hath sinned, in them shall he die. Yet ye say, The way of the Lord is not equal. Hear now, O house of Israel; Is not my way equal? are not your ways unequal? When a righteous man turneth away from his righteousness, and committeth iniquity, and dieth in them; for his iniquity that he hath done shall he die. (Ezekiel 18:20-27 KJV).*

Lesson:
God will bring the world to justice; everyone who has ever lived on earth will face his judgment throne. Some people will be exonerated and be awarded heaven, but others will be cast into hell fire. Only people who have confessed Jesus Christ as their Lord and served him well on earth will inherit God's kingdom.

How can anyone inherit heaven with good works since humans have sinful nature? How can anyone be able to successfully justify him or herself in the presence of God with personal righteous standard? Humans need an advocate on God's Day of Judgment! Jesus Christ is the only deity who adequately fit the position. God will honor whatever request he makes on behalf of his followers on God's Day of Judgment. Hence, all people should consider it a good investment to declare their faith in Jesus Christ, and serve him faithfully. He is the only deity who is qualified to help anyone pass God's imminent judgment, and also help him/her gain entrance to heaven.

Prayer:
Dear God, I understand that Jesus Christ is the only deity who has power to earn anyone eternal life, so what am I waiting for? I want to immediately confess Jesus Christ as my Lord. In fact, I will do it right now! I (*mention your name*), I confess Jesus Christ as my Lord and Savior. I believe he died for my sins, and resurrected to give me eternal life. Therefore, I give my life to him. I will faithfully follow Jesus Christ from today, and I will serve him with all my heart throughout the days of my life. Please forgive my past sins, and write my name in the

book of life. Please make me forever fit for your kingdom. For in the name of Jesus Christ I made my faith declarations.

Amen.

« DAY 316 »

Believers Must Be Aware Of Signs Of End Time, And Prepare For Rapture

Focus Passage: 2 Timothy 3

Christians are to be careful and ensure that they are aware of evil practices that symbolize End Time. Christians must ensure that they do not participate in those evil practices. The scripture warned,

> *"But mark this: There will be terrible times in the last days. People will be lovers of themselves, lovers of money, boastful, proud, abusive, disobedient to their parents, ungrateful, unholy, without love, unforgiving, slanderous, without self-control, brutal, not lovers of the good, treacherous, rash, conceited, lovers of pleasure rather than lovers of God— having a form of godliness but denying its power. Have nothing to do with such people"* **(2 Timothy 3:1-5 NIV).**

Lesson:
In the last days, evil will perpetrate and dominate the earth; Christians must ensure they do not participate in such evils, since God will punish whoever does so. However, while some evil signs of end time are predominant - such as homosexuality, others are not. Some subtle signs of end time include pride, self-righteousness, lust of money, blasphemy, and others which are itemized in 2-Timothy 3:1-5. Since evil signs of end time manifest in multiple ways, believers must be sensitive to approach them with the power of Holy Spirit. We must allow God's Spirit to instruct us in dealing with those evil factors! We must understand that bible required us to out rightly reject evil practices of end time! Again, we must not tolerate them, but reject them! God is counting on Christians to be his true ambassadors on earth. We must represent him well, so that people can have clear understanding of his righteous standard and comply with it. Jehovah will honor any of his children - whether group or individuals - who choose to promote his righteous standard and make him proud.

Prayer:
Dear God, please save me from evil practices that have consumed our society! Give me grace and confidence to stand up for your righteousness, and do your will at all times. Do not let me follow multitude to do evil, but let my deeds and actions glorify your holy name. I also pray for my brethren throughout the world that you will empower us to promote your bible standard - without any form of compromise. Let Christians throughout the world be your true representative, so that your light of gospel can continue to shine in this evil world. For in the name of Jesus Christ I make my requests.

Amen.

« DAY 317 »

God Retains His Supreme Dominance Over All The Creations

Focus Passage: Ezekiel 20, 21

Israelites rejected God with their actions by turning to idol worship. However, God insisted that he would rule over them by force and claim his supremacy. God said,

> "As I live, saith the Lord God, surely with a mighty hand, and with a stretched out arm, and with fury poured out, will I rule over you: And I will bring you out from the people, and will gather you out of the countries wherein ye are scattered, with a mighty hand, and with a stretched out arm, and with fury poured out. And I will bring you into the wilderness of the people, and there will I plead with you face to face. Like as I pleaded with your fathers in the wilderness of the land of Egypt, so will I plead with you, saith the Lord God. And I will cause you to pass under the rod, and I will bring you into the bond of the covenant: And I will purge out from among you the rebels, and them that transgress against me: I will bring them forth out of the country where they sojourn, and they shall not enter into the land of Israel: and ye shall know that I am the Lord" ***(Ezekiel 20:33-38 KJV)***.

Lesson:
All people must serve God with fear and trembling since he is God of gods and Lord of lords. Humanity cannot ignore the fact that the Creator has supremacy over all things. He will do whatever he is determined to do - and no one can stop him. As far as heaven is farther from the earth, so is God more powerful than humanity. Therefore, no one should underestimate the power of the Creator. Humanity should not disrespect God by submitting to other deity. In other words, we must not serve idol! God is the only deity that people must serve with all truthfulness. Our time and efforts must be dedicated to the praise of God's name only. An act of idol worship - whether worship of money, material, or people - are detestable to God! As far as the Creator is concerned, whoever engages in idol worship will not see his face on the last day. Such person will be rejected from the gate of heaven, but be cast to hell fire. Hence, people of all nations and lands must understand that Jehovah will visit idol worshipers with fierce anger accompanied by heavy punishments.

Prayer:
Dear God, what do I gain by serving idols? Nothing, absolutely nothing! Idols have eyes but they cannot see; they have legs, but they cannot walk! Idols are nothing but vain imaginations that can never measure up to God's power! In fact, virtual idols are human hallucination that leads to vanity! Therefore, I confess my sins of idol worship today. I am sorry for rejecting you to promote sinful habits. I turn a new leaf today, and I will not serve idols anymore! I will faithfully serve you - the only living God. I yield my complete life to you today; I confess your Son Jesus Christ as my Lord and personal Savior. I will keep a consistent relationship with you, and I will serve you with all my mind and strength. Please keep me faithful to you throughout the days of my life. For in the name of Jesus Christ I make my requests.

Amen.

« DAY 318 »

Gospel Evangelization Is Not A Choice But A Must For All Christians

Focus Passage: 2 Timothy 4

The scripture emphasized that Christians must preach gospel of Jesus Christ to other people, so that they can have opportunity to become born-again also. It is written,

> "...I give you this charge: Preach the word; be prepared in season and out of season; correct, rebuke and encourage—with great patience and careful instruction. For the time will come when people will not put up with sound doctrine. Instead, to suit their own desires, they will gather around them a great number of teachers to say what their itching ears want to hear. They will turn their ears away from the truth and turn aside to myths." *(2 Timothy 4:1-4 NIV).*

Lesson:

Gospel evangelization is not a choice but a must for all Christians! We are commanded to preach gospel of Jesus Christ to people of every nation and land. We must preach gospel of Jesus without reservations! Christians must preach gospel when convenient and when not convenient. We must evangelize gospel without giving preference to church titles. Everyone must evangelize gospel whether he/she is a church member, a pastor, a teacher, a deacon, an evangelist, a bishop, or a pope! God expects us to prosper for him at all cost, and we must make sizable efforts to populate his kingdom! Jehovah will reward any Christian who prioritizes gospel evangelization above any other spiritual exercise. An imperishable crown of glory would be awarded for the fellow in heaven. However, a person who hoards gospel will remain at the mercy of God's judgment!

Prayer:

Dear God, please empower me to faithfully preach gospel of Jesus Christ to other people. Help me to get over my selfishness to start sharing gospel with others so that they can have their own opportunity of salvation! Energize me through your Holy Spirit to proclaim your name on the mountain, and in the valley. Let me promote your gospel from coast to coast, so that people of different race and culture can hear gospel and be saved. Also, give me courage to invite neighbors, friends, and family to church so that they can hear gospel as well. Most importantly, please let me remain your loyal child so that I can remain fit for your kingdom. For in the name of Jesus Christ I make my request.

Amen.

« DAY 319 »

Christians Must Be Cautious To Avoid Anything Transforming Into An Idol In Their Lives

Focus Passage: Ezekiel 22, 23

God labeled Israelites as harlots for practicing idolatry; they would face due consequence if they refuse to repent. Jehovah handpicked a prophet as a talking point and warned,

> *"Therefore, Oholibah, thus says the Lord God: 'Behold, I will stir up your lovers against you, from whom you have alienated yourself, And I will bring them against you from every side"* **(Ezekiel 23:22).**

Lesson:
Christians are not allowed to serve two masters. We are required to serve God only - and nothing more! No child of God should compare his/her Creator with any other deity. Jehovah is God, and he is the only deity that humanity must serve. Meanwhile, idol worship is not limited to image worship only. An idol may appear in form of material, money, people, and others. In short, anything that takes the place of God in our heart is an idol! A smart phone, laptop, and pocket-book may become an idol. In fact, if care is not taking, a person's wife, husband, and/or a child can become an idol. Nothing must take over God's position in our heart. Anyone who claims to be God's child must ensure that he/she has an undivided attention when it turns to serving God. It is important to emphasize that history has proven that God detest idolatry more than any other form of sin. The Creator has gone an extra mile to prove his point in ancient time; he has wiped out nations, and disowned his own children for the sake. He can do the worse again! Therefore, all people ought to fear God and give him due honor with full (and undistracted) worship.

Prayer:
Dear God, please help me to give you an undivided attention, so that you can be happy with me always. Do not let me be trapped into idol worship. Please forgive my past sins of idolatry; help me to stop whatever may be claiming rivalry with you in my life. Let me start to serve you with full devotion, so that you can be pleased to shower your grace and goodness on my life - now and always! For in the name of Jesus Christ I make my requests.

Amen.

« DAY 320 »

God Reserves Priceless Eternal Rewards For His Faithful Children

Focus Passage: 1 Peter 1

Children of God are encouraged to endure their trials and temptations for the sake of eternal reward that is set before them. Believers must stay close to God with unwavering faith to receive incorruptible crown of glory on the last day. It is written,

> *"In all this you greatly rejoice, though now for a little while you may have had to suffer grief in all kinds of trials. These have come so that the proven genuineness of your faith—of greater worth than gold, which perishes even though refined by fire—may result in praise, glory and honor when Jesus Christ is revealed"* **(1 Peter 1:6-7 NIV).**

Lesson:
Every child of God ought to endure whatever challenge of faith that he/she may face since the effort would be rewarded in heaven. God will crown Christians who endure persecutions and trials of faith in the last days. Christ has warned believers not to assume that Christianity would always be "bread-and-butter" experience. Christianity would come with rigorous challenge. Some Christians would be persecuted to the point of death! However, no Christian who endures faith unto the end would be ashamed. God has reserved eternal rewards for people who are pious in faith! Some honor may come in this life, but no honor would be comparable to eternal rewards preserved in heaven. Hence, all Christians are encouraged to stand firm with Jesus Christ and keep their testimony to earn God's priceless eternal rewards.

Prayer:
Dear God, please keep me in faith, and let me remain consistent with bible standard without any form of compromise. Empower me through your Holy Spirit to endure trials and temptations that may come my way, so that I can hear your resounding words of appreciation in heaven - "Weldon my good servant!" Please make me forever fit to qualify for your incorruptible crown of glory. For in the name of Jesus Christ I make my requests.

Amen.

« DAY 321 »

No Human Should Meddle With God's Business Uninvited

Focus Passage: Ezekiel 24, 25, 26

Sin caused a rift between God and Israelites, and the former turned his back against his own children. The incident created vacuum of opportunity for the enemy nations to strike. However, God promised to temper judgment with mercy. He will forgive his children's sin and afflict those who attack them. God said to Ezekiel,

> *"Son of man, because Tyre has said against Jerusalem, 'Aha! She is broken who was the gateway of the peoples; now she is turned over to me; I shall be filled; she is laid waste.' "Therefore thus says the Lord God: 'Behold, I am against you, O Tyre, and will cause many nations to come up against you, as the sea causes its waves to come up"* **(Ezekiel 26:2-3).**

Lesson:
No human should meddle with God's business uninvited. It would result to a failed mission, and God would be provoked! For example, issues that relate with God's servants are sensitive, and no one should meddle uninvited. God's servants are answerable to God; they are not answerable to us. Some servants of God may obviously live double-standard lifestyle and be inconsistent with the bible; however, it is not anyone's business to chastise them - unless God specifically ask for it. In addition, people should take caution to deal with activities that relate with gospel expansion. Since, evangelism is the heartbeat of God; he would frown at anyone who interferes with the prosperity of his works. In addition, Jesus Christ also warned that an undue criticism of manifestations of the Holy Spirit is regarded as unpardonable sins **(Matthew 12:31-32).** Hence, since some issues are sensitive and could provoke God's unprecedented actions, believers must be cautious to deal with them. Instead of irrational behaviors that may cause us to suffer punishments, we should grow up to live according to bible standard. We should gauge our lifestyles with God's requirement of holiness and faithful services which would earn us blessings on earth, and in heaven. ["Therefore, laying aside all malice, all deceit, hypocrisy, envy, and all evil speaking, as newborn babies, desire the pure milk of the word, that you may grow thereby" **(1 Peter 2:1-2)**].

Prayer:
Dear God, please help me to mind my own business and be careful in dealing with sensitive issues. Please do not let me engage in any activity that may provoke you! Instead of meddling with your business uninvited, let me mind my business of giving you thorough and faithful services that will be applauded in heaven. Help me to live a positive lifestyle that will earn everlasting life of peace and prosperity in heaven. For in the name of Jesus Christ I make my requests.

Amen.

« DAY 322 »

Believers Should Advance In Thoughts And Actions To Honor Their Faith Profession

Focus Passage: 1 Peter 2

All Christians are expected to grow in faith, and be productive for their Master - Jesus Christ. No Christians should remain one static position as the scripture emphasized,

> *"Therefore, laying aside all malice, all deceit, hypocrisy, envy, and all evil speaking, as newborn babies, desire the pure milk of the word, that you may grow thereby"* **(1 Peter 2:1-2).**

Lesson:
God requires Christians to build and maintain good relationship with him. He does not expect anyone to remain a baby Christian. Babies drink milk, but adults eat solid food! Mature Christians conduct themselves honorably among gentiles, and they are productive for God (*1 Peter 2:11-12*). Therefore, anyone who professes to have known God for a period of time must be able to bear fruits for Jesus Christ. However, Satan would keep insensitive Christians busy with petty factors that would rob them of their blessings. The enemy would manipulate baby Christians to have limited thinking. Their thoughts and practices would promote malice, fighting, immorality, jealousy, pride, and the like. In as much a Christian engages in such evil practices, he/she would find it difficult to advance in faith; such person cannot bear abiding fruits for God. Hence, any Christian who expects God's blessings on earth (and in heaven) must lay aside petty sins, and all other evil acts to make God happy.

Prayer:
Dear God, please help me to be a serious Christian who will not be disappointed on the last Day of Judgment. Help me to have focus and live a consistent lifestyle that will glorify your name. Please do not let me be trapped into sinful and fleshly activities that contribute little or nothing to your kingdom. Help me to grow and mature in faith, so that devil can be ashamed, and your name be glorified. Let my life bring you praises and honor always. Please bless me in this life, and also count me worthy to inherit your eternal kingdom. For in the name of Jesus Christ I make my requests.

Amen.

« DAY 323 »

It Is Unwise For Anyone To Compare Him Or Herself With God

Focus Passage: Ezekiel 27, 28, 29

A person who compares him or herself with God is not wise. Even Satan attempted to equate himself with God and it backfired! The traitor would have to suffer eternal consequence for his action in hell. The scripture revealed Satan's action that backfired,

> *"... 'Thus says the Lord God: "You were the seal of perfection, full of wisdom and perfect in beauty. You were in Eden, the garden of God; every precious stone was your covering: The sardius, topaz, and diamond, Beryl, onyx, and jasper, Sapphire, turquoise, and emerald with gold. The workmanship of your timbrels and pipes was prepared for you on the day you were created. "You were the anointed cherub who covers; I established you; you were on the holy mountain of God; you walked back and forth in the midst of fiery stones. You were perfect in your ways from the day you were created, till iniquity was found in you. "By the abundance of your trading You became filled with violence within, And you sinned; Therefore I cast you as a profane thing out of the mountain of God; And I destroyed you, O covering cherub, From the midst of the fiery stones. "Your heart was lifted up because of your beauty; You corrupted your wisdom for the sake of your splendor; I cast you to the ground, I laid you before kings, That they might gaze at you"* **(Ezekiel 28:12-17).**

Lesson:
Humans are nothing without God, and we should not attempt to equate ourselves with him. God offers us whatever support that we may enjoy today: peaceful atmosphere, sunshine, rainfall, and the rest. Without God's supports, we will all live miserable lives! Our lives completely depend on him, and we are absolute zero without his support! Therefore, all people should realize this fact and humbly submit themselves to the Creator. We must not attempt to compare ourselves with God, since the action will incur dire consequences. All people must reverence God and proclaim: God is God; he is stronger than humanity; he possesses autonomous power, and he is the judge of the earth! Jehovah will be pleased with our attitude of gratitude and shower his goodness on our lives. Anyone who prioritizes giving adequate honor to God will not regret, but will have much blessings to show forth.

Prayer:
Dear God, you are God of gods, and Lord of lords! You are bigger than what people say, and there is no word to express your greatness and supremacy over the earth. You are my God, my Rock, and my Lord. I am determined to yield my full life for you. I will serve you, honor you, and do your will throughout the days of my life. Please keep my faith resolute in you, and help me to remain humble at your feet to be worthy of your blessings at all times. Please prosper me in all my ways, and let me have many benefits to show forth - forever! For in the name of Jesus Christ I make my requests.

Amen.

« DAY 324 »

Christians Are Responsible For First-Class Love For Their Family

Focus Passage: 1 Peter 3

Family members are required to be reasonable with each other - for especially, those who profess to be Christians. The scripture challenged Christians as written,

> "Wives, in the same way submit yourselves to your own husbands so that, if any of them do not believe the word, they may be won over without words by the behavior of their wives, when they see the purity and reverence of your lives. Your beauty should not come from outward adornment, such as elaborate hairstyles and the wearing of gold jewelry or fine clothes. Rather, it should be that of your inner self, the unfading beauty of a gentle and quiet spirit, which is of great worth in God's sight. For this is the way the holy women of the past who put their hope in God used to adorn themselves. They submitted themselves to their own husbands, like Sarah, who obeyed Abraham and called him her lord. You are her daughters if you do what is right and do not give way to fear. Husbands, in the same way be considerate as you live with your wives, and treat them with respect as the weaker partner and as heirs with you of the gracious gift of life, so that nothing will hinder your prayers. Finally, all of you, be like-minded, be sympathetic, love one another, be compassionate and humble" **(1 Peter 3:1-8 NIV).**

Lesson:
Children of God must be responsible for the welfare of their family members to glorify God (1 Peter 3:1-8).
As far as heaven is concerned, there is no rule of exception for true love. God's children must love other people as Christ love and died for them. However, despite the universal law of love, family members take precedence since they are the closest people around. Family members deserve our first-class attention, and we must start our love expression to them. Husband must love his wife; wife must love her husband, parents must love their children, and children must love, honor and respect their parents. Any child of God who hates or ignore his/her family members is simply not practicing true Christianity! How can a Christian claims to have successfully helped others while he/she has neglected his/her family members? Truly, some family members are bound to have differences, but that must not prevent anyone from performing due diligence to his/her family. Every child of God must to make significant efforts to put devil to shame in his/her family by demonstrating true and thorough Christ' love to them.

Prayer:
Dear God, please help me to love my family, and be your true ambassador in their lives. Help me to play positive roles that will uphold healthy relationship in my home. Let me be a true and godly husband/wife/child/grandchild so that your light can shine supremely in my life. At the same time, help me to extend the same love for my friends and neighbors, and to the outside world for the sake of your glory. Let your light so shine through me to glorify your name in people's lives. In addition, please let the world recognize your true love and respond

to the salvation of your Son Jesus Christ in order to make heaven. For in the name of Jesus Christ I make my requests.

Amen.

« DAY 325 »

Any Nation That Violate God's Universal Order Is At The Brink Of Downfall

Focus Passage: Ezekiel 30, 31, 32

Any nation that suppresses God's supreme constitution of holiness in favor of an ungodly standard will surfer heavy punishments from God. Jehovah will judge a rebel nation with heavy punishments; he will make them pay for their abominable actions. The Creator promised to punish Israel and its surrounding nations for their rebelliousness. Ezekiel prophesied,

> "Thus says the Lord: "Those who uphold Egypt shall fall, and the pride of her power shall come down. From Migdol to Syene those within her shall fall by the sword," Says the Lord God. "They shall be desolate in the midst of the desolate countries, and her cities shall be in the midst of the cities that are laid waste. Then they will know that I am the Lord, when I have set a fire in Egypt and all her helpers are destroyed. On that day messengers shall go forth from me in ships to make the careless Ethiopians afraid, and great anguish shall come upon them, as on the day of Egypt; for indeed it is coming!" (Ezekiel 30:6-9).

Lesson:

Any nation that fails to honor God of heaven and respect his supreme order of holiness will face his justice. No nation or empire is above God's order. Any nation that arrogates itself as the ultimate power and violates God's supreme order is at the brink of downfall. Nations will live and go, but God will remain forever! Of course God himself formed nations; he respects their rule of justice, however not at the detriment of his universal standard! Jehovah will not underscore the fact that he is the ultimate deity with final authority; he will not appreciate anyone, nation, or land to tamper with his supreme order. In order words, God's universal rule of laws are not subject to humans' review - which are love, impartial justice, and heterosexual marriage (marriage between man and woman). Any nation that arrogantly meddles with those universal laws will not go scot-free, but face trial in God's own court of justice! Hence, nations and lands must cherish God and submit to his universal rules in order to prosper.

Prayer:

Dear God, please save our country from making mistakes that would cause them to suffer irreparable loss. Let our leaders and people in authority submit themselves to your will; let their decisions lead to blessings and not causes. Let the judicial system exercise justice with godly mindset and respect your universal orders! Please save our land from making mistakes that would help Satan flex his muscles to hurl it to a downfall. Please let your light prevail over darkness in our land, so that your name can be praised always. Please do these things, and many more! For in the name of Jesus Christ I make my requests.

Amen.

« DAY 326 »

Christians Have Bounty Of Goodness Available For Them On Earth And In Heaven

Focus Passage: 1 Peter 4

Christians are to utilize Christ's experience of death and resurrection to their advantage. No Christian should live under sinful influences of Satan since Christ has already won them victory. The scripture stated,

> *"Therefore, since Christ suffered for us in the flesh, arm yourselves also with the same mind, for he who has suffered in the flesh has ceased from sin, that he no longer should live the rest of his time in the flesh for the lusts of men, but for the will of God. For we have spent enough of our past lifetime in doing the will of the Gentiles—when we walked in lewdness, lusts, drunkenness, revelries, drinking parties, and abominable idolatries"* **(1 Peter 4:1-3).**

Lesson:
Jesus Christ has engaged in war against Satan and won victory for his followers; therefore, no child of God should live a defeated life. Satan has lost his battles against us, and now, we must live in victory. Believers must celebrate victory in God through the empowerment of the Holy Spirit. We have the Holy Spirit of God available to help for all exploitations. We can live pleasant and pleasurable lives in the presence of God; we can live in holiness and be in tune with heaven always. The Holy Spirit of God can empower us to love people during difficult time. He (Holy Spirit) can energize us to live sacrificial lives and be productive for God's kingdom. Yes, Holy Spirit can give us needed courage to be effective evangelists! Indeed, Christians are the most fortunate people on earth: Bounty of goodness are available at our disposal on earth, and plentiful riches are waiting for us in heaven. No one on earth is as fortunate as Christians! Congratulations to people who have confessed their faith in Jesus Christ - for victory shall be their portions forever! Anyone who esteems to live a triumphant life on earth must submit to Jesus Christ and confess him as Lord, since there is no better alternative to his guaranteed security.

Prayer:
Hallelujah I am a child of God. Praise God, I am a victor on earth, and Satan has lost battle over my life. Victory of Jesus Christ is my portion, and I will rejoice in the salvation of the Lord - forever! Please God baptize me with your Holy Spirit to keep serving you in truth and Spirit. Let your Holy Spirit empower me to stand upright with you, and let him lead me into all righteousness. Please keep me alive for your purpose, and let gospel fire continue to burn in my bones. Let me live above sin, and please keep my feet firm within your gate to remain fit your blessings. For in the name of Jesus Christ I make my requests.

Amen.

« DAY 327 »

God's Servants Are Held With High Standard In The Presence Of God

Focus Passage: Ezekiel 33, 34

Gospel ministers are to follow bible principles and properly lead so that people can faithfully serve God. A minister who fails to adequately occupy his position may not go scot-free, as God emphasized to Ezekiel,

> *"When I say unto the wicked, O wicked man, thou shalt surely die; if thou dost not speak to warn the wicked from his way, that wicked man shall die in his iniquity; but his blood will I require at thine hand. Nevertheless, if thou warn the wicked of his way to turn from it; if he do not turn from his way, he shall die in his iniquity; but thou hast delivered thy soul"* **(Ezekiel 33:8-9 KJV).**

Lesson:
God's servants are held with high standard in the presence of God, since they represent God among people. They have God's backing to bind and loose as deem fit. In fact, Jesus stated that his servants would do the "Impossibles" for the sake of his glory. However, God's servants have high price to pray for their honor: Since they have heaven's mandate, they are held with high standard and accountability. Their efforts go straight to God, and they will heavily pay for their loose disobedience. Therefore, God's servants are expected to fear God, and never give in for sinful external influences. They must preach undiluted word of God to promote his kingdom. No minister of God is ought to submit at the feet of politicians. No gospel minister ought to be found with prostitutes. He or she cannot abuse the less privileged people under whatever circumstance. More importantly, every minister of God must speak undiluted word of God without fear of reprise. Every gospel minister must uphold the fundamental principles of the bible and promote it! God - the grand master - has preserved his prestigious rewards for his faithful servants. They will reap the fruits of their labor in this life, and in heaven also!

Prayer:
Dear God, please uphold your servants in righteousness, and give them grace to faithfully serve you. Assist your servants to lead by example, and empower them to preach irresistible gospel. Let your servants be fearless in speaking your truth! Give them courage and boldness to promote bible standard. Please prosper your servants in their personal lives and ministries. Help them to overcome trials and temptations, and let them live triumphant lives on earth and make it to heaven! For in the name of Jesus Christ I make my requests.

Amen.

« DAY 328 »

Brethren In Christ Are To Promote Love And Unity

Focus Passage: 1 Peter 5

Brothers and sisters in Christ must respect each other and live in true love. Everyone must make a decisive effort to promote unity in the body of Christ. The scripture emphasized,

> *"Likewise you younger people, submit yourselves to your elders. Yes, all of you be submissive to one another, and be clothed with humility, for "God resists the proud, but gives grace to the humble." Therefore humble yourselves under the mighty hand of God, that He may exalt you in due time"* **(1 Peter 5:5-6)**.

Lesson:
Believers in Christ are to stay with each other in love. We must be honest with one another, and promote unity. God expects us to be our "brothers' keepers" which means we must seek the welfare of every brother and sister. In fact, a true Christian is not supposed to be selfish and think about him or herself only. A true Christian must make effort to provide for fellow believers who are in need. How can someone call him/herself a Christian and not feed his/her hungry fellow? How can someone claim to love Christ and seek downfall of another brother/sister? Will Christ be happy with someone who is abusive of his fellow Christian? Definitely not! Christ does not play games, he will reject hypocritical Christians and shut his door of heaven against them **(Matthew 25:41-46)**. Hence, anyone who aims heaven must practice honest Christianity that bible required. In addition, a true believer is expected to share his/her faith with other people, since heaven is not meant for few people only. Christ came to save the whole world, and we must spread his gospel as far as possible to ensure that people escape punishment of hell fire.

Prayer:
"Love lifted me!
Love lifted me!
When nothing else could help,
Love lifted me!"

Dear good Lord, please help me to demonstrate true love to other people, for especially fellow Christians. Also, please help the church to practice true love that you required. Let brethren put aside segregation and self-righteousness, but let them put on Christ righteousness with all humility. Empower believers throughout the world to share their faith with other people, so that unbelievers can come to your knowledge (of Jesus Christ) and be saved. Please let Christ' love conquer us all! For in the name of Jesus Christ I make my requests.

Amen.

« DAY 329 »

God Won't Allow His Name To Be Marred; He Will Defend Himself Like A Mighty Warrior

Focus Passage: Ezekiel 35, 36

Children of Israel profaned the name of God with their evil practices, but the Creator promised to clean it up. Since Israelites were having difficulty in pleasing God and giving him due honor, he promised to help them out. Jehovah promised,

> *"I will give you a new heart and put a new spirit within you; I will take the heart of stone out of your flesh and give you a heart of flesh. I will put my Spirit within you and cause you to walk in my statutes, and you will keep my judgments and do them. Then you shall dwell in the land that I gave to your fathers; you shall be my people, and I will be your God. I will deliver you from all your uncleannesses. I will call for the grain and multiply it, and bring no famine upon you. And I will multiply the fruit of your trees and the increase of your fields, so that you need never again bear the reproach of famine among the nations"* **(Ezekiel 36:26-30).**

Lesson:

God cannot (and he will not) allow his name to be dragged in the mud. He will rise like a mighty soldier to defend his name - under whatever circumstance. Since he is supreme, Jehovah will overrule our human imperfections to glorify his name. (Also, an unpleasant circumstance that happen to a child of God will not mare God's name. The Creator is best at turning a terrible situation into an excellent one). Therefore, no human should underestimate the power of God. No one should take God for granted and predict his next line of action - it will backfire! If anyone spills mess on God's name, he will clean it up. He would forgive the action, but he may not let the consequence go unaccounted. The Creator may return with heavy rod of correction on his insolent child. Therefore, it is absolutely a gamble exercise for anyone to underestimate the power of God. The best any child of God can do is to give God due honor, and serve him well! Such pious exercise will incur sure blessings, and not curses. Hence, anyone who bears "child of God" must honor his heavenly father with an indelible commitment.

Prayer:

Dear God, I understand that you are great in power and plentiful in mercy. You will forgive sins and pardon iniquities. However, I do not want to take you for granted in order to avoid your wrath. Therefore, please help me to be careful in dealing with you. Help me to serve you with fear and respect. Let me walk before you with dignity, and let me faithfully serve you throughout the days of my life so that I can qualify for your overwhelming blessings in this life, and in heaven also. For in the name of Jesus Christ I make my requests.

Amen.

« DAY 330 »

People Who Cautiously Practice Christianity Will Indeed Meet God In Heaven!

Focus Passage: 2 Peter 1

Nominal Christians have no place with God. Who are the nominal Christians? People who profess to love God, but do otherwise! God expects anyone who professes to be his child be adept in following bible principles and demonstrating godly virtues. The scripture stated,

> *"But also for this very reason, giving all diligence, add to your faith virtue, to virtue knowledge, to knowledge self-control, to self-control perseverance, to perseverance godliness, to godliness brotherly kindness, and to brotherly kindness love. For if these things are yours and abound, you will be neither barren nor unfruitful in the knowledge of our Lord Jesus Christ"* **(2 Peter 1:5-8).**

Lesson:
People who cautiously practice Christianity with the hope of satisfying God and go to heaven are smart, because they will indeed meet God in heaven! God reserves his best place for those committed individuals in heaven. Anyone who professes to be a true Christian must have godly virtues. Such person must have notable characteristics which are not limited to self-control, perseverance, kindness, and love (agape love). Nothing attracts God's attention than observing someone following God's laws and faithfully serving him. Also, a good Christian ought to bear fruits for God's kingdom, and also be relevant to his/her society. In short, a good Christian must bear positive fruits in all aspects of life.

Prayer:
Dear God, please help me to live a life that is relevant to your kingdom. Also, let my life be relevant to people around me. Give me grace to demonstrate godly virtues that will lead to the glorification of your name. Empower me through your Holy Spirit to serve you with beauty and honor, so that I can prosper in this life, and in heaven also. For in the name of Jesus Christ I make my requests.

Amen.

« DAY 331 »

People Who Trust God Shall Rise Above Their Challenges
Focus Passage: Ezekiel 37, 38, 39

Can dry bones rise again? Yes indeed! God spoke to Prophet Ezekiel that Israelites who have lost virtues and have become dead as bunch of dry bones would rise again to fulfill their destiny. Ezekiel recounted his experience,

> *"And he said unto me, Son of man, can these bones live? And I answered, O Lord God, thou knowest. Again he said unto me, Prophesy upon these bones, and say unto them, O ye dry bones, hear the word of the Lord. Thus saith the Lord God unto these bones; Behold, I will cause breath to enter into you, and ye shall live: And I will lay sinews upon you, and will bring up flesh upon you, and cover you with skin, and put breath in you, and ye shall live; and ye shall know that I am the Lord. So I prophesied as I was commanded: and as I prophesied, there was a noise, and behold a shaking, and the bones came together, bone to his bone. And when I beheld, lo, the sinews and the flesh came up upon them, and the skin covered them above: but there was no breath in them. Then said he unto me, Prophesy unto the wind, prophesy, son of man, and say to the wind, Thus saith the Lord God; Come from the four winds, O breath, and breathe upon these slain, that they may live. So I prophesied as he commanded me, and the breath came into them, and they lived, and stood up upon their feet, an exceeding great army"* **(Ezekiel 37:3-10 KJV).**

Lesson:
Dry bones can rise again; dry bones will rise again, and dry bones shall rise again for those who trust God! Anyone or group of people who put their trust in God may experience short trials and afflictions, but they will eventually rise above them all. Children of God will not remain under influences of the enemies forever. God will rise up like a mighty soldier to defend his own people. Yeah, he will defend his children and help them overcome their limitations. What is dry bone? Dry bone can be compared to an experience of spiritual dryness. It can occur as unfavorable medical or physical condition. Such experience usually occur to inflict pain and horror on God's people; however, since nothing goes beyond his power, God will defend his own people and fight their battles. He will do whatever necessary to liberate them from their afflictions and give them victory. However, a child of God who intends to have lasting victory over dry bone experience must understand that he/she must serve God well. Sure victory is only reserved for people who have complete dependence in God as the scripture emphasized, *"The angel of the Lord encamps all around those who fear Him, and delivers them"* **(Psalm 34:7).**

Prayer:
Dear God, please turn all dry bone experience in my life into active bone experience. Let me start to experience healing and restoration in every area of my life that has been subjected to sickness. Let the strength of God come upon me to be able to do exploits and go extra miles for the sake of your kingdom. Let me receive inner strength to talk and walk boldly in proclaiming the gospel of Jesus Christ so that people may have salvation opportunity. Also, let all my life endeavors return to success, and let me prosper in the land of the living. Please do these and many more. For in the name of Jesus Christ I make my requests. Amen.

« DAY 332 »

Christians Should Consider Bible As Their Main Standard To Judge Between Good And Evil

Focus Passage: 2 Peter 2

The scripture warned Christians to beware of false prophets and false teachers who manipulate people for their selfish ambitions. Both the deceptive leaders and their followers will pay for their actions on God's Day of Judgment. It is written,

> *"But there were also false prophets among the people, even as there will be false teachers among you, who will secretly bring in destructive heresies, even denying the Lord who bought them, and bring on themselves swift destruction. And many will follow their destructive ways, because of whom the way of truth will be blasphemed. By covetousness they will exploit you with deceptive words; for a long time their judgment has not been idle, and their destruction does not slumber"* **(2 Peter 2:1-3).**

Lesson:
Christians are to be watchful of practices and teachings that are contradictory to the bible. We must use bible as our measuring standard to judge between good and evil. We must base our judgment on bible principles - and nothing more! If a teaching, prophecy, and/or any other spiritual activity does not comply with the bible, we must reject it. As God's children, we must be firm with the truth and ensure that our activities comply with the bible. Every Christian must personally study his/her bible to know what God expects from him/her. It is everyone's responsibilities to develop personal relationship with God and grow in his grace. Yes, we may need mentors/teachers for guidance, but bible must be considered as the final authority. God will honor anyone who practice true Christianity and remain consistent with his word.

Prayer:
Dear God, please help me to be watchful and not to fall to the traps of false teachers. Let me only entertain teachings that are consistent with your word. Let bible be my measuring standard to judge between good and evil; let me reject activities that lack bases in your word. Help me to be firm with the truth, so that I can remain rapturable and meet you in heaven on the last day. For in the name of Jesus Christ I make my requests.

Amen.

« DAY 333 »

Heaven Retains God's Perfect Creativity Reserved For The Saints

Focus Passage: Ezekiel 40, 41

Prophet Ezekiel was privileged to receive revelation of heaven, and he described his experience. He said,

> "Then he (God's angel) went to the gateway which faced east; and he went up its stairs and measured the threshold of the gateway, which was one rod wide, and the other threshold was one rod wide. Each gate chamber was one rod long and one rod wide; between the gate chambers was a space of five cubits; and the threshold of the gateway by the vestibule of the inside gate was one rod. He also measured the vestibule of the inside gate, one rod. Then he measured the vestibule of the gateway, eight cubits; and the gateposts, two cubits. The vestibule of the gate was on the inside" **(Ezekiel 40:6-9)** ..."He measured the width of the entrance to the gateway, ten cubits; and the length of the gate, thirteen cubits. There was a space in front of the gate chambers, one cubit on this side and one cubit on that side; the gate chambers were six cubits on this side and six cubits on that side. Then he measured the gateway from the roof of one gate chamber to the roof of the other; the width was twenty-five cubits, as door faces door" **(Ezekiel:11-13)** ..."After that he brought me toward the south, and there a gateway was facing south; and he measured its gateposts and archways according to these same measurements. There were windows in it and in its archways all around like those windows; its length was fifty cubits and its width twenty-five cubits. Seven steps led up to it, and its archway was in front of them; and it had palm trees on its gateposts, one on this side and one on that side" **(Ezekiel:24-26)**.

Lesson:
Heaven is an indescribable place of glory. Heaven is a place not made by human; it was planned, designed, and constructed by God himself. No human word would be suitable enough to describe the beauty of heaven. A place created with divine wisdom, heaven enjoy absolute perfection! The planning, design and construction - were in perfect standard. The Creator crafted heaven for himself to enjoy his royalty on his created universe. He specially created it to fit his pleasurable desires. However, he has decided to share his treasured home with humanity on the last day. Unfortunately despite the blank check given to us, only few people will be qualified to enjoy the blissful place. Only people who have accepted Jesus Christ as God's Son and have confessed him as their personal Lord and Savior will go to heaven! Hence, all people must humbly submit to God and confess his Son Jesus Christ as their personal Lord and Savior.

Prayer:
"Jerusalem on high; my song and city is, my home whene'er I die, the center of my bliss. O happy place! When shall I be, my God, with thee, to see thy face?" O dear good Lord, please make me qualify for heaven. I want to see and feel the perfection of your beauty. I want to taste your dessert and eat your dinner. I want to eat the food of angels. I want to experience perfect peace and joy that are beyond the limited version that earth can offer. I want to live eternally with you in heaven. I understand that Jesus Christ is the only license to heaven, and everyone must confess him as his/her Lord to be saved. Therefore, I confess him (Jesus Christ) as your Son, and I accept him as my personal Lord and Savior. O Jesus Christ, please

rapture me on the last day to enjoy the benefits of heaven forever! For with faith in Jesus Christ I make my requests.

Amen.

« DAY 334 »

End Time Is Here, And Jesus Christ Will Soon Return To Rapture His Saints

Focus Passage: 2 Peter 3

Have skeptics criticized Christians about End Time theory? Yes, they have. They have attacked Christians' teaching of End Time and Rapture. To them, end time and rapture are fallacy. However, whether critics believe bible or not, rapture event will occur and end will come to this earth. Bible warned Christians to abstain from people who may be persuading them to doubt the second coming of Jesus Christ. It is written,

> *"This second epistle, beloved, I now write unto you... That ye may be mindful of the words which were spoken before by the holy prophets, and of the commandment of us the apostles of the Lord and Saviour: Knowing this first, that there shall come in the last days scoffers, walking after their own lusts, And saying, Where is the promise of his coming? for since the fathers fell asleep, all things continue as they were from the beginning of the creation. For this they willingly are ignorant of, that by the word of God the heavens were of old, and the earth standing out of the water and in the water: Whereby the world that then was, being overflowed with water, perished: But the heavens and the earth, which are now, by the same word are kept in store, reserved unto fire against the day of judgment and perdition of ungodly men. But, beloved, be not ignorant of this one thing, that one day is with the Lord as a thousand years, and a thousand years as one day. The Lord is not slack concerning his promise, as some men count slackness; but is longsuffering to us-ward, not willing that any should perish, but that all should come to repentance. But the day of the Lord will come as a thief in the night; in the which the heavens shall pass away with a great noise, and the elements shall melt with fervent heat, the earth also and the works that are therein shall be burned up..."* **(2 Peter 3-9 KJV)**.

Lesson:

Teaching about End Time and second coming of Jesus Christ (Rapture) is very important, and it is justified by the bible (Matthew 24). The second coming of Jesus Christ is imminent and everyone is to prepare for this event. Indeed due to our impatient human nature, we may be tempted to doubt the promised return of Christ; however, we are encouraged to remain unwearied because of the precious price involved. We must understand that God's calendar is different from ours. Our count of one thousand years is similar to his count of one day (2 Peter 3:8). Therefore, we should not be tempted to assume that we have fully understood God and his timing. Our job is to believe and obey his instructions! End Time is imminent; rapture event will happen, and the saints will be taken to heaven. People who have accepted Jesus Christ as God's Son, and have confessed him as their personal Lord and Savior will escape the punishments of hell fire to be with God in heaven forever! (Rev. 21:8).

Prayer:
Dear God, please qualify me for your kingdom. Give me patience and confidence needed to remain in faith unto the end. Let my faith confession in Jesus Christ and his second coming be absolute, and do not let me trust deceivers who are manipulating people to doubt his second coming. Please keep my fire of faith burning, and let me continue to serve you with all faithfulness from now until you return to take me home! For in the name of Jesus Christ I make my requests.

Amen.

« DAY 335 »

Jesus Will Save Whoever Comes To Him – With No Restriction To Any Religion

Focus Passage: Ezekiel 42, 43, 44

God distant himself from Israelites due to their sins, but he will eventually forgive and redeem them. The Creator will restore his children, and keep them under his watchful eyes to ensure they are not stray anymore. Ezekiel shared his revelation of God's plan as stated,

> "And the glory of the Lord came into the house by the way of the gate whose prospect is toward the east. So the spirit took me up, and brought me into the inner court; and, behold, the glory of the Lord filled the house. And I heard him speaking unto me out of the house; and the man stood by me. And he said unto me, Son of man, the place of my throne, and the place of the soles of my feet, where I will dwell in the midst of the children of Israel for ever, and my holy name, shall the house of Israel no more defile, neither they, nor their kings, by their whoredom, nor by the carcases of their kings in their high places" **(Ezekiel 43:4-7 KJV).**

Lesson:

Sin caused enmity between God and man, but the gap of separation will not last eternally. Jehovah will merge the gap and redeem his people. He has presented his Son Jesus Christ to mediate and restore his people back to their Creator. Through him (Jesus Christ) people will receive forgiveness of sins; they will receive redemption and restoration. It is written
"For God so loved the world that He gave His only begotten Son, that whoever believes in Him should not perish but have everlasting life **(John 3:16)."**

Since Christ was chosen by God to save humanity from their sins, all people ought to believe and serve him. Through him we will receive forgiveness of sins, and through him we will obtain the gift of eternal life. Christ will not reject anyone; he will save whoever comes to him whether the person professes to be a Christian, a Jew, a Muslim, a Hindu, a Buddhist, or other. Also, a gentile who comes to Jesus Christ will receive his salvation. Anyone who confesses Jesus Christ as Lord and accept him as his/her personal Lord and Savior will be saved **(Romans 10:9-10).**

Prayer:

Dear God, I come today to receive forgiveness of my sins so that I can inherit your everlasting kingdom. I understand that repentance and salvation can only be obtained through your Son Jesus Christ; therefore, I confess him (Jesus Christ) as Lord and I accept him as my personal Savior. I will follow the footstep of Jesus from today and forever. Please write my name in the book of life, and let me remain qualified for your kingdom. For in the name of Jesus Christ I make my requests.

Amen.

« DAY 336 »

Christians Are To Humbly Confess Their Misdeed To God To Receive Forgiveness

Focus Passage: 1 John 1

All people – whether Jews or gentiles – are encouraged to faithfully interact with God through his Son Jesus Christ in order to receive forgiveness of their sins. It is written in the scripture,

> *"This is the message we have heard from him and declare to you: God is light; in him there is no darkness at all. 6 If we claim to have fellowship with him and yet walk in the darkness, we lie and do not live out the truth. But if we walk in the light, as he is in the light, we have fellowship with one another, and the blood of Jesus, his Son, purifies us from all sin. If we claim to be without sin, we deceive ourselves and the truth is not in us. If we confess our sins, he is faithful and just and will forgive us our sins and purify us from all unrighteousness. If we claim we have not sinned, we make him out to be a liar and his word is not in us"* ***(1 John 1:5-10 NIV).***

Lesson:

Christians are expected to relate with God with all honesty. We are expected to be open and be truthful to him. We are to confess our misdeed to him; ask for his forgiveness, and have genuine repentance. Also, we are to humbly seek God's help to live the lives acceptable to him. (We should daily seek his face through prayers to receive his indwelling Holy Spirit for empowerment to live righteous lives). However, God takes no pleasure in arrogant Christians who believe they have understood everything about God and would not need further commitment. God will distant himself from those who proclaim self-righteousness as a means of gaining entry to heaven. The Creator expects us to humbly relate with him and daily seek his face with true worship. However, Satan rejoices over sinful and self-righteous people, and he is always ready to gain their sinful moments to carry out his evil deed. Hence, Christians are to be watchful and humbly live the lives expected of them so that devil will have no occasion to glorify himself over them. God reserves his eternal rewards for people who always trust him for help, strength, and support.

Prayer:

Dear God, please keep me honest with you always so that I can qualify to enjoy all your benefits. Help me to be truthful in my approach; let my confession of sins be genuine, and let my repentance be genuine. Please daily fill me with your Holy Spirit to live pure and acceptable life, so that I can qualify to inherit your kingdom. Please let Satan be ashamed over my life, and let all his attempts to lock me in sin fail. Empower me through your Holy Spirit to live acceptable and victorious life always! For in the name of Jesus Christ I make my requests.

Amen.

« DAY 337 »

God Requires Our Consistent Relationship In Order To Bless Us

Focus Passage: Ezekiel 45, 46

Daily worship must not be considered as a difficult exercise to God. Israelites were obligated to offer their sacrifices to God on a consistent basis to establish a long-term relationship with him. God required,

> *"You shall daily make a burnt offering to the Lord of a lamb of the first year without blemish; you shall prepare it every morning. And you shall prepare a grain offering with it every morning, a sixth of an ephah, and a third of a hin of oil to moisten the fine flour. This grain offering is a perpetual ordinance, to be made regularly to the Lord"* **(Ezekiel 46:13-14).**

Lesson:
Believers are required to maintain consistent relationship with God in order to obtain his benefits. We are not expected to keep casual relationship with him, but our activities to him must be honorable. We must daily offer our sacrifices of prayer and praises to him to keep our relationship with him growing. As it applies to any other relationship, our understanding of the Maker can only grow when we spent ample time him. This means we have to spend ample time in his presence with quality spiritual exercise - prayer and praises. Besides, there is grace and strength to obtain from the Creator when we consistently worship him every morning and every evening. Our consistent services will unlock his door of blessings, and we will be able to enjoy his unmerited grace and favor. The heavenly Father will lavish his true worshipers with every necessary benefit to ensure that their services in his presence are not found wanting.

Prayer:
Dear God, how awesome you are to desire worship from a little person like me! You are beautiful beyond descriptions, and I will give you what you deserve. Since nothing is more important to you than my sacrifices of true and thorough worship, I will give it to you. All I am asking is grace and power to do so. Please enable me with strength to offer you my best prayer and praises at all times. Help me to worship you on a consistent basis so that I can qualify for your benefits. Let my fellowship offerings always bring honor to your holy name - from now and evermore! For in the name of Jesus Christ I make my requests.

Amen.

« DAY 338 »

Believers Must Focus To Receive Incorruptible Heavenly Treasures

Focus Passage: 1 John 2

The scripture challenged all Christians to care less about the world, but care more about heaven. Earthly treasures will perish but heavenly treasures will abide forever. The scripture charged,

> "Do not love the world or the things in the world. If anyone loves the world, the love of the Father is not in him. For all that is in the world—the lust of the flesh, the lust of the eyes, and the pride of life—is not of the Father but is of the world" **(1 John 2:15-16)**.

Lesson:
All Christians are challenged not to be obsessed with the cares of the world. We must not chase the earthly pleasures as if they are our only hope. As true followers of Jesus Christ, we must consider serving God as our topmost priority. We must not forget that this world will soon vanish, and heaven will become our permanent home.

Prayer:
Dear God, please help me to set my priority right. Assist me to prioritize cares of heaven above the cares of the earth. Do not let me be obsessed with worldly cares that will soon perish. Help me to faithfully serve you and prepare for heaven where incorruptible treasures are stored. For in the name of Jesus Christ I make my requests.

Amen.

« DAY 339 »

A Person That Serves Jesus Christ Will Receive God's River Of Life

Focus Passage: Ezekiel 47, 48

God will heal, reward, and restore his saints in heaven. They will live beyond any painful experience they might have survived on earth as the scripture explained that an important river of God will flow to all regions of God's kingdom to heal and restore saints from their past trauma. Ezekiel had an encounter with God and he shared his experience,

> *"Then said he unto me, These waters issue out toward the east country, and go down into the desert, and go into the sea: which being brought forth into the sea, the waters shall be healed. And it shall come to pass, that every thing that liveth, which moveth, whithersoever the rivers shall come, shall live: and there shall be a very great multitude of fish, because these waters shall come thither: for they shall be healed; and every thing shall live whither the river cometh. And it shall come to pass, that the fishers shall stand upon it from Engedi even unto Eneglaim; they shall be a place to spread forth nets; their fish shall be according to their kinds, as the fish of the great sea, exceeding many. But the miry places thereof and the marishes thereof shall not be healed; they shall be given to salt. And by the river upon the bank thereof, on this side and on that side, shall grow all trees for meat, whose leaf shall not fade, neither shall the fruit thereof be consumed: it shall bring forth new fruit according to his months, because their waters they issued out of the sanctuary: and the fruit thereof shall be for meat, and the leaf thereof for medicine"* **(Ezekiel 47:8-12 KJV).**

Lesson:
The river of God gives life. It heals all bruises, and it grants perfect peace of God. God's river of life has its source from the heart of Jesus Christ. Anyone who drinks from the river will not be thirsty again; the fortunate fellow will have divine assurance of going to heaven. God's river of life is automatically apportioned to anyone who gives his or her life to Jesus Christ. A person who confesses Jesus Christ as his or her personal Lord and Savior will have peace on earth and in heaven also.

Prayer:
Dear God, please let your river of life flow into my heart. I open the door of my heart and I am ready for you today! I confess and believe that Jesus Christ is the Son of God, and I accept him as my personal Lord and Savior. I believe that my name is now written in the book of life, and I will enjoy eternal life with you God in heaven. All my declarations and prayers are made through the name of Jesus Christ.

Amen.

« DAY 340 »

Earth Is Our Temporary Home, But Heaven Is Our Permanent Home

Focus Passage: 1 John 3

All Christians must remain focus and faithfully serve God. We must always remember that though we live in the same world with unbelievers, we do not share the same final destination with them. Our main objective is to see God and enjoy his everlasting fellowship in heaven. The scripture reminds us about this and said,

> *"Behold what manner of love the Father has bestowed on us, that we should be called children of God! Therefore the world does not know us, because it did not know Him. Beloved, now we are children of God; and it has not yet been revealed what we shall be, but we know that when He is revealed, we shall be like Him, for we shall see Him as He is. And everyone who has this hope in Him purifies himself, just as He is pure"* **(1 John 3:1-3).**

Lesson:
Earth is our temporary home, but heaven is our permanent home. We Christians must not allow the influences of the temporary home to cause us to lose heaven. We must cautiously walk our pilgrimage journey on earth so that we can be accepted to heaven. We must abstain from sin and live holy lives before God – at all times.

Prayer:
Dear God, please help me to live a purposeful life on earth. Help me to always remember that this earth is a temporary home and heaven is a permanent home. Let me please you in all ramifications so that I can be warmly welcome to heaven at the last day. Please do not let me be condemned and go to hell fire. For in the name of Jesus Christ I make my requests.

Amen.

« DAY 341 »

God Will Fulfill His Plans On His Children Under Whatever Condition!

Focus Passage: Ezra 1, 2

God inspired a gentile king to sponsor the reconstruction of his Holy Temple. Despite his idolatry backgrounds, King Cyrus of Persia encouraged all Jews to go back to their home land and repair the damaged God's temple at Jerusalem. The king also commanded all his citizens to offer Jews materials and financial supports. The scripture reported,

> *"Now in the first year of Cyrus king of Persia, that the word of the Lord by the mouth of Jeremiah might be fulfilled, the Lord stirred up the spirit of Cyrus king of Persia, that he made a proclamation throughout all his kingdom, and put it also in writing, saying, Thus saith Cyrus king of Persia, The Lord God of heaven hath given me all the kingdoms of the earth; and he hath charged me to build him an house at Jerusalem, which is in Judah. Who is there among you of all his people? his God be with him, and let him go up to Jerusalem, which is in Judah, and build the house of the Lord God of Israel, (he is the God,) which is in Jerusalem. And whosoever remaineth in any place where he sojourneth, let the men of his place help him with silver, and with gold, and with goods, and with beasts, beside the freewill offering for the house of God that is in Jerusalem"* **(Ezra 1:1-4 KJV).**

Lesson:

God can use anyone for the purpose of glorifying his name. Also, he can use anyone to bless his children. The Creator retains his divine ability to command either a king or a servant to serve his unprecedented purposes that he has ordained for his children. If God has a plan for anyone, he will fulfill it – under whatever condition! The almighty God knows how to make things perfectly work out for his children. Nobody can stop God from performing his goodly wishes over his children.

Prayer:

Dear God, please let all your promises over my life come to pass. Let all situations and circumstances of life work to my advantage. Let me triumph in all situations, and let my life become an embodiment of your testimony. For in the name of Jesus Christ I make my requests.

Amen.

« DAY 342 »

Christianity Is Not A Wishy-Washy Religion That Entertain Selfish Ideologies

Focus Passage: 1 John 4

Christians must not be naïve; we must identify what we believe, and we must not allow anyone to fool us! The scripture warned,

> *"Beloved, do not believe every spirit, but test the spirits, whether they are of God; because many false prophets have gone out into the world. By this you know the Spirit of God: Every spirit that confesses that Jesus Christ has come in the flesh is of God, and every spirit that does not confess that Jesus Christ has come in the flesh is not of God. And this is the spirit of the Antichrist, which you have heard was coming, and is now already in the world"* **(1 John 4:1-3)**.

Lesson:
Christianity is not a wishy-washy religion that everybody brings his or her selfish ideologies. Christianity is God's religion that was established by Jesus Christ. The religion has God's ideas, but not our ideas! Therefore, every Christian must hold firm to his faith in Jesus Christ without wavering. No Christian should appreciate any doctrine that lacks bases in the scripture. We must confirm sermons, teachings, and prophecies with the scriptures. We must reject erroneous teachings, and we must faithfully follow Jesus Christ. There is no doubt that our honest and dedicated services to God will incur divine blessings. The faithful children of God will shine in this world – and they will shine in heaven also!

Prayer:
Dear God, please save me from becoming a victim of antichrist who mislead people with false teachings. Please help me to hold firm to my faith in Jesus Christ. Help me to diligently study the scripture, and help me to apply the principles of the scripture to my life. Let me prosper in this world and in heaven also. For in the name of Jesus Christ I make my requests.

Amen.

« DAY 343 »

Great Things Are Done For God When People Operate In Unity

Focus Passage: Ezra 3, 4

Exile Jews were authorized to return home and rebuild their precious city of Jerusalem. All the released captives were excited to see their dreams come true, and they were in full agreement to launch a sound project that will revamp God's temple destroyed by the Babylonians. The returned Jews were very excited about their miraculous breakthrough, and they praised God in one accord – to the extent that their enemies heard their testimony songs from a far distance. The scripture reported,

> *"Then Jeshua with his sons and brothers, Kadmiel with his sons, and the sons of Judah, arose as one to oversee those working on the house of God: the sons of Henadad with their sons and their brethren the Levites. When the builders laid the foundation of the temple of the Lord, the priests stood in their apparel with trumpets, and the Levites, the sons of Asaph, with cymbals, to praise the Lord, according to the ordinance of David king of Israel. And they sang responsively, praising and giving thanks to the Lord: "For He is good, For His mercy endures forever toward Israel. Then all the people shouted with a great shout, when they praised the Lord, because the foundation of the house of the Lord was laid"* **(Ezra 3:9-11)**.

Lesson:

Great things are done for God when people operate in unity. In fact, devil cannot withstand a group of Christians that operates in unison. However, it is unfortunate that we believers sometimes allow Satan to manipulate us through rivalry and divisions. Christian sects claim superiority over each other. Meanwhile, while believers are busy entertaining divisions, Satan continues to gain ground. The enemy is utilizing every opportunity to attack the church. The church must endeavor to lay aside all differences. We must praise and serve God together. Great things – and greater things – will happen in Christian fold if we can practice love and celebrate unity. The unity of brethren will honor God, and it will put devil to shame. Unity will also turn to become blessings for all children of God.

Prayer:

Dear God, please let your sincere love reign among Christians. Let us give room for your Holy Spirit to operate in our lives. Help us to lay our differences aside, and serve you together in one accord. Let all churches submit to the feet of Jesus Christ and operate in love. Empower the Christian folds to be more sensitive – so that none of Satan's scheme will prosper. Let us stand firm and be your true ambassadors that will be warmly welcome to heaven. For in the name of Jesus Christ I make my requests.

Amen.

« DAY 344 »

Believers Must Pray For Holy Spirit's Help To Practice True Love

Focus Passage: 1 John 5

Anyone who claims to love God must prove so by loving his Son Jesus Christ. The fellow must also extend his/her love to other fellow believers. The scripture stated,

> *"Whoever believes that Jesus is the Christ is born of God, and everyone who loves Him who begot also loves him who is begotten of Him. By this we know that we love the children of God, when we love God and keep His commandments"* ***(1 John 5:1-2).***

Lesson:
God required us (his children) to love him with all our heart. We must have unconditional love for him; we must also love our fellow believers. However, genuine love cannot come from mortal men (and women). Humans are selfish and biased; therefore, we need supernatural power of God to help us conquer our limitations. Such power can only be given by the Holy Spirit of God. Hence, believers should daily seek God through prayers to receive the empowerment of his Holy Spirit, whom will help us do the unspeakable! The divine Spirit of God will energize us to love God and our fellow brethren dearly.

Prayer:
Dear God, please baptize me with your Holy Spirit to exercise true and genuine love towards you and other brethren. Let the Holy Spirit empower me to live an acceptable life in your presence, so that I can qualify to receive your overwhelming benefits, and also that your name be glorified among the people. For in the name of Jesus Christ I make my requests.

Amen.

« DAY 345 »

Believers Are Not Allowed To Prioritize Personal Interests Above God's Interests

Focus Passage: Haggai 1, 2

God called Israelites' attention to the secrets behind their poverty. They remained in suffering because they have failed to set their priority right. Israelites have prioritized their personal interests above God's interest; therefore, they would remain in their terrible situations until they put God first. God showed the escape route and said,

> *"Ye have sown much, and bring in little; ye eat, but ye have not enough; ye drink, but ye are not filled with drink; ye clothe you, but there is none warm; and he that earneth wages earneth wages to put it into a bag with holes. Thus saith the Lord of hosts; Consider your ways. Go up to the mountain, and bring wood, and build the house; and I will take pleasure in it, and I will be glorified, saith the Lord"* **(Haggai 1: 6-8 KJV).**

Lesson:
We children of God are not allowed to prioritize our personal interests above God's interests. We must consider God's interest to be primary – while our personal interests become secondary! God is always challenged to help when people adequately prioritize their objectives. The blessings of God will forever abide with people who put him first in their lives.

Prayer:
Dear God, please help me to put you first in my life. Help me to love and serve you with a pure heart, so that I can have all my life expectations met. For in the name of Jesus Christ I make my requests.

Amen.

« DAY 346 »

False Teachers Will Rob Insensitive People During End Time

Focus Passage: 2 John 1

Christians are warned of numbers of false teachers that will rise up during period of *End Time*. The false teachers will utilize various techniques to manipulate people and rob them of their money and materials. They will rob people of their salvation, and many will be hauled to hell fire! The scripture warned,

> *"For many deceivers have gone out into the world who do not confess Jesus Christ as coming in the flesh. This is a deceiver and an antichrist. Look to yourselves, that we do not lose those things we worked for, but that we may receive a full reward"* **(2 John 1:7-8).**

Lesson:
During End Time, the world will witness the surge of fake bible teachers, prophets, pastors, and/or others. The deceivers will rise with various schemes to manipulate people into losing their money, material, and salvation. Christians are warned to be careful not to fall victims of those deceivers. Believers are to be close to their bible, and diligently read it to understand the mind of God. We must ensure not to believe any theory that lacks basis in the bible. Believers must be prayerful to hold on to bible truth since it would go unpopular in this promiscuous world! We must be careful not to allow cares of this world take heaven away from us. If we indeed stand firm with our testimony of Jesus Christ, Jehovah will bless us with his everlasting rewards in heaven.

Prayer:
Dear God, Please save me from deceptive teachers who manipulate people to losing their salvation. Help me to stay firm with gospel truth. Let me be close to my bible and read it always for better understanding. Let my devotion be meaningful to you, and please keep my feet firm within your gate. Keep me firm to remain qualify for your eternal kingdom, and let me ever be worthy of your imperishable crown of glory in heaven! For in the name of Jesus Christ I make my requests.

Amen.

« DAY 347 »

God Is Gracious And Loving; He Will Forgive Any Repentant Sinner

Focus Passage: Zechariah 1, 2, 3, 4

Israelites sinned, and God removed his protection to punish them; however, Jehovah promised to forgive and restore his people. He will also severely deal with enemy nations that have taken advantage of Israelites' miseries. God promised Israel and said,

> *"For thus saith the Lord of hosts; After the glory hath he sent me unto the nations which spoiled you: for he that toucheth you toucheth the apple of his eye. For, behold, I will shake mine hand upon them, and they shall be a spoil to their servants: and ye shall know that the Lord of hosts hath sent me. Sing and rejoice, O daughter of Zion: for, lo, I come, and I will dwell in the midst of thee, saith the Lord. And many nations shall be joined to the Lord in that day, and shall be my people: and I will dwell in the midst of thee, and thou shalt know that the Lord of hosts hath sent me unto thee. And the Lord shall inherit Judah his portion in the holy land, and shall choose Jerusalem again. Be silent, O all flesh, before the Lord: for he is raised up out of his holy habitation"* **(Zechariah 2:8-16 KJV).**

Lesson:
God is tough with sin, and he will not kindly behold a stubborn sinner. However, God is also loving, gracious and forgiving; he will kindly deal with any sinner who turns to him to seek his forgiveness. Jehovah will glorify his name in the life of anyone who is humbled enough to say "sorry" for his/her mistakes. No matter the magnitude of a sin, God will forgive repentant sinners! Meanwhile, God's security and provisions will be available for people who maintain consistent relationship with him. The Creator will watch over them and satisfy them with grace and mercy, so that unbelievers can be challenged to serve him also. Hence, people who have ongoing relationship with God should take it seriously and be more diligent. Also, people who have turned their back against God, and those who have never yield should turn a new leaf. They should come close to God and serve him well, since their rewards will be in heaven.

Prayer:
Dear God, I yield my life to you to serve you with honesty, humility, and integrity. Please help me to maintain a consistent relationship with you, so that I can enjoy your many benefits in this life and in heaven also. For in the name of Jesus Christ I make my requests.

Amen.

« DAY 348 »

People Who Serve God Will Possess Their Possessions On Earth, And Much More In Heaven

Focus Passage: 3 John 1

Apostle John commended and prayed for Gaius having heard that he was steadfast in true love of Jesus Christ. John wrote,

> "The Elder, To the beloved Gaius, whom I love in truth: Beloved, I pray that you may prosper in all things and be in health, just as your soul prospers. For I rejoiced greatly when brethren came and testified of the truth that is in you, just as you walk in the truth. I have no greater joy than to hear that my children walk in truth. Beloved, you do faithfully whatever you do for the brethren and for strangers, who have borne witness of your love before the church. If you send them forward on their journey in a manner worthy of God, you will do well, because they went forth for His name's sake, taking nothing from the Gentiles. We therefore ought to receive such, that we may become fellow workers for the truth *(3 John 1-8)*."

Lesson:
People who serve God well on earth will have immeasurable benefits to receive from him in heaven. However, their rewards will not be limited to heaven only. Since God see all things and cares for his own people, he will furnish his people with some benefits on earth. The Creator will honor his faithful servants on earth with many benefits which are not limited to joy, peace, and soundness of mind. Faithful servants of God will be bold like lions on earth and they will possess their possessions. God's faithful children will be immovable in the sight of adversity; they will be strong to take down mountains and level valleys. In fact, the list of benefits reserved for God's faithful children is endless! Hence, people who associate themselves with God should serve him will diligence. Heavenly bound people should remain focus and be committed with thorough worship to the living God, since they will derive many benefits for their services in this world, and in heaven also.

Prayer:
Dear God, please help me to serve you well on earth with all honesty, and remain committed to you unto the end. Let my services receive your pleasurable attention so that I can be blessed in this world and in heaven also. Please keep me close to you always so that I can do what is acceptable and rewarding. For in the name of Jesus Christ I make my requests.

Amen.

« DAY 349 »

God Will Fight For His People, And They Shall Have Rest

Focus Passage: Zechariah 5, 6, 7, 8

Israelites wandered away from God and suffered, but their Creator promised to draw them closer and redeem them. Israelites will recover their losses, and they will have God's name to praise. God said,

> *"And it shall come to pass, that as ye were a curse among the heathen, O house of Judah, and house of Israel; so will I save you, and ye shall be a blessing: fear not, but let your hands be strong. For thus saith the Lord of hosts; As I thought to punish you, when your fathers provoked me to wrath, saith the Lord of hosts, and I repented not"* **(Zechariah 8:13-14 KJV).**

Lesson:
God cares so much for his people; he will forgive their sins and help them recover their losses. Distressing situations will become things of the past for God's children, and they will still have God's name to praise. However, people who oppress God's children; people who deprive them of their rights, and those who rejoice over their failures will pay a heavy price for their actions. God will defend his own people, but punish the wicked ones. The consequences of wicked acts may surpass anyone's imaginations. Hence, it is beneficial to be at the right side of God and be blessed than to be on his negative side and incur his hash judgment! All people ought to honor God and also support his children so that things can work accurately for them.

Prayer:
Dear God, please keep me at the right side of history to receive your blessings. Guide and guard me to make decisions that are pleasant to you so that I can be blessed! Let me be supportive of your works and your people. Let my actions contribute to the progress of your people, and also let me make positive contributions to your kingdom, so that it can be well with me in this life and in heaven. For in the name of Jesus Christ I make my requests.

Amen.

« DAY 350 »

Immorality Will Reign During End Time And Some Insensitive Believers Will Derail

Focus Passage: Jude 1

Christians are warned to beware of surge of immoral activities on the last day, which if care is not taken, would cause many believers to backslide from faith. It is written,

> *"...These are murmurers, complainers, walking after their own lusts; and their mouth speaketh great swelling words, having men's persons in admiration because of advantage. But, beloved, remember ye the words which were spoken before of the apostles of our Lord Jesus Christ; How that they told you there should be mockers in the last time, who should walk after their own ungodly lusts. These be they who separate themselves, sensual, having not the Spirit"* **(Jude 1:16-19 KJV).**

Lesson:
Present days Christians are living at a crucial time when their faith would be tested with fire, and believers must ensure to stand firm with their beliefs or else, Satan will attempt to claim glory over their lives. Believers are now exposed to some theories that lack basis in the bible. Our society promotes behaviors that contradict bible, and we are forced to adopt them. Believers are now being brainwashed through media to believe and accept practices of homosexuality - which is unbiblical! Worse still, some professed Christians now proclaim that Jesus Christ was just a man (and not God in human flesh). Also, some preachers broadcast eternal salvation - and argue that salvation cannot be lost through sin! It is unfortunate that many naive Christians are falling for these deceptions! However, sensitive Christians would escape dangers of hell fire by engaging in personal bible study and upholding their traditional bible beliefs. Every serious Christian ought to daily read his/her bible to understand God's mind and affirm the truth. Also, we should pray for God's guidance to understand the scripture. More importantly, believers should be careful in selections of associations and spiritual leaders. Any church, denomination, or bible teacher/preacher/pastor/prophet that contradict bible fundamentals must not be followed. Every Christians must be heavenly conscious, and ensure to serve God in Spirit and truth **(John 4:24).** A serious Christian who does his/her due diligence and follows bible truth to the end will escape hell and meet God in heaven.

Prayer:
O dear good Lord please save me from heresies so that I will not lose my soul to Satan in hell fire! Save me from false teacher, preacher, prophet, and others who manipulate bible for their selfishness. Save me from Satan's agents whose purposes are to deceive people and send them to hell! Save me from our society impositions that are forcing people to adopt immoral opinion against bible principles. Help me to stand firm, and serve you with contrite heart so that I can remain qualify for your eternal kingdom. Please empower me through your Holy Spirit to do what is just and acceptable in your presence at all times. For in the name of Jesus Christ I make my requests.
Amen.

« DAY 351 »

God Is Merciful, But No One Should Live In Sin And Expects God's Grace To Abide

Focus Passage: Zechariah 9, 10

House of Judah sold their lives to sin, but God promised to buy them back with his gracious love. The outcast children of God will be favored as God promised,

> *"I will strengthen the house of Judah, and I will save the house of Joseph. I will bring them back, because I have mercy on them. They shall be as though I had not cast them aside; for I am the Lord their God, And I will hear them"* **(Zechariah 10:6).**

Lesson:
God is loving and forgiving, and he will forgive our sins and bless us if we turn to him. The ever-gracious Lord will show us his loving-kindness and redeem our lands. He will also wipe off our painful memory and replace it with senses of calmness, peace, and joy. However, despite his ever available enduring love, the Creator still warned that we do should take him for granted. We must not live in sin and expect his grace to abide. God will punish unrepentant sinners in hell fire; therefore, we must have a genuine relationship with him always. Our acts of sin repentance must be genuine for God to reckon well with us and bless us. Also, we must obey God's instructions and serve him well before we can receive his abiding blessings. The heavenly Father will only remain happy with us if we can serve him with dignity and honor.

Prayer:
Dear God, please help me not to take your grace for granted. Help me to love you with all my heart; let my relationship with you be genuine. Please help me to exercise genuine repentance whenever I commit sin, so that I can remain on your good side to receive your abundant blessings. Let your Holy Spirit empower me to faithfully serve you so that I can qualify to inherit your eternal life. Please bless me today, tomorrow, and forever! For in the name of Jesus Christ I make my requests.

Amen.

« DAY 352 »

Only Those Who Have Confessed Their Faith In Jesus Christ Will Go To Heaven

Focus Passage: Revelation 1

End Time season is here; Jesus Christ will appear in the sky; he will rapture believers to heaven and leave unbelievers behind on earth to suffer torments from Satan. Believers will eventually live permanently with God in heaven, while the unbelievers will permanently live with Satan in hell fire. Scripture announced the second coming of Jesus Christ as quoted,

> *"Behold, He is coming with clouds, and every eye will see Him, even they who pierced Him. And all the tribes of the earth will mourn because of Him. Even so, Amen"* **(Revelation 1:7).**

Lesson:
Jesus Christ will return to earth to transport his followers to heaven. Everyone on earth will witness this event, but not everyone will participate in it. Only people who have confessed their faith in Jesus will go to heaven; those who have rejected Christ as God's Son and those who have refused to accept him as their personal Lord and Savior will not go to heaven. Christ will transform his true followers to heaven where there shall be eternal righteousness, peace, and joy. Those who end up with Jesus Christ will live permanently with him in his kingdom; however, unbelievers will have their part in hell, where there shall be torments and horror. Hence, people who have confessed their faith in Jesus Christ should hold firm with their conviction; those who have not confessed Jesus Christ as their personal Savior should immediately do so, since there is no any other way through which anyone can be saved - except through him **(Acts 4:12).**

Prayer:
Dear Jesus Christ, I understand that you are the Savior of the world, and all believers must confess you as Lord to be saved. Therefore, I confess you as my personal Lord and Savior, and I yield my complete life to you! Please help me to stand firm with my conviction, and baptize me with your Holy Spirit to live acceptable life before you, so that I can remain qualify for your eternal kingdom. Please count me worthy in your kingdom! Thank you Jesus Christ for your saving grace.

Amen.

« DAY 353 »

Jehovah Will Advance His Goodness For His People – And Nothing Can Stop Him

Focus Passage: Zechariah 11, 12

Dwellers of Jerusalem have lived in fear and oppressions of their surrounding nations, but God promised them guaranteed safety. The City of Jerusalem would prosper and flourish despite hostility suffered from their enemies. God said,

> *"On that day I will make the clans of Judah like a firepot in a woodpile, like a flaming torch among sheaves. They will consume all the surrounding peoples right and left, but Jerusalem will remain intact in her place"* ***(Zechariah 12:6 NIV).***

Lesson:
God will protect his own people, and offer them much benefit. External influences and pressures that children of God may suffer on earth would not be strong enough to stop God from performing his goodness in their lives. Since nothing can stop God, he will advance his goodness in his people's lives; he will not stop until he has made his children's faces shine. God's children will have upper hands over their enemies; they have unquenchable Spirit of God dwelling in them, therefore they are bound to succeed. Congratulations to people who have made their choices to serve Jehovah and also follow the footsteps of his Son Jesus Christ - They will prosper in this life, and they will also prosper in heaven. People who have not registered a relationship with God should do so by confessing Jesus Christ as their Lord and personal Savior.

Prayer:
Dear God, I understand that you are the only one who has guaranteed security. You have enough strength to save and bless people. Therefore, I swear my allegiance to follow you. I yield my life to you, and I will faithfully serve you throughout the days of my life. Please anoint my head with your oil of gladness, and make my face shine. Please overflow me with your grace, and empower me through your Holy Spirit to live a life acceptable to you always. Please defend my interest in this life, and let me remain qualify for your eternal riches in heaven. For in the name of Jesus Christ I make my requests.

Amen.

« DAY 354 »

God Delights In People That Honor Their Confession Of Faith With Full Devotion

Focus Passage: Revelation 2

God convicted Ephesians' church as imperfect, and challenge it to straightening up its rough edges, or else it would miss great opportunities designed for it. God who is the owner of all churches said to Ephesians' Church,

> "I see what you've done, your hard, hard work, your refusal to quit. I know you can't stomach evil, that you weed out apostolic pretenders. I know your persistence, your courage in my cause, that you never wear out. "But you walked away from your first love—why? What's going on with you, anyway? Do you have any idea how far you've fallen? A Lucifer fall! "Turn back! Recover your dear early love. No time to waste, for I'm well on my way to removing your light from the golden circle" **(Revelations 2:2-5).**

Lesson:
Christianity requires seriousness; anyone who claims to be a Christian must take his/her relationship with God seriously, and serve him well. Sin separates us from God, and we must run from the acts. If anyone falls from grace and backslide, he/she should humbly confess the sin committed to God and genuinely repent. No Christian should sit on the fence, but everyone must honor his/her confession of faith in Jesus Christ and serve him with full devotion. God loves diligent and dedicated people, he will honor those who serve him with consciousness of going to heaven. Also, he will honor people who put him first in whatever they do. Doors of opportunity will open for people of God, and Christ will ensure that his name is praised in their lives in all ramifications. Hence, all people should serve God well and yield their complete life to him.

Prayer:
Dear God, please help me to be honest with you in everything I do. Do not let me cover up sins, but help me to exercise genuine repentance, so that I can be on your good side to receive your eternal blessings. Please teach me how to seriously serve you so that I can be found fit for the second coming of your Son Jesus Christ! Also, help me to serve you well so that I can qualify for your blessings on earth. Empower me with your Holy Spirit and anoint me with grace so that I can prosper in the land of the living. For in the name of Jesus Christ I make my requests.

Amen.

« DAY 355 »

od Standard Of Righteousness Won't Change; Humans Are To Comply

Focus Passage: Zechariah 13, 14

Israelites had enjoy practicing idolatry which has made them suffer terrible punishments from God; however the Creator promised to rid them out of their sins. God will give them a change of mind and remove evil practices from their land. Evil dwellers of the land would be ashamed when God's scepter of righteousness is lifted up. God promised the nation of Israel,

> *"On that day, I will banish the names of the idols from the land, and they will be remembered no more," declares the Lord Almighty. "I will remove both the prophets and the spirit of impurity from the land. And if anyone still prophesies, their father and mother, to whom they were born, will say to them, 'You must die, because you have told lies in the Lord's name.' Then their own parents will stab the one who prophesies" (Zechariah: 13:2-3 NIV).*

Lesson:
God has a standard of righteousness that cannot be broken; he will not change his mind, but humans are to change their mind to comply with his standard. God's principles remain immovable and unchangeable; he will not compromise those principles based on our "evolving" beliefs and practices. We humans may rationalize and come up with excuses, but Jehovah will remain immovable, and he will judge the world based on his set rules. Therefore, people of our generation should sit tight and serve God according to his standard. We should clearly define God's expectations according to bible standards and comply with them. We should desist from trivializing issues that are important to God. The Creator expects us to change from our sinful ways, and turn to him with purity. We must revere God and serve him with dignity so that he can bless us. If we make God happy with our holy living, he will make us happy with his benefits: Rain will fall in its time, and sun will shine according to schedule. However, if we disobey God and take him for granted, his imminent judgments loom over us. People who walk against God's laws will have themselves to blame in hell - unless they exercise repentance before it is too late.

Prayer:
Dear God, I understand that you are God of grace and mercy, but you are also God of fire and brimstone. You will not tolerate evil but you will judge evildoers; those who refuse to repent from their sinful ways will suffer consequences for their actions. Therefore, I submit myself to you today. I come to say, "I will obey your instructions and serve you well." I am sorry for my sins and I repent from them all. As from today, my total life is dedicated to you, and I will serve you faithfully throughout my life! Please write my name in the book of life and keep me heavenly worthy. For in the name of Jesus Christ I make my requests.

Amen.

« DAY 356 »

Definition Of Christianity Goes Beyond Lip Services

Focus Passage: Revelation 3, 4

Every child of God is expected to maintain a distinct relationship with his/her Maker. No "sitting on the fence," no "one-leg-in and one-leg-out" practices allowed. Whoever claims to be a Christian must do so whole-heartedly, or else he/she will be rejected at the gate of heaven. God said through his word,

> *"I know your works, that you are neither cold nor hot. I could wish you were cold or hot. So then, because you are lukewarm, and neither cold nor hot, I will vomit you out of My mouth. Because you say, 'I am rich, have become wealthy, and have need of nothing'—and do not know that you are wretched, miserable, poor, blind, and naked— I counsel you to buy from Me gold refined in the fire, that you may be rich; and white garments, that you may be clothed, that the shame of your nakedness may not be revealed; and anoint your eyes with eye salve, that you may see. As many as I love, I rebuke and chasten. Therefore be zealous and repent"* **(Revelation 3:15-19).**

Lesson:

Anyone who claims to be a Christian should examine him or herself if indeed he/she deserves to go to heaven. God will not save anyone based on title and personal claims, he will save people based on their confession of faith and the type of relationship they keep with him. Anyone who professes to be a Christian should not engage in lip service. He/she should not keep distant relationship with God. A good Christian ought to have personal and growing relationship with God. He/she is expected to be close to God and constantly read his/her bible. The person supposed to be part of a local fellowship/church and be involved in services that honor God. Also, a good Christian is expected to read and understand God's law and carefully follow them. A good Christian calls God his Father; he calls Jesus his/her Savior. A good Christian supports good courses and promotes welfare of others. A good Christian daily seek God's face and ask for God's indwelling Holy Spirit to live an acceptable and overcoming life in this world. Ultimately, a good Christian is in expectant of Christ' return, and carefully watches his/her steps in order to qualify for rapture. At the end of it all, Christ will call a good Christian to heaven - A home specially preserved for his saints.

Prayer:

Dear God, "Am I a good Christian?" Well, I come humbly before you today for your assessments. Please check me out, wash me, and keep fit for your kingdom. Convict me of my mistakes, and help me to repent from them all. Keep my heart pure, and baptize me with your Holy Spirit to live a committed life before you. Edify me with your word, and keep me forever fit for your rapture. Please let me qualify to hear the blast of your trumpet on the last day so that I can be transported to heaven! Let me qualify to receive your crown of glory in heaven, and partake in your eternal banquet! For in the name of Jesus Christ I make my requests.

Amen.

« DAY 357 »

God Watches Over His Own Children; He Identifies Them Among The Multitude

Focus Passage: Psalm 74, 75, 76

Israelites suffered terrible blows from their enemies and lamented to God for his rescue. The people cried and beg God to defend them for the sake of his name. Israelites lamented,

> *"We do not see our signs; There is no longer any prophet; nor is there any among us who knows how long. O God, how long will the adversary reproach? Will the enemy blaspheme your name forever?* **(Psalm 74:9-10).**
>
> In addition, Israelites turned their distressing situations into prayers and said, *"Remember this, that the enemy has reproached, O Lord, and that a foolish people has blasphemed your name. Oh, do not deliver the life of your turtle dove to the wild beast! Do not forget the life of your poor forever. Have respect to the covenant; for the dark places of the earth are full of the haunts of cruelty"* **(Psalm 74:18-20).**

Lesson:
Deliverance and salvation will come to people of God in their distressing situations. Horrible circumstances cannot overpower God's children because they have God's Spirit residing in them. Besides, God watches over his own children, and he recognizes their voices among the multitude. Just like any parent, God recognizes our voices - his own children! He will come to us in time of need. He will defend our interests and fight our battles. God will plead our causes and save us from the enemies. Meanwhile, when God arise on our behalves, the enemies are in trouble! God will make them pay more than they have stolen. Jehovah will beat down the enemies until they have become completely irrelevant. Enemies of God's children will have much to suffer. They will suffer many casualties in an unprecedented manner. God will leave the enemies of righteousness an impression that will last their lifetime. Hence, if God be for us (children of God), who can be against us? Let every believer shout a loud hallelujah!

Prayer:
"I am so glad I belong to God, I am so glad I belong to Jesus Christ who is the defender of his people!" Indeed I am glad that Jehovah is my Father who will take care of my business. He will defend me from the snares of the fowlers and save my soul from adversity. God the Creator of universe will serve my interest in all ramifications for the sake of his glory. Satan and all his forces will be ashamed over my life, and God alone will be glorified! I am a strong believer of God's power. Salvation of Jesus Christ is my heritage forever! Praise God, and bless his Son Jesus Christ forever!

Amen.

« DAY 358 »

Jesus Volunteered To Save Humanity When No One Else Would

Focus Passage: Revelation 5

God asked for a volunteer to create pathway for saving humanity, no one volunteered except Jesus Christ. He was the only heavenly being that was willing to pay the heavy price involved. Bible described the scenario that led to salvation path of humankind (as John explained in Revelation),

> *"And I saw in the right hand of Him who sat on the throne a scroll written inside and on the back, sealed with seven seals. Then I saw a strong angel proclaiming with a loud voice, "Who is worthy to open the scroll and to lose its seals?" And no one in heaven or on the earth or under the earth was able to open the scroll, or to look at it. So I wept much, because no one was found worthy to open and read the scroll, or to look at it. But one of the elders said to me, "Do not weep. Behold, the Lion of the tribe of Judah, the Root of David, has prevailed to open the scroll and to lose its seven seals."* **(Revelation 5:1-5)**. *"...But one of the elders said to me, "Do not weep. Behold, the Lion of the tribe of Judah, the Root of David, has prevailed to open the scroll and to lose its seven seals." And I looked, and behold, in the midst of the throne and of the four living creatures, and in the midst of the elders, stood a Lamb as though it had been slain, having seven horns and seven eyes, which are the seven Spirits of God sent out into all the earth. Then He came and took the scroll out of the right hand of Him who sat on the throne"* **(Revelation 5:5-7)**.

Lesson:

Jesus Christ among other heavenly beings had a chance to volunteer to come to earth for the purpose of saving humanity. Christ the Son of God surrendered to his Father's will, and he said "Father send me." He accepted the bitter-sweet scroll from God which contained the master plan for the operation. The scroll - which signified the contract - did not contain anything admirable, yet Jesus was willing to accept its terms for the purpose of granting salvation opportunity for humanity. The prime goal of the contract is that humanity must be liberated from Satan's entrapment and be saved. The details of the contract include suffering that the Messiah must undergo to achieve his goal: He must be willing to face brutal treatments from Satan and people he intend to save; He must be willing to bear various kinds of abuse and ultimately die in the hands of the enemies. However, several horrific factors itemized in the contract did not terrify Jesus. He understood that no one else would volunteer if he refused; therefore, he was willing to give all it takes to save us. Hence, salvation comes to earth. The Savior would be born, and everyone who believes in him would be saved. Anyone who accepts Jesus as true Son of God and confesses him as his/her personal Lord and Savior will be saved. (Romans 10:9-10).

Prayer:

Dear Jesus Christ, I thank you for sacrificing your life on the cross for the purpose of saving my soul. I thank you for liberating me from Satan and the punishment of hell fire. I am giving my life to you today – sweet Jesus! I confess that you are Christ the Son of God. I believe that you died on the cross and resurrected to give me life. Therefore, I confess you as my personal

Lord and Savior. Please write my name in the book of life, and keep me heavenly worthy. Thank you again Jesus Christ for your saving grace.

Amen!

« DAY 359 »

God's Grace Have Limits – Stubborn Sinners Should Watch Out

Focus Passage: Psalm 77, 78

A Psalmist could not stop wondering why Israelites enjoy abusing their God-given opportunities. Despite much goodness they have received, the people remained ungrateful and continued to upset God with their sinful actions. The psalmist said,

> "...Yet He had commanded the clouds above, and opened the doors of heaven, had rained down manna on them to eat, and given them of the bread of heaven. Men ate angels' food; He sent them food to the full. He caused an east wind to blow in the heavens; and by His power He brought in the south wind. He also rained meat on them like the dust, Feathered fowl like the sand of the seas; And He let them fall in the midst of their camp, All around their dwellings. So they ate and were well filled, For He gave them their own desire" **(Psalm 78:23-29).**

The psalmist lamented, "*How often they provoked Him in the wilderness, and grieved Him in the desert! Yes, again and again they tempted God, and limited the Holy One of Israel. They did not remember His power: The day when He redeemed them from the enemy, When He worked His signs in Egypt, And His wonders in the field of Zoan*" **(Psalm 78:40-43).**

God despised Israelites for their persistent sinful actions as the psalmist explained, "*For they provoked Him to anger with their high places, and moved Him to jealousy with their carved images. When God heard this, He was furious, and greatly abhorred Israel, So that He forsook the tabernacle of Shiloh, The tent He had placed among men, and delivered His strength into captivity, And His glory into the enemy's hand. He also gave His people over to the sword, and was furious with His inheritance. The fire consumed their young men, and their maidens were not given in marriage. Their priests fell by the sword, and their widows made no lamentation. Then the Lord awoke as from sleep, like a mighty man who shouts because of wine. And He beat back His enemies; He put them to a perpetual reproach.* **(Psalm 78:58-66).**

Lesson:

Evil has consequences, and people who engage in it will have much price to pay later. Anyone who persists in evil will eventually regret his/her action and pay heavy price. The Creator will extend his grace on sinners - but not for an indefinite period. Meanwhile, the price of disobedient acts is rough, tough, and tense! Hence, it is advantageous to honor God and receive his blessings than receiving his punishments. Evil people should change from their wickedness; unrepentant sinners should turn a new leaf - to receive God's favor and benefits. The emphatic truth that must remain resonating in everyone's mind is that "Jehovah will rule supremely over the earth; he will bless his own people, but punish the wicked people with darkness and brimstone of hell fire."

Prayer:
Dear God, I prefer to receive your benefits than your punishments. I have made up my mind to honor you and be devoted to you. I will not practice wickedness, and neither will I support wicked people. My choice will remain to faithfully serve you so that I can receive your benefits in this life, and in heaven also. Please empower me with your Holy Spirit to do things that are right and are acceptable to you, so that I can remain fit for your eternal kingdom. For in the name of Jesus Christ I make my requests.
Amen.

« DAY 360 »

Some Horrific Event Will Precede The Second Coming Of Jesus Christ

Focus Passage: Revelation 6

Seven mysterious seals were opened in heaven which uncovered the deep secrets of end time. Some of the details are mind-boggling - but they are true. God's angels detailed secrets of the seals that Christ (the Lamb of God) opened in heaven about end time. The seals represent:

1. *Triumphant strength of Jesus Christ who will conquer the whole earth.* **(Revelation 6:2).**
2. *End Time conflicts that would claim many lives.* **(Revelation 6:4).**
3. *Significant scarcity that would make earth inhabitants suffer.* **(Revelation 6:5).**
4. *Death will be rampant, which would hurt humans' souls deeply.* **(Revelation 6:8).**
5. *Martyrs (those who died from persecutions) will ask God to revenge their bloodshed.* **(Revelation 6:10).**
6. *Earthquakes will be rampart, and all earth inhabitants would live in fear.* **(Revelation 6:12-17).**

Lesson:

Events of end time have been sanctioned by God in heaven, and earth inhabitants have no choice than to experience them. The scriptures emphasized what events would precede Christ's second coming **(Revelation 6).** Situations would be bad for earth inhabitants: Earthquakes, famine, diseases, wars, and other unpleasant circumstances will develop. Many would wish they were never born! While earth still bleed in pains, Christ will appear in the sky to rapture his followers to heaven to live with him for a period of time **(Acts 1:11).** Unbelievers would be left behind on earth to relate with the devil who would claim total control. Satan will have opportunity to flex his muscles and do whatever he likes against earth inhabitants. He will manipulate earth inhabitant and prepare them to receive eternal condemnation of God. Other events will follow, and Christ' Millennia reign would be established on earth - Revelation 20:4, (but Satan would have sealed his followers with evil signs of 666 - **Revelation 20:1-3).** God's judgment will follow Millennia reign of Christ; all earth inhabitants will face their Creator to accounts for their activities and receive judgment. God will award his eternal kingdom to Christ followers, and haul unbelievers to the eternal lake of fire known as hell fire **(Revelation 21; Revelation 14:11).**

Prayer:

Dear God, please count me worthy for heaven - there is nothing interesting on earth to enjoy after rapture! Please I want to go with Jesus Christ whenever he returns! I understand that Jesus Christ is the only way that leads to heaven, therefore I open the door of my heart to him today! I believe that Jesus is the Son of God and he is the savior of the world. I confess him (Jesus Christ) as my personal Lord and Savior. I give him my complete life, and I swear my allegiance to follow him throughout the days of my life. I confess my sins, and repent from them. From now on, I am fully belonged to Jesus, and I will remain with him forever! Hallelujah Christ is the king and he is my savior - Heaven is my final home!
Amen.

« DAY 361 »

Humility And Repentance Are The Solutions To Sin And Its Consequences

Focus Passage: Psalm 79, 80

A psalmist begged God to tamper justice with mercy over Israel, or else they would forever suffer for their sins, and their end would be worse than that of infidels. The psalmist pleaded,

> *"O remember not against us former iniquities: let thy tender mercies speedily prevent us: for we are brought very low. Help us, O God of our salvation, for the glory of thy name: and deliver us, and purge away our sins, for thy name's sake"* **(Psalm 79:8-9 KJV)**.

Lesson:
Humility and repentance are the solutions to sin and its consequences. Anyone who aims at obtaining mercy of God should be humble enough to confess his/her sins to God, and ask for forgiveness. Confession of sin does not demean anyone, neither does it underrate dignity. Confession of sin symbolizes humility and seriousness; it shows integrity. A person who genuinely confesses his/her sin will receive forgiveness from God. Christ will wash away his/her sins. The fellow will receive God's grace and strength to maintain more stability in order to overcome future temptations. However, a prideful and self-righteous person has lost the opportunity of forgiveness; he/she has lost the opportunity of personal improvement also. Stubborn and unrepentant sinners cannot find a place with God - since God detest them! As the Scripture stated, *"Though the Lord is on high, yet He regards the lowly; but the proud He knows from afar"* **(Psalm 138:6)**.

Hence, anyone who values forgiveness and also intent to have spiritual growth and personal improvement should exercise repentance from his/her sins. Great doors of opportunity will forever open for humble people who care to walk with God in integrity.

Prayer:
Dear God, I understand that humility comes before honor, and I must exercise repentance before I receive forgiveness. Therefore, I submit myself at your feet to ask for your forgiveness. I am sorry for all my past mistakes; I repent from them, and promise to start living rightly with you. I will serve and obey you according to your expectations. Please give me grace to give you my best efforts so that you can be happy with me always - and so that I can qualify for your tremendous blessings in this life, and in heaven also. For in the name of Jesus Christ I make my requests.

Amen.

« DAY 362 »

God Will Award Imperishable Crowns Of Glory For His Saints In Heaven

Focus Passage: Revelation 7

God will reward faithful followers of Jesus Christ with his new heaven and new earth. Believers of Jesus Christ from all walks of life will be honored by God. The scripture explained,

> *"...After these things I looked, and behold, a great multitude which no one could number, of all nations, tribes, peoples, and tongues, standing before the throne and before the Lamb, clothed with white robes, with palm branches in their hands, and crying out with a loud voice, saying, "Salvation belongs to our God who sits on the throne, and to the Lamb!"* **(Revelation 7:9-10)**. *People who have suffered for the sake of their faith will robe in royal apparels; they will forget their pains. It is written, "They shall neither hunger anymore nor thirst anymore; the sun shall not strike them, nor any heat; for the Lamb who is in the midst of the throne will shepherd them and lead them to living fountains of waters. And God will wipe away every tear from their eyes"* **(Revelation 7:16-17).**

Lesson:

There is no regret in serving God, but there are great rewards for serving God. People who faithfully serve God in this earth will receive huge rewards from God in heaven. The almighty God will honor Christ followers with imperishable crown of glory; they will have their past painful memories replaced with the good ones. Christ's saints will dine and wine with him in heaven; they will sing new songs to his praise, and they will also remain in perfect peace forever. Indeed those who have confessed Jesus Christ as their Lord and Savior while on earth will rejoice in the bosom of the Almighty forever! However, cruel people, and those who have denied the lordship of Jesus Christ will not have a place in heaven. Their place will be hell fire, where Satan and all his demons would be condemned forever.

Prayer:

"Jerusalem on high, my song that city is, My home whenever I die, the center of my bliss; O happy place! When shall I be, My God, with Thee, to see Thy face?"

Dear God, please I want to go to heaven after I have left this earth. I do not want to end up with the devil in hell, but I want to be perpetually situated in heaven - where there shall be eternal peace and joy. Please count me worthy! I understand that no one can qualify for heaven except his/she has confessed Jesus Christ as Lord; therefore, I declare today that I (*mention your name*) confess Jesus Christ as my personal Lord and Savior. I believe he is the Son of God, and through him all people will receive forgiveness of sin. I confess my sins to you Lord, and I repent from them. As from today, I will faithfully serve you with all my heart, and I will do this till Christ return to rapture me home. Please keep my feet standing within your gate, and let me forever fit to enjoy eternity life with you in heaven! For in the name of Jesus Christ I have made my requests.

Amen!

« DAY 363 »

God Is A Disciplined Deity; He Will Not Stand By Wicked People

Focus Passage: Psalm 81, 82, 83

Deliverance is not a difficult task for God; however, he would not deliver Israelites because of their persistent sins. God said,

> *"Oh that my people had hearkened unto me, and Israel had walked in my ways! I should soon have subdued their enemies, and turned my hand against their adversaries. The haters of the Lord should have submitted themselves unto him: but their time should have endured for ever. He should have fed them also with the finest of the wheat: and with honey out of the rock should I have satisfied thee"* **(Psalm 81:13-16 KJV).**

Lesson:
God will bless his children; he will save and deliver them from trouble. He will keep watch over them to ensure their enemies could not prevail over them. However, the Almighty God will only perform his great miracles for people who serve him well. He will not stand by wicked and unrepentant sinners in their sinful practices so that unbelievers would not mock his name. Those who have turned their back against God will have many benefits to lose; they will suffer casualties from their enemies, but children of God will have upper hands during adversity and sail unto victory! Since God is such a disciplined deity, all people ought to honor and serve him according to his expectations to receive his blessings.

Prayer:
Dear God, please keep me fit to receive your blessings always. Help me to stay clear of sins and walk worthy of your expectations. Keep me save within your radar so that I can continue to enjoy your grace of peace, protection, and prosperity. Please keep me ever worthy of your benefits! For in the name of Jesus Christ I make my requests.

Amen.

« DAY 364 »

Terrible Events Will Succeed Rapture Event; Everyone Ought To Confess Jesus As Lord Before It Is Too Late

Focus Passage: Revelation 8

Jesus Christ the Lamb of God opened 7 seals in heaven, and the 7th seal unfolded the great tribulations that would befall earth inhabitants after rapture. The 7th seal has 7 trumpets that were blown separately. The 1st through 4th trumpets invoked great damages to the earth to the extent that God's angel bitterly lamented in heaven. The scripture described,

> *"The fourth angel sounded his trumpet, and a third of the sun was struck, a third of the moon, and a third of the stars, so that a third of them turned dark. A third of the day was without light, and also a third of the night. As I watched, I heard an eagle that was flying in midair call out in a loud voice: "Woe! Woe! Woe to the inhabitants of the earth, because of the trumpet blasts about to be sounded by the other three angels!"* **(Revelation 8:12-13 NIV).**

Lesson:
God's power will shake our present earth during the last days to symbolize the forthcoming of Jesus Christ. Also, the pro-rapture events that the world will experience will surpass what anyone has ever experienced. The great news is that people who have reserved their faith in Jesus Christ, and as confessed him as their personal Lord and Savior will escape pro-rapture events. While others suffer on earth, they will remain with Jesus Christ in heaven to dine and wine with him! While saints rejoice in heaven, Satan will torments earth inhabitants with many horrific events. Therefore, it is advantageous that people confess Jesus Christ as Lord and personal Savior before it is too late. Christ salvation will no more be relevant after rapture event! Everyone should come humbly before Jesus Christ and be saved to enjoy in heaven, and not regret in hell.

Prayer:
Dear God, I understand that this world will suffer terrible tribulations after rapture event; therefore, I want to be raptured! I confess Jesus Christ as my personal Lord and Savior. I confess my sins, and repent from them. From now on, I dedicate my complete life to Jesus Christ, and I promise to serve him throughout the days of my life. Please write my name in the book of life to inherit your eternal life in heaven. For in the name of Jesus Christ I make my requests.

Amen.

« DAY 365 »

God Inhabits Praises Of His People, He Will Bless His True Worshippers

Focus Passage: Psalm 84, 90

The scripture congratulates people who dwell in God's presence to give him quality praises. They will be refreshed, and they will not lack good things from their God. It is written,

> *"Blessed are those who dwell in your house; they will still be praising you. Blessed is the man whose strength is in You, Whose heart is set on pilgrimage. As they pass through the Valley of Baca, They make it a spring; the rain also covers it with pools"* **(Psalm 84:4-6).**

Lesson:
God loves to inhabit the praises of his people; he delights in it greatly, and he will forever bless people who make singing praises their constant practice. Hence, people who know how to praise God well should not relent in their efforts, since they will have huge rewards to receive in due time. Any Christian that expects God's special attention must constantly sing songs of praises to his Holy Name.

Prayer:
Dear God, please teach me how to praise you! Let me praise you with my best efforts. Let attitude of bringing you gratitude becomes my lifestyle. Please reward my good efforts with your much benefit, and let me enjoy your blessings in this life and beyond! For in the name of Jesus Christ I make my requests.

Amen.

« Note To The Reader »

Dear Friend,

Before you ever thought of purchasing this book, God has already planned to bless you with it. He has established a pattern through which He will help you discover His purpose for your life. You are such an awesome person specially created by the Creator to live a fulfilled life on earth, and showcase His glory. The Scripture attested,

"Before I formed you in the womb I knew you; before you were born I sanctified you; I ordained you a prophet to the nations" (Jeremiah 1:5 NKJV).

I have prayed for you that this book would fulfill God's divine purpose for your life. My hope is that our time together in analyzing details of the bible and establishing how they are relevant to our lives has reignited your confidence in our sovereign God's control, and has refreshed your hope in the certainty of heaven.

I would love to hear from you. Feel free to connect with me on my blog and subscribe to receive my regular newsletters and email devotionals.

May the Lord bless you as you serve Him and patiently wait for his benefits!

James Taiwo
www.jamestaiwo.com

« Connect With James Taiwo »

On his blog: **www.jamestaiwo.com**

Email: **contact@jamestaiwo.com**

Facebook: **https://www.facebook.com/jamestaiwoJT**

Twitter: **https://twitter.com/theJamesTaiwo**

"Wisdom is the principal thing a person must venture to get. Once obtained, it will brighten his face and forever change the course of his destiny"

- James Taiwo -

« About The Author »

James Taiwo is the founder and senior pastor of **World Outreach Evangelical Ministry Inc, New York City**. He is also the publisher of Trumpet Media Ministries. He obtained a Doctor of Theology Degree from Lighthouse Seminary, Beebe Arkansas. He also obtained a Master of Science Degree in Environmental Engineering from Polytechnic University, New York.

Displaying multiple talents, James Taiwo practice Civil and Environmental Engineering, preaches gospel, and plays saxophone. He has written over 1000 free articles online, and still counting. Also, as an engineer and a preacher, Dr. Taiwo continues to implement various means of diversifying gospel to adapt to the fast changing technology of our days.

Made in the USA
Las Vegas, NV
22 August 2023

76451141R00226